ENDING EUROPE'S WARS

Jonathan Dean

ENDING EUROPE'S WARS

The Continuing Search for Peace and Security

A Twentieth Century Fund Book

Published in association with the
Union of Concerned Scientists

The Twentieth Century Fund Press ◆ New York ◆ 1994

The Twentieth Century Fund sponsors and supervises timely analyses of economic policy, foreign affairs, and domestic political issues. Not-for-profit and nonpartisan, the Fund was founded in 1919 and endowed by Edward A. Filene.

Published in association with the Union of Concerned Scientists, Washington, D.C.

Library of Congress Cataloging-in-Publication Data

Dean, Jonathan.
    Ending Europe's wars : the continuing search for peace and security / Jonathan Dean.
        p.   cm.
    "A Twentieth Century Fund book."
    Includes bibliographical references and index.
    ISBN 0-87078-196-0
    1. National security—Europe.   2. Europe—Politics and government—1989-   3. Europe—Defenses.   I. Twentieth Century Fund.
    II. Title.
    D2009.D43   1994
    327.1′72′094—dc20
                                                                94-26796
                                                                CIP

Cover Design and Graphic Illustration: Claude Goodwin
Manufactured in the United States of America.

*This book is dedicated to those whom I owe most
for their love and help:*

my father, Kenneth Dean

my wife, Theodora

*my brother, David,
and his wife, Mary*

FOREWORD

The sad events in Bosnia, the march of folly in Africa, and the continuing violence along the edges of the former Soviet Union sometimes obscure the towering and positive international events of our time: the end of the Soviet Empire and of East-West divisions in Europe. But it should not be surprising that the fall of the Berlin Wall and the rapid collapse of communist regimes across Eastern Europe have reopened a host of questions about U.S. national interest and the relevance of existing security structures and institutions. For the United States, for NATO, and for the former Warsaw Pact nations, there is neither precedent nor natural order to fall back upon now that the familiar certainties of cold war rivalries have been removed. Threats to security surely exist, but their nature is obscure and unpredictable. In fact, after the massive failure to anticipate the end of the Soviet system, we have reason to question our ability to know exactly what it is we should fear, let alone how to protect against it.

The challenge of ensuring Western security is more complex than ever, involving not only the nations of Europe but also the architects of the old order, particularly the United States. New ventures like the Partnership for Peace and the continuing expansion of the European Union are important elements, but they only partially clarify the problem. One can speculate about the future shape of European security arrangements only with great difficulty and modesty. For within whatever arrangements emerge, there will be important new players, including a unified Germany, a more cohesive European community, modernizing Central and Eastern European countries, and a Russian state whose political complexion remains uncertain.

We still seem some distance from the day when there will be consensus about the fundamentals of the European situation. The questions that cannot be answered perhaps outnumber the things we can count upon. How far, for example, can the European Union be pushed? Maastricht, after all, was a breathtakingly close call. When will Germany begin to assert its national interest like any other "normal" country? And, sooner or later, the Germany that does so will be immensely strengthened by the successful digestion of its eastern component. What sort of *European* cultural and political identity is really possible? There are even those who argue that the media "dominance" of the United States is blocking such a ripening of a European personality.

Perhaps most significantly, policymakers on both sides of the Atlantic are gingerly feeling their way on the most fundamental question concerning future security arrangements: Just what are the various publics of these democracies willing to support in terms of expense, risk, and action? It has been much noted in recent years that true democracies do not make war on one another. In the absence of a life-and-death threat, such as that posed by the former Soviet Union, the question is just what will incite them to act. Kuwait suggests one answer, Bosnia quite another.

In this context of complex and unanswered questions, the Twentieth Century Fund has sponsored a number of studies of the new foundations of American foreign policy, including several that focus specifically on America's relations with Europe and European security institutions. Many of these issues are discussed in a forthcoming volume by Tony Smith, *America's Mission: the United States and the Global Struggle for Democracy.* Two years ago, we published *Securing Europe* by Richard Ullman; shortly thereafter, *The Consequences of Peace* by James Chace addressed many of these questions. We currently have under way studies by David Calleo, Robert Art, Henry Nau, Michael Mandelbaum, John Ruggie, and Walter Mead, which also address these questions. In this way, we hope to contribute to the thinking, and even education, of an American public that must be engaged if we are to develop a new democratic consensus about foreign policy.

We hope to publish fresh and insightful analyses of where we have been, where we stand today, and where we are likely to be in the near-term future. The Fund was fortunate therefore that Jonathan Dean, arms control adviser to the Union of Concerned Scientists, was among those intrepid enough to venture into these uncertain waters. Dean's background as a U.S. ambassador and negotiator and his particular experiences in arms control and disarmament make him especially well suited to the task. Any new security structure, after all, is likely to include a network of arms control restrictions and confidence-building measures as well as new codes and rules of military behavior for the states of Europe.

Dean addresses a number of key questions confronting policymakers today, including America's precise interests in Europe, the outlook for the evolution of the security relationship between the United States and Europe, the future of NATO, and the role of nuclear weapons in the new European security system. He provides us with a road map for the near-term development of European security. His research, analysis, and advice should be welcomed by all those in American policy-making circles who recognize what an immense stake we have in the successful reconstruction of a secure set of arrangements in Europe.

This volume is, in one respect, an unusual venture for the Fund: the work was supported jointly, and the book is being copublished with the Union of Concerned Scientists. On behalf of the Fund's trustees, I want to thank Ambassador Dean for his efforts in exploring this important topic and to thank the Union for their cooperation.

RICHARD C. LEONE, *President*
The Twentieth Century Fund
May 1994

CONTENTS

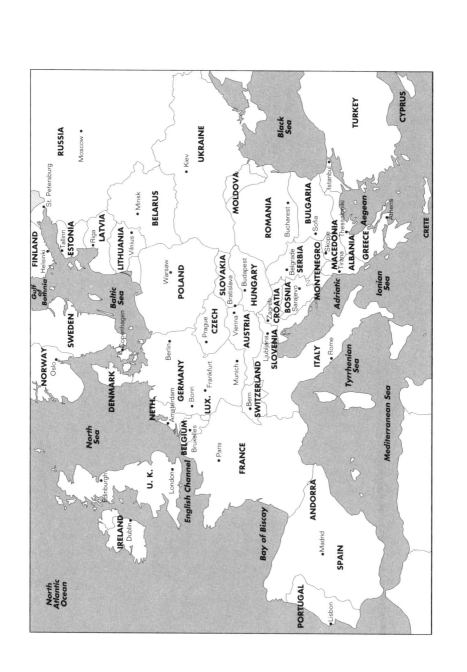

PREFACE

The end of the cold war has had three main consequences: The first is a sharp drop in the risk of global nuclear war—although not total elimination of that risk. The second is the liberation from totalitarian rule of the peoples of Eastern Europe and the Soviet Union, along with the dissolution of the Soviet Union as such.

The third main consequence of the end of the cold war is the sudden emergence of the multilateral world security system hoped for by the founders of the United Nations but frozen in cold war animosity for half a century.

This new worldwide security system, imperfect and fragmentary, is already on trial for its future existence. Its survival and growth depend to a large extent on the capability of the institutions that compose the European regional security system to do their main job of creating a reasonably safe environment in which violence and the threat of catastrophe through nuclear weapons are minimized. This book evaluates these institutions and their prospects for realizing their potential of preventing conflict and rapidly ending conflict when it occurs.

Europe still has the worst security problems of any of the world's regions, both as regards controlling nuclear weapons and with respect to ethnic and nationalist struggles. Europe also has the most developed array of institutions and procedures to cope with conflict history has ever seen. The governments supporting this security system, including those of the United States and the European Community and, up to now, Russia, have at their disposal the greatest assemblage of military and economic resources on earth. If these governments cannot use all these instruments of multilateral security to deal effectively with Europe's security problems, then it is unlikely that the same governments, which provide the bulk of the resources underpinning the UN system, can make the worldwide system of multilateral security work. Europe is the test case for the worldwide system.

This book is divided into four main parts; the thread that connects them is the record of success or failure in preventing or controlling armed conflict between states and inside them. The story begins with Mikhail Gorbachev's remarkable achievement, helped by insightful Western diplomacy, in the nearly bloodless dismantling of Stalinism in the USSR and of the Soviet empire in Eastern Europe, paving the way for the peaceful reunification of Germany. A salient feature of these historic developments is that they avoided the serious violence they could have entailed. The second part of the book discusses the security problems that have since arisen in Europe, including the Russia-Ukraine confrontation, which has placed at serious risk the entire structure of nuclear arms control, and the ethnic conflicts in Yugoslavia and in several Soviet successor states. This section also assesses future developments that could threaten European security. Among the possibilities reviewed are a resurgent Germany; moves toward autocratic government in Russia; escalation of ethnic conflicts to interstate war and the eruption of new localized fighting; and the growing confrontation between Europe and fundamentalist Islam.

The third section evaluates the strengths and weaknesses of the broad array of institutions that have been developed in Europe to deal with security problems and prevent conflict: a reformed NATO; the NATO-sponsored North Atlantic Cooperation Council and Partnership for Peace, the two umbrella organizations that bring together the members of NATO with the states of Eastern Europe, Russia, and the other Soviet successor states; the Conference on Security and Cooperation in Europe (CSCE), the pan-European organization with emphasis on conflict prevention; and the European Union with its defense arm, the Western European Union. This part of the book also describes the regime of arms control and confidence-building measures that governs the relationships among the armed forces of the European states and Russia, reducing competition and suspicion and creating the mutual confidence indispensable for political and economic cooperation. Finally, it assesses the capability of these institutions to deal with the actual problems which confront them today and may do so in the future.

In the first years after the end of the cold war, all the institutions of European security have performed poorly in their job of preventing or damping down conflict. Unless they can do better—the concluding chapters of the book describe several possibilities for improvement—these institutions will fall into disuse and their member states may move toward greater military autonomy, with implications in some cases for nuclear weapons capability.

However, this is not a "doom book" prophesying catastrophe. It tries to take an objective view not only of the failures but also of the successes of the post-cold-war period in Europe in avoiding the further spread of violence and of the real creativity that has brought a wide range of new multilateral structures and procedures to prevent future conflicts. The goal of a conflict-free Europe is still distant. But a great deal can be done to move in that direction and to avoid security threats now on the horizon.

"Security" is the absence of fear and reasons for fear. It is a broad term covering many aspects: domestic public order, economic security, environmental security, and military security. This book focuses on military security, which involves conflict and systematic armed violence between states or within their borders. Although it does not make continual reference to the other, wider dimensions of the concept of security, it has been written in vivid awareness of them.

I acknowledge with gratitude the real help I have received in writing this book from the Union of Concerned Scientists and from the Twentieth Century Fund, and also from the Ford Foundation and the United States Institute of Peace. I have received a great deal of discerning assistance from Nancy Moser and Teri Grimwood, who did the main work of compiling the manuscript, and from Wendy Silverman, Melanie Allen, Tara Magner, Peter Allen, James Macdonald Baker, and Muge Kinacioglu, whose skilled research provided many important facts and ideas. In particular, I want to thank Steven Greenfield of the Twentieth Century Fund for incisive and insightful editorial guidance. Where the book makes its points clearly, it owes much to him.

PART I

THE END OF THE SOVIET SYSTEM

THE FORMER SOVIET UNION AND ITS NEIGHBORS

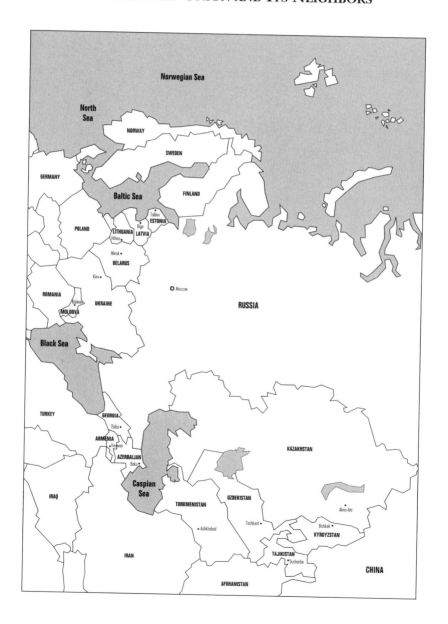

1

THE DAM BREAKS:
DISSOLUTION OF THE SOVIET UNION

When it came, it was like a force of nature, an earthquake or a tornado, or perhaps more like the sudden collapse of a huge dam, with torrents of pent-up water crushing everything flat before it.

Within seven years from the designation of Mikhail Gorbachev as general secretary of the Communist Party of the Soviet Union (CPSU) in March 1985, the harsh realities of the cold war system in Europe were swept away. The Soviet police state, communist control over Eastern Europe, the Iron Curtain—all were gone. The menacing NATO-Warsaw Pact military confrontation in Europe, the largest, costliest, and potentially most destructive peacetime concentration of armed forces in human history, had dissipated, and with it, the looming threat of a third world war in Europe that could spread to global nuclear annihilation. Outside Europe, the Soviet Union dropped its expansionist policy in Afghanistan, Angola, and Ethiopia. It was the end of worldwide political confrontation as well.

The communist governments of Eastern Europe fell, and the Soviet Union agreed to withdraw all its forces from Eastern Europe, to cut by two-thirds the heavy armaments of Soviet conventional forces west of the Ural Mountains, 1,400 miles from the Soviet border with Poland, to withdraw tactical-range nuclear weapons, and to take many strategic-range forces off alert. Germany was peacefully unified. After the abortive coup of August 1991, the Communist Party of the Soviet Union was banned, and the Soviet Union itself dissolved into Russia and eleven other republics, in the process conceding independence to the three Baltic states. These developments transformed the global political system to a greater extent than either world war.

Europeans called this enormous spate of changes "the revolution of 1989," since many of the events, including the sudden dissolution of East German police controls at the Berlin Wall, took place in the two hundredth anniversary year of the French Revolution. But better than the idea of a revolution pursued by force of arms, the image of a natural cataclysm captures more accurately the suddenness, the broad extent, the increasing uncontrollability of the process, as well as the nearly complete lack of deliberate violence in these events, aside from many deaths in Romania. The image of a dam break and ensuing flood is perhaps most pertinent because it embodies the cumulative pressure of the desires of millions of East Europeans and Soviet citizens for radical change, built up over years of frustration under totalitarian repression.

For years, the collapse had been predicted. As early as the 1950s, the first leaders of "front line" West Germany, Chancellor Konrad Adenauer and Social Democratic opposition leader Kurt Schumacher, had insisted that the success of Western states in providing economic prosperity and democratic freedoms would exercise irresistible attraction on the populations of the communist-dominated states of East Europe. Even before that, many Western critics had insisted that the Leninist-Stalinist system in the Soviet Union would collapse because of its own internal contradictions, among them the incompatibility of centralized control with the demands of an increasingly complex economy for independent judgment and autonomous action by individuals.

The main factors contributing to the collapse were also well known: the resolute containment of Soviet expansion by Western governments whose determination was documented by the deaths of thousands of American and Allied soldiers in Korea and in Vietnam and by the willingness of the Western states to undertake a vast program of armament at great cost; the stubborn East European resistance to absorption in the Soviet system, periodically punctuated by overt and sometimes bloody resistance; and the silent longing of the Germans to reunify their country. Early unsuccessful Western efforts to topple the communist governments of Eastern Europe through isolation had been replaced by decades of patient Western effort to develop relations with both the governments and their populations, demonstrating an underlying willingness to cooperate that gravely undermined efforts of leaders to present the NATO countries as inexorably hostile. Above all, the increasing failure of the communist economies and of their science and technology to keep up with Western progress and increasing knowledge of that failure among Eastern populations eroded the foundations of the totalitarian system.

But, despite obvious weaknesses, the Soviet system lumbered on. The continuing use of force and threat of force in the police states of Eastern Europe and the Soviet Union concealed the growing cracks and fissures in the communist system and gave it an aspect of eternity.

When the breakup came, its immediate cause was the efforts of Mikhail Gorbachev to make limited adjustments in the Soviet system. Gorbachev, a self-possessed leader of insight and considerable political courage, came on the scene after years of stagnation under the leadership of Leonid Brezhnev and his moribund successors. Gorbachev's own statements over the ensuing seven-year period, including his political testament, *Perestroika*,[1] and his comments after the failed August 1991 coup against him show him to be a convinced reformer, dedicated to his own vision of Soviet communism, who wanted to modernize the existing system. But Gorbachev was not an isolated phenomenon. He represented and articulated the views and the values of an increasing number of Soviet professionals—scientists, lawyers, economists, and others who wanted to protect their material possessions, their scope for professional action, and their lives against the arbitrary incursions of the totalitarian police state.[2]

It is evident from Gorbachev's account of his program in *Perestroika* that, in his efforts to reform the Soviet system under the slogans of *glasnost*, or active participation in public debate, and of *perestroika*, or restructuring the Soviet system, he intended to rid the Soviet system of its counterproductive rigidities, to improve the system—not to risk the system itself. But the fear that had held together the czarist Russian empire and then the Stalinist empire, fear based on the increasingly effective readiness of the rulers to use repressive force and terror—and the acceptance by most of the citizens of the East European states and the USSR that this was the given order of affairs—was rapidly dissolved after the codeword *glasnost* signaled relaxation of police repression and after no reprisals were taken against those who took advantage of it.

Even when matters were getting out of hand in Eastern Europe, Gorbachev was not willing to authorize the use of repressive force in Eastern Europe to hold together the Warsaw Pact or, with limited exceptions in the Baltic states and Georgia, to permit its use inside the Soviet Union. This restraint dissolved the cement holding together the rigid structures of a system that in its heyday rightly had been called the "empire of fear," and allowed the pent-up pressures behind the dam of the totalitarian state to burst through.

As a man who had come up through the ranks of the Communist Party of the Soviet Union, Gorbachev fully realized the stultifying effects of bossism and corruption. But as a leader from inside the system, he made a fundamental miscalculation as to the elements that held it together. There were some positive bonds of support for ideology, some realization of mutual benefit, and some support from national sentiment in the Slavic republics. But, as foreign and domestic critics had pointed out from the outset of the Leninist-Stalinist system, often so long ago that the correctness of their insight had faded from view, the Soviet system was based on terror. Once Gorbachev relaxed repression in order to carry out his reform programs and refused to use it when the dam began to crack, the entire system collapsed.

Gorbachev was no principled Gandhi-like proponent of nonviolent change. He was deceitful, as he showed in his attempt to suppress details on the extent of the 1986 Chernobyl disaster and by his surreptitious agreement to use of force in the Baltics, and as he needed to be in order to advance to the top in the authoritarian Soviet system. Nonetheless, the central factor in the developments of the Gorbachev years and Gorbachev's vital contribution to these developments was his refusal to use repressive force.

We sketch here some major steps taken by the Gorbachev government to invigorate the seized-up totalitarian system of the Soviet Union.[3] It is a compelling story from many viewpoints: It illustrates the enormous scope and intricate development of the mechanisms of control in the modern totalitarian state, giving some idea of the complexity of Gorbachev's task. Faced by the requirement to obtain the acquiescence of the very system he was changing for each step of change, Gorbachev did not pause for discussion but autocratically and smoothly removed component after component of the totalitarian system and replaced them with components of more democratic nature. The masterful management of this operation, its lack of violence and of effective opposition from within the system until the last desperate coup, was a remarkable political achievement. Most important for our present purpose, this brief account illustrates the difficult political and economic heritage of the successor states and the immense political mortgage they have to cope with.

PROGRESS ON HUMAN RIGHTS

Beginning in 1986, Gorbachev began a program of institutional reforms. Initially, this process took the form of isolated individual administrative decrees, but by 1988, wholesale reform of the Soviet system was under way. Step by step, and accompanied by considerable Western pressure, the Soviets reformed their legal and penal systems. By the end of 1988, nearly all political prisoners had been released from Soviet camps. The notorious, catch-all gag rule of the Soviet system, Article 190–1 of the

Soviet penal code, which made "defamation" of the Soviet Union a felony punishable by sentence to labor camp, was abolished in the course of a widespread reform of the penal and judicial systems. Censorship was dismantled gradually.

In addition to actions righting injustices to individuals, the Gorbachev government introduced many far-reaching general reforms in the field of civil liberties. Public demonstrations were legalized (July 1988). Jamming of foreign broadcasts was finally ended, opening the access of Soviet citizens to a wider range of information on the outside world and also on developments inside the Soviet Union. Worker strikes, previously repressed by force as criminal antistate activities, were legalized (October 1989), but the government was given the right to prohibit strikes by decree in key segments of the economy, including energy and transportation. A new law on freedom of the press abolished official censorship (June 1990), which, however, continued in various forms. State control was also exercised through allocating paper for publishing, in tight supply. In July 1990, Gorbachev ended party control over Soviet Union television and radio stations. However, the openly critical Leningrad program "Vyzglad" was taken off the air, and radio and television remained open to influence by Gorbachev's government.

Religious freedom was established for the first time in the Soviet Union, which had from the outset followed a policy of suppressing organized religion. The new law (September 1990) gave equal status to all religions and charitable organizations, allowed proselytizing, and establishment of seminaries. During this period, previously rigorous barriers to emigration were progressively lifted. In 1990, about 450,000 Soviet citizens received permission to emigrate, and over 4 million went abroad as tourists. Jewish emigration was at the rate of about 180,000 per year in 1990. (The figure for 1986 was under 1,000.) In May 1991, the Supreme Soviet moved to complete legislation freeing departure from the USSR for Soviet citizens desiring to emigrate or travel.

Even before the emergence of Gorbachev as Soviet leader, the Soviet Union was slowly opening up on human rights; Gorbachev's actions greatly accelerated this trend. The early improvements in human rights came about partially as the result of domestic social change—urbanization and the growth of professional groups that wanted to protect their own prerogatives and privileges. It came about partially as the result of external pressure from the United States and from European Community member states arguing that the Soviet Union must fulfill its human rights commitments under the 1975 Helsinki Accords of the Conference on Security and Cooperation in Europe (CSCE) and subsequent CSCE agreements. It should be kept in mind that Brezhnev signed the 1975 Helsinki

Accords and accepted most of what was agreed to on protection of human rights in the Madrid follow-up meeting of CSCE before his death in November 1982. Well before Gorbachev's emergence, the Soviet Union was evolving toward a "civic society."

ELECTIONS

Under the classic Leninist-Stalinist system, only the Communist Party of the Soviet Union and its party-controlled mass organizations were permitted to exist as political organizations. The party selected all political candidates, and only one for each elected position. Election procedures were a travesty of the secret ballot: In nearly all cases, voters marked their ballot at a table in plain view of election officials, almost always party officials. A curtained booth was provided for dissenters, whose identities were immediately established through its infrequent use.

Departures from these traditional totalitarian practices in the Gorbachev era were far-reaching but not complete. In June 1987, on an experimental basis, elections for local Soviets and district court judges based on multiple candidates took place in seventy-six electoral districts. A constitutional reform instituted by Gorbachev in late 1988, intended to elicit initiative and enliven the routine performance of the Supreme Soviet, established a bicameral legislature. The Congress of Peoples Deputies became the forum for general political debates and for changes in the Soviet constitution, while the Supreme Soviet was restricted to legislative functions. This reform was imitated in the fifteen republics of the Soviet Union, including Russia, where it later caused grave difficulty for the government of Boris Yeltsin.

The March 1989 elections to the Soviet Congress of Peoples Deputies brought further advances but not fully free elections. One-third of the seats, including Gorbachev's own, were reserved for representatives of the Communist Party or of communist-dominated social and political organizations. Counting those who ran unopposed, fewer than one-half of the members were chosen by competitive popular vote with more than one candidate. Nonetheless, Communist Party leaders in Moscow and Leningrad were thrown out of office. The Congress elected the 542 members of the Supreme Soviet, the full-time Soviet legislature. In televised proceedings at the outset of its session, members of the USSR Supreme Soviet for the first time questioned prospective cabinet ministers proposed by Gorbachev, causing eleven of his nominations to be withdrawn.

The following year (April 1990), the Congress of Peoples Deputies amended the Soviet constitution to eliminate the Communist Party's monopoly of political power as "the guiding force of Soviet society" (Article 6), and passed a law providing the legal basis for a multiparty system, with equal treatment for political groups that met certain requirements. Significantly, no nationwide political parties were established. The task exceeded the organizational and economic resources available, and there was no basis for it in existing political attitudes. Throughout 1990, new elections were held in the constituent republics. Boris Yeltsin, one-time CPSU regional secretary brought by Gorbachev to head the Communist Party of the city of Moscow and then fired in 1987 from the Politburo for overzealous pressure for reform, was elected in March 1990 by a 90 percent vote in his Moscow election district to the Supreme Soviet of the Republic of Russia and then elected by the membership of that body as its chairman. Gorbachev had a rival—and a successor. Convinced reformers began to migrate from Gorbachev to Yeltsin, who, though far from an intellectual, selected a group of talented advisers whose suggestions he took seriously.[4] In June 1991, after a constitutional change providing for elections for a popularly elected president of the Russian Republic, Yeltsin was elected with 57 percent of the vote. Electoral democracy had come to Russia in the first general suffrage election ever held there.

Although it ultimately proved unsuccessful in holding together the Soviet Union, reform of its structure and increased power-sharing between the central government and the fifteen constituent republics belongs to this abbreviated list of Gorbachev's moves toward democracy in the USSR. In April 1990, after several false starts, the Supreme Soviet passed a "Law on the Delimitation of Powers Between the USSR and the Federation's Constituent Parts," reforming the 1922 treaty that had established the legal structure of the USSR. The draft was heavily criticized from the outset by Yeltsin and other republic leaders who pointed out that, under it, the union government retained full authority over such fields as energy, production, transportation, and communications. Up to the last day of his rule, Gorbachev tried again and again, in successive redrafts of this law, to find agreement on a new formula for power-sharing among the constituent parts of the USSR. But his efforts were to end in total failure; pent-up resentment against Moscow's centralized rule was too strong.

ECONOMIC REFORM

For the first five years of his rule, Gorbachev's economic reforms were timid, partial, and unsuccessful; it seems clear that the free-market concept remained alien to him until the end. Above all, he did not move to free prices or to privatize the Soviet Union's huge state-owned basic industries. Instead, he created a chaotic mixture of ineffective old operations and weak new elements.

Initially, Gorbachev's economic policy followed the pattern of his efforts in other sectors of Soviet society: pep talks, efforts to energize workers and management by exhortation, an unpopular campaign against alcoholism, and a crackdown on corruption, always endemic in the Soviet system and especially prevalent under Brezhnev. Privately owned cooperatives for repairs of all kinds had existed for a long time. In effect, they were private businesses restricted to a handful of employees, members of the cooperative, in practice, its employees. In May 1988, the law governing cooperatives was broadened, permitting cooperative restaurants among others. The expanded cooperatives had a bad start. For seventy years, the Soviet leadership, increasingly conferring privileges on itself, had been preaching egalitarianism, and Soviet citizens considered personal profit odious. Those hardy Soviet citizens willing to start cooperatives in the face of social pressures were on the margin of society and included some criminal elements. Local officials harassed start-up cooperatives with high taxation and refused to make available premises for their businesses.

The right of individuals to lease land for a fifty-year period was promulgated by decree in August 1988, but the Supreme Soviet did not convert the decree to enduring law until February 1990, adding a right to inherit for the family of the lessee, but not its sale to others—a compromise between proponents and opponents of private property. The compromise found few takers because of fears that the arrangement could be arbitrarily eliminated in the future and because of the practical difficulty of convincing existing cooperatives or state farms to part with good land and working equipment. In March 1990, the Supreme Soviet passed a law on ownership that for the first time legalized ownership of the means of production. Individuals could now own equipment, own or co-own small businesses or "labor partnerships," or own shares in larger businesses. Legislation establishing a stock exchange was passed (December 1990). But, in comparison with his innovations in domestic political institutions and foreign policy, Gorbachev's economic policy lagged far behind. Again and again, he balked at freeing prices.

FOREIGN POLICY

Soviet foreign policy under Gorbachev was more responsive to his lead than domestic policy, and changes in it were even more radical than changes in Soviet domestic policy. Cooperation and the common search for peace replaced confrontation and ideological competition. In terms that since have become familiar, Gorbachev presented the conceptual basis for the new policy in his book *Perestroika*, written in September 1987, and in his major speech at the United Nations in December 1988. He emphasized the growing interdependence of world states because of the emergence of global issues like the environment, which affect all states and are beyond the power of individual governments to deal with. "Today, the preservation of any kind of closed societies' is impossible. . . . The world economy is becoming a single organism." Gorbachev stated that, in urgent cases, cooperation among states to cope with general problems of humanity should have priority over the struggle between the forces of capitalism and socialism. This revoked the long-standing Marxist-Leninist concept of an ultimate showdown between the rival forces. Gorbachev repeatedly stressed that nuclear war would mean the end of the human species and could not be won, urging that nuclear weapons be abolished. He argued that security is indivisible (no state could have enduring security at the cost of others) and that the search for military superiority must be relinquished and replaced by defensive doctrine.[5]

This radical shift in foreign policy is a key to understanding the outcome of Gorbachev's rule in the Soviet Union. The global struggle between imperialism and socialism, sometimes expressed in the concept of hostile encirclement of the USSR, was, together with the continuing subjection of the non-Slavic population of the USSR, the ultimate justification for the existence of the Soviet totalitarian regime. It justified the Communist Party's monopoly of power, actions to seal off the outside world, the militarization of Soviet society, and the command economy. When Gorbachev eliminated that justification, presenting the outside world not as hostile but as potentially cooperative, he eliminated the justification for the totalitarian state and its regime of terror, a change paralleled by his action to eliminate the Communist Party's constitutional monopoly of power in domestic affairs. He also eliminated the main justification for communist rule in Eastern Europe.

Gorbachev's contributions to a new Soviet philosophy of foreign affairs were startling in their acceptance of an interdependent, interconnected world in which universal human values were to receive precedence over national interests. Yet it was understandable that outsiders mindful of the Soviet Union's combative, aggressive foreign policy of past generations remained skeptical. In three key areas—relinquishment of quantitative Soviet superiorities in nuclear, chemical, and conventional weapons; relinquishment of Soviet political control over Central and Eastern Europe; and relinquishment of Soviet support for Marxist or revolutionary groups throughout the world—Gorbachev showed he was serious.

ARMS CONTROL

It was in arms control that Gorbachev made his most deliberate and rapid demonstration of desire to enter on a new relationship with the West. Within months of his designation as general secretary, Gorbachev accepted the main Strategic Arms Reduction Talks (START) limits proposed by the United States: a 50 percent reduction in strategic-range missiles to a limit of 1,660 for each country and a warhead ceiling of 6,000—in return for agreement to relinquish its Strategic Defense Initiative (SDI) program of defense of ballistic missiles. Later, Gorbachev relinquished this condition.

In April 1986, Gorbachev proposed new conventional arms control negotiations for Europe to replace the long-lasting, unproductive negotiations on Mutual and Balanced Force Reductions. In December 1988, he showed he meant business in this new proposal by announcing in his speech at the UN large unilateral reductions of Soviet forces, which included 240,000 active-duty military personnel, 10,000 tanks, 8,500 artillery pieces, and 800 combat aircraft from the Western USSR and Eastern Europe. The withdrawals included six tank divisions from East Germany and Hungary, which were disbanded on schedule. In September 1986, the Soviet Union agreed in the Stockholm Document of the CSCE to an extensive system of prenotification and of observation of field activities of ground forces in Europe that included the first Soviet agreement to on-site inspection on the territory of the USSR, later to become a commonplace.

In December 1987, when Gorbachev signed the Intermediate-range Nuclear Forces (INF) Treaty on intermediate-range nuclear weapons, he agreed to destroy all Soviet ground-based missiles with ranges between 500 and 5,500 kilometers—twice as many Soviet as U.S. missiles—and to extensive on-site verification. The last missiles were destroyed without incident in summer 1991.

These actions had great impact in convincing publics in the Western states that Gorbachev was sincere in proposing a new relationship. They also had strong impact on public opinion in Eastern Europe and were a material factor in the events that ensued there.

In June 1990, at the Washington Summit, Presidents Bush and Gorbachev also signed a bilateral agreement to destroy the chemical weapons stocks of both countries down to 5,000 tons by the year 2000 and to destroy production facilities, together with establishment of extensive verification measures. This agreement gave impetus to the multilateral treaty prohibiting possession or production of chemical weapons negotiated by the United Nations Disarmament Conference in Geneva and signed in Paris in January 1993.

Gorbachev's next arms control move was even more significant. The Soviet Union agreed in the Conventional Forces in Europe (CFE) negotiations to cut its holdings of major conventional weapons deployed in the western USSR to one-third of their level before the negotiations began. Gorbachev agreed to eliminate the huge Warsaw Pact superiority in tanks, artillery, armored combat vehicles, combat aircraft, and attack helicopters deployed west of the Ural Mountains in return for token reductions of the same arms by the NATO countries.

At the Paris Summit meeting of heads of state and government of the countries participating in the Conference on Security and Cooperation in Europe in November 1990, Gorbachev gave final approval to a series of confidence- and security-building measures providing for advance notification and outside observation of large-scale ground-force activities in the western USSR and agreed to establishment of several permanent CSCE peacekeeping institutions which, together with the INF and CFE treaties, form important components of the emerging post-cold war security system in Europe.

In July 1991, at their Moscow Summit meeting, Presidents Bush and Gorbachev signed the Strategic Arms Reduction Treaty. Once it enters into force, this START Treaty will provide for reduction of strategic-range nuclear forces of both countries by about one-third, with stringent verification. The Soviet Union agreed to eliminate one-half of its force of SS–18 missiles, the heavy missiles that carried warheads strong enough to destroy a large portion of U.S. fixed silo-based nuclear missiles in an attack initiated by the USSR. This provision alone would sharply reduce the possibility of a successful Soviet surprise attack on the United States.

After the failed August 1991 coup, in his last major arms control move, Gorbachev responded positively in October 1991 to President Bush's proposal for worldwide withdrawal of surface-to-surface and sea-based tactical-range nuclear weapons and for withdrawal of strategic nuclear arms from alert. Gorbachev pledged that many of the withdrawn tactical warheads would be dismantled. Gorbachev's de facto successor, Boris Yeltsin, went even further in signing the START II agreement providing for reduction of all ground-based missiles equipped with multiple warheads. But in four key major types of armaments—intermediate-range missiles, strategic-range missiles, chemical weapons, and major conventional armaments—the Soviet Union under Gorbachev voluntarily moved to eliminate the quantitative superiorities that had been the essence of the Soviet military threat during most of the cold war.

THE END OF SOVIET EXPANSIONISM IN THE THIRD WORLD

Gorbachev also acted to end the Soviet invasion of Afghanistan and the Soviet expansion in the Third World through the massive arms transfers and the presence of thousands of Soviet and other Warsaw Pact political, economic, and military advisers that had extended the East-West confrontation in Europe into a global challenge for over thirty years.

In January 1987, eight years after the trumped-up Soviet invasion of neighboring Afghanistan in December 1979, the Gorbachev government declared a unilateral six-month cease-fire. Soviet forces were withdrawn on schedule from Afghanistan (December 1989), with Soviet commander General Boris Gromov marching alone across a railroad bridge to Soviet territory as the last Soviet soldier to leave the country. In Latin America, the Soviet Union stopped military aid to the Sandinista regime of Nicaragua and played a constructive role in bringing about the free elections that drove the Sandinistas from power (November 1990). In Africa, the Soviets ended their support of Marxist governments in Mozambique, Angola, and Ethiopia.

By the end of Gorbachev's rule, with the exception of Cuba, no client states remained of the Soviet Union's once-numerous footholds in the Third World. The worldwide politico-military confrontation between the United States and the Soviet Union, which had mobilized much of the world in costly and dangerous military confrontation, which had motivated bloody wars in Korea and Vietnam, and which could have triggered all-out nuclear war between the Soviet Union and the United States, was at an end. Gorbachev symbolized the new policy of positive cooperation by voting at the UN for common action against Saddam Hussein of Iraq and by joining the United States in cosponsoring a new round of Mideast peace talks.

GORBACHEV MOVES TO THE RIGHT

Within months of the high point of detente, which came with Gorbachev's agreement in mid-July of 1990 to membership of a united Germany in NATO, a chill wind blew through Europe as right-wing reaction set in the Soviet Union. Gorbachev rejected far-reaching economic reform, dropped his reform-minded advisers, appointed hard-liners to head the Soviet interior ministry and police forces, and condoned or even authorized the use of force to repress efforts of the Baltic states to achieve independence.

Underlying this sudden shift was the fact that internal Soviet debate over decentralization of economic and political power had finally become serious. Slowly, despite his efforts to temporize, Gorbachev was forced to a point where he had to relinquish his approach of gradual administrative reform and to choose between radical change or reaction. He was not given the time to make the choice.

During 1989 and early 1990, Yeltsin was emerging as the spokesman of the reformists. Despite Gorbachev's strenuous efforts to do so, he failed to prevent Yeltsin's election as president of the Supreme Soviet of the Russian Federation (May 29, 1990). Gorbachev, a keen judge of shifting political forces, made tentative moves toward alliance with Yeltsin. He agreed that several of his economic advisers headed by Stanislav Shatalin should meet with Yeltsin's advisers and jointly develop what became known as the Shatalin Plan or the 500-day plan for rapidly carrying out the main initial moves toward a market economy in the Soviet Union.

But suddenly, Gorbachev shifted his position. In September 1990, he presented to the Supreme Soviet a President's Plan, which pulled back from the Shatalin Plan and maintained the authority of the central government in farming, taxation, and currency. A month later, he presented yet another Gorbachev Plan to the Supreme Soviet, which completely dropped the concept of a transition to a market economy within a specified period of time.

Further developments seemingly documented Gorbachev's cooperation with reactionary elements. In January 1991, units of the Soviet armed forces, acting for a spurious Committee of National Salvation, attacked the buildings of the Lithuanian parliament in Vilnius and killed sixteen unarmed civilians seeking to defend the premises. The following week, Soviet forces staged a raid in Riga, Latvia. Gorbachev claimed not to have been informed of either action until after the fact, but few believed Gorbachev's denials that he had authorized the raids or at least had advance knowledge of them. In the face of statements of support for the governments of the Baltic republics from Boris Yeltsin, a very large pro-Baltic demonstration in Moscow convened by Yeltsin supporters, and of widespread protests from Western governments, the attempt to quell the Baltic republics by force was not pressed further at the time.

Nonetheless, Gorbachev continued to press elements of his reform program. In March 1991, he submitted a revised draft of the Union Treaty to the republic governments. This version was based on the opposite principle from that of November 1990. In the new draft, all power was to be reserved to the republics except that which they explicitly delegated to the central government. It provided for a loose federation in which the republics themselves would rule on secession and on new members. The central government would have responsibility for defense and foreign policy but could not decide on issues of war and peace on its own. Although the important issue of an agreed criterion for the division of revenues was not resolved, the new treaty called for revenues to be raised by the republics and shared with the central government. On April 23, Gorbachev, Yeltsin, and other republic heads initialed the new draft treaty.

Gorbachev had apparently reconciled himself to playing a limited role under this treaty as possible future president of a Soviet central government with limited powers, almost as limited as those of a constitutional monarch. But it was precisely this treaty that was the source of Gorbachev's fall from power. The day after signature of the new Union Treaty, in a closed session of the Central Committee, Communist Party conservatives demanded an accounting from Gorbachev, listing the failures of his policy in the declining economy and in public order. Gorbachev accused his critics of plotting to return the country to totalitarian dictatorship.

On the eve of Gorbachev's July 31 summit meeting with President Bush to sign the START Treaty, another mysterious Soviet raid on Lithuanian border posts took place, with the evident intent of undermining the summit meeting. A few days earlier, on July 24, after a tough all-night session with republic heads, Gorbachev announced that the main details of the new Union Treaty had been agreed upon and that the remaining issue of how much taxation revenue would be given the central government by the republics would soon be solved. The treaty was to be signed the next month, on August 19.

The treaty would have in practice placed the main assets of the Soviet economy in the hands of the Yeltsin government of the Russian Federation and its radical economists, almost all of whom had migrated from Gorbachev to Yeltsin during Gorbachev's shift to the right in the fall of 1990. This shift of responsibility would have made defense and armament production, as well as the size of the Union armed forces, dependent on revenues that would be raised and controlled by the republics, sums that would almost certainly be drastically cut within a short time. This action catalyzed the determination of Gorbachev's conservative opponents, whose power would be drastically curtailed by the new treaty, to remove him.

THE AUGUST COUP AGAINST GORBACHEV

The eight chief conspirators, calling themselves the State Committee for the State of Emergency, comprised Gorbachev's own hand-picked chief aides. Claiming that its objective was to restore law and order in the USSR and prevent chaos, anarchy, and civil war, the junta took control over all aspects of social and economic life on August 19, 1991. The timing of the action was almost certainly determined by the desire of the plotters to block the signature of the new Union Treaty, scheduled to take place the same day in Moscow. In fact, when they finally went on trial in spring 1993, the plotters stated they had acted to prevent the dissolution of the Soviet Union through the treaty.

The conspirators confined Gorbachev to his holiday home at Foros in the Crimea, claimed that he was unwell and had resigned from office in favor of Gennadi Yanayev, and moved troops into Moscow and several other larger cities. But they lacked the resolve and the solid military support to establish their rule by force, and after courageous resistance by

Yeltsin and his followers, the coup dissolved. Gorbachev returned to Moscow August 21 and resumed power, but only formally.

The coup was the last paroxysm of the old order in the Soviet Union. It had momentous consequences: Resistance to the coup marked the political coming of age of the Russian public, which showed courage and determination like that shown by the prodemocracy demonstrators in Eastern Europe. When the conspiracy bubble burst, it dispelled for a time at least the fears of imminent civil war. And it radically diminished the authority of the main institutions of the old order—the KGB, the armed forces, and military-industrial complex. Boris Yeltsin achieved a commanding position in Russian politics on the basis of demonstrated courage and leadership.

These events proved that both foreign and domestic forecasters of a coup in the Soviet Union had been right. But the forecasters, domestic and foreign, all appear to have made the same mistake. Imbued with the experience of Stalinist totalitarian ruthlessness, continued even though routinized in the Brezhnev period, nearly all had assumed that, if a coup did take place in the Soviet Union, it would be successful, at least for a time, because it would be carried out with total ruthlessness and repression, at the cost of considerable bloodshed.

In the event, the coup was a total failure because of the lack of determination to use repressive force. Gorbachev's resistance to bloodshed seems to have spread to the conspirators, who do not seem to have killed a single person intentionally. The plotters failed to kill Gorbachev when they approached him at his vacation residence in the Crimea and thus missed the action that would have made irrevocable their own personal commitment to the coup. They failed to capture Yeltsin, the obvious center of resistance to them, or Anatoli Sobchak, the popular mayor of Leningrad who opposed them. The troops surrounding the Russian Federation's "White House" on August 19–20 in Moscow were instructed not to fire and in fact were not issued live ammunition. The three young men who died in the siege perished in isolated episodes, not organized action by the armed forces. Marshal Yazov told his officers to avoid civilian casualties and pulled his troops out of Moscow after only two days without firing a shot.

In fact, the plotters were not ruthless old-line Stalinists. Instead, they were the top *apparatchiki* of the Soviet Union, the defenders of its main institutions—the military, military production complex, the KGB, and the Communist Party. Their manifesto addressed to the Soviet population made no mention of socialism or Marxism-Leninism. They finally acted, not when Gorbachev downgraded the Soviet Communist Party, agreed to withdraw Soviet forces from Eastern Europe, or made peace with the

United States and NATO, but on the eve of the signature of the Union Treaty, which would have meant the end of their own institutional pre-eminence.

Gorbachev returned from house arrest absorbed in his own experience and wholly unaware of the far-reaching change that had taken place in the minds of Yeltsin's adherents in a few dramatic days. Pale and dazed, he told a press conference on August 22 that the coup had not shaken his belief in the "socialist" ideal. On the basis of the new party program approved in July, he said, there was still the possibility of uniting all that was progressive in the party. The party must be reformed and become "a living force of Perestroika—I am a convinced adherent of the socialist idea."[6]

But Moscow demonstrators were already tearing down the statue of Felix Dzerzhinsky, the ruthless Polish-born leader of Lenin's secret police, in the small square in front of KGB headquarters. The next day, as Gorbachev tried to thank the Supreme Soviet of the Russian Federation for its help in defeating the coup, Yeltsin sneeringly flourished in Gorbachev's face a proclamation suspending the Communist Party on the territory of the Russian Federation.

The Soviet Union Dissolves

The smoke and noise of the falling bastions of institutional Soviet power after failure of the coup tended to obscure an even more far-reaching development—the dissolution of the Soviet Union itself. The defeat of the coup and the discrediting of the chief institutions of forceful repression of the Soviet Union—the military, the interior ministry, and the KGB—dissolved the bonds of fear that had maintained control over the civilian population everywhere in the Soviet Union and severed the bonds of fear that held together the Soviet Union itself.

The coup had a shock-wave effect in this regard. During 1989 and 1990, most of the Soviet Union's fifteen component republics had declared their intention to seek some form of independence, and Armenia had decided to undertake a plebiscite on the subject. However, before the coup, only Lithuania and Georgia had formally proclaimed full independence from the Union of Soviet Socialist Republics. But Estonia and Latvia seceded on August 19. On August 24, the Ukrainian parliament announced its intention to secede if confirmed by a plebiscite on December 1. Belarus declared its independence (August 25), Moldavia (August 27), followed by Azerbaijan (August 30), Uzbekistan (August 31), Kyrgyzstan (August 31), Tajikistan (September 9), Armenia (September 21), and laggard Turkmenistan on October 27. The Russian Federation and Kazakhstan each declared its laws to be sovereign, with precedence over Soviet Union law.

On August 29, 1990, the Russian Federation and Ukraine signed an agreement on economic and defense cooperation. Ukrainian leader Leonid Kravchuk announced he was attempting to organize a summit meeting of the heads of the fifteen Soviet republics in Kiev or Minsk to discuss economic union. Gorbachev would not be invited but would be informed of the outcome. It was generally accepted that some link with Ukraine and Kazakhstan was essential for the economic survival of the Russian Federation, by far the largest component of the Soviet Union. Kazakhstan with a large Russian population (over 40 percent), was regarded as cooperative.

Gorbachev sought to adjust to the new situation by announcing still another draft of the Union Treaty, this time calling for a Union of Sovereign States. He hurriedly dissolved the Supreme Soviet (August 29) and established a State Council composed of the heads of government of the republics, scheduled to become the governing body of the future Union of Sovereign States. The State Council meeting of September 6 recognized the independence of the three Baltic states. In November, a new draft treaty establishing a loose confederation was tentatively agreed by the State Council. But Ukraine, Uzbekistan, Moldova, Georgia, and Armenia did not participate in this meeting.

This was Gorbachev's last effort. The decisive event came on December 1, when the Ukrainian electorate confirmed the decision to declare independence of Ukraine. At that point, Yeltsin, who had been willing to give at least superficial support to Gorbachev's efforts to form a political and economic union, declared Gorbachev's efforts a failure. Yeltsin shifted to the concept of complete elimination of central power and its replacement by understandings agreed among the republics themselves.

THE COMMONWEALTH OF INDEPENDENT STATES

On December 7, 1991 the New Commonwealth of Independent States was founded in a meeting of Ukrainian, Russian Federation, and Belarus leaders near the Belarus capital Minsk. By the end of the month, the other nine republics except for Georgia, riven by civil war, had joined.

The agreement of Minsk and that of Alma-Ata, the capital of Kazakhstan, where the republic leaders met (December 23, 1991) in order to symbolize the equal status of the Central Asian republics and to formalize their original understanding, took the form of a treaty of cooperation among twelve independent, equal sovereign republics, akin in this sense to the 1950 Treaty of Rome among the founding members of the European Community. The participating states committed themselves to provide equal treatment to one another's citizens living on their territory (about 60 million persons, including about 25 million Russians), to respect one another's borders, ensure freedom of movement of citizens within the commonwealth, to respect the borders of all participating states, and to cooperate with one another in politics, economics, education, health care, environment, science, transportation, communications, foreign policy, and defense.

The participants established common institutions, including a Council of Heads of State, a Council of Heads of Government, ministerial committees on foreign affairs, defense, economics and finances, transportation, social security, and internal (police and public order) affairs. They agreed that the Russian Federation would take over the Soviet Union's permanent seat on the UN Security Council. They established a joint command over strategic nuclear forces, temporarily appointed Marshal Yevgeniy Shaposhnikov as its commander, adopted an agreement on control and supervision of nuclear weapons, and agreed to meet further to divide up nonstrategic military forces. The participants declared that the commonwealth was neither a state nor a supranational institution. All decisions would be made by consensus, with each republic having a single equal vote. Russian was designated as the working language.

The Minsk participants declared the Union of Soviet Socialist Republics dissolved.[7] Gorbachev resigned on December 25, and the rump Supreme Soviet voted the USSR (and itself) out of existence on December 26, 1991. Yeltsin began to pay the Soviet armed forces. He took possession from Gorbachev of the Kremlin and of the suitcase with the Soviet nuclear weapons codes, which corresponded in symbolic significance to the royal regalia, the crown and scepter, of the Russian czars.

AN EVALUATION

The climactic events of the second half of 1991—the anti-Gorbachev coup, the weakening of the main institutions of Soviet power, the dissolution of the USSR, its replacement by the Commonwealth of Independent States, and the beginnings of free-market economic reforms at least in the Russian Federation were the logical climax of Gorbachev's withdrawal of the linchpin of totalitarian terror from the old Soviet Union.

It is significant in this context that the dissolution of the mighty USSR was without violence. Not a shot was fired to preserve history's largest empire. Once again, Gorbachev refrained from attempting to hold onto power through force, although resort to force was by this time probably impractical. This absence of violence was Gorbachev's final pride. He said in his resignation speech, "Not once have I regretted that I did not take advantage of the post of General Secretary to rule like a czar."[8]

This was a remarkable achievement. But was the absence of violence in the dissolution of the Warsaw Pact and the Soviet Union a positive virtue on the part of Gorbachev, or was it something else? Robert
Cullen, an American journalist with considerable experience in the Soviet
Union, thinks it was something else, a failure of nerve. He questions
"whether the Russians still possessed the capacity for cruelty required of
any imperial power. . . . The Russian leaders were no longer capable of the
violence that would hold their inner empire together."[9] Cullen draws a
parallel between the decline of the Soviet Union and the dissolution of the
British Empire after World War II. He cites British historian Corelli Barnett,
who ascribes the decline of hard-headed British imperial toughness to
sentimental liberal values propagated by British public schools from the
1830s on, a development that caused the British elite not to think of British
interests, but for example, of Indian interests.[10] In this view, although
Cullen does not put it that way, the civic culture that emerged in Soviet
cities in the 1960s, 1970s, and 1980s could be considered equivalent to
British liberalism in its sapping effects.

Cullen may well be right as far as the irresolute anti-Gorbachev conspirators are concerned. Changes in the values of political elites have again
and again been associated with the decline of political systems, from the
time of classic Rome to the end of Spanish grandeur in the seventeenth century, to the fall of the old regime in France in 1789, and to the end of the
czarist system in Russia itself. Gorbachev's own actions and statements
do demonstrate a radical change in elite values. At the same time, it is
hard to believe that this disciple of KGB chief Yuri Andropov, this man
who had come up through the ranks of the CPSU, and who in the words
of Andrei Gromyko, not a bad judge of political toughness, had "teeth of
steel," experienced a failure of nerve rather than having acted on the basis
of deliberate decision as regards his abstention from the use of force.

The next chapter describes how, parallel to these events in the Soviet
Union, a torrential political deluge swept away the entire structure of
Soviet control over Eastern Europe in less than a year.

2

SLIPPING OFF THE YOKE:
THE LIBERATION OF EASTERN EUROPE

The suddenness and rapidity of the withdrawal of Soviet control from Central and Eastern Europe and the liberation of the peoples of Eastern Europe from communist police-state regimes were remarkable aspects of these events. In a tidal wave of interconnected developments, within a year from the fall of the Berlin Wall in November 1989, communist governments were swept from all the states of Eastern Europe.

With the exception of Romania, the most remarkable aspect of the liberation of Eastern Europe was its lack of violence.

Since the origins of the cold war in East-West disputes over the treatment of defeated Nazi Germany, the Soviet Union had demonstrated rock-hard determination to maintain its political, economic, and military domination over Eastern Europe. From the viewpoint of Soviet leaders, the fact that the Marxist-Leninist system had expanded to Eastern Europe was an essential legitimization of communism within the Soviet Union itself and evidence for the ultimate worldwide victory of Marxism. Thirty ground-force divisions, the cream of the Soviet army, held the area in a steel fist. And the Soviet Union had repeatedly used its troops to eliminate dangers to Soviet control over Eastern Europe. In 1953, it repressed an uprising of Berlin workers that had started with riots over work norms and wages. In 1956, it brutally suppressed the Hungarian uprising, a serious attempt to withdraw from Soviet domination. In 1968, it repressed the "Prague Spring," an effort by the Czechoslovak Communist Party leadership to introduce twenty years ahead of time substantially the same "socialism with a human face" that Mikhail Gorbachev was seeking in his campaign of *perestroika*.

In particular, Western and Soviet leaders alike considered the Soviet hold over East Germany, the German Democratic Republic (GDR), to be unshakable. The GDR was the keystone of the entire Warsaw Pact system. The Soviet hold over that country was the guarantee that there would never again be a German attack on Russia as there had been in 1914 and again in 1941, the last one leaving 16 million dead to the long-suffering Soviet people, who had also lost as many to Stalin's climb to total power.

Most Western and most Soviet leaders considered that serious conflict in Germany would be a certain cause of World War III, the final Armageddon. As many saw it, the fatal sequence of events could start with popular unrest in East Germany that exceeded the control of local police. Volunteers from West Germany would join in the fighting. The Soviet General Staff would order repression of the uprising by Soviet forces. NATO leaders would order an alert of their forces. Misreading the signal, Soviet leaders would order an all-out attack on NATO forces in West Germany. Given their heavy numerical preponderance, the Soviet forces would push back NATO forces and drive toward the North Sea and English Channel. To prevent this, the president of the United States would authorize use of tactical nuclear weapons. The Soviets would respond in kind. To demonstrate its determination to continue to resist, the United States would then carry out a limited strike on Soviet territory with strategic nuclear weapons. This possibility, provided for in contingency planning from a time of clear U.S. superiority in strategic nuclear weapons, had with the increase of Soviet nuclear forces become a "window of vulnerability," because the next anticipated action was full-scale Soviet strategic nuclear attack on the United States.

Despite these fearsome premonitions, in October 1990, only fourteen months from the establishment in August 1989 of a coalition government between the communists and anticommunist Solidarity leaders in Poland, Germany was peacefully united and the governments of all the Warsaw Pact states had been replaced. By 1991, Soviet troops had completely withdrawn from Czechoslovakia and Hungary. By 1992, all combat troops had left Poland. Withdrawals from East Germany, to be completed in 1994, were ahead of schedule. The Warsaw Treaty Organization had been definitively dissolved, as had its economic counterpart, the Council for Mutual Economic Assistance (CMEA).

In the entire process, there were some cases of brutality by national police in repressing popular demonstrations, but recorded deaths were very few. The exception was several hundred dead in Romania, where dictator Nicolae Ceausescu was the only East European political leader to attempt to retain power by force. Czechoslovaks called their nonviolent liberation from Soviet control the "Velvet Revolution." The term was applicable to the entire process in Eastern Europe. The forty-year-old Soviet yoke had not been cast off through resolute military action by local populations. There had been demonstrations by hundreds of thousands of East Germans and Eastern Europeans, highly courageous in the light of the violent repression that most feared, given the past actions of their own police states and of Soviet armed forces. But not one Soviet soldier fired a shot in defense of Soviet domination over an area that most inhabitants and most Westerners had believed the Soviets were determined to hold at any cost. Instead, Soviet troops were ordered not to use force. In place of widespread conflict leading to global nuclear war, the course of events so feared by NATO leaders, the Soviet yoke slipped smoothly off the shoulders of the long-repressed populations of the Warsaw Pact states.

A "New Relationship"

Gorbachev's moves toward development of a new relationship between Moscow and the Warsaw Treaty states were, like his approach to domestic reform, cautious at the outset. In *Perestroika*, written during September–October 1987 when Gorbachev dropped out of public view for a six-week period, he declared that "political relations between the socialist countries must be strictly based on absolute independence. . . . The independence of each Party [sic], the sovereign right to decide the issues facing its country and its responsibility to the nation are the unquestionable principles." However, in the next paragraph, Gorbachev refers to "the interests of world socialism" in an unmistakable echo of the vocabulary of the "Brezhnev doctrine" justifying Soviet military intervention in Czechoslovakia; he says that each socialist government must take into consideration and balance "both its own and common interests."[1]

The positive implication of Gorbachev's arms control moves for greater independence of individual Warsaw Treaty states was clearer than these initial political pronouncements. The underlying message for the non-Soviet members of the Warsaw Pact was unambiguous: The Soviet Union was engaged in serious dismantling of the massive East-West military confrontation in Europe that had held the non-Soviet states of the Warsaw Pact in tight regimentation for forty years. If Gorbachev thus endorsed the view that the danger of attack by German irredentists and their NATO allies was receding, then the fundamental rationale for the tight Soviet hold over the states of Eastern Europe was dissolving.

Gorbachev's support of political reform in Eastern Europe became more explicit with the passage of time. In his momentous speech of December 1988 before the UN, Gorbachev said "the principle of freedom of choice" as regards the institutions of society and external alliances "is mandatory . . . Freedom of choice is a universal principle that should allow for no exceptions. Its non-recognition is fraught with extremely grave consequences for world peace."

When it came to practice, Gorbachev carried out these statements. He did not resist in January 1989 when representatives of the Polish government, the Catholic Church, and Solidarity agreed in Warsaw to "Round-Table" talks on sharing power between Solidarity and the Polish communists, or a month later, when the Central Committee of the Hungarian Communist Party agreed to something that Gorbachev had thus far decried in the Soviet Union, the formation of independent non-communist political parties. To the contrary, after a February 1989 visit to Moscow, Hungarian Premier and Communist Party chief Karoly Grosz reported that, after reviewing the history of the 1956 Soviet invasion of Hungary and the 1968 invasion of Czechoslovakia, Gorbachev had spoken against any foreign intervention in the affairs of the Eastern European states and had accepted the existence of a multiparty system in Hungary. Gorbachev went still further. In a widely reported telephone call to General Secretary Mieczyslaw Rakowski (August 1989), he brought the Polish Communist Party to reverse its refusal to enter a coalition government to be dominated by Solidarity.

In its advanced stages, the process of slipping off the Soviet yoke took different forms in different Eastern European states. In Poland, communism was overthrown by a tripartite coalition of workers, the Catholic Church, and Polish intellectuals inclined toward social democracy. In East Germany, communism was toppled by East Germans voting with their feet for a higher living standard and by other East Germans courageously demonstrating under the leadership of reform communists and of social democratic intellectuals. In Hungary, communism was toppled by a group of communist leaders themselves veering toward social democracy. In Czechoslovakia, it was the university students who in the last stage precipitated the downfall of the communist dictatorship. In Romania, Bulgaria, and Albania, Communist Party leaders sought to maintain their hold on power by radically reforming the Communist Party itself, what Gorbachev had tried to do in the USSR. But in no case was the development as sudden as it appeared to the outside world.

POLAND

After two months of heavy strikes at the Lenin shipyard in 1980, a workers' group known as Solidarity was permitted by the Polish authorities to form an authorized trade union with the right to strike and to work independently of the communist-led Polish unions. From the outset, Solidarity leaders emphasized a nonviolent approach designed to limit police repression and, above all, Soviet military intervention. In 1981, Solidarity overreached itself tactically and posed an ultimatum to the Polish government, demanding a nationwide referendum on establishing a noncommunist government if the government failed to give Solidarity access to media and local free elections. The day after these demands were raised, the Polish government under General Wojciech Jaruzelski imposed martial law (December 1981). It is probable that this action, taken under considerable Soviet pressure, was also motivated by a desire to avoid Soviet military intervention. Solidarity leaders, including founder Lech Walesa, were imprisoned but later amnestied (July 1986).

In the late 1980s, responding to the same economic pressures as were plaguing the Soviet economy, the Polish government once again tried to reduce subsidies and increase prices. Once again, Polish workers went on strike, first at Nowa Huta and then at the Lenin shipyards (August 1988). Walesa demanded reorganization of the Polish government. At the end of the year, the Central Committee of the Polish United Workers Party (the Communist Party) decided that Solidarity should be conditionally legalized for a two-year trial period (January 1989). The following month, round-table talks began between the Polish government and Communist Party, Solidarity, and the Catholic Church. The steadily increasing standing of the Catholic Church was as important as the comeback of Solidarity in determining the final outcome.

The intention of Polish communist leaders on entering the round-table talks was not power-sharing. It was to co-opt prominent noncommunist personalities who could help the party gain support from the Polish public for economic reforms that had previously floundered on public resistance. Success of these reforms, communist leaders calculated, would enable them to retain power.

Similar considerations motivated parallel actions by the leadership of the Hungarian Communist Party—they believed that by coopting noncommunist groups they could retain decisive power. Both leadership groups made the same mistake Gorbachev made—they vastly overestimated popular support for the communist approach and underestimated pent-up aversion to it.

Step by step, the Polish communists ceded positions. They agreed to hold partially free elections in summer 1989, in which 65 percent of the seats in the Polish lower house or Sejm would be held for communists, and 35 percent would be open to free election, as would all seats in the Polish Senate. At the end of the election process, Solidarity held 99 of 100 Senate seats and all of the 161 electable seats in the Sejm (June 1989). In August, an all-party coalition government was finally formed under Solidarity leader Tadeusz Mazowiecki after Gorbachev prevailed on the Polish communists to participate. Mazowiecki was the first noncommunist head of government in a Warsaw Pact state. It was a remarkable achievement of persistence, courage, and tactics by the Solidarity leadership and their supporters in the Polish population.

In December 1990, Walesa emerged as the first directly elected president in Polish history. And in October 1991, Poland held its first free elections for the national parliament since 1926, when the patriotic general Josef Pilsudski, victor over the Soviet invasion of 1920, took over the government. Only 43 percent of the Polish electorate participated in the 1991 elections. The Polish election law had no requirement that political parties must obtain a stated minimum percentage of the vote in order to be represented in parliament. The result was representation in the Sejm of twenty-nine separate political parties, many representing only 1 or 2 percent of the popular vote. Mazowiecki's Democratic Union, the largest single party, received only 13 percent of the popular vote.

The situation was ominously similar to that of the Weimar Republic in the 1920s where a like number of parties in shifting unstable coalitions created weak and ineffective government amid very difficult economic conditions. And economic difficulties were mounting in Poland. Real income in 1991 was down one-third from the level of 1989, itself low. Unemployment was at 2 million, 10 percent of the work force of 20 million, and forecast to increase to 18 percent, or 3.5 million, by the end of 1992.

Given these conditions, President Walesa had difficulty in getting a coalition together, finally appointing Jan Olszewski prime minister. At last, Poland had a freely elected president and a freely elected government. But the new government was committed to backing away from the rigors of economic "shock therapy." The symbol of shock therapy, Finance Minister Leszek Balcerowicz, was fired in the turnover.

HUNGARY

The Gorbachev-era development in Hungary lacked the drama of Polish events, with Solidarity's long and courageous struggle against an oppressive regime. Yet the Hungarian developments brought the first free parliamentary elections among Warsaw Pact states, and it was also the actions by the Hungarian government that brought down the hard-line Erich Honecker regime in East Germany. Moreover, against the background of bitter popular resentment of the bloody 1956 Soviet repression of the Hungarian uprising, the Hungarian government took the lead among the non-Soviet Warsaw Pact states in demanding withdrawal of Soviet troops from its territory and in insisting on rapid and complete dissolution of the Warsaw Pact and of the CMEA, the Soviet-directed committee for economic coordination of the East European states.

The turnover within the Hungarian Communist Party began early. On the same day in June 1987 when Gorbachev was purging the Soviet Politburo in Moscow, two old-line communists, the president of Hungary (and the general secretary of the Hungarian Communist Party) and the prime minister, were pushed out of office in Budapest. Their replacements, Karoly Nemeth and Karoly Grosz, belonged to a new breed of communist leaders who argued for free elections, more than once predicted they would lose these elections, and stated that if they lost, they would honor the outcome and accept it peacefully. The following year, long-time party leader Janos Kadar, who had taken over during Soviet repression of the 1956 uprising and had introduced several partial moves toward market economy, was removed as party chief and replaced by Grosz. Forty percent of Central Committee members were also replaced (May 1988).

In February 1989, the Central Committee approved the formation of independent political parties and abandoned its constitutional role as leading political force of the nation, a full year before the Soviet Union undertook similar actions. At a time when Walesa and his fellow Solidarity leaders were struggling inch by inch for power-sharing with the Polish Communist Party under the threat of strikes, the Hungarian Communist Party leadership was voluntarily conceding power to other groups, in the absence of public pressures, but anticipating those pressures. The Hungarian party leaders met with opposition political forces and in September 1989 reached agreement with them on the text of a new constitution and on holding multiparty elections in June 1990. Communist Party leaders believed that by negotiating reform and devolution of power from above, they could retain political power and be elected as the decisive element of a coalition government in the coming elections.

While these developments were taking place, the Hungarian government in January 1989 signed the concluding document of the Vienna Conference on Security and Cooperation in Europe (CSCE) Follow-Up meeting, which included a provision ensuring that citizens of CSCE states should have the freedom to enter and leave their countries. In March 1989, the government signed the UN Protocol on Refugees, which obliges signatory states not to force political refugees to return home. These new obligations conflicted with a provision of the Hungarian-East German Treaty of 1969, which committed each government not to allow citizens of the other state to depart from its territory without showing a valid exit visa—in other words, each government pledged itself to act as police officer to maintain the Iron Curtain for the other.

On August 31, in a momentous meeting in East Berlin between Hungarian foreign minister Gyula Horn and East German foreign minister Oskar Fischer, Horn ended a tense session by telling Fischer that, in the view of the Hungarian government, its obligation under the UN convention was more binding than the 1969 treaty it had made with the GDR. It would return the thousands of East Germans flocking to Hungary to East Germany, but only if the East German government committed itself to let these people leave East Germany if they wished.[2] German chancellor Helmut Kohl and foreign minister Hans-Dietrich Genscher pled with Hungarian leaders to let the East Germans pass over their borders. Gorbachev is reported to have left the final decision to the Hungarians.[3]

On September 11, the Hungarian government announced that it had suspended its 1969 agreement with the GDR government. In practice, the Hungarians had aligned themselves with noncommunist Federal Germany against the communist GDR. Within the next thirty-six hours, 20,000 East Germans who had been waiting in camps in Hungary were in Austria, waiting to be moved to Federal Germany by train. The figure had risen to 30,000 by the beginning of October, when mass demonstrations in East German cities became the center of attention.

During March and April 1990, the Hungarian general elections took place. The hopes of Hungarian communist leaders that they would continue to hold a position of decisive influence were not fulfilled. The new government was formed by the conservative Democratic Forum, with the Small Holders Party and Christian Democratic Party as its smaller coalition parties, giving the government a total of 229 seats in a 386-seat parliament. The Hungarian Communist Party, renamed the Socialist Party, got only 33 seats, a miserable showing. It was the first Hungarian free election since the Soviet takeover of Eastern Europe.

After the elections, the main opposition party, the liberal Alliance of Free Democrats, pressed the newly elected government to begin negotiations on Hungarian withdrawal from the Warsaw Pact. In a resolution of June 1990, the Hungarian Parliament voted 232 to 0 in favor of this move. Already in March, the old communist-dominated government had opened negotiations for withdrawal of Soviet forces from Hungary in the hope of improving its chances in the forthcoming general elections. Subsequently, Hungarian political leaders explained that a major factor in the urgency with which they pressed for agreement on withdrawal of Soviet troops from Hungary and for dissolution of the Warsaw Pact and the CMEA was their desire to bring about these changes while Gorbachev was still in power; Hungarian leaders increasingly feared a right-wing coup in the Soviet Union that would suspend Gorbachev's decisions.

Leaving aside East Germany as a special case because of the influence of West Germany, Hungary moved fastest of the East European states in establishing a freely elected parliamentary system, respect for human rights, and the rule of law. We have seen how Hungary's adherence to CSCE and UN commitments on human rights triggered the chain of events in the summer of 1989 that led to German unification. A year later, in recognition of these real achievements, the Council of Europe admitted Hungary to full membership (November 1990), the first former communist state to meet its criteria.

CZECHOSLOVAKIA

The Gorbachev changes reached the Czechoslovak Communist Party in 1987. Aging president Gustav Husak resigned in favor of Milos Jakes (December 1987). On the August 1988 twentieth anniversary of the 1968 Soviet invasion of Czechoslovakia, a crowd of 10,000 demonstrators in Wenceslas Square calling for democratic reforms was broken up by Czechoslovak riot police. However, later in the year, at a meeting of the Communist Party's Central Committee, Prime Minister Lubomir Strougal and his deputy were forced to resign (October 1988). At the beginning of 1989, a small group of demonstrators in Prague commemorating the twentieth anniversary of the suicide by self-immolation of the Czechoslovak student Jan Palac in protest against the Soviet invasion was again put down by the riot police. Vaclav Havel, a playwright and a leading dissident, was arrested, sentenced, and later released on parole.

The decisive turning point in slipping off the communist yoke in Czechoslovakia came in November 1989 after police again broke up a demonstration and were rumored to have killed a student. An umbrella organization of protest groups called Civic Forum was founded on November 19 and staged a much larger rally of 200,000 on November 20, calling for a countrywide sympathy strike on November 27. On November 24, the Politburo of the Czechoslovak Communist Party resigned, but Havel dramatically charged before a crowd of 200,000 that these changes in the party leadership were a "fraud" and that the old system continued. On November 27, millions of workers throughout Czechoslovakia joined in a two-hour sympathy strike against the regime. Power-sharing talks between the Communist Party leadership and Havel and other Civic Forum leaders began. A coalition government with a majority of noncommunists was established in December 1989. Free elections took place in June 1990. Civic Forum and its allies received a majority of seats: Havel was reelected president of Czechoslovakia after having first been elected to that office by the parliament the previous December.

The Czechoslovaks had carried out a nonviolent Velvet Revolution. Even the reported death of a protesting student the previous November at the hands of police was subsequently revealed to have been based on a misunderstanding. The revolution left Czechoslovakia a small state of 16 million people, 50,000 square miles, with gross national product in 1988 of $158 billion, the only central Eastern European country with a prewar record of democracy and a political culture of solid middle-class values, whose population showed tenacity and quiet obstinacy rather than the audacity of the Poles, and with a leader in President Havel who was better able than others in Eastern Europe to grasp and to articulate the essence of the repressive, dreary communist experience.

But, in 1991, the Civic Forum coalition of students, intellectuals, social democrats, anticommunists, and reform communists split, as Solidarity had broken up in Poland, into a right-wing free enterprise group under Finance Minister Vaclav Klaus, with others grouped around President Havel. Economic reform slowed in 1991 as tensions increased between Czechs and Slovak nationalists.

Many Slovaks considered that since the independence of Czechoslovakia in 1918, their earlier patronizing tutelage at the hands of Austrians had continued in the hands of the better-educated, more affluent Czech population. In the 1990s, Slovakia, still an agrarian economy punctuated with a few now tottering large-scale industries including a tank plant for Soviet-designed T–72 tanks, was suffering the social consequences of economic reform, especially higher unemployment than in the Czech lands. Even Christian Democratic Slovak premier Jan Carnogursky, a former political prisoner and a strong supporter of Havel and Civic Forum, came out for separation, as did the coalition of former communists and nationalists led by Vladimir Meciar. Public opinion polls showed a considerable majority in both parts of the country for the continuation of common government, but the level of support was dropping in Slovakia.

As thirteen rounds of discussion between Czech and Slovak leaders on power-sharing ended without results in November 1991, President Havel asked the national assembly to pass a law providing for a national referendum on the subject. Havel's effort was rejected by the parliament. Finally, in November 1992, the Czechoslovak Federal Parliament voted for separation of the two parts of the country, an action that came into effect on January 1, 1993. The powerful wave of anticommunism and anti-Soviet nationalism that had brought the liberation of Eastern Europe from the Soviet system had developed into a flood of pure nationalism and the democratic state of Czechoslovakia had fallen victim to it.

THE BALKAN COUNTRIES

The Balkan communist countries, Romania, Bulgaria, and Albania, had far less experience with parliamentary democracy than the northern tier of East Germany, Poland, Hungary, and Czechoslovakia. They had remained under Ottoman Turkish colonial rule well into modern times. Romania and Bulgaria gained independence from the Ottomans only in the late 1870s. Albania did not do so until 1912. Characteristically, all three states were personal dictatorships rather than being ruled, as in the north, by a clique of top communist leaders, each with a regional power base of his own. This system to a degree limited the absolute rule of the party general secretaries and acted to replace them in situations of political or economic crisis. And unlike the ruling cliques of the northern tier, the Balkan dictators made little effort in the 1980s to devolve power through "round-table" power-sharing after Gorbachev began his reforms in the Soviet Union. All three dictators, Nicolae Ceausescu of Romania, Todor Zhivkov of Bulgaria, and Ramiz Alia of Albania (who had taken over when dictator Enver Hoxha died in 1985 after a rule of forty years), opposed Gorbachev-style reforms, although Zhivkov did institute some of them. None of these countries had Soviet forces stationed in them, and Gorbachev's pro-reform influence on them was weaker than in the northern tier. These dictators, too, were swept away following the revolutionary changes in the north, but there were significant differences. In Romania, Bulgaria, and Albania, the old regime was ousted and replaced by groups of their own communist colleagues. For a time at least, the communists remained in power under different labels.

In Romania, Ceausescu's program of paying off Romania's foreign debt at any social cost led to blackouts and energy shortages in 1987, 1988, and 1989. Police ruthlessly repressed the most recent of a series of revolts by Romanian coal miners in Brasov (October 1987). In June 1988, about 50,000 Hungarians demonstrated in Budapest against Ceausescu's plan to raze about 7,000 villages in Transylvania largely occupied by Hungarians and to replace them by 500 agro-industrial complexes featuring high-rise apartment houses. Ceausescu rejected protests by the Hungarian government and ordered the Hungarian consulate in Cluj-Napoca closed.

In November 1989, after the Polish and Hungarian communists had ceded power and after the fall of the Honecker government in East Germany, Ceausescu was unanimously reelected to another five-year term as general secretary of the Romanian Communist Party. Yet his reign was to end in the next month.

On December 16, in the Transylvanian town of Timisoara, the Romanian Security Police attempted to deport Laszlo Tokes, a Hungarian Lutheran pastor who had criticized the Romanian government for mistreating the Hungarian minority. Ceausescu ordered the Security Police to open fire on 10,000 Hungarian demonstrators. They did so, and many hundred were killed; even today it is not clear how many. In Bucharest, Ceausescu was booed and shouted down in a demonstration of 10,000 (December 21). The Romanian Security Police killed at least thirteen people, but the crowd would not disperse. The following day some elements of the armed forces joined the demonstrators in storming the Central Committee Building. Ceausescu and his wife, Elena, fled but were captured by the military, tried for genocide, and executed on December 25, 1989.

The Council of National Salvation, a group of communist leaders who later claimed they had long been plotting to depose Ceausescu, named one of their members, Ion Iliescu, interim president. In an election held in May 1990 after only a week's preparation, the National Salvation Front headed by the same anti-Ceausescu communist leaders won 67 percent of the seats in Romania's two-house parliament, and Iliescu was elected president with 85 percent of the vote.

In Bulgaria, the final crisis came in November–December 1989. Early in November, the Bulgarian environmentalist group Eco-Glasnost held a demonstration of close to 10,000 in Sofia. Zhivkov, in power since 1954, unexpectedly resigned as president and general secretary and was replaced as party general secretary by Petar Mladenov. Early in December, opposition groups including Eco-Glasnost merged to form the Union of Democratic Forces. The Central Committee of the Bulgarian Communist Party purged the Politburo and the Central Committee itself of hard-line members and expelled Zhivkov from the party. Later he was placed on trial for embezzlement. Open elections were held in June 1990. The Bulgarian Socialist Party, the renamed but basically unchanged Communist Party, gained a majority of 211 of 400 seats in the national parliament against the poorly organized, multigroup Union of Democratic Forces.

Albania, a tiny state of 3 million and 11,000 square miles, the last holdout among East European communist states, held its first free elections in March 1991. As in Bulgaria and Romania, the party of former communists, the Party of Labor of Albania, won the election. It won 162 of 250 seats, while the Democratic Party of Albania won only 65. The countryside voted en masse for communist candidates, while a gerrymandered election law favored rural districts. In June 1991, after a series of violent demonstrations in the cities and a three-week general strike, the communist government resigned and was replaced by a coalition government headed by Ylli Bufi, who promised new elections soon. These were held in March 1992: The noncommunist Democratic Party won 62 percent of the vote and formed the government; the Socialist (Communist) Party received only 25 percent of the vote.

SOVIET INTENTIONS

Did Gorbachev deliberately work toward smooth dissolution of the Soviet position in Eastern Europe on the basis of a preexisting plan, having concluded even before he came to power that the Soviet position there was in the long-term unsustainable? It is clear that use of force by Soviet troops in Eastern Europe would have tightened and mobilized the old totalitarian system within the Soviet Union, an outcome that would have destroyed Gorbachev's attempts to restructure that system. Soviet armed repression in Eastern Europe could also have resulted in worldwide nuclear war. It would certainly have destroyed Gorbachev's efforts to establish a more cooperative relationship with the United States and Western Europe.

A few of Gorbachev's conservative nationalist critics, like Colonel Viktor Alksnis of the Soyuz faction in the Supreme Soviet, and Colonel General Igor Rodionov, the commander during the Soviet army massacre of Georgian demonstrators in Tbilisi in April 1989, darkly intimated, in the tradition of German Reichswehr officers in 1919, that the Gorbachev leadership had with deliberate forethought deprived the Soviet armed forces of the fruits of victory, in this case the Soviet Union's smashing military victory over the Third Reich. And in his report to the 28th CPSU Congress, Foreign Minister Eduard Shevardnadze claimed "yes, in principle, we did foresee the changes. We sensed their inevitability."[4]

Most probably, however, the Soviet leadership had no preconceived plan. The initial impulses for change in Eastern Europe were unplanned byproducts of change in the USSR. Gorbachev's initial *glasnost* reforms in the Soviet Union brought negative reaction from conservative communists in the USSR. To bolster his domestic program, Gorbachev then urged reform in Eastern Europe. Under the influence of reform elements in most Eastern European countries, their publics mobilized and become more assertive. The Soviet leadership refused military intervention, and the process got out of hand.

The question of Gorbachev's original motivation is relatively unimportant in comparison to the consequences of these actions. What is clear is that Gorbachev's actions and statements in favor of *glasnost* and *perestroika* in the Soviet Union encouraged moves toward independence in Eastern Europe. Cumulatively, these statements dispelled the pervasive fear of armed repression that was the heritage of the Stalin and Brezhnev eras, making it feasible for reformers, nationalists, and thousands of ordinary citizens to dare to resist the status quo. It is also clear that Gorbachev and his colleagues rapidly understood what was going on in Eastern Europe and quickly decided not to use force and make the best of it. Soviet armed forces did not intervene at any stage in the Central and Eastern European countries where they were deployed, the German Democratic Republic, Poland, Czechoslovakia, or Hungary, although they were in a position to do so decisively, at least in terms of the initial effects of intervention. Nor did they seek to enter neighboring Romania or Bulgaria. Reports that Gorbachev gave explicit orders to Soviet forces in Eastern Europe not to intervene are highly plausible. In any event, Soviet forces did not do so in a single instance.

GERMAN UNIFICATION

The four main allies of World War II—France, the United Kingdom, the United States, and the Soviet Union—had put every effort into defeating Nazi Germany, but they could not agree what to do with Germany once it was defeated. From one viewpoint, this disagreement was not difficult to understand: Since the rise of the nation-state in sixteenth-century Europe, no enduring place had been found for Germany among the European states. In the immediate sense, the World War II allies broke over the issue of allocating reparations to the USSR from the part of defeated Germany occupied by the Western allies. The Soviet Union, which had nearly been destroyed by Hitler's ferocious 1941 attack, was not satisfied that its growing control over East Germany provided sufficient assurance against future misuse of German power. Consequently, it made repeated efforts to regain its role in joint control over West Germany as well. In furtherance of this objective, in 1952, Soviet leaders proposed creation of a unified neutral Germany. Later versions of the proposal foresaw unification through free nationwide elections, which is what took place nearly forty years later.[5]

But even if Stalin had in fact been prepared to relax his hold on East Germany and to permit genuinely free elections in return for a more certain control of Germany's foreign and military policy, the concept still could not have worked. No Western leader could trust the Stalinist Soviet Union not to seek increasing influence over a Germany united in this way. No Western leader could trust the recently defeated Germans to responsibly undertake such a difficult role in Europe. There was no general European framework in which a limited Germany could have been fitted. So the division of Germany continued for decades as the best solution achievable at the time, but at a high continued cost of a massive military confrontation that could erupt into a third world war and of totalitarian rule over the population of East Germany, as well as of the East European states.

Forty years later, all of these conditions had changed fundamentally. West Germany had been successful in establishing a functioning federal democracy, with political and social institutions that functioned as well as any in the world, including an effective parliament; an independent judiciary; and successful division of power in a federal system. Germany had carried out meticulous prosecution of Germans for war crimes and a conscientious program of material restitution and reparation for Nazi crimes. Its civilian-controlled armed forces had been purged of the vices of Prussian discipline while retaining military effectiveness. It had functioning political parties (showing their age like political parties throughout the industrialized world, but still more healthy than most); strong trade unions with an important role in cooperative management of the economy through legally ensured positions on the board of directors of all larger companies; and independent public media run by hypercritical intellectuals. West Germany's political system had absorbed and integrated the interests of 10 million German expellees and refugees from former German territories and from East Germany without developing political extremism.

Germany's success in building a functioning democratic system was so evident that, as German unification came into sight, public opinion polls in all the European countries that had suffered war or occupation by Nazi invaders, including the Soviet Union itself, showed that astoundingly high majorities welcomed the idea of German unification. This was a remarkable, spontaneous "report card" for forty years of practicing German democracy.

Moreover, forty years after the early Soviet proposals for German unification, there was a functioning international framework into which a unified Germany could be smoothly and securely fitted. It was composed of the increasingly strong European Community, which had brilliantly justified the insight of its creators that the best way to deal with defeated Germany, at least West Germany, was to embed it in a system of economic and political cooperation, and of a NATO alliance of which Federal Germany had for decades been a responsible and fully contributing member, and also of new security institutions like the Conference on Security and Cooperation in Europe.

WHY SO RAPIDLY?

These fundamental changes from the cold war conditions that had brought the division of Germany explain to some extent why German unification, once impossible, had become more possible. But why did German unity come about so rapidly and unexpectedly?

Largely because of one key element that had been discounted in most outside analyses and those made by West Germans, too—the East German population. Over the years, the assumption had grown that the populations of all of the East European communist states, and especially the orderly, disciplined East Germans, should be discounted as important political factors. Moreover, it was widely believed that the East German regime was the toughest and most ruthless among the satellite regimes and, as we have noted, that the Soviet Union would maintain its dominant position in East Germany by force if necessary. None of these key assumptions proved correct.

In hindsight, it is possible to identify the factors that came together so suddenly during 1989 to create the political dam burst of German unification. We have already described some of these precipitating factors: Gorbachev's encouragement of reform among the ruling communist parties of Eastern Europe, his toleration of power-sharing in Poland and Hungary at the beginning of 1989, and the Hungarian decision to open Hungary's borders with the West and not to enforce travel restrictions of the East German regime, with tens of thousands of East Germans voting with their feet for the West German system over their own.

Then came demonstrations by hundreds of thousands of East Germans in Leipzig, Dresden, and East Berlin calling for domestic political reform, the failure of the East German communist leadership to use force against the demonstrators, a failure in which the severe illness of East German political leader Erich Honecker may have played an important role, and the fall of the Berlin Wall.[6]

These events came so rapidly that they took on the quality of a political avalanche, to use our preferred metaphor, a dam burst or tidal wave that no one, not even the Soviets, dared to stop. We have noted the important role in these events of the positive qualities of Federal German society. But, ironically, Germany's dark past also was a factor. No outsider wanted to take the risk of seriously crossing the Germans in East or West for fear of ultimate negative consequences.

The crucial factor in the nearly bloodless unification of Germany was the smoothness and rapidity with which the Soviet Union under Gorbachev adjusted to the new situation after the fall of the Berlin Wall, although Gorbachev had good help from the United States, Federal

German, and other Western governments. As late as the summit meeting with President Bush at Malta at the beginning of December 1989, Gorbachev described the outlook for German unity in the same terms that he had repeatedly used over the past five years of his rule: The division of Germany was a fact of history. Realism required acceptance of the fact that there were two German states. This is the way it was and that way it would remain. But less than eight weeks later, in his Moscow meeting with the newly designated East German prime minister, reform communist Hans Modrow, Gorbachev accepted German unification as a probability.

It is probable that, ultimately, Gorbachev could not have blocked German unification except through the use of force, which would have entailed the risk of war with the NATO alliance and which would in any event have cost him not only the possibility of improved relations with the Western countries but also the continuation of his entire program to reform the Soviet Union. However, convictions were very strong among Soviet leaders and people that the best way to ensure that the terrible sacrifices of the Great Patriotic War against Hitler had not been in vain was to maintain the Soviet hold on East Germany and to keep Germany divided. Under the influence of these ingrained feelings, Gorbachev might well have postponed and delayed for a considerable time. If he had done so, there is considerable possibility that in East Germany and in the Soviet Union, opposition to the final outcome might then have coalesced, that violence might have been used by the East German regime or the Soviet military, and that the final result might have been conflict.

It was part of Gorbachev's political genius that he recognized the considerable dangers of this course and that he moved with rapidity to avoid them. Even so, if the German unification issue had been at the center of public attention in the Soviet Union at the time it was being negotiated, instead of disputes over Gorbachev's own program of domestic reforms, it is probable that the Gorbachev government would not have felt itself free to act as it did.

Once the decision of principle was achieved, several additional factors accounted for the smoothness and speed with which the actual process of German unification took place within a mere twelve months. Other factors were the pressure of the East Germans migrating into West Germany in late 1989 and early 1990 at the rate of 2,000 per day, and fear in West Germany and other Western countries of abrupt change in Soviet policy or in Soviet leadership. In the light of Gorbachev's swing to the right in the fall of 1990 under the pressure of dissatisfaction and opposition to his domestic policy, the view is not baseless that what Gorbachev agreed to in the first six or seven months of 1990 might not have been politically feasible only a few months later.

Another factor that made for speed in the unification process was the enlightened posture of the U.S. administration. President Bush and his officials registered very quickly the fact that German unification was not a problem or a catastrophe for the United States but, instead, the positive fulfillment of forty years of resolute and farsighted containment policy by the United States and its allies. Also of great importance was the agreement by the Soviet Union and the Western allies not to interfere with the details of German unification as a domestic process. The wartime victors over Nazi Germany were entitled to such interference by the rights they had reserved for themselves after defeat of Nazi Germany with regard to German unification. Instead, they decided to limit their prerogatives to the external aspects of German unification.[7]

A further important factor in the speed of the unification process was the decision, ratified through the March 1990 East German elections, to extend the Federal German Basic Law to East Germany rather than to draft a complete new constitution for a united Germany. In practice, this meant extension of the domestic system and foreign policy commitments of the existing Federal Republic to East Germany. This outcome marginalized the East German reform groups that desired to make a new beginning with East German society, to find a more humane "third way" between Soviet communist and what East German reformers considered the extreme *laissez-faire* capitalism of the Bonn state. Ironically, the East German reformers did not realize that what they sought already existed to a large degree in Federal Germany's social market economy. Bonn's takeover was handled with considerable tact, even though the reformers claimed they had been pressed too hard. The decision to apply the Basic Law, whose value as a framework for the democratic process had been demonstrated by experience, made it possible to do in months what would otherwise have taken years in a messy process of drafting a new constitution.

A further factor making for speed of the unification process was the agreement of the four powers to the German desire that there should be no peace treaty negotiations with Germany. If a peace conference on Germany had taken place, over forty countries would have participated in what would have inevitably have been a long process. Federal German leaders considered that Germany had worked its way back to civilized society with its own programs of restitution to Israel, Poland, and to individual victims of Naziism, also with its meticulous prosecution of war crimes, and that it would not be right to put a united German government in a situation like that of the negotiators on the Versailles Treaty after World War I. The existence of the CFE Treaty, a framework into which restrictions on German armed forces could be folded in a nondiscriminatory way, was also important in smoothing the way to unification.

Nonetheless, even after movement toward democracy started in Poland, most observers in East and West considered East Germany would be the last to make concessions to domestic reformers. The East German regime was among the most conservative in the Warsaw Pact. East German leader Erich Honecker openly rejected the idea of German unity. The political and economic systems of the two German states were, he said, as incompatible as fire and water. Honecker openly opposed the idea that the GDR should emulate Soviet political reforms and had even censored Soviet publications that described Gorbachev's *perestroika* program before permitting their circulation in East Germany. Honecker and his colleagues had close links with Soviet conservatives. GDR leaders joined outside observers in considering the East German population orderly and disciplined.

However, in a fateful move at the beginning of the 1980s as the political crisis over deployment of new Soviet and U.S. medium-range INF missiles reached its peak, Honecker decided to try to exploit the strong desire of the East German population for peace and arms control in order to improve his own public-opinion standing. In fact, backing for arms control was the only source of widespread support the GDR regime ever received from the East German population. The substantive position of the East German Protestant Church on this topic was very close to that of the GDR regime, so Honecker allowed the church slightly increased latitude to host discussion groups on East-West relations and current events. These informal discussion circles, courageously protected by the church, which wished to make good in this way for its own lack of determination in opposing the Hitler dictatorship, eventually generated the political reform groups that played a vital role in the overturning the East German communist leadership in the second half of 1989.

But, beyond this relatively small handful of reformers, the decisive element in German unification was the East German people, who in the tens of thousands broke out of their prison state through Austria and Czechoslovakia and later, directly across the inner German border, and who demonstrated against the East German regime and its police in the major cities of East Germany until they swept aside the Berlin Wall and obliged leaders in East and West to grant them the unification they demanded.

The courage and determination of these East Germans were among the major surprises of German unification. The absence of a violent response from the East German leadership was another. The Socialist Unity Party (SED) regime under Honecker was among the toughest in the Warsaw Pact. Yet Honecker did not move to use force when acute problems arose in East Germany. We have cited the main reason for this—clear signals from Gorbachev that Soviet military would not intervene against East German citizens.

A second reason, perhaps a critical one, was that Honecker himself was seriously ill with liver cancer at the critical moment for SED decisions on using force. If Honecker had been healthy and politically active, it seems quite possible that, even without Soviet backing, he would have decided on heavy use of force against the East German demonstrators in Leipzig and Dresden. As a consequence, the process of German unification could have become far more dangerous.

THE EAST GERMANS ACT

In August 1989, hundreds of East Germans crossed into Austria from Hungary. On September 11, the Hungarians opened their borders. At the end of September, the East German regime permitted the transit to West Germany of over 10,000 East Germans who had been camped out on the grounds of the Federal German Embassy in Prague clamoring to go to West Germany. On October 3, in an effort to stem the blow, East German authorities banned all foreign travel by East German citizens. The next day, there was a mass demonstration of 10,000 East Germans at the Dresden railroad yards as demonstrators tried to board the East German trains taking their fellow East Germans from the West German Embassy in Prague to West Germany. Two days later, Gorbachev was in East Berlin on the same platform with his estranged political ally Honecker to celebrate the fortieth anniversary of the establishment of the GDR. On this occasion, Gorbachev is said to have urged Honecker once again to show flexibility and to move with the times. However, Gorbachev seemed to have given up in this effort when he stated emphatically and prophetically at the end of the visit that "he who is too late will be punished by life."

For Honecker, it was already too late. Demonstrations in East Berlin, Leipzig, and Dresden of about 10,000 people each protesting the travel ban and calling for reform of the GDR system were broken up by the East German police. But on October 9, a much larger demonstration of 50,000 to 70,000 people headed by leaders of church discussion groups appeared in Leipzig. Egon Krenz, then state security chief of the GDR, claims that he countermanded orders by Honecker to use deadly force in this demonstration. In any event, the demonstration was probably the watershed event for the end of the communist regime in East Germany.

On October 16, over 100,000 Leipzigers demonstrated against the SED government, with at least 30,000 demonstrators in Dresden. On October 18, Krenz got a majority vote in the SED Politburo to force Honecker out of power and to appoint Krenz himself as successor. But the East Germans were not satisfied with a state security head as Honecker's successor. Over 300,000 protesters turned out in Leipzig and 100,000 in

Dresden (October 23). Within a week, the Leipzig demonstrators were no longer calling for reform of East German institutions, but for unification with the Federal Republic.

On November 1, the East German government reopened the border with Czechoslovakia; 50,000 East Germans used this route to flee to Federal Germany within a week. Five of the eighteen members of the SED Politburo resigned on November 3. But this did not satisfy the East German population. On November 4, a huge crowd of over 500,000 demonstrated in East Berlin calling for democratic institutions and elections. Hans Modrow, reformist SED leader from Dresden, was nominated prime minister on November 8. The next day, November 9, 1989, the GDR government announced that exit visas would be granted to all citizens.

But the GDR population did not wait to be issued the visa applications. They crowded in the thousands to the crossing points into West Berlin. After seeing the number of people involved, the East German police apparently decided on their own to let them through. The Berlin Wall, a symbol of police repression for nearly thirty years (since August 1961), had fallen. On hearing the news, the Federal German Bundestag, in session in Bonn, spontaneously broke into "Deutschland uber alles." Millions of people throughout the world joined the Germans in celebrating the end of the world's most notorious monument to political oppression.

THE INTERGOVERNMENTAL PHASE

By the beginning of 1990, as East German migration to West Germany continued at rates of over 100,000 a month, unaffected by Chancellor Kohl's agreement with GDR prime minister Hans Modrow to move toward a confederate status for the two German states, German leaders on both sides had realized that the goal would have to be full unification and that it would have to happen rapidly. Gorbachev had conceded to Chancellor Kohl and Foreign Minister Genscher that unification could take place if a united Germany could be fitted safely into a European security order, and agreement had been reached on the mechanism through which this goal was to be sought, the Two-Plus-Four talks (negotations between the two German states and the four wartime Allies).

Some future historians may consider the momentous agreements reached during 1990 on the German unification issue as mere implementing actions. However, the situation in and around Germany remained highly delicate. The whole process of reaching decisions was much like defusing a gigantic land mine. At any moment, acute problems could have arisen—through the actions of the huge throngs in East Germany, or also in the Soviet Union, where the powerful conservative opposition to

Gorbachev had been distracted from foreign issues by controversy over dismantling the Stalinist state, or through disputes among the Western allies. All these dangers were avoided by the skill of the leaders involved.

In early February 1990, Federal Republic of Germany foreign minister Genscher flew to Washington in a successful effort to gain the Bush administration's support for an accelerated program of unification. A few days later, Secretary of State James Baker conveyed Washington's support to Soviet leaders in Moscow. An important breakthrough came when Chancellor Kohl and Foreign Minister Genscher flew to Moscow to confer with Gorbachev and reported after their discussions that Gorbachev had unambiguously committed the Soviet Union to accept German unification, with the process of unification and its timing to be determined by the Germans themselves. Then, during the late February meeting in Ottawa of NATO and Warsaw Pact states to discuss President Bush's proposal for an "Open Skies" system of aerial observation, agreement was reached to handle the external aspects of German unification in negotiations in the Two-Plus-Four talks, with the first meeting to be held in May.

.   The East German round-table conference of communist and other political parties called GDR-wide elections for March 1990. The results were clear and decisive. The Christian Democrats and their Free Democratic allies won an absolute majority of seats and formed a coalition government with the Social Democrats and all other political parties except the Communist Party, now renamed the Party of Democratic Socialists (PDS). Lothar de Maiziere, a prominent Protestant layman and lawyer who had defended East Germans charged with political crimes at a time when it was dangerous to do so, was elected prime minister. The Social Democrats did poorly, with under 22 percent of the vote, undermining their hopes of victory in the all-German elections that were to take place later in the year. The PDS received only 16 percent of the popular vote. Counted together, the unhappy political parties of indigenous reform like New Forum received only 5 percent of the popular vote.

A treaty on monetary economic and social union between the two German states that initiated the formal process of unification and provided for a single currency, the Deutsche Mark (D Mark), in all of Germany, was signed in March and went into effect in July. Fatefully, Chancellor Kohl overruled the advice of the West German Bundesbank and insisted on exchanging one Western D Mark for each relatively worthless East German mark for private accounts of individuals. A thousand-page unification treaty that performed the enormous task of extending the entire legal system of the Federal Republic to East Germany was signed in August. Its entry into effect on October 3, 1990, was the legal basis for the formal act of unification that took place the same day.

INTERNATIONAL STATUS OF THE UNIFIED GERMANY

That the expanded German state would continue as a member of the European Community was supported and expected by all, and formal action to this effect took place in June 1990. For both the Western countries and the Soviet Union, the main issue of German unification, once the Soviet Union had given up hope of preventing or delaying it and had relinquished its initial effort of December 1989 to influence the process of domestic unification, was the military status of the unified German state, whether Germany would be neutral or a member of NATO or some other organization and what restrictions should be placed on the military potential of a unified Germany.

The Western countries viewed the possibility of a military neutral united Germany with great apprehension; they believed it would as in the past create conditions of deep instability in Europe as Germany see-sawed between East and West trying to maximize its influence and to find its own optimum security, losing all trust from the West, playing with the idea of military alliance with the Soviet Union, with the phantom of German domination of Europe. German political leaders saw the lessons of German history the same way. Although Chancellor Kohl often warned outsiders against charging younger generations of Germans with responsibility and guilt for Hitler's crimes, he even more frequently warned his fellow Germans of the dangers that would befall them if Germany again became a "wanderer between the worlds." Kohl wanted the united Germany to fit into the same integrated framework that had bought so much success to West Germany. Western leaders were convinced they had the answer to controlling Germany's past destructive behavior in the integration process that they had been pursuing toward Germany since the late 1940s, enveloping, integrating, and embracing Germany and its economic, political, and military potential into a larger cooperative framework.

As regards NATO itself, Federal Germany had fit well into the integrated staff that had inculcated habits of cooperation in place of long-standing national rivalries. Federal Germany had no general staff or mobile logistics of its own; it could not launch a major independent military operation. Western leaders wanted to keep this framework and to extend it to the whole of Germany. Dissolution of NATO's integrated staff could mean the "renationalization" of Germany's defense policy and of German armed forces and the end of the ingrained habits of cooperation that had made NATO effective.

This last point about NATO's continued effectiveness was important because Western leaders had other considerations in mind than controlling the negative potential of a united Germany. They believed that a militarily effective NATO would be needed as guarantor of the peace in post-cold war Europe. Despite moves toward reform, the Soviet Union would remain the most powerful country of the continent. It continued to have a largely autocratic system, open to sudden changes of policy by decision from the top or by political coup. Europe had been the most conflict-ridden area of the world during the twentieth century. The human cost of this condition had been enormous in the past. It could be even higher in the event of future conflict. Some insurance against the repetition of conflict was needed at least until it became unambiguously clear that the new European set-up could function without it.

For NATO to function as an effective guarantor, there were two main requirements: the continued presence in Europe of a significant U.S. military contingent and continuing German membership in NATO. In reality, these two requirements amounted to a single one: Without German contingents, NATO would not be militarily effective, and without German membership and German willingness to accept continuing deployment of sizable U.S. forces on German territory, in practical terms, there could not be a militarily significant U.S. military presence in Europe.

Without German membership in NATO and without a militarily significant U.S. troop presence in Europe, there would probably still be a rump NATO composed of the United Kingdom, France, and NATO members other than Germany. But such a grouping could neither effectively guarantee the new European structure nor the security of a united Germany. Politically, a rump NATO would almost certainly have the objective of counterbalancing both Germany and the Soviet Union. In such a situation, there would be many possibilities for the growth of frictions, misunderstandings, resentments, and military competition, no matter what controls might be placed on the armed forces of a united Germany. Europe would be back again in the unstable situation in and around Germany that had preceded both World War I and World War II.

There was a further, more immediate danger in the situation: If the question of whether a united Germany should become a member of NATO developed into a long-running dispute between the Western countries and the Soviet Union, this argument could cause deep alienation between the two sides. Moreover, this question could readily develop into a major divisive domestic political dispute inside the united Germany, splitting the German electorate down the middle and activating all the old suspicions and resentments in Germany and outside it.

Fortunately for all, the NATO membership issue never achieved its destructive potential. The main reason for this was that the Soviet Union no longer had the leverage of earlier years to trade off relaxation of Soviet control over the domestic policy of the GDR in return for neutralization. After the East German population took power in its own hands and swept aside the communist dictatorship, the Soviet Union no longer had this concession to make. Enforced neutrality for a united Germany had no attraction on its own. In fact, the Soviet Union's own Warsaw Pact allies rejected the idea of German neutrality in a Warsaw Pact foreign ministers meeting in Prague in March 1990.[8] Czechoslovakia's foreign minister, dissident Jiri Dienstbier, stated in a press conference that neutrality would be the worst alternative for Germany, and Polish foreign minister Krzysztof Skubiszewski said neutrality would foster the tendencies of a united German government to seek to play an independent great-power role.

After a pause in spring 1990, to enable the Soviets to take stock, negotiation over the issue of Germany's external status resumed momentum. At the Washington Bush-Gorbachev summit (May 31–June 1, 1990), President Bush put forward a number of possible assurances to Gorbachev: The president said NATO would soon announce a revised strategy that would make it even more evident that the future NATO, even with German membership, would not be a threat to the Soviet Union; the United States would also drop its opposition to strengthening and institutionalization of the CSCE, which the Soviets had been pushing as a Pan-European security system and as an ultimate successor for both NATO and the Warsaw Pact. Following agreement by the German government to these points, President Bush said NATO would abstain from moving its forces into former GDR territory; that the expanded Federal Republic would renew its pledges to abstain from nuclear, biological, and chemical weapons; and that Germany would also compensate the Soviet Union for withdrawal of its troops and for loss of trade with the GDR.

A few days later, President Bush made good his forecast about a new NATO strategy. At the London Summit on July 5–6, NATO leaders proposed an agreement with the Warsaw Pact on nonuse of force, invited Gorbachev to address the North Atlantic Council, stated that nuclear weapons would henceforth be considered "weapons of last resort," and announced that NATO commanders would prepare a new strategy moving away from "forward defense" in Germany.

These actions consolidated Gorbachev's domestic political position in time for the key session on Germany's international status with Chancellor Kohl in Stavropol on July 16–18.[9] The session had been preceded by several Genscher-Shevardnadze meetings. Gorbachev and Kohl finalized some existing understandings and added others of their own until a completed picture of Germany's future military status was agreed, and later taken over in the Two-Plus-Four Treaty, or "Final Settlement With Respect to Germany."[10] The version given here is a composite of what was agreed at Stavropol with what is set forth in the Two-Plus-Four Treaty agreed two months later in September 1990:

1. The united German state would not produce, possess, or dispose of nuclear, chemical, and biological weapons and would continue to be bound by the 1968 Treaty on Non-Proliferation of Nuclear Weapons.

2. The united German state would accept the limitations of the CFE Treaty on major conventional armaments allocated to West Germany as the maximum levels for its own holdings of these weapons. In other words, a unified Germany would not claim a larger allocation of weapons because of the accession of East Germany.

3. Within three to four years, the united Germany would reduce its active-duty military personnel to a maximum strength of 370,000 men of which no more that 345,000 men would be assigned to ground and air forces taken together. Despite the fact that the main weapons of German ground and air forces would be limited, in order to restrict the military potential of the unified German state, the Soviet Union considered it essential that the total number of active-duty German military personnel also be limited. As we will see in our discussion of the CFE Treaty later in this book, the Soviet conclusion was logical: If arms are limited, but military personnel are not limited, it would be possible for German armed forces to increase the manpower of units equipped with permitted weapons, like the infantry component of tank divisions, to build up infrastructure, or to train additional personnel on the permitted arms, creating conditions for rapid expansion of German forces after a decision to nullify the treaty. Soviet leaders remembered well how the German Reichswehr had done just this under the Versailles Treaty. Because Germany did not wish to be "singled out" or discriminated against by undertaking a limitation not undertaken by other states, as defeated Germany had been compelled to do in the Versailles Treaty after World War I, Federal Germany asked for and received commitments from the four wartime allies that they would undertake a parallel limitation on their military manpower deployed in the CFE area of application in follow-on talks to the CFE negotiations.

4. The Soviet Union agreed to withdraw all its armed forces from Germany by 1994. The huge heavily armed force that had occupied the heart of Europe and locked together the entire Soviet system in Eastern Europe would be withdrawing without firing a shot.

5.   After receiving the return of its full sovereignty through dissolution of the remaining four-power occupation rights, the government of unified Germany could decide to remain a member of NATO.

6.   The Gorbachev-Kohl agreement included some special understandings on military activities on the territory of the GDR. The intent of these measures was to demonstrate in a visible way that German unification would not bring important military benefits to Germany or other NATO states: Until withdrawal of Soviet forces from the GDR was completed in 1994, no forces under NATO command would be stationed in the area, German forces could be deployed there, but they would be "territorial" forces, not under NATO command.

7.   No nuclear weapons or delivery systems intended for nuclear weapons could be stationed in this part of Germany. Dual-purpose delivery systems (artillery, missiles, aircraft) could be stationed there, but only in a conventional role. East German territory was to be permanently denuclearized. Because East German territory is no more than 150–200 miles wide, the military significance of this measure is rather limited, but its political and symbolic significance is considerable.

For its part, the Soviet Union agreed at Stavropol to withdraw all its forces, close to 400,000 men in 1990, from Germany by 1994. This key decision was eased by the fact that the Soviet leadership had already decided the previous year to withdraw all forces from Eastern Europe and had also accepted early in 1990 an accelerated timetable for withdrawal from Hungary and Czechoslovakia. Nonetheless, Gorbachev's willingness to agree to such a rapid timetable for withdrawal of the far larger Soviet force from Germany was a further demonstration of his political realism: Given the changes in East Europe, the Soviet troops in Germany were in a dangerously exposed position and were already showing signs of a drastic drop in morals, evidenced by desertion, sale of equipment, and so on.

In the Stavropol meeting with Gorbachev, Chancellor Kohl eased the pain of Soviet decisions on German membership in NATO by agreeing to pay the Soviet Union for expenses of withdrawing Soviet troops from East Germany, including provisions for construction of new housing in the USSR for withdrawn forces, and to pay for the adverse economic consequences of German reunification for the Soviet Union, particularly the contracts for products to be supplied by GDR plants or to be purchased by the GDR from the Soviet Union. Two German-Soviet agreements on these issues were worked out later. The total cost of unification in payments to the Soviets was about 30 billion marks.

GERMANY'S EASTERN BORDERS

The August 1945 Four-Power meeting at Potsdam had definitively awarded the Soviet Union the formerly German northern part of East Prussia, but it had left open until a final peace treaty with Germany the final determination of Poland's borders. What was involved was the southern half of East Prussia, and the Oder-Neisse line, which had been Poland's western border with the GDR ever since the Soviet Union had at the end of World War II expelled 6 million Polish inhabitants of Eastern Poland, incorporated 70,000 square miles of Poland in the Soviet Union, and compensated Poland by giving it 40,000 square miles of German territory up to the Oder-Neisse. The GDR had accepted the Oder-Neisse line as final in a bilateral treaty with Poland in 1950, the Federal Republic had accepted it in a 1970 treaty, subject to a final peace treaty. As the possibility of German unification became more real in 1989, all four anti-Hitler wartime allies made statements to the effect that a united Germany would have to accept the Oder-Neisse line as final.

Only Chancellor Kohl remained silent on this subject during a visit to Poland in November 1989 just after the fall of the Berlin Wall and in his Ten-Point program of confederation issued on November 28, 1990. In the face of mounting statements of concern from Poland, other European states, and inside Germany, Kohl obstinately argued that Germany could not act definitively on the border issue until it had become unified and sovereign. One of Kohl's apparent motives for resisting pressures for a more accommodating position was to block entry by the right-wing Republican party to the Bundestag. The party might have won enough conservative CDU votes in the Bundestag elections scheduled for the end of 1990 to make it impossible for a CDU government to remain in power. Finally, Kohl had to concede that earlier action could be taken in the form of parallel resolutions from the Federal German Bundestag and East Germany Volkskammer (June 1990) pledging that an all German government would accept the Oder-Neisse border. After the official unification of Germany on October 3, 1990, Germany and Poland signed a treaty, ratified by Germany in May 1992, which established definitive borders for Poland, which thus took over 25 percent of prewar German territory.

TIGHTENING THE LINKS WITH THE EUROPEAN COMMUNITY

Two French leaders, France's President François Mitterrand and Jacques Delors, president of the Executive Commission of the European Community, rapidly concluded that it would be essential to even more firmly embed a more powerful united Germany in the European Community. Since the establishment in 1951 of the first of the European

Communities, the Coal and Steel Community, or Schuman Plan, the process of tying postwar Germany into a cooperative grouping of other European states and of achieving thorough integration and development of common aims what armies had failed to do, to provide a framework in which Germany could develop a secure international identity and constructively apply its great talents, had been progressing. Once it had been decided to carry out German unification through extending the Federal German Basic Law and Federal German institutions to the GDR, the issue of principle was automatically resolved. As a part of an enlarged member state, the East German territory and economy would become part of the European Community. President Delors provided rapid Community action to implement the decision.

President Mitterrand considered that further expansion of the European Community toward a common currency and political union was essential to bind the new Germany even more firmly. Mitterrand met with Chancellor Kohl early in 1990 and obtained his agreement to move in this direction. Kohl fully realized that he had to meet the security concerns of France and Britain over German unification as he had met Soviet concerns.

Fortunately, the instrument was at hand. Expansion of the European Community would help to overcome the concerns of France and other Community member states over the prospect of a larger united Germany. Prime Minister Margaret Thatcher, far less enthusiastic about expansion of the European Community, had sought to bind the united Germany more tightly through ensuring its membership in NATO. Both efforts succeeded. At a special EC meeting of heads of government in Dublin (April 1990), Chancellor Kohl tactfully abstained from asking for the increased voting rights in the EC to which a unified Germany would in theory have been entitled by size, and he met worries of some less-developed EC members that German payments into the EC development fund would be cut because of the greatly increased needs of East Germany for West German economic support. The Federal Republic dropped earlier delaying tactics on moving toward a single European currency and endorsed this objective, as well as the objective of European political union. The meeting gave orders to expedite drafting of the new treaties on both points, the treaties that were signed in Maastricht in December 1991.

CULMINATION

On October 3, 1990, Germany was unified. In December 1990, the first all-German elections were held, and the Christian Democratic-Free Democrat coalition government under Chancellor Kohl received a solid majority. One important chapter of European history ended; another began.

German unification brought into being a state of mixed characteristics. Germany had a GNP of 2.5 trillion DM in 1990 (about half that in dollars), third in the world after the United States and Japan. It is the world's leading trading nation. But it is a small country of 357,000 square kilometers, smaller than France, Spain, or Sweden, a third smaller than Germany at the end of World War II. Germany's 79 million population includes 6 million foreigners, a source of future problems.

The process of unification brought clarity on a nonthreatening military status and on German borders. The German reaction to unification was restrained and sober. At last, Germany had found the right place for itself in Europe, and it was likely to add greatly to leadership and decisionmaking in an expanding European Community. At the same time, few states had as many political mortgages and burdens.

PART II

EUROPE'S NEW SECURITY PROBLEMS

THE FORMER YUGOSLAVIA TODAY

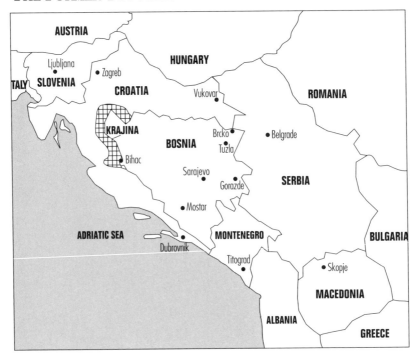

THE CAUCASUS

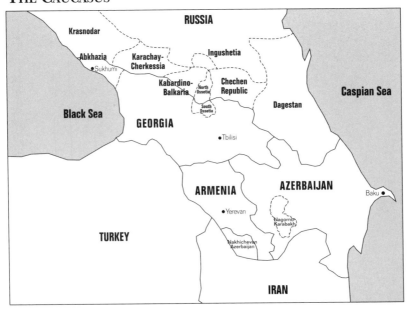

3

DARK SKIES OVER MOSCOW

In the 1990s, Europe has three well-recognized, pressing security problems: nationalist-ethnic violence in many European states, the most uncontrolled in the former Yugoslavia and in the Soviet successor states; the still-dangerously incomplete agenda of nuclear arms control in Russia, Ukraine, Belarus, and Kazakhstan; and gnawing uncertainty, likely to last for many years, over whether reform forces will prove strong enough to prevent the Russian polity from developing toward autocratic nationalism that could pose a serious threat to the security of neighboring states and of the rest of Europe and the United States as well.

Three longer-term issues also threaten European security: First, as a consequence of the inability thus far of multilateral institutions concerned with European security—the United Nations, the Conference on Security and Cooperation in Europe (CSCE), and the Western European Union (WEU)—to deal more effectively with ethnic conflict, the discrediting and hollowing out of these institutions reduce their capacity to cope with future crises and threaten a return to a system of competitive, autonomous nation-states. Second, the mounting tendency in the Western countries to consider the Islamic states as an ultimate mortal enemy could develop into a self-fulfilling prophecy. A related issue is the inability to cope with the rising pressures of migration, an inability that is undermining the democratic substance of all Western states. Another problem, acute voter disaffection with long-serving cold war political parties in all West European countries probably means an extended period of weak and divided government in Europe to cope with these problems.

RUSSIA AND ITS ROLE

The economic well-being and political stability of the twelve independent successor states of the former Union of Soviet Socialist Republics
(and also the three Baltic states) depend to a considerable degree on the
largest and most developed of them all—the Russian Federation. The
smaller states on the periphery of Russia—the Baltic states, Belarus,
Ukraine, Moldova in the west; the three Transcaucasus republics, Georgia,
Armenia, Azerbaijan; and the five Central Asian republics, Kazakhstan,
Uzbekistan, Tajikistan, Turkmenistan, and Kyrgyzstan—are all sovereign
states in the formal sense. But their future depends to a large extent on the
economic and security policies of the huge Russian Federation. Russia
has nearly 77 percent of the territory of the old USSR (6.5 million square
miles, as compared to the 3.7 million square miles of the United States);
51 percent of the former Soviet Union's population (147 million people);
half of its food output; great mineral wealth, including 75 percent of the
coal mined in the former USSR (and half of the world's coal reserves);
90 percent of Soviet oil and 75 percent of natural gas production; well
above 50 percent of Soviet industrial production; and two-thirds of its
armed forces, nuclear and conventional.

As well as important economic assets, Russia has substantial social
strengths. Among them are a highly literate population (99 percent,
with 96 percent enrollment in secondary schools), especially strong in
natural sciences and engineering. Although weak, there were some pre-
communist traditions of local self-administration, formation of voluntary
groups, and private initiative. During the post-Stalin period, there was
continual growth of noncommunist cultural associations, illicit free enterprise that produced an estimated fifth of Soviet GNP, and a continual
effort on the part of the growing number of white-collar professionals to
protect themselves against arbitrary police-state practices.[1] As a result of
some degree of civic culture, a pattern of beliefs concerning the political
role of the individual and interpersonal relations grew in the Brezhnev
years and formed the basis for Mikhail Gorbachev's *glasnost* policy.

In Boris Yeltsin, the Russian Federation has had a tough leader of
proven courage and political resourcefulness. At the same time, Yeltsin is
a lonely figure whose health may, as often reported, be seriously weakened and who is largely without a supporting team that could provide a
range of possible successors.[2] Yeltsin's direct supporters include a small
number of informed democrats and a larger number of people whose attitudes incline them toward a democratic position but who are not fully
schooled in the dynamics and institutions of democracy. More numerous than convinced democrats, a large number of Russian citizens are

antitotalitarian in their rejection of the repressive practices of the past, their skepticism toward the executive, and their suspicion of actions that have the smell of authoritarianism.

Among the most important assets of the new Russia is a favorable international environment. This consists not only of the absence of overt enemies, but also a clear understanding by the world's industrialized states of the stakes involved in the success or failure of Russia and other former Soviet republics and their willingness to help economically and politically. Paradoxically, what made the world so fear the Soviet Union— its vast nuclear arsenal—remains in place as the main reason for outside concern about the future of Russia and other successor states with nuclear weapons. The possibility that this nuclear arsenal could in one way or another get out of control will probably ensure continuation of the industrial states' support for Russia; as many are aware both inside and outside Russia, in the absence of these weapons, Western interest in Russia's future would be much less. At the same time, Western concerns over nuclear weapons in Russia and the three other republics where they have been deployed, as well as over Russia's relationships with the surrounding republics, could also grow into a serious political obstacle to continued assistance.

A Stormy Beginning

There is wide agreement that the future of Russian relations with the outside world is dependent on the consolidation of functioning democratic institutions in Russia, and that this process in turn depends in large degree on the state of the domestic economy. During 1992 and 1993, the first years of the new Russia, the economy tottered. The government gained control of its own finances only in December 1991 as the Soviet superstructure collapsed. It tried hard to bring the deficit under control. It freed most prices, slowed the issuance of new money, slashed the state budget, and made radical cuts of up to 80 percent in arms procurement. In the weeks immediately following freeing of prices, the cost of many items went up by more than 250 percent. These increases kept the food stores empty. Food riots took place in several cities.

Some Russian experts predicted social strife, including mounting local violence, strikes, street riots and demonstrations, an upsurge of individual and organized crime, and conflict of civil war dimensions, leading to an authoritarian regime with a program of putting an end to disintegration of civil society and restoring law and order.[3] Many outside experts predicted the same outcome. Robert Gates, director of the Central Intelligence Agency, predicted a disintegrating economy, acute shortages of food and fuel, mass unemployment, disintegration of the armed forces, ethnic conflicts, and "the most significant civil disorder" since 1917, possibly culminating in a return to authoritarian rule.[4]

Against the background of these potential dangers, in the last six months of 1992 and the first half of 1993, the Yeltsin government endured a bitterly hostile relationship with the Russian Federation Congress of Peoples Deputies. Elected in March 1990, over 85 percent of Congress members had held *nomenklatura* positions under the old regime. The Congress's right wing, about one-third of its members, was composed of representatives of nationalist, authoritarian political groups divided mainly by their continued allegiance to state control of the economy or by its repudiation. Outright Yeltsin supporters numbered fewer than one-third of the deputies. The balance was held by a loose caucus of more moderate Russian nationalists and managers of the megacompanies and state farms of the old command economy, typified by a group called Civic Union.

By the end of 1992, after protracted political battles with the Congress, President Yeltsin lost his right to govern by decree and was forced to jettison his lead economic reformer, Prime Minister Yegor Gaidar, apparently in a deal to gain agreement of Civic Union supporters to a spring referendum. Yeltsin was obliged to accept a new Prime Minister, Viktor Chernomyrdin, from the ranks of Civic Union. One of Chernomyrdin's first actions was to reimpose price controls on some foods. Yeltsin's pro-Western foreign minister, Andrei Kozyrev, was repeatedly attacked by the Congress for his pro-Western policy.

However, the widespread famine predicted for the winters of 1991 and 1992 was averted. Food was in good supply, although at high prices. Partially as a result, living standards for individuals fell by 50 percent in 1992 from the already low 1991 level. High inflation not only wiped out the savings of the former beneficiaries of the communist system; it deprived the Russian economy of its biggest potential source of investment, domestic savings, as well as almost totally discouraging private foreign investors. Long lines of sidewalk vendors in nearly every large Russian city selling old shoes, hats and dresses, or a single cucumber or sausage gave pathetic evidence of deprivation—and of popular reaction in the next elections.

Russian industrial production went down another 20 percent in 1992, making for a cumulative decrease of about 40 percent from already low 1990 levels, and dropped still further in 1993. In the critical energy sector, oil production in mid-1993 was running at a rate of 350 million tons a year, a reduction of nearly half from the average annual figure of 600 million tons in the 1980s. It seemed probable that Russia, once a major oil exporter, would have to import it by 1995.[5] Russian GDP for 1993 was 12 percent less than that of 1992, and 29 percent below 1991, with estimates for a further drop in 1994. In 1994, 35 percent of the Russian population would have incomes below the official poverty level. However, official unemployment figures for 1993 were still only 1.4 percent of the work force, a record low for industrialized countries, although unofficial estimates put the figure considerably higher when titular employment and underemployment were calculated in.[6]

Gaidar's "shock therapy" was for the moment still in place without him. Its main components were rapid freeing of most prices (but not energy prices or housing), heavy cutbacks in public spending to reduce the dangerously large budget deficit, and the beginning of privatization of state enterprises through a 10,000-ruble voucher issued to all Soviet citizens for the purchase of company shares. But the policy had failed in one major objective, restricting the growth of Russia's money supply for public credits. Viktor Gerashchenko, chairman of the Central Bank of Russia, appointed in July 1992 by antireform forces in the Russian Supreme Soviet, increased the money supply by about 30 percent a month for several months straight. Between July 1 and October 1, 1992, the bank printed over 2 trillion rubles. The bank also made available more than 1 trillion rubles in credit to large companies, whose intercompany loans also increased from a total of 39 billion at the beginning of 1991 to 3.2 trillion in mid-June 1992. As a result of pumping in all this money while production was dropping drastically, the monthly inflation rate rose from 8 percent in July 1992, when Gerashchenko was appointed, to 25 percent in December. The ruble–dollar exchange rate, a good indicator of public confidence in the future of the Russian economy, dropped from 200 rubles to the U.S. dollar at the beginning of 1992 to about 1,000 to the dollar in mid-1993.

Much of the credit expansion was generated by Central Bank loans to big enterprises that continued to provide the bulk of Russian social services: nursery schools, clinics, and hot meals as well as employment. But much of it was direct government payments to citizens in the form of increased wages and pensions, which partly explain Yeltsin's surprising success in the referendum held in April 1993. Of the 69 million Russian voters who participated in the referendum (about 63 percent of the electorate), better than 57 percent stated that they had confidence in Boris Yeltsin as president of the Russian Federation. An amazing 53.7 percent approved the socioeconomic policies of the Yeltsin government despite all the deprivations that had accompanied them. A slim majority rejected the idea of early presidential elections urged by Yeltsin's opponents, while a majority of over 70 percent supported early elections for the Congress of Peoples Deputies.[7]

Yegor Gaidar and Western experts like Anders Aslund of Sweden and Jeffrey Sachs of the United States worried about uncontrollable hyper-inflation in Russia if the issuance of credit and money was not stopped.[8] They feared hyperinflation would make money and productive effort value-less and bring mass reaction on the streets. For their part, adherents of Civic Union and a gathering number of critics of shock therapy in the West claimed that cutting off credits to the big state-owned companies would close down most enterprises and bring hyperunemployment instead of hyperinflation, thus pushing the Russian masses out onto the streets.

Heading off adverse popular reaction while making radical changes in Russia's economy was indeed the central issue for Russian politicians. The otherwise courageous Mikhail Gorbachev had flinched from that risk in his timid economic policy, worsening the situation for his successors. Adherents and critics of shock therapy agreed on at least one thing: They insisted that, unless their advice were followed, the result would be mass uprisings followed by authoritarianism and the end of the Russian exper-iment with democracy. Boris Yeltsin said in December 1992, citing the poet Alexander Pushkin, "I fear the Russian mass, aroused and pitiless."[9]

Adding to the misery of daily life in Russia, the crime rate went up by about 20 percent in 1991 and 30 percent during 1992. A large part of the increase arose from economic deprivation, but the biggest cause was the removal of ruthless suppression under the communist regime. Deterrence of crime does not work well in societies like that of the United States, where successful prosecution is sporadic and uneven. But, even taking account of typically falsified statistics, deterrence did work under the relentless police-state conditions of the Soviet Union because repression was consistent, thorough, and brutal. Russia's chief public order official, Major General Vyacheslav Ogorodnikov, made the point clearly in a press conference in mid-1992, "People do not believe they will be pun-ished anymore for committing crimes. They know the system has broken down. They are less afraid of this system now than they used to be." This was the dark reverse side of Gorbachev's reluctance to use force against Soviet citizens, continued by Yeltsin in Russia. It was reported at the end of 1992 that about 3,000 identifiable criminal organizations were oper-ating in Russia. Half their revenue was spent on bribing officials. Cases of corruption and bribe-taking went up 27 percent in 1992.[10]

By the middle of 1993, some economists were claiming that the Russian economy had reached its low point and an upward trend had set in. The Central Bank increased interest rates for new credit. Credit creation was down and the government's budgetary deficit was being held to 10 percent of GDP. Inflation was below 20 percent per month. Coal prices were freed. The private sector now employed about 40 percent of Russian

workers. Russia had a foreign trade surplus for 1993. World Bank officials at this point wanted the big Russian firms to stop taking credits to
maintain employment artificially so that unemployment could be shifted
to a less expensive social safety net, and they wanted to make subsidies to
large military plants dependent on rapid conversion to marketable civilian products.[11] But this modest economic progress appeared to end with
the December 1993 elections, which brought a parliament even more
hostile to reform.

POLITICAL DEFICITS

Russia has never had a functioning democracy. Although there were
the beginnings of a working parliament, the Duma, in the early 1900s,
Russia was for centuries ruled by absolute monarchy until that was
replaced by totalitarian rule in 1917. The Russian political tradition was
of subservience to autocratic authority. By the time the Soviet Union dissolved, convinced adherents of the official ideology formed only a small
minority of the population. Even so, after the collapse, for a large part of
the Soviet population, there was no positive system of beliefs to substitute
for the general orientation, however unsatisfactory, that had been provided by the official ideology. The result, especially among the older population, was a feeling of worthlessness, powerlessness, of not having
achieved anything positive after years of hard work, a classic case of
absence of positive beliefs, or "anomie." The old system also left a legacy of low social trust and high mutual suspicion. After the collapse, social
cohesion, such as it was, suffered badly. As elsewhere in Europe, strong
nationalism rushed in to fill the vacuum. Russian national feeling had in
spite of all remained strong throughout the seventy years of Bolshevism.
So there was already a foundation for this development.

Public opinion polls reflected these attitudes. In a Times Mirror
Center poll taken in November 1992, 51 percent of Russians believed a
strong leader was the best solution to their problems; only 31 percent
considered democracy an answer. More than 52 percent disapproved of
the political and economic changes of the past several years, an interesting contrast to the referendum five months later, when the percentage
approving the economic policies of the Yeltsin government was the same.
Dislike for other ethnic groups was on the increase, as was the view that
parts of neighboring countries really belong to Russia.[12] The semiannual
European Community *Eurobarometer* reported on a poll, also from
November 1992, that only 37 percent of respondents favored a free-market system; 44 percent were against. Nearly 60 percent said life had been
better under the old Soviet system, while 18 percent said life was better

under the present political system. Thirty-three percent believed that a dictatorship was possible within a year.[13]

On paper, the post-Soviet Russian political system was a strong parliamentary democracy. In practice, Russia's political institutions were weak, with overlapping and conflicting authority. Political power was widely dispersed—one criterion of democratic government—but there was no generally agreed allocation of authority to individual components of the system as in the United States and elsewhere in the west. President Yeltsin was titular head of government but had little authority vis-à-vis the Congress and the Supreme Soviet. His veto could be overturned by a simple majority. He had no constitutional authority to dissolve the Congress of Peoples Deputies or the Supreme Soviet for new elections, as he later nonetheless did. The Central Bank was not responsible to the executive for policy direction or for the issuance of money, but to the Supreme Soviet. The prime minister had no authority over foreign and defense policy; this was exercised by the president. As Yeltsin and the Russian legislature continued in deadlock, Yeltsin governed throughout 1992 through the authority to issue emergency decrees granted him by the legislature in December 1991; the Congress rescinded this authority at the end of 1992.[14]

The Soviet-era Russian constitution itself was ridiculously easy to amend; it had been loaded with over 300 often conflicting amendments since 1990. The vice president of Russia, Aleksandr Rutskoi, feuded with Yeltsin and belonged to a different political party, similar to the situation that prevailed in the early days of the American republic. Ruslan Khasbulatov, the chairman or speaker of the Congress as well as of the subordinate standing legislature, the Russian Supreme Soviet, who had also stood at the barricades with Yeltsin during the August 1991 coup, turned into a major Yeltsin opponent.[15]

Yeltsin was nearly impeached after vituperative clashes with Khasbulatov and the antireform majority of the Congress of Peoples Deputies in legislative sessions in December 1992 and March 1993. He was widely criticized by his own supporters for failure to use the great popularity he had gained out of frustrating the August 1991 coup to establish a nationwide political party of his supporters, call new elections, and adopt a new constitution. Yeltsin himself admitted this error, even though chaotic conditions of this early period would have made it very difficult to hold new elections, and even more difficult to draft a new constitution and put it to a vote. Yeltsin was also criticized for neglect of day-to-day decisionmaking in the effort to be a national leader above politics, and for oscillating between unwise compromise with his opponents and assertive, sometimes autocratic, behavior.[16]

In actuality, in his first two years, Yeltsin's record as president of a sovereign Russia was quite good. He brought the economy through a very difficult period, survived the worst attacks of the hostile majority in the Congress of Peoples Deputies and Supreme Soviet, succeeded in organizing a referendum in which the Russian people expressed approval of his performance, and used the prestige from this victory to launch moves toward a new draft of the constitution and new elections that would eliminate the Congress of Peoples Deputies and replace it with a new, democratically elected parliament. He almost succeeded in doing all of this without violence.

YELTSIN'S REGIONAL PROBLEMS

In addition to staving off the Russian parliament, Yeltsin was engaged in a second political front against regional authorities. In early June 1993 he convened a constitutional assembly of 700 representatives of the republics and other administrative subdivisions of the Russian Federation, heads of regional administrations and parliaments, political parties, and interest groups. Yeltsin's motive was clear: to contain the hostile majority in the Congress through this new body. Unfortunately for him, most representatives of Russia's regional authorities wanted to increase their own power at the expense of central government.

Even Stalinism had had a hard job in controlling centrifugal tendencies within Russia. With liberalization, one of the major dangers threatening the country was that of total disintegration. With five levels of government (Russian Federation, republics, region, city, and district) in most areas, some of them controlled by unreconstructed communists, some by supporters of free enterprise struggling to liberate themselves from central government control, and some by ethnic minorities seeking autonomy, central government authority at the end of the line was often weak and ineffective. Yeltsin had to resort to the Napoleonic system of prefects, appointing local presidential representatives to assure that regional authorities carried out his decrees. Nonetheless, these decrees were widely ignored. The State Procurator reported that in 1992 local or regional authorities in Russia had made 16,000 official decisions overriding and violating nationwide laws.[17] Even worse, most of the regional and local authorities were withholding much of the revenue they had collected for the Federation.

Reflecting these dynamics, the constitutional convention of regional representatives focused on debate between supporters of strong powers for the central government and those calling for more authority for the 89 component subdivisions of the Russian Federation (21 mainly ethnic republics, 6 *krays*, 50 *oblasts*, often called regions in Western terminology, 1 autonomous oblast, and 11 autonomous *okrugs*). The argument over division of revenues and authority between the federal government and the components of the Federation expanded to a dispute between republics and regions as to their relative status and powers. The government of Tatarstan, one of the most militant ethnic republics, insisted that the new constitution declare the republics to be "sovereign entities" with standing superior to that of the regions and other subdivisions. On the other hand, regions like Sverdlovsk and the Far East region claimed status as autonomous republics in order to boost their own authority. One motive driving the efforts of the more numerous regions to gain equal status with the republics was that the latter were obligated to turn over to the central government a far smaller fraction of their tax revenue than the regions.

Underlying the regional issue were problems of national minorities. Russia is divided into at least 100 nationalities. Of Russia's 147 million people, over 30 million are non-Russian, mainly Turkic. All of Russia's twenty-one autonomous republics, named after non-Russian ethnic groups that are often outnumbered by Russians within republic boundaries, have declared their "independence" from Russia. One of them, Chechnya, formally seceded from Russia in October 1992, though this has not been recognized. The autonomous Tatar republic voted in a referendum in March 1992 to become a sovereign state.

DISSOLUTION OF THE RUSSIAN PARLIAMENT AND NEW ELECTIONS

The increasingly bitter conflict between the Congress of Peoples Deputies and Yeltsin came to a violent end in September–October 1993 with Yeltsin's decree dissolving the Congress and the Supreme Soviet of Russia and his use of military force to carry out the expulsion from the building of the Supreme Soviet of about 150 hard-line reform opponents who resisted with armed force.

Yeltsin returned from vacation in August 1993, insisting that new parliamentary elections must take place by the end of the year. He told the press that his greatest political mistake had been to fail to dissolve the parliament immediately following the collapse of the August 1991 anti-Gorbachev coup and that he would not make the same mistake again. On September 16 he defiantly reappointed reformist Yegor Gaidar as first deputy prime minister. On September 20, the Russian Supreme Soviet reconvened. At its meeting planned for September 22, the Supreme Soviet planned to repass the budget law passed in July and twice vetoed by Yeltsin. If implemented, it would have increased the government deficit to about 25 percent of GDP and pushed Russia into hyperinflation. Also on the agenda of the Supreme Soviet were draft laws that would have eliminated Yeltsin's veto powers such as they were and made resistance to decisions of parliament a criminal act.

Yeltsin acted on September 21 with a decree disbanding the Supreme Soviet and the Congress of Peoples Deputies and calling for elections in December to a new Federal Assembly. The Supreme Soviet responded the same day by impeaching Yeltsin on the charge of having attempted a political coup against legal authority and proclaimed Vice President Alexander Rutskoi acting president of Russia. Rutskoi and Supreme Soviet chairman Ruslan Khasbulatov remained in the building of the Russian Supreme Soviet, brought in about 600 armed adherents, and tried to fortify the building. The defense was organized by the National Salvation Front, a hard-line organization of extreme nationalists and unreformed communists that Yeltsin had vainly sought to ban.

On September 29, Yeltsin ordered the rump Supreme Soviet of about 150 deputies to leave the building, now surrounded by Interior Ministry troops, by October 4. On October 2–3, supporters of the Supreme Soviet staged mass riots in Moscow, seized the office of the Moscow mayor by force, and, publicly urged by Rutskoi and Khasbulatov, attacked the main Moscow Ostankino television station. On October 4, the government brought in army troops with tanks and shelled the rump parliament into surrender. Few missed the irony of the main site of this conflict: The shell-battered, smoke-blackened Moscow White House had been the scene of Boris Yeltsin's courageous resistance, Khasbulatov at his side, to the instigators of the August 1991 coup, the place where he had completed the dismantlement of the Stalinist dictatorship begun by Mikhail Gorbachev. For the second time in two years, the world watched with transfixed attention as Moscow's fragile political structure tottered on the edge of a bloody abyss.

The outcome was less certain than it appeared; Congress supporters nearly succeeded in taking the Ostankino television station and the General Staff proved reluctant to act against them. In one version, even Yeltsin himself was unable to sway them in a 2:00 A.M. visit on October 4, and only decisions by individual subcommanders of elite units in the Moscow area brought the intervention of their units. Rutskoi and Khasbulatov erred in accepting and encouraging armed resistance, which gave Yeltsin grounds to use superior force. They would probably have fared better with passive resistance. Nonetheless, with total dead on both sides at about 150 persons, the outcome was much less bloody than many events of modern Russian history.

In the aftermath, Yeltsin dissolved elected local Soviets throughout the country and said new regional bodies would be chosen in the

December elections, which would also decide on a new constitution for Russia. He revoked his own decree of September 23, which set new presidential elections for June 1994, and said the next presidential elections would not be held until 1996, when his own term expires. He also dissolved the Supreme Court, which had declared illegal Yeltsin's decree dissolving the Supreme Soviet. Western governments were shocked by Yeltsin's constitutional coup and the ensuing violence; nonetheless, they saw no alternative than to support him.[18]

THE NEW RUSSIAN CONSTITUTION

The new constitution of the Russian Federation, replacing the 1978 version, was adopted December 12, 1993, on the basis of the simple question, "Do you agree to the constitution of the Russian Federation? Yes or no?" Just 52 percent of the total votes cast (about 55 percent of the 107 million-strong total electorate participated in the vote), representing about 28 percent of eligible voters, were affirmative.

The new constitution, drafted by Yeltsin's own advisers, reverses the relationship in the 1978 constitution and provides for a strong president with a relatively weak parliament. Article I declares, "The Russian Federation/Russia is a democratic, federative rule of law state with a republican form of government." (The two designations "Russian Federation" and "Russia" are to have equal validity.) The constitution assures a wide spectrum of human rights, including free speech and free press and the right to private property, including ownership of land, as well as the right to housing and free medical care.

The president of Russia is head of state and commander-in-chief of the armed forces, and also chairman of the still not fully developed Security Council. The president appoints cabinet members and senior officials. These are subject to confirmation by the parliament, but the president can dismiss the cabinet without agreement of parliament. He can veto legislation, in which case a two-thirds vote is required to overrule. He can either reject or ignore two successive parliamentary votes of no confidence in the cabinet and can then dissolve the lower house or State Duma for new elections if it again votes no confidence or if it refuses to confirm the president's choice of prime minister. (Given the forbiddingly large protest vote in the December 1993 elections, it is unlikely that Yeltsin would wish to call new elections soon or that this provision gives him the leverage he sought.) The new constitution provides that the president can issue decrees without specific authorization of parliament; presidential decrees cannot contravene the constitution or existing laws. The president can temporarily take over executive powers in the regions. The new constitution makes impeachment of the president much more difficult than did the 1978 version.

The Federal Assembly or parliament of the Russian Federation consists of two chambers, the Federation Council, the upper house, and the Duma, or lower house. Perhaps fatefully, in the December 1993 elections, both were chosen only for a two-year term ending in December 1995. Thereafter, the Duma will be elected every four years. The Federation Council will not be elected again; two representatives from each will be appointed by the governments and assemblies of the republics and regions. The Federation Council approves presidential proclamation of martial law or emergency, confirms appointment of judges, and approves legislation passed by the Duma. The Duma passes laws and budgets and votes of confidence in the cabinet.

The constitution provides for an independent judiciary including a constitutional court. All of the eighty-nine republics, regions, and other territories into which Russia is divided will have equal rights, and all will be subject to federal laws and decrees. The earlier move to give the regions and republics greater autonomy was dropped. This shift, at least on paper, toward central government is a probable source of future trouble. The Yeltsin government showed its awareness and its willingness to be flexible about its enhanced status in concluding a bilateral treaty with Tatarstan in mid-February 1994. Tatarstan will, at least for a time, retain its own constitution. Moscow has accepted that a relatively low share of locally raised taxes will be turned over to the central government. The Yeltsin government indicated its readiness to reach similar understandings with other republics.

THE 1993 ELECTIONS

Formally, the new constitution will be more difficult to amend than its predecessor. Constitutional amendments will require a two-thirds vote of the Duma and a three-quarters vote of the Federation Council. Nonetheless, the strong showing of the opposition in the December 1993 elections assures continued controversy over the content of the constitution as well as all other political subjects.[19] The clear winner in the elections was Vladimir Zhirinovsky, a nationalist populist demagogue with an uncanny ability to put into words the stream of consciousness of the man in the street, heading his misnamed Liberal Democratic Party. The Liberal Democrats led all others in getting nearly 23 percent of the nationwide vote, far better than the 15 percent received by the reformist Russia's Choice, the closest competitor. In fact, the election results left proreform groups with just about the same one-third of seats in the new Duma they had had in the old Supreme Soviet, with antireform elements holding more than 40 percent of the seats, an increase of roughly 10 percent in their strength in the old parliament.

Despite their earlier claims that Yeltsin's proposal for new elections in 1993 was illegal, the parties of the antireform opposition, including the Agrarian Party, Communist Party, and the Liberal Democrats, legitimated the December 1993 elections through their willingness to participate in them. Thirteen political parties qualified under the government decree establishing conditions for competing in the elections, which included the collection of 100,000 signatures for each party. Finally, there was a nationwide system of political parties—a definite gain for the Russian political system, whatever the election outcome.

The election system provided for 178 members of the Federation Council, two for each republic or region, and 450 members of the State Duma. Each voter had a separate ballot for the Federation Council. For the Duma vote, modeled on the successful Federal German election system, each voter had two ballots, one for direct election of a single candidate by plurality in each of 225 single-member districts and the other for a nationwide candidates list of individual parties; the remaining 225 seats were divided according to the percentage of the nationwide vote received by each party. The more than 1,000 foreign election observers reported no significant election fraud or violence.[20]

In the initial sessions of the Federal Council, Vladimir Shumeiko, a first deputy prime minister and close aide of President Yeltsin, was elected president or chairman of the Federation Council, the upper chamber of the legislature. Ivan Rybkin, a leader of the Agrarian Party of procommunist collective farm managers, was elected president of the State Duma by a bare majority. The reformists and their allies could muster enough strength in the Duma to block votes of nonconfidence or impeachment, but they could not control the parliament's agenda. On the other hand, it rapidly became clear that Zhirinovsky's ultranationalist Liberal Democrats were prepared to cooperate with the Communist Party and its Agrarian Party allies.

SIGNIFICANCE OF THE ELECTIONS

The outcome of the December 1993 elections was a great shock and surprise to President Yeltsin and the Russian reformers, who had predicted an easy election victory after their favorable showing in the April referendum and the forcible dissolution of the old Russian parliament. It was also a shock for the supporters of reform in the outside world. It should not have been such a great surprise. Russian and foreign observers and opinion polls had documented growing economic dissatisfaction and nationalism. Polls just prior to the elections had predicted the outcome with fair accuracy. In contrast to the April referendum, where Yeltsin supporters controlled the public media and there had been little organized opposition, in the December 1993 elections, all viewpoints were represented by at least rudimentary nationwide political parties. By all accounts, opposition groups, including Zhirinovsky's Liberal Democrats and the communists, made far better use of their television opportunities than progovernment parties. Besides, nine months of further deprivation and economic misery had intervened between the two votes.

Boris Yeltsin declared that the adverse election outcome was a protest vote against increasing impoverishment of Russians; that is, that the main reason for the near-catastrophic outcome was economic protest. Zhirinovsky, with continued threats to "nuke" Japan and Germany, to "annihilate" NATO, and to use a "mystery weapon" against Bosnian Muslims, said with some accuracy that his main role had been to articulate the deep humiliation of many Russians over Russia's seemingly unending decline from superpower status to Third World conditions. In any event, the elections do not appear, as had been hoped, to have made Russia more governable. Instead, they increased the authority both of Yeltsin and of his opponents and thus sharpened their confrontation. Yeltsin's position was strengthened through the additional powers conferred on him by a legally and more or less democratically adopted constitution. The antireform parties were legitimated by their election in a free vote.

Although the antireform parties were essentially the same forces that backed the anti-Gorbachev coup in 1991, that had opposed reform in the old parliament, and that had sought to retain power and prevent new elections by backing the armed sit-in at the Russian Supreme Soviet, they now represented actual voters and their credentials would have to be accepted. The strength of the opposition parties would have to be taken into account if Yeltsin wished to give the appearance of constitutional rule. This meant a slowdown in economic reform and a more nationalistic tone in government policy.

The success of antireform forces in the elections were an even greater shock to Western governments and publics than Yeltsin's dissolution of parliament and his forcible seizure of the Moscow White House. Zhirinovsky's considerable voter support and his deliberately extremist statements brought immediate comparisons with Adolf Hitler and Weimar Germany. There were urgent new calls to extend NATO membership to Poland, the Czech and Slovak Republics, and Hungary. Clearly, the immediate problem for the Yeltsin government from Zhirinovsky and his continued outrageous statements was not domestic. Zhirinovsky was not running the Russian government even though he had some prospect of winning the presidential elections to be held by June 1996 if he did not discredit himself first. The problem was the mutually reinforcing spiral of alienation and doubt that his emergence had brought to relations between the Western countries and Russia. Yeltsin's inability to call for new elections in the face of the strong nationalist showing strengthened the position of Prime Minister Viktor Chernomyrdin, whose more conservative approach could make it feasible to pull together majorities in the Duma for individual pieces of legislation.

RESULTS FOR ECONOMIC POLICY

Did the outcome of the 1993 elections decisively block economic reform in Russia? In his first substantive commentary on the elections and again at the Moscow summit meeting with President Bill Clinton in January 1994, Boris Yeltsin said Gaidar and his policies would stay in place. President Clinton criticized the International Monetary Fund (IMF) for excessively stringent conditions for loans to Russia and urged a two-track policy of continued reform and an improved social safety net for Russian workers who might lose their jobs because of the breakup or bankruptcy of the big state-owned concerns. The idea as articulated by the American economist Jeffrey Sachs, who had advised the Russian government, was to cut back on government credits being given big state-owned firms to pay their redundant workers, which was blocking privatization and fueling inflation. Instead, Western governments should make available noninflationary hard currency to pay the costs of unemployment compensation to be distributed by the Russian government, and retraining costs, while the big firms would be broken up and privatized or even closed down completely. Sachs estimated the cost of this support program at $14 billion for the first year.

But even as President Yeltsin proclaimed the continuation of reform, Prime Minister Chernomyrdin told the State Duma that the government would not allow "ill-considered leaps forward and unreasonable shock actions." In any event, the possibility was slim that the concept of noninflationary outside financing of a social safety net for Russia could succeed. Western countries, mired in recession and battling unemployment of their own, were unlikely to make available large sums to support the unemployed in Russia. Sadly, after much fumbling, this probably was the right formula for outside help. But, even though less so than in Russia, the Western economies too were captured in the recession-bound aftermath of cold war emphasis on military production. As a result, there was not going to be any rapid Russian transition to a free-market economy and democracy. Instead, a long and uncertain road lay ahead.

The West's past record on delivery of economic aid to Russia was poor. In 1992, the United States organized a Western aid program of $24 billion; $15 billion was actually paid. In 1993, the Group of Seven (G-7) industrial countries promised $28 billion plus a $15 billion debt renegotiation. It did agree to stretch out Russia's debt payments, but delivered less than $2 billion of support for short-term currency stabilization and about $6 billion in export credits, falling $20 billion short of its pledge. In most cases, Russia itself failed to meet Western or IMF preconditions. In a wave of postelection recriminations, Western experts blamed the International Monetary Fund for ineptitude in not transferring to Russia more of the available credits. In a telling response, IMF director Michel Camdessus pointed out that if Western governments had wanted to, they could have made available more direct grant aid to Russia. Instead, they preferred to extend credits through the IMF, which was obliged to adhere to its standard, worldwide conditions for lending. Camdessus said that the main difficulty of the Russian government in meeting IMF conditions had been its continuing deadlock with the Russian parliament. In fact, in their efforts to drum up domestic support for extending aid to Russia in a period of recession and high unemployment at home, Western governments had almost universally exaggerated the significance of what they could do, creating high expectations in Russia and then disappointing them.

Postelection comments by Vice President Albert Gore and Deputy Secretary of State-designate Strobe Talbott to the effect that there would now have to be less shock and more therapy were claimed by Russian reformers to have caused Yeltsin to conclude that there had to be a pause in reform policy. In mid-January, Yegor Gaidar announced his resignation, claiming the new Russian government had failed to assure adequate support for his reform program. This was followed by the resignation of Finance Minister Boris Fyodorov, a combative reformer who had done his best to prevent the Central Bank from printing more money. The two leading foreign economic advisers of the Russian government, Jeffrey Sachs and Swedish economist Anders Aslund, also resigned. Prime Minister Chernomyrdin, his own position strengthened by the troubles of the reformers, pledged to continue with economic restructuring, but he also proclaimed an end to "free-market romanticism." Commenting on the resignations of Sachs and Aslund, Chernomyrdin said the mechanical transfer of Western economic ideas to Russian soil had done more harm than good; there had to be a Russian solution. By mid-January, the ruble had dropped from 1,000 to the U.S. dollar to about 1,600.[21]

The first Chernomyrdin postreform budget continued but only modestly cut back the huge credits and subsidies to state-owned industrial and agricultural enterprises. In January 1994, in further signals of gathering political conservatism, Valery Zorkin, former chief justice of the Supreme Court, who had been fired by Yeltsin in September when the Court declared unconstitutional Yeltsin's dissolution of the Russian parliament, was voted back onto the Court by other justices. And the Duma used its new constitutional powers to amnesty both the conspirators of the 1991 anti-Gorbachev coup and Rutskoi, Khasbulatov, and other leaders of the September 1993 parliamentary sit-in.

Yeltsin and the Military

President Yeltsin established new armed forces for Russia in May 1992, after it proved impossible, because of the insistence of Ukraine and other successor republics on establishing their own independent armed forces, to keep the elements of former Soviet conventional forces together in the framework of the newly established Commonwealth of Independent States. The Russian professional officer corps, hurled in a matter of months from privileged status in the Soviet Union to humiliation, confusion, and economic misery, with many of its members living in temporary shacks or tent cities, still represents one of the major components of the Russian polity.[22] Their counterparts in Ukraine and elsewhere have similar importance. Although the armed forces supported Yeltsin in his 1991 election bid for the presidency of the Russian Federation and Yeltsin claimed their backing in the April 1993 referendum,[23] there was some evidence that in the parliamentary elections of December 1993, a majority supported Zhirinovsky and his Liberal Democrats. Small wonder: the plight of the Russian military typified the humiliation of Russia.

Urged by his reform supporters to appoint a civilian defense minister, President Yeltsin opted for Soviet tradition in naming a military officer, Pavel Grachev, the most prominent of the officers who came to his defense during the anti-Gorbachev coup. He did appoint a civilian, Andrei Kokoshin, a leading exponent of "defense sufficiency" and arms control in the Gorbachev period, as one of the deputy ministers. In June 1992, Yeltsin appointed Colonel General Viktor Dubynin as first deputy minister and chief of staff. Dubynin had been commander of Soviet forces in Poland and had a hard-line reputation. To meet right-wing pressures, the president subsequently appointed as another deputy minister Colonel General Boris Gromov, the last Soviet commander in Afghanistan and later deputy Soviet interior minister under Boris Pugo, one of the leaders of the August 1991 anti-Gorbachev coup. Just before the coup, Gromov had signed a manifesto calling for military dictatorship of the USSR.

The Russian military and security services generally supported Yeltsin's foreign and domestic policies in 1992 and 1993, but they were able to frustrate his commitments to withdraw all troops from the Baltics and apparently contemplated concessions to Japan over the Kurile Islands. In July 1992, Foreign Minister Andrei Kozyrev accused the military of fomenting the insurgent "Transdniester Republic" in Moldova by supplying it with weapons—and also of preparing a coup against Yeltsin.[24] Swashbuckling army corps commander General Alexander Lebed and his Fourteenth Army remained in military control of the Transdniester Republic despite Yeltsin's public commitment that the army would be withdrawn.

After the October 1993 storming of the parliament building, observers inside and outside Russia anxiously viewed the Russian military for signs of increased influence on policies of the Yeltsin government. Russia watchers considered this a key indicator both of the health of democracy in Russia and of the future of Russian policy.

The evidence was mixed. In late 1993, Yeltsin again raised soldiers' salaries and pensions and exempted them from income taxes. In November, he relinquished the previous year's plan to reduce the Soviet armed forces to 1.5 million men, stating that the lower level would not be enough for the missions of the Russian armed forces. At the same time, he approved a new doctrine for the Russian armed forces. Perhaps motivated by concerns over China, the new military doctrine restricted the concept of no first use of nuclear weapons adopted under Brezhnev to possible conflict with countries that had no nuclear weapons. It dropped the concepts of defense sufficiency or defense with limited objectives popularized by Gorbachev. But the new statement of doctrine also contains many worthwhile concepts, among them civilian control over the military. Moreover, in contrast to earlier documents of this type, an extensive summary was made public.[25]

Reflecting the views of Defense Minister Grachev and other senior officers, Yeltsin reversed his earlier acquiescence to Polish and Czech membership in NATO, becoming ever more energetic in his opposition as the NATO Summit approached in mid-January 1994. Urged by the military, the Russian government also pressed for changes in the geographic sublimits of the Conventional Forces in Europe (CFE) Treaty to permit deployment of more Russian forces in the Caucasus, threatening to withdraw from the treaty unless Western signatories agreed.

At the same time, Yeltsin was not effusive in praise of the Russian military or of Defense Minister Grachev after the October uprising at the Russian parliament. In a subsequent interview, he said, "My defense minister could not make up his mind. There was a period of uncertainty when the troops did not arrive. Apparently, he had been given too much responsibility and he doubted whether the soldiers would follow his orders." Outside military experts saw signs of hasty, makeshift operations in the tactics and units used to assault the Moscow White House.[26]

In little more than two years, elements of the Russian military twice saved Yeltsin from disaster—in August 1991 and in October 1993. He owed it a big debt. With Zhirinovsky, a potential rival for the presidency of Russia, actively seeking support of the military, it was clear that Yeltsin was dependent on its loyalty. But he had been all along. What had saved him from military coups was recognition by the military leadership of the acute difficulties of Russia's situation. The top brass had no solutions of their own. Moreover, the Russian military was politically divided from top to bottom in the same way as was the entire Russian population.

RUSSIAN FOREIGN AND DEFENSE POLICY

Aside from the increasingly controversial Russian relationship with neighboring republics, the foreign and defense policy of Russia as it evolved in the early 1990s posed no serious problems to the countries of the Western coalition or to Western Europe as such. Although a postelection trend is evident not to identify too closely with Western policy, especially U.S. policy, Russian foreign policy has generally been one of cooperation with the West on such matters as a Mideast political settlement, Iraq, arms control, and, for the most part, on the Yugoslav civil war and other peacekeeping issues.

Given national electoral gains, cooperation is likely to become less automatic with the passage of time. Russian foreign policy will increasingly seek opportunities, both symbolic and real, to demonstrate independence from the United States. A few areas of friction have already emerged. During the bruising encounters between President Yeltsin and the antireform majority of the old Congress of Peoples Deputies, the right wing repeatedly charged that Yeltsin and even more, Kozyrev, were subservient to U.S. and European Community foreign policy. In postelection statements, both Yeltsin and Kozyrev emphasized still more that Russia has its own unique "Eurasian" foreign policy stance, representing the interests of Russia alone. At the United Nations, Russia adopted a more overtly pro-Serb position and was reluctant to back President Clinton's proposals for air attacks on the Serbs and Croats and engaged in independent, uncoordinated policy of its own with the Bosnian Serbs. In May 1993, Russia used its first post-Soviet veto in the UN Security Council to reject a mandatory assessment to pay the continued costs of UN peacekeepers in Cyprus, previously funded by voluntary contributions. The vote was not a significant one, but it was a warning shot that the period of automatic Russian compliance in the Security Council was over.

A second area of friction was Russian arms sales abroad. In 1992, Russian military exports amounted only to $2.5 billion compared to U.S. sales of about $15 billion, though the Soviet Union had led the United

States in arms transfers during much of the cold war period. However, the pledges of Yeltsin and Gaidar that Russian arms sales would continue resulted in sales to China of SA–10 surface-to-air missiles and of a large number of modern combat aircraft. The idea that Russia was building up the forces of a potential rival brought criticism even from Russian defense experts. Russia also sold three submarines to Iran, shifting the naval balance of local powers in the Persian Gulf. Despite trade sanctions levied by the United States against a Russian rocket engine company, Glavkosmos, in May 1992, the Russian government proceeded to implement the company's $400 million sale to India of rocket engines that the Bush and Clinton administrations considered to be usable for strategic-range missiles and thus a violation of the export control rules formulated by the countries belonging to the Missile Control Technology regime. (Russia was not a member, but had promised to adhere to regime rules.) Before it was resolved, the dispute brought punitive postponement by the United States of a scheduled visit to Washington of Prime Minister Viktor Chernomyrdin. In June 1993 came a similar case of sale to Libya by Russia of rocket fuel ingredients.[27]

Almost certainly, there will be further frictions of this kind. But it is improbable that differences over policies toward third countries will develop into truly serious crises unless there is general change in the orientation of the Russian government. The exception, to which we turn later, is Russian policy toward neighboring states. The Yeltsin government is committed to cooperation with the Western countries as a way of maintaining Russia's international status and a flow of economic aid from the West. Similar considerations will affect decisions of most future leaders.

In distinction to Russian policy toward the Western states, which is largely political and economic, the main emphasis of long-term security policy is on dangers on Russia's unstable southern periphery, where long-standing fears of Islamic fundamentalism combine with actual conflict to cause serious concerns—and, probably, on possible long-term problems with China. This orientation plays a role in difficulties with neighboring states to the south.

DOES RUSSIA POSE A CONVENTIONAL MILITARY THREAT TO THE WEST?

After decades of concern over the possibility of massive Soviet ground-force attack on Western Europe, it is natural that there are still some apprehensions in the West over the possibility of some repetition of the threat. With respect to the actual capabilities of the Russian armed forces, these fears are residual rather than real. Gorbachev's rule was a period of troop withdrawal, large force cuts, and efforts to redefine the role of the Soviet armed forces. The main developments included withdrawal of Soviet forces from Afghanistan, large unilateral cuts, agreement to withdraw Soviet forces completely from Germany and Eastern Europe, and conclusion of the Treaty on Conventional Forces in Europe (CFE) providing for massive cuts in Soviet conventional forces. The institutional power of the Soviet armed forces was further cut back by Gorbachev following the participation of Defense Minister Dmitri Yazov in the unsuccessful August 1991 coup and by the dissolution of Soviet central power that ensued.

The three interrepublic meetings of December 1991 that established the Commonwealth of Independent States also brought agreement to set up "under unified command a common military-strategic space including unified control over nuclear weapons." The armed forces of the former USSR were placed under Commonwealth control, exercised through a council of the heads of state and of the heads of government of the republics and a committee of the republic ministers of defense. Marshal Yevgeniy Shaposhnikov, Gorbachev's last defense minister, was named commander. Shaposhnikov established a joint command over strategic forces, and also over remaining armed forces and border troops. He proposed that the strategic forces command should include nuclear forces, missile and air defense, naval forces, airborne units, transport aviation, and central logistics—plus offensive air components and ground forces.

This ambitious scheme would have left the individual republics with only local defense ground forces, while Russia with the bulk of former Soviet forces controlled their defense policy. It failed. At the same December 1991 meetings, leaders of three republics—Ukraine, Moldova, and Azerbaijan—declared that their governments intended to establish their own conventional armed forces. In fact, the Commonwealth arrangement merely papered over an ongoing controversy among the successor states over dividing up Soviet conventional forces. Soon after the August 1991 coup, Ukraine, followed by Belarus, Kazakhstan, and other republics, laid claim to major Soviet military units and armaments on their territory. By 1992, all the successor republics had decided to establish their own armed forces, taking over components of former Soviet units to do so. They had also formally agreed on dividing up the major conventional armaments that would remain after CFE reductions.

In the most important case, President Leonid Kravchuk of Ukraine, nervous over muttered threats from Yeltsin's entourage about possible Russian military intervention in Ukraine with regard to nuclear weapons and the Crimea, declared himself commander-in-chief of all forces on Ukrainian territory and ordered all personnel in these units to take an oath of allegiance to the Ukrainian state. Early in 1992, Ukraine cut the communications link between Moscow and military units on its territory and took over the military communications network. Ukraine was especially interested in airborne and tank divisions on its territory, combat aircraft, including heavy bombers, and the Black Sea fleet based at Sevastopol. In the fall of 1992, Ukraine assumed "administrative" control of CIS units equipped with strategic nuclear weapons, meaning that it fed and paid the personnel of these units, who were also required to undertake an oath of allegiance to Ukraine.

In mid-June 1993, Marshal Shaposhnikov finally announced the failure of efforts to establish joint Commonwealth forces and replaced the Commonwealth's integrated staff with a liaison staff charged with promoting coordination and cooperation among the armed forces of the individual republics. [28] The Commonwealth of Independent States continues as an institution of military, political, and economic coordination and for specific tasks like peacekeeping operations. At the December 1993 meeting of Commonwealth heads of government in Turkmenistan, Boris Yeltsin was elected president for the first six months of 1994. The office will rotate like the presidency of the Council of the European Union. Unquestionably, in the military, political, and economic spheres, the Commonwealth is a device for legitimizing Russian influence over neighboring republics. The latter do however gain security and economic benefits from it, and most will also energetically seek to maximize the advantages of their independent status.

The armed forces of the former Soviet Union, numbering at their peak about 4.5 million men together with an enormous amount of armaments, are now partially dispersed, probably irreversibly, among eleven other successor republics as well as Russia. Taking into account the loss of Eastern European forces and the effects of the CFE Treaty, one-half of the Warsaw Treaty's peak conventional strength has now dissipated. It is beyond the capabilities of even an economically restored, resurgent Russia to fully restore the conventional military power of the former Soviet Union. The enforced Soviet alliance with the Eastern European members of the Warsaw Pact, whose armies provided a total of 1.5 million soldiers, cannot be restored. East Germany's military potential has been incorporated into the Federal Republic. Although the forces of the remaining Eastern European states have since become much smaller and will remain so, in most situations of potential conflict, most of these countries would resist Russia rather than ally themselves with it. Russia has concluded a defensive alliance with Armenia, Kazakhstan, Uzbekistan, Kyrgzstan, and Tajikistan, but even if these states could be called on for some joint enterprise with Russia, their forces are weak. Of the remaining republics, Belarus has linked itself with the Russian economy and may ultimately rejoin Russia. Given its population of 10 million, its military potential is limited. Georgia and Azerbaijan joined the Commonwealth belatedly in 1993 under Russian pressure. Moldova and even Ukraine are in a dependent economic relationship with Russia, especially for energy supplies, but they retain their separate military identity. The three Baltic states are hostile toward Russia. Under extreme circumstances, Russia might be able to pull the forces of several neighboring republics into a military alliance resembling the former Warsaw Pact, but its military value would be uncertain, among other reasons because shortage of funds is likely to keep all the component armies weak. Whether Ukraine will be able to maintain its national and military independence is a key indicator of Russian intentions and military potential.

The strength of Russia's armed forces in early 1993 was estimated at about 2.7 million, still a very large force, numerically though not qualitatively. Plans to drop to 1.5 million within the next few years have been suspended in favor of a level of 2 million, but maintaining the higher level might not be feasible in economic terms. Russian ground and air force personnel are limited to 1.4 million under the CFE–IA agreement. (This figure does not include naval personnel or personnel of the strategic nuclear forces.) At the end of 1993, the Russian army was estimated at 630,000 officers and only 544,000 enlisted men. In part, this unbalance reflected the fact that compliance with conscription call-up remained below 50 percent; in Moscow, it was only about 5 percent in 1992. Even if Russia planned to introduce an effective conscription system in the future, its population base had shrunk by 50 percent, 200 million fewer than that of the European Community. Training was minimal and force readiness was at a very low level. Most unit commanders focused on the day-to-day physical survival of their units. In a 1992 survey, 70 percent of officers contacted considered that their units were incapable of carrying out their military missions.[29] In the fall of that year, despite energetic efforts, the army deputy chief of staff had great difficulty in collecting a small force of 2,500 men to send to quell unrest in the Caucasus. In mid-1993, Foreign Minister Kozyrev quipped that even if Russia wanted to increase its 800-man peacekeeping force in the former Yugoslavia, it did not have the men.[30] Later, when Russia promised the UN and the Bosnian Serbs to send a battalion of Russian soldiers to Bosnia, it had to take half of them from peacekeeping duty in Croatia.

Corruption in the armed forces was widespread, reflecting economic pressures. Thousands of officers were formally charged with corruption. Many sold equipment to keep themselves and their units fed; even Defense Minister Grachev was accused by Yeltsin opponents of misusing his position to gain a private dacha. If already harsh economic conditions worsen and supply, pay, and rations to individual units of the Russian forces are interrupted, there is a possibility that some units will engage in foraging and robbery at the point of a gun; this has already taken place on an isolated basis in some republics.

Production of arms and military equipment was once 60 percent of Soviet industrial output. Procurement of armaments was cut by 80 percent in the Russian Federation budget for the first six months of 1992, leaving money only for spare parts. At the end of 1993, expenditures on arms and equipment remained 78 percent below the 1989 level.[31] Figures for 1992 of weapons manufacture by category showed why there was such heavy pressure to sell Russian arms abroad: Bomber production fell from 700 in 1988 to 20; tank production from 3,500 in 1988 to 675; artillery pieces from 2,000 to 450; in 1992, Russia built only five military helicopters. These figures might go up in future, but any expansion of Russian arms production would be relatively slow, domestically contentious, and highly visible, leading to pointed enquiries from foreign aid donors of economic aid.[32]

In a hearing before the Senate Armed Services Committee at the beginning of 1992, the director of the Defense Intelligence Agency, Lieutenant General James Clapper, stated that the military capabilities of all the successor states including the Russian Federation were "in profound decline." CIA director Robert Gates said in the same hearing that the threat to the West of deliberate attack by Commonwealth armed forces "has all but disappeared for the foreseeable future." General Clapper agreed.[33]

Conventional armed forces in this condition—decreasing numbers, low morale, limited training, and degenerating equipment—could not again become a direct threat to European security in a short time. To do so in the long term would require considerable economic revival and political leadership capable of overcoming domestic opposition to military adventurism and of bringing at least Belarus and Ukraine into close military cooperation with Russia. As long as Russia does not have effective control over Ukraine, no sudden attack to the West would be feasible. To achieve this degree of influence would require many years of concentrated effort and would be highly visible, not in the least owing to the systematic exchange of information and the on-site inspections taking place under the terms of the Conventional Forces in Europe Treaty and of agreements concluded in the Conference for Security and Cooperation in Europe.

Russia does pose potential security threats to Europe, but they do not include short-term risks of direct aggression. The greatest security problems for the West from Russia arise in connection with the huge arsenal of nuclear weapons still deployed in Russia and other successor states, from the possibility that Russian involvement in quarrels along its borders could at some point lead Russia back toward militarized imperialism and into wider interstate war that might have a Western connection, and from the possibility that developments in these areas or in Russian domestic politics could bring alienation between Russia and Western supporters of Russian democracy. Here, the potential conflict which is of greatest concern to European security is that between Ukraine and Russia, in part, over nuclear weapons. Moreover, with deep cuts in personnel, equipment, and force readiness, the temptation for Russia will be considerable to place greater reliance on its own nuclear weapons. Above all, the fear of what nuclear-armed Russia might in the future become lies like a dark cloud over Western relations with Moscow.

4

RUSSIA AND ITS QUARRELSOME NEIGHBORS

Conflicts in neighboring republics have brought new strains into Russia's domestic and international politics. Its responses have increased Western suspicions of Russian intentions, and foreign criticism has revived the old communist feeling of being beleaguered by the outside world. Russia's troubles with its former Soviet brethren can be grouped in three geographic areas: First, the six republics to the west of Russia—the Baltic states (Estonia, Latvia, and Lithuania), Belarus, Ukraine, and Moldova, with a population of about 75 million; Russia's frictions with Ukraine are the worst of these problems. Second, the three small Transcaucasus republics to Russia's southwest—Georgia, Armenia, and Azerbaijan—with a total population of only 15 million, are all engulfed in ethnic conflicts; some of these have already become interstate wars and could spread still further. The problems in Russia's own neighboring Caucasus ethnic minirepublics are connected. Third, the five Central Asian republics east of the Caspian Sea and south of Russia—Kazakhstan, Turkmenistan, Uzbekistan, Tajikistan, and Kyrgyzstan—with a total population of about 50 million people, are all in political and intellectual ferment. In this area, old-line communists, Islamic fundamentalists, and more or less democratic socialists compete for influence. Bloody civil war has already broken out in Tajikistan.

Russia is linked to these conflict areas in many ways, including proximity and the fact that 25 million Russians are still living in the other republics, particularly in Ukraine and Kazakhstan.[1] Russian nationalists have repeatedly charged that the Yeltsin government has been negligent in dealing with the interests of these Russians in the "near-abroad." In their public statements after the impressive nationalist showing in the December 1993 elections, President Boris Yeltsin and Foreign Minister Andrei Kozyrev became more vehement that the interests of these Russians must and would be defended. Throughout history, of course, protection of nationals abroad has repeatedly provided grounds for military intervention in other countries.

Russia is also directly linked to the republics by the continued stationing in most of them of Russian troops. As of the end of 1993, the rough figures for Russian ground forces in the Soviet successor republics were the following: Latvia, 15,000; Estonia, 5,000; Belarus, 30,000; Moldova, 3,000–8,000; Georgia, 20,000; peacekeeping forces in Tajikistan, 15,000–20,000; joint forces with Turkmenistan, 34,000; Uzbekistan's armed forces number about 15,000, of which some 6,000 are Russian officers. Russian antiaircraft and antimissile units and air force units also remain deployed in many republics.[2] The newly adopted military doctrine of the Russian Federation makes clear that a priority objective of Russian armed forces is "the maintenance of stability in regions adjoining the borders of the Russian Federation."[3] In itself, this objective is understandable. It is doubtless a major objective of U.S. armed forces to maintain stability in neighboring countries even if this objective is not publicized as boldly as in Russia. But the intervention of Russian armed forces in neighboring republics, especially in Georgia, have caused increasing concern.

THE WESTERN REPUBLICS

Russian political relations with the Baltic states are not good. The Baltic states wrested their independence from an unwilling Soviet Union shortly before its demise, and all three have passed laws that make it difficult for their large Russian minorities to obtain citizenship or hold political office. Withdrawal of Russian troops, a major issue for these newly independent states, has proceeded in politically motivated fits and starts. All have left Lithuania; the complete withdrawal from Latvia, except for the personnel of a radar warning installation, is scheduled for August 1994; under 5,000 are still in Estonia. These states remain tightly linked to the Russian economy, and Russia has sought to use economic pressures to protect its citizens; Gorbachev ordered suspension of oil deliveries to Lithuania in 1991, and Yeltsin temporarily suspended supplies of natural gas to Estonia in mid-1993. Frictions over treatment of ethnic Russians will probably continue, but all three states receive considerable political support from the Scandinavian countries, the European Community, and the

United States, and should hold their own unless the Russian government adopts truly extreme policies.

Belarus has close economic relations with Russia but has declared that it is militarily nonaligned. A domestic political struggle is in progress between advocates of continued independence of Belarus and supporters of outright reunification with Russia. Even if the former gain the upper hand, the very close relationship with Russia will probably continue.

Russia has serious security difficulties in Moldova, much of which was pulled away from Romania by the 1939 Molotov-Ribbentrop Pact. About 64 percent of Moldova's 4.3 million inhabitants are Romanian speakers, 14 percent are Ukrainians, and 12 percent Russians, with the remainder small minorities like Gagauzi and Bulgarians. When Moldova declared its sovereignty in June 1990, the Russian Transdniestrian Soviet Socialist Republic at Tiraspol on the western border of Ukraine declared its own independence from Moldova. A group composed predominantly of old-line communist Russians, but with some Ukrainian and Moldovan participation, had seized the richest, most industrialized section of Moldova. The population of this area is about 780,000; 28 percent Ukrainian, 25 percent Russian, and 40 percent Romanian. Leaders of the secessionist area claimed they were acting in anticipation of agreement by the Moldovan and Romanian governments to incorporate Moldova into Romania.

Fighting broke out in November 1991 between the secessionists, including units of the Russian Fourteenth Army, and the Moldovan government. By July 1992, when a cease-fire was declared, about 1,000 people had been killed. A peacekeeping force of the Moldovan army, Russian army, and local secessionist forces has been operating since. The situation remains highly flammable, with the potential for interstate war spreading to Romania, Moldova, Ukraine, and possibly Russia. However, Moldovan president Mircea Snegur, who campaigned for unification earlier, argues that a majority of Moldovans now do not want union with Romania. Snegur signed an economic union agreement with Russia in September 1993 and has even offered the Transdniester region negotiation on a federative relationship, a possibility he earlier rejected. The Conference on Security and Cooperation in Europe (CSCE) has sent repeated mediation missions to the area.

Russo-Ukrainian relations have emerged as the most strained among the former republics of the USSR to Russia's west. Ukraine's population of nearly 52 million includes over 11 million Russians. (For its part, Russia has almost 4 million Ukrainian residents.) In modern times, Ukraine has never had any extended period of independence. Soon after Ukraine's declaration of independence, in December 1991, marked the end of the Soviet Union, Russia and Ukraine quarreled over economic policy, over the price of Russian oil and natural gas, over dividing the personnel and armaments of the conventional armed forces of the former Soviet Union, including the Black Sea Fleet, as well as over possession of the rich Crimea, which Khrushchev had turned over to Ukraine in 1954 as a political gesture to mark the 300th anniversary of Ukraine's union with Russia, and, most sensitive of all, over control of that portion of the Soviet nuclear arsenal deployed in Ukraine.

Overnight, Ukraine became public enemy number one in the declarations of Moscow politicians. In return, a draft of Ukraine's official statement of defense policy declared Russia to be its main enemy. Although Russia had signed CSCE commitments pledging not to change existing borders in Europe by force or threat of force, it hung back from explicit acceptance of Ukraine's borders. Many Russians, including some senior officials, could not psychologically accept that Ukraine, for 300 years an integral part of Russia, was irrevocably gone. Formally accepting Ukraine's borders would mean accepting the permanent loss of the Crimea, Russia's Florida and California combined.

Although right-wingers in both countries urged resort to force, the Russo-Ukraine quarrel simmered down for a while in the summer of 1992, when Yeltsin reached agreement with Ukrainian president Leonid Kravchuk to place the aging Black Sea Fleet under joint command until 1995, when it was to be divided between the two countries. But the quarrel flared up again a year later as Black Sea Fleet sailors refused to accept Ukrainian orders under the joint Ukrainian-Russian command arrangement, and as Russia doubled the price of oil to Ukraine.

In June 1993, Presidents Leonid Kravchuk and Boris Yeltsin agreed to divide the fleet immediately, but with Russia continuing to use the port of Sevastopol. Then, in September, Kravchuk, hard-pressed by Ukraine's continued economic decline, agreed to sell Ukraine's half of the fleet to Russia, and also to transfer nuclear weapons in Ukraine to Russia. The Ukrainian Vrchovna Rada, or parliament, canceled the sale of the fleet and Ukraine defense minister Paton Morozov said the Rada would never accept the nuclear part of the deal. The old Russian Supreme Soviet passed a resolution in May 1992 stating that Khruschev's cession of the Crimea to Ukraine should be nullified. A second resolution in July 1993 declared Russian sovereignty over Sevastopol. Sevastopol's old-line communist local government supported this declaration. In January 1994, the overwhelming majority of Russian inhabitants of the Crimea (more than 70 percent of the 2.7 million population of the Crimea is Russian) voted in a regional president, Yuri Meshkov, pledged to unification with Russia and to holding a referendum on establishing "an independent Crimea in union" with other members of the Commonwealth of Independent States, "although at this time" not explicit reunification with Russia. President Kravchuk said Meshkov had exceeded his powers and canceled the referendum, but it was held as an opinion poll.

The Ukrainian economy was in free fall amid a three-way confrontation between parliament, president, and prime minister similar to Russia's, but still worse in its inability to tackle problems of government deficits and fast-flowing credits to large concerns. Ukraine's population is divided into three major groups: anti-Russian Ukrainians in the west, Russians in the east on the border with Russia; and a large group of Russified Ukrainians in the middle. Only the West Ukrainians have traditionally had deep-rooted hostility toward Russia. Unless real hostility solidifies in the middle group, it is hard to believe that Russo-Ukraine frictions, serious and numerous as they are, will lead to serious bloodshed between the two countries. But they could do so. New parliamentary elections scheduled for March 1994 promised to bring a stronger contingent of West Ukrainian nationalists into the parliament, while, as Ukraine's economy crumbled with hyperinflation, Russians in East Ukraine and the Crimea thought more and more about rejoining Russia. Most of them had voted in 1991 for Ukrainian independence and secession from the Soviet Union because they thought Ukraine would be more prosperous than Russia. Theoretically, the highest possible degree of regional autonomy for the ethnic Russian areas within the borders of Ukraine or even peaceful cession of East Ukraine and the Crimea to Russia together in return for a large Russian economic indemnity to Ukraine might be possible solutions, but Ukrainian-Russian relations would probably have to get still worse before these solutions became feasible. Civil war in Ukraine was a distinct possibility. If it took place, it could trigger Russian military intervention, and Europe's worst post-cold war international crisis.

TRANSCAUCASUS

Gorbachev's *glasnost* policy was a signal to people in Eastern Europe and in the Soviet Union itself that the Kremlin would no longer use force to suppress dissent. Among the side effects of this policy was the eruption of ethnic violence in Nagorno-Karabakh, a small (population 150,000), predominantly Armenian autonomous region transferred by Stalin in 1923 to the control of the Azerbaijan Republic. In February 1988, the Armenian-dominated Nagorno-Karabakh Soviet requested union with Armenia. Fighting between Armenians and Azeris broke out soon after and has continued ever since. In December 1989, the Armenian Supreme Soviet declared the unification of Armenia and Nagorno-Karabakh, although no other country has recognized the annexation.

Moscow, the United Nations, and the CSCE have all tried to bring about a lasting cease-fire and negotiation for a political settlement in Nagorno-Karabakh. Despite Azerbaijan's larger population (7 million) to Armenia's (3 million), and its effective blockade of energy supplies to Armenia, the Armenians achieved success after success in the fighting. Armenian advances brought the fall of one Azeri government in 1991 and of a second one in the late spring of 1993. An estimated 6,000 were killed by the end of 1992 in a conflict that had become interstate war.

By that time, the Armenians had captured not only the Karabakh enclave, but also considerable surrounding territory. By September 1993, they had taken a fifth of Azerbaijan's territory, much of it to the south of Nagorno-Karabakh, including a sixty-mile stretch along the Iranian border. About a million Azeris had been displaced; many were seeking refuge in neighboring Iran, which has up to 20 million Azeris, a Turkic people, within its own borders.

Both Iran and Turkey, which also has a common border with Azerbaijan, warned Armenia to rein in its offensive, as did Russia, which has important interests in oil-rich Azerbaijan. In September 1993, President Heidar Aliev of Azerbaijan took the initiative to offer peace talks with Armenia. Reversing Azerbaijan's earlier (October 1992) withdrawal from the Commonwealth of Independent States, he applied to rejoin. Russia brokered cease-fire talks between Karabakh and Azerbaijan in September 1993. The CSCE too has held a series of dialogues between Armenia, Azerbaijan, and Karabakh as a prelude to sending a large number of observers once a dependable cease-fire is achieved. In March 1994, the Armenian and Azerbaijan governments did sign a formal cease-fire under Russian auspices, but it did not hold.[4]

GEORGIA

The Georgian parliament declared independence from the USSR in April 1991. After a series of erratic, despotic actions, Georgian president Zviad Gamsakhurdia was overthrown in bloody fighting in January 1992. Former Soviet foreign minister Eduard Shevardnadze was appointed president of Georgia and subsequently popularly elected. But fighting continued between Georgian troops and supporters of Gamsakhurdia. There was still worse conflict between fiercely nationalistic Georgians, who make up only 70 percent of Georgia's 5 million people, and the 25 percent of its population represented by three ethnic minorities with whom the Georgians have long dealt roughly: Ossetians and Abkhazians on Georgia's northern borders with Russia, and Adzharians on the southwest border with Turkey.

Abkhazia, long a separate principality before its forcible incorporation into the Soviet Union in the 1920s, called for independence from Georgia in March 1989. Sporadic fighting broke out. In July 1992, after Abkhaz separatists issued a new declaration of autonomy, Georgian troops occupied Sukhumi, Abkhazia's main city. The predominantly Muslim Abkhazians number only about 120,000, some 20 percent of Abkhazia's population. But they received help from small neighboring Caucasian republics in Russia, most of which want to secede, and a considerable amount of free-lance military assistance from Russians, both in munitions and personnel. Georgia made repeated charges of official Russian involvement, disclaimed by Moscow. An Abkhaz offensive in July 1993 against the Georgian occupants of Sukhumi ended in a Russia-brokered cease-fire that was supposed to be monitored by the UN. Only twelve of eighty-eight UN observers had arrived by September, when the Abkhazians, breaking the truce, launched a new offensive which drove Georgian forces personally led by President Shevardnadze out of the city.

With Georgian government forces defeated in Abkhazia, followers of ousted leader Gamsakhurdia launched a new uprising against Georgian government troops and moved toward the capital, Tbilisi. A desperate Shevardnadze, after repeatedly rejecting Russian intervention, now appealed for it. As the price of Moscow's support, he reversed himself and joined the Commonwealth of Independent States, and in February 1994 signed a bilateral pact with Russia. The treaty formalized Russia's use of three military bases including the Black Sea port at Poti. As Yeltsin arrived in Tbilisi to sign the agreement, Georgia's deputy defense minister was assassinated, apparently in protest against the treaty, and the defense minister himself threatened resignation because of Russian pressure. As this deal was being negotiated, Russian troops spread out to defend the rail line from Tbilisi to the Black Sea, and the Gamsakhurdian rebellion rapidly died out with the reported death of its leader. Meanwhile, Swiss diplomat Eduard Brunner, acting for the UN, and Russian deputy foreign minister Boris Pastukhov mediated an agreement between Abkhazia and Georgia, providing for deployment of international peacekeeping forces to supervise the cease-fire put in place after Abkhazians gained control of Sukhumi and for continuation of political talks between Georgia and Abkhazia. In a Washington visit in March 1994, Shevardnadze obtained President Clinton's support for a UN mandate giving peacekeeper status to Russian troops monitoring the cease-fire in Abkhazia. Shevardnadze expressed the hope that a mandate would provide some measure of outside control over the activities of these forces.

Fighting between Georgians and Ossetians living in Georgia (they number 90,000) started in September 1989. A year later, the South

Ossetian Supreme Soviet declared its territory a separate state, aiming for union with North Ossetia, which is inside the borders of Russia (the total population of North and South Ossetia is 300,000). A cease-fire went into effect in South Ossetia in June 1992 with a peacekeeping force composed of Russians, Georgians, and Ossetians. Ethnic violence then erupted in North Ossetia between North Ossetian Christians and Ingush Muslim peasants from the neighboring republic. Like many other non-Russian minorities, the Ingush had been deported far away during World War II for alleged collaboration with the Germans. Later, they returned to find that their fields in this rocky, land-poor area were occupied by Ossetians, and they tried to take them back by force. Russian troops were sent in. The president of neighboring secessionist Chechnya, an ex-Soviet air force general, threatened to intervene to expel Russian forces. (Chechnya refused to participate in the December 1993 Russian elections, claiming independent status.) The Stockholm International Peace Institute estimates that there are thirty current territorial disputes in the Caucasus.[5] Russia seems to be recapitulating many of its eighteenth- and nineteenth-century efforts to wrest control of the Black Sea area from the Ottoman Empire and Persia, and to be seeking to move its forces back to earlier Russian and Soviet positions along the borders of Iran and Turkey.

CENTRAL ASIAN REPUBLICS

Small mountainous Tajikistan adjoins Afghanistan and China. About 80 percent of its 5.6 million population are Sunni Muslims; the largest group, the Tajiks, speak a Persian dialect. A regional power struggle between the traditional communist hierarchy in northern Tajikistan and secular and Muslim reform elements in the south developed into a bloody war with religious overtones, with an estimated 20,000 killed and 300,000 refugees by mid-1993. In May 1992, an unusual alliance of Muslim fundamentalists, modernizing anticommunists and local leaders from southern and eastern Tajikistan forced old-line communist leader Rakhmon Nabiyev to take them into a coalition government in Dushanbe, the capital. In September, they forced Nabiyev to resign at gunpoint and took over the government. Fighting broke out between the two groups. Moscow intervened to save small Russian units taken hostage. President Islam Karimov of neighboring Uzbekistan, another old-line communist leader, sent armed help to the Nabiyev forces, while the fundamentalists reportedly received arms, training, and volunteers from Gulbuddin Hekmatyar, the hard-line Afghan faction leader whose forces were at the time shelling Kabul in a power struggle similar to that in Dushanbe.

In December 1992, pro-Nabiyev forces, aided by Russians and Uzbeks, recaptured Dushanbe. Nabiyev was replaced by Emomali

Rakmonov, also an old-line communist, who consolidated power through repression, though raids from revenge-seeking Afghans continued. Russia built up the 201st Russian Motorized Infantry Division in Tajikistan with thousands of Russian soldiers at double pay and also sent in a division of border guards. It persuaded adjacent states to participate, mainly symbolically, in a CIS joint peacekeeping force in Tajikistan, of which the 201st Division is the main component. Speaking of the Afghan raids across the Tajikistan border and reflecting Russian fears that Islamic fundamentalism and political chaos could spread north, President Yeltsin said in July 1993, "Everyone must realize that this border is in effect Russia's." The Tajik government eventually agreed to convert its currency to new rubles, tying its economy to that of Russia. However, part of the deal was a statement of willingness by the Tajikistan government to conduct political talks with leaders of guerrilla groups.[6] Although most fighting died down by the end of 1993, this conflict was not yet over.

Resurgence of Russian Imperialism?

By spring 1994, Moldova, Georgia, and even Nagorno-Karabakh and Tajikistan were quiescent if not peaceful. Russian forces had consolidated their position in Georgia and Tajikistan. The Russian Fourteenth Army was still ensconced in the Transdniester region. Moldova, Georgia, Azerbaijan, Armenia, and Tajikistan were all linked more tightly with the Russian economy. Russian diplomacy and in most cases, Russian armed forces, had played an important role in diminishing the fighting.

Although most of these conflicts have been small-scale, for the small states actually involved in them, the costs have been very high. In addition to the loss of life, the consequences for the economy and for democratic development in these mainly poor states have been disastrous. In all four cases there was barbarous warfare involving poorly controlled irregular forces, arbitrary rule, wholesale restriction of democratic processes, unjustified killing of civilians, and widespread destruction of economic resources.

For Russia, the consequences are also bad. The economic costs of military intervention are heavy, and Russia's overstrained budget cannot afford them. Managing the involvement of Russian troops and seeking conciliation are a drain on the time and energy of Russian leaders. The conflicts risk bringing in outside nations like Afghanistan, Turkey, and Iran. Moreover, there are damaging repercussions for the Russian domestic political process. The continuous fighting on the western and southern borders of Russia, often involving Russian troops, helps to maintain an atmosphere of crisis and a high degree of emotional mobilization in Russian politics. Above all, the Russo-Ukraine dispute keeps negative sentiments boiling on both sides.

These conflicts provide a dangerous dynamic for nurturing extreme nationalism in all the peoples of the successor states, especially Russia. Politicians like Vladimir Zhirinovsky deliberately play on these emotions, emphasizing the deteriorating situation of Russians in the neighboring republics. The Russian government cannot insulate itself from these pressures. Boris Yeltsin's press spokesman Vyacheslav Kostikov said as the new Federal Assembly convened in January 1994 that in Yeltsin's policy "undisputed emphasis in foreign policy will be given to protection of Russia's national interests and the rights of Russians and Russian-speaking people . . . on the basis of pan-national solidarity." Yeltsin had already made a vain effort to gain dual citizenship for Russians living in neighboring republics at the CIS Council meeting in Turkmenistan in late December 1993. Foreign Minister Andrei Kozyrev drew heavy criticism both locally and in the West for remarks in January 1994 (later revised) to senior Russian officials to the effect that Russian troops should remain in the Baltic republics and other former Soviet republics in order to protect Russian citizens and to avoid a security vacuum that might be filled by forces hostile to Russia.[7]

In short, the conflicts in neighboring republics appear to be pushing Russian policy in the direction of reversion to the militaristic imperialism of the past, and to be pushing it toward the autocratic development feared by many Russians and foreigners alike. The non-Russian republics reacted nervously to Yeltsin's suggestion in the spring of 1993 that the United Nations should delegate to Russia a special role "as guarantor of peace stability in regions of the former USSR."[8] Foreign Minister Kozyrev later complained that Russia was bearing the burden of peacemaking in the border states with no outside help. He again urged UN participation or at least UN endorsement of these efforts.

There is a real dilemma here for Russia and for the international community. Whatever past history, should 200,000 Ossetians, 120,000 Abkhazians, or 100,000 Armenian residents of Nagorno-Karabakh— populations the size of a small city—be allowed to use their claims for internationally recognized independence or union with other states to cause bloody wars? These conflicts represent a potential security threat both to Russia and to other countries. The ineffective governments of the neighboring republics are generally unable to cope with them on their own. Often, the policy of these governments toward local minorities has precipitated the problem in the beginning. Secretary of State Warren Christopher complained at the CSCE Council of Foreign Ministers meeting in late 1993 of repeated human rights violations in Turkmenistan and Uzbekistan, which both have old-style authoritarian governments. Once conflict breaks out, the governments are too weak to cope with it. Western public opinion is presently disinclined to support sending yet another outside peacekeeping force to these trouble spots, although Russia has repeatedly requested such forces. Consequently, Russia must either stand by as Russian citizens are endangered and conflicts occur near the borders of Russia itself, or it must intervene, risking inevitable criticism from public opinion in the neighboring republics and from Western governments and publics.

Since mid-1993, triggered mainly by events in Georgia and later by the strong nationalist showing in the Russian elections, Western criticism of Russian actions in neighboring republics has intensified. For example, in early 1994, British defense minister Malcolm Rifkind told participants in an annual gathering of security experts in Munich that Russian efforts to regain control over the former Soviet empire were "the most likely threat to the security of Europe."[9] The concerns engendered by the possibility of the Russian expansionism could alienate Western political opinion and reduce vital Western economic and political support for Russian democracy.

BORDER DISPUTES

In addition to the seething ethnic quarrels on its borders, Russia and its neighboring republics have potential border disputes with nearly all of their many neighbors, including Finland, the Baltic states, Turkey, Iran, Afghanistan, China, and Japan. In its formal agreements, the Commonwealth of Independent States declared existing republic borders to be inviolable, but the Soviet Academy of Sciences claimed in early 1991 that there were about sixty-six unresolved border disputes among the former Soviet republics. Of twenty-three interrepublic borders in the old Soviet Union, only three were not contested—Latvia's borders with Ukraine and with Belarus, and Belarus's border with Russia.[10]

Mark Smith of the London-based Royal United Services Institute for Defense Studies has described twenty of these border disputes:[11] In addition to serious territorial arguments between Russia and Ukraine, there are actual or potential disputes between Lithuania and Poland; Estonia and Russia; Russia and Lithuania (over Kaliningrad, a part of Russia taken over from Germany after World War II, but with access for Russia only via Lithuania); Belarus and Lithuania; Poland and Belarus (where there are former Polish territories on which Polish minorities still live); Poland and Ukraine, where there is also a Polish minority; Slovakia and Ukraine (the Soviet Union incorporated a small portion of prewar Czechoslovakia); Ukraine and Moldova, where Ukraine holds northern Bukovina, part of the Romanian territories annexed by Russia under the Ribbentrop-Molotov Pact. Moldova has protested to Ukraine against Ukraine's incorporation of Bukovina, which Ukrainians for their part consider a traditional part of Ukraine.

NUCLEAR DANGERS FROM RUSSIA AND THE SUCCESSOR REPUBLICS

The main security threat today facing both Europe and the United States arises from the continued deployment of many thousands of nuclear weapons amid the turbulent political environment of four Soviet successor republics—Belarus, Ukraine, Kazakhstan, and especially Russia itself. As central Soviet power collapsed, Russia moved rapidly to gain control over Soviet nuclear forces. Gorbachev handed over the nuclear codes for the USSR's strategic weapons to Russian president Yeltsin on December 25, 1991. In establishing the Commonwealth of Independent States in early December, the leaders of Russia, Belarus, and Ukraine agreed to aim for total nuclear disarmament and in the meanwhile to establish a common military command over nuclear weapons. In subsequent meetings, they were joined by Kazakhstan, the fourth republic where strategic-range weapons of the former Soviet Union were deployed.

Most non-Russians considered the Commonwealth's nuclear command a fig leaf for Russian control over nuclear weapons deployed in the other republics, but the heads of the CIS governments were promised a veto right over any use of nuclear weapons. Russia pledged to dismantle all strategic- or tactical-range nuclear weapons brought from the other republics to Russia with opportunity for observers from the republics to oversee the destruction. As regards tactical weapons, dismantling was sporadically monitored by Ukraine and the other two republics.

The United States strongly preferred, as a more predictable arrangement, that all nuclear weapons of the former Soviet Union be placed under the sole control of Russia. When it became evident that this would not be possible because of resistance from the other three republics, the Bush administration moved with great skill and speed to associate the three with the as yet unratified START I Treaty. In protocols to that treaty signed at Lisbon in May 1992, the three republics joined Russia, as the main successor state of the USSR, in undertaking the obligations of the treaty. Their heads of government also pledged in letters to President Bush to adhere to the Nuclear Non-Proliferation Treaty (NPT) as nonnuclear states in the "shortest possible time."

Late in December 1991, Ukraine, Belarus, and Kazakhstan agreed to send all tactical-range nuclear weapons on their territories to Russia by the next July. This target was met. The Russian government has reported the complete withdrawal of approximately 15,000 tactical nuclear weapons from Eastern Europe and the other former Soviet republics and it has begun to dismantle these weapons at the rate of about 2,000 per year, somewhat higher than the rate at which the United States is dismantling its withdrawn tactical warheads. There have been repeated reports, none as yet confirmed, that some tactical warheads slipped out of the collection net. Some tactical nuclear weapons remain deployed at various locations inside Russia; the security of warhead custody at some of these locations has been questioned.

The Bush administration also acted with initiative in moving to reduce the Russian arsenal of deployed nuclear weapons still further through the START II Treaty, signed in January 1993. When implemented, the treaty will eliminate multiple warheads on land-based missiles and reduce nuclear warheads deployed on strategic-range missiles to a level of about 3,000 in each country.

Pushed by Congress, the Bush and Clinton administrations provided money to help Russia and other successor states in transporting and safe-guarding withdrawn warheads, constructing a new storage facility for them in Russia, and instituting or improving controls to block export of nuclear weapons components. By mid-1993, Congress had made $1.2 billion available for this purpose, although the funds were spent very slowly. The administration also agreed to purchase from Russia up to 500 tons of highly enriched uranium for weapons, which would be converted to nuclear fuel by diluting it with low-enriched uranium. All these actions were aimed at reducing the many risks that arose from collapse of the Soviet Union's effective if totalitarian control over nuclear weapons. Between them, the Russian and U.S. governments had apparently smooth-ly picked up the pieces of the former Soviet Union's nuclear capability and reassembled them in a new, safer pattern.

THE PROGRAM RUNS INTO TROUBLE

However, by December 1992, when the Ukraine parliament, the Vrchovna Rada, recessed without ratifying the START I Treaty, it had become evident that this carefully planned program was in considerable difficulties, most of them caused by the nationalistic feud between Ukraine and Russia. The Russian Supreme Soviet ratified START I but made exe-cution of its ratification dependent on ratification by the other three republics and on their adherence to the NPT Treaty. The U.S. Senate, rat-ifying START I in October 1992, had insisted on similar conditions for implementation. In March 1993, Belarus ratified START I and signed the NPT. Kazakhstan ratified START I and then signed the NPT in December. But Ukraine had not acted.

Ratification hearings on START II, a bilateral treaty between the United States and Russia without participation of the other three republics, began in early 1993 in the old Russian Supreme Soviet, but the treaty was already being opposed by right-wingers. The latter claimed that its provisions would give undue advantage to the United States. In particular, they criticized treaty provisions calling for destruction of all land-based missiles with multiple warheads, including the much-feared Soviet SS–18s, while permitting deployment of more submarine-launched multiple warhead missiles by the United States than Russia, with its smaller number of submarines, would be able to match. Given the continuing vendetta between Yeltsin and the Russian parliament, it seemed better to delay further Russian action on the treaty until after the new elections, when the new Duma would have to continue ratification proceedings. Unfortunately, this calculation was frustrated by the results of the December 1993 elections for the Duma, which raised serious questions about prospects for START II ratification. In any event, neither Russia nor the United States would ratify START II until Ukraine moved on START I and NPT.

At the end of 1993, Belarus still had 54 single-warhead missiles deployed on its territory. Kazakhstan had 104 missiles and 40 long-range bombers with a total of about 1,400 warheads. Ukraine had 175 multiple-warhead missiles and 21 bombers with a total of about 1,800 warheads. More than two-thirds of former Soviet strategic nuclear weapons, including nearly 6,000 missile-mounted warheads and over 100 bombers with about 700 warheads, remained deployed in Russia, together with large reserves of warheads and fissile material for weapons.

Ukraine's frictions with Russia over armed forces continued to grow during 1992 and 1993. There was hostility over dividing the conventional forces of the former Soviet Union between Russia and Ukraine as Ukraine assumed control of armed forces on its territory, including the bulk of the modern tank force the USSR had deployed against NATO, nuclear-capable Bear H and Blackjack bombers—the key air component of Soviet strategic forces—and the Black Sea Fleet. These disputes came against the background of bitter disagreement over the Crimea and over the price of Russian oil deliveries to Ukraine, which Russia, staggering under the weight of its own economic reform, wanted to increase. Most of all, there were problems of national pride and sovereignty. The Russian government treated Ukraine's government like a spoiled younger sibling. The Russian ambassador in Kiev was reported to have advised his foreign colleagues not to set up shop permanently in Kiev because Ukrainian independence would be a short-lived affair.

Gradually, as the arguments continued, possession of the nuclear weapons deployed in Ukraine and even the issue of their legal ownership, claimed by Russia, became a symbol of national independence for Ukraine. Ukrainian parliamentary opinion, strongly antinuclear after the Chernobyl disaster of 1986, gradually shifted until a majority appeared to support retention of nuclear weapons. Ukraine had asked for $2.8 billion to compensate it for expenses of dismantling the big strategic-range missiles, for a share of proceeds from Russian sale of fissile material to the United States, and for binding security guarantees from the United States and Russia, but it was not obtaining satisfaction on any of these counts. A majority of Ukrainian parliamentarians appeared to be moving toward a position where Ukraine would ratify START I and would permit dismantling and destruction of Ukraine's aging SS–19 missiles but would hold onto its 46 more modern SS–24 missiles with 460 warheads until it became clearer that Ukraine's security vis-à-vis an unstable and unfriendly Russia was assured. A number of Rada deputies had come to believe that permanent retention of at least some nuclear weapons was the only effective assurance of Ukraine's safety and continued independence.

These approaches, of course, would mean indefinite postponement of Ukraine's signature of the Nuclear Non-Proliferation Treaty. Some Ukrainians, without much knowledge of the difficulty of altering the text of the NPT, suggested that the treaty be amended to accommodate a special temporary category of "threshold nuclear states," to include Ukraine. Meanwhile, Ukraine moved toward tighter physical control over nuclear delivery systems and warheads deployed on its territory. As a result, access to warheads for Russia's maintenance technicians became tighter. Russia claimed Ukraine's weapons were in a dangerous state of neglect. For the moment, Russia maintained control of the electronic locks mounted on strategic-range missiles deployed in Ukraine, Kazakhstan, and Belarus to prevent unauthorized firing. But Ukraine had physical control over the approximately 1,800 warheads deployed on its soil with the capability to override or bypass Russian electronic locks and to retarget the missiles within a matter of months, although it could not do so without being observed. Because it is difficult although not impossible to convert 3,000–5,000-mile strategic-range missiles to shorter trajectories, attention focused on the 400 or so warheads for air-launched cruise missiles deployed in Ukraine; these appeared to be under full Ukrainian control.

Throughout 1993, the new Clinton administration played a successful mediating role with Russia and Ukraine—a role welcomed by Ukraine and tolerated by Russia. Finally, during President Clinton's Moscow visit in mid-January 1994, he and Presidents Yeltsin and Kravchuk signed an agreement providing for removal of all strategic warheads from Ukraine within three years. Portions of the agreement were kept confidential, evidently to improve President Kravchuk's leverage with his fractious parliament, but it appeared that Russia would cancel part of Ukraine's huge debt to Russia in payment for the fissile material from already withdrawn tactical warheads. The United States would make advance payment to

Russia for low-enriched uranium fuel it imported from the conversion of fissile material of withdrawn nuclear warheads. Russia in turn would send 100 tons of low enriched uranium to Ukraine to fuel its power reactors. After START I entered into force and Ukraine signed the NPT, the United States and Russia would extend security guarantees to Ukraine based on existing CSCE commitments to respect the territorial integrity of states. The guarantees would provide that border changes could be made only by peaceful and consensual means, and that signatories would refrain from economic coercion and would also seek immediate UN Security Council assistance to Ukraine if the latter were attacked by a nuclear aggressor. The United States would pay Ukraine a minimum of $175 million to meet dismantling costs and would make available an initial $155 million in economic aid with a commitment to double this amount if Ukraine undertook significant economic reforms, a commitment rapidly made good during Kravchuk's visit to Washington in March 1994.

In February, the Ukraine parliament ratified the START I Treaty but, in a close vote, held back on authorizing the Ukrainian government to sign the Non-Proliferation Treaty. The emergence of a still more refractory and nationalistic parliament was forecast in the March 1994 elections. It was unclear what future action the Ukrainian parliament would take, but the chances nonetheless seemed fairly good for ultimate settlement.[12]

SOME CONSEQUENCES

The United States and Russia, together with the major European Community countries, have been making great efforts to bring Ukraine to fulfill the obligations it undertook at Lisbon. There is a great deal at stake for all these countries. If they fail, intensification of Ukrainian-Russian military tensions will occur, with a continuing atmosphere of hypertension and ultimate significance attached to every tiny action by either side whether planned or coincidental. Many Ukrainians fear commando raids by Russian Spetsnaz troops to take possession of the warheads by force. Russian commanders are aware that it would probably not be feasible to seize all of the warheads before some could be fired, but this fear illustrates the depth of Ukrainian concern. In short, Ukraine's continued possession of nuclear weapons would almost certainly bring continuing, dangerous deterioration of relations between Russia and Ukraine.

Another casualty of failure to settle could be the Nuclear Non-Proliferation Treaty itself. If Ukraine refuses to carry out its commitment to sign NPT for whatever reason, the prospect of indefinite extension of the treaty in the 1995 review conference would be seriously undercut. States with the technological capacity to build nuclear weapons would be cautious about committing themselves forever not to develop nuclear weapons in the face of an open demonstration that the international non-proliferation regime was incapable of effectively preventing the emergence of new nuclear powers. Withdrawal of North Korea from the NPT, which North Korea threatened in early 1993, could have the same effect: For example, it was reported that, during the July 1993 Group of Seven (G–7) meeting in Tokyo, Japan declined to subscribe to a joint statement calling for unlimited extension of the NPT even though Japan had endorsed a similar statement at the previous year's G–7 meeting. The Japanese government explained it needed more time to consider the issue, although the successor government did commit itself to indefinite extension.[13]

If considerations like these resulted in an extension in 1995 of the Non-Proliferation Treaty for only a short period of time, say five or ten years, rather than indefinitely, this would create a very difficult situation. Many nonnuclear states would want to use subsequent review sessions to extract specific commitments from the nuclear weapons states to abolish nuclear weapons. Such commitments are unlikely to be forthcoming and the NPT could as a result collapse.

For the United States, continued failure of Ukraine to adhere to the NPT and thus to fulfill the requirements of both the U.S. Senate and the Russian parliament for implementing START I could also mean the collapse of the SALT-START regime of bilateral strategic arms control with Russia and potential anarchy in the U.S.-Russian nuclear relationship. Something might be rescued from the START treaties through executive agreement between the two governments to carry out some of the reductions and other actions prescribed in the treaties, but at some point the legislatures of both countries would probably object to carrying out arms reduction without a firm treaty commitment.

POSTRATIFICATION PROBLEMS

Even if Ukraine signs NPT and both START treaties begin to be implemented, many serious problems with regard to nuclear weapons in the former Soviet Union will remain. Implementation can take up to ten years for both START treaties. But if the Ukrainian government collapses or there is civil war in Ukraine between Ukrainian nationalists and Russian citizens of Ukraine, possibly with Russian intervention, all three groups might attempt to seize Ukrainian nuclear weapons. Moreover, there is always the possibility of accidental launch or warhead discharge from negligent handling in the confused and disorganized conditions of the successor states. Russia claimed that Ukrainian missile silos were damp, with an increasing danger of electrical short circuit, and that there were rocket fluid leaks and accumulations of explosive hydrogen around warhead nose cones.

Other worries, highly pertinent for Russia and the other three republics as well, are the possibility of forcible seizure, theft, or illegal sale of deployed warheads or stored warheads and fissile material. Given endemic conditions of ethnic clashes, increasing activity of criminal gangs, and widespread corruption among officials and military personnel in Russia and the republics, these concerns are serious. There is a risk that nuclear weapons in Russia or the other three republics could be taken over by political extremists or terrorists, perhaps as blackmail to involve outside powers like the United States or the European Union in quarrels like those between Ukraine and Russia or Armenia and Azerbaijan. There have been repeated reports of an attack in January 1990 by Azeri nationalists on a nuclear weapons storage site in Baku.

Leakage from the Soviet successor republics of knowledge, components, and materials to the outside world is also an endemic problem. Several thousand trained nuclear physicists and nuclear weapons experts, most poorly paid or unemployed, are scattered among the former Soviet republics, as are a large number of nuclear research laboratories and civilian power reactors. Some republics might in time seek to develop their own nuclear weapons. But the more immediate risk is of hard currency sale of nuclear expertise and components to Third World countries like Pakistan, North Korea, Iran, and Libya. There have already been reports that Iran has made job offers to Russian nuclear arms designers. Reports that North Korea sought to recruit Russian missile experts have been confirmed.

Control over export of nuclear materials from the former Soviet Union has been lax and irregular. No serious breach of security is yet known, but control mechanisms remain ineffective in all republics and the number of incidents is increasing. In 1992, there were a hundred reported cases of attempted sale of low-enriched uranium from nuclear power reactors in the former Warsaw Pact states, most of them masquerading as weapons-grade material. In 1990 and 1991, the Soviet central government sold nuclear power plants to Pakistan and to India—two mutually hostile, undeclared nuclear powers—without requiring that those countries accept full-scope safeguards on all their nuclear operations. Russia has apparently been selling India heavy water for plutonium reactors. The majority of uranium processing plants of the former Soviet Union are in the Asian republics of Kyrgyzstan and Tajikistan, now beyond the control of Moscow, increasing the possibility of unregulated hard currency sales to Third World countries, especially close-by Pakistan, India, and Iran. Russia's record on selling of long-range missile components gives reason for concern. Important Russian sales to Brazil as well as India are in the works.

Even if they are ratified and enter into effect, the START treaties themselves have serious shortcomings. They provide for withdrawing nuclear warheads and missiles from field deployment, but they do not provide for irreversible reductions. That is, the treaties do not obligate Russia or the United States to dismantle or destroy either nuclear warheads or strategic-range missiles, with the significant exception of the destruction of SS–18 missiles provided for in START II. Otherwise, both warheads and missiles can be retained and stored without limit. There is also no mutual obligation of Russia and the United States to account for or to dismantle the tactical warheads withdrawn in parallel unilateral action from deployment outside national territory, although each country has said it would dismantle a considerable number, and this process is going on in the United States and Russia but without verification arrangements. And although President Clinton in September 1993 proposed an international agreement to end the production of fissile material for weapons, there is as yet no such agreement.

Russia is apparently prepared to dismantle strategic warheads withdrawn from the other republics under START I, but there is no mutual U.S.-Russian obligation to destroy warheads, no provision for full accountability, and no mutual obligation to place the fissile material from these weapons in internationally maintained and monitored storage. All this means indefinite continuation of risks of forcible seizure, theft, or illegal sale in Russia.

This review of nuclear risks from Russia is based on the assumption that the Russian government continues a policy of cooperation with the Western countries. Among the worst risks of a politically unstable, nuclear-armed Russia is that this may not always be the case. A right-wing nationalist government in Russia might use its possession of nuclear weapons to threaten other states. In the absence of further agreements, a future nationalistic-authoritarian Russian government could, without breaking out of the START Treaty, rapidly expand its stocks of stored nuclear warheads, causing acute international alarm and starting a new arms race. If it then wanted to withdraw from START, Russia could in a matter of months double its deployed nuclear force of about 6,000 warheads under START I back to over 10,000.

The implications of the general situation described here are vast: Maintenance and command and control have degenerated in Russia. There are increasing risks of accidental warhead explosion or accidental launch. The Soviet early warning system, large segments of which are scattered in the neighboring republics, is more prone than before to false alarms. The iron discipline of the communist system has dissipated, and troop motivation and control are more uncertain. In the circumstances, launch on warning will probably be the rule for the Russian as it was for the Soviet government.

Although the former Soviet Union is believed to have produced over 46,000 warheads since 1949,[14] there is no accurate inventory of Russian holdings of warheads or weapons-grade fissile materials. The United States has agreed to help establish alternate power sources, but in 1994 Russia was still operating three dual-purpose plutonium reactors for energy purposes, producing weapons-grade plutonium at the same time and will continue to do so for several years. The United States has funded the design of a new, long-term Russian repository for storing fissile material, but under best circumstances, construction of this facility will take six to ten years. The purchase by the United States from Russia of 500 tons of highly enriched uranium for downgrading and conversion to power reactor fuel is useful but will take twenty years to complete. Beyond that, it is not a definitive solution to these problems: As the deal was being discussed, it shocked Western experts to learn from Boris Yeltsin himself that Russia possessed far more weapons-grade highly enriched uranium than Western intelligence agencies had estimated.[15]

The most immediate of all of these problems is a political one—nervous reaction from the outside world to continuing evidence of political instability in Russia, combined with its continuing possession of very large nuclear arsenals. As with negative developments in the Russian polity or in Russian relations with surrounding republics, this hostile Western reaction may be the greatest immediate danger from nuclear weapons in the former Soviet Union. Mutually reinforcing suspicions could spiral, among other things severely undermining Western public support for various forms of aid to Russia and other republics. We deal with these nuclear weapons problems further in the last chapter of this book.

A LONG-TERM FORECAST

Overall, considering the difficulties it faced in the first few years of its separate, post-Soviet existence, Russia has at least made a definite start toward becoming a functioning democracy, although nothing has been finally settled. The Yeltsin government moved through a stormy transition from authoritarian rule with a minimum of the organized violence whose occurrence was so widely feared both inside and outside Russia. The fatalities in the fighting between adherents of the old Supreme Soviet and the government troops were not numerous, and the December 1993 elections were without violence. In this sense, the Yeltsin government was able to build on the remarkable record of epochal change without major violence that was Gorbachev's greatest achievement. Whether it will be possible to build further on this record is the major open question on Russia's future—and of the future security of Europe. And the central difficulty about Russia is that there will be many, many years of uncertainty and mixed results before a conclusive, positive answer can be possible. On the other hand, a definitive negative outcome could take place rapidly at any point in this period.

In the early 1990s, many observers compared the state of the Russian Federation with that of Weimar Germany, where acute inflation and economic misery combined with rampant nationalism to lead to Hitler's totalitarian rule. Others saw in Boris Yeltsin a counterpart of Alexander Kerensky, the social democrat whose shaky hold on the post-czarist Russian polity was broken by Lenin's Bolshevik coup in late 1917; these analysts clearly expected a new dictator. In August 1991, a few days after the failure of the anti-Gorbachev coup, Secretary of Defense Richard Cheney suggested that the future might bring outbreaks of violence, conflicts between the republics and between ethnic and national groups within the republics, and further deterioration of the economy, generating labor strife, possible famine, widespread popular disorder, and massive refugee flows to neighboring countries.[16] In opening the Moscow CSCE conference on human rights in September 1991, Gorbachev himself predicted that dissolution of the Soviet Union into independent republics would bring a flood of refugees, armed conflicts, ethnic hatreds, and looting and pillaging of cities and villages. To many observers, Russia appeared like a mountain of gunpowder waiting for a match.

Many such predictions seem to rest in part on a concept of the Russians as a potentially nihilistic mob that continually hovers on the verge of lawless and immensely destructive rampage, motivated by an innate spirit of *buntarstvo*, anarchic rebellion against all that exists, which, if it erupts, can be repressed only by terror.[17] Dostoyevsky's Grand Inquisitor represents all mankind—but Russians are meant—as rebellious slaves waiting to ferociously tear down the institutions of civilization and drench the earth with blood. In reflections on his sojourn at the czarist court in St. Petersburg in the early nineteenth century, the ultraconservative writer Joseph de Maistre considered that the final authority of government in Russia must rest on the executioner in order to prevent a rampage of peasants and serfs like the *jacquerie* of the French Revolution. These concepts, widespread in Russian political thinking, may reflect the deep-seated apprehensions of a serf-holding minority over the possibility of widespread uprising, reinforced by actual experience with anarchist activities and the chaotic disintegration of czarist rule.

However, the predicted explosions did not take place, at least not within Russia itself. The traditional contention that Russians have a deep-rooted cultural tendency to destructive violence, cruelty, and aggression that distinguishes them from other populations in a similar state of social disorganization is much overdrawn. Specific historical circumstances elicit and emphasize such characteristics. Nonetheless, political and ethnic conflict in the republics neighboring Russia indisputably is the deadly enemy of democratic and economic development.

Moreover, the current ethnic conflicts are not the end of the instability caused by the USSR's collapse. Beyond the pitched battles in Azerbaijan or Tajikistan, it is hard to believe that, in a situation of economic deprivation and many old resentments, the Russian Federation will indefinitely find it possible to resolve the claims of Tatars, Bashkirs, Chechens, or Yakuts in a nonviolent way, or that all of these groups will refrain from the use of force against Russians.

Clearly, the future of Russia and the other Soviet successor states depends heavily on the degree of progress they make toward economic well-being over the next twenty years. Representatives of the center-right Civic Union faction often hold up the economy of China as a better model than Yeltsin's reform program. But, leaving aside Chinese agriculture, which is almost completely privatized, the Russian economy is in actuality already rather like the Chinese, a mixture of a state industrial sector operating as a nationwide welfare institution and an expanding private sector, often unofficial and sometimes illegal.[18] There is a vital difference: China remains unabashedly authoritarian.

Many analysts assume that if the principal republics—Russia, Belarus, Ukraine, Kazakhstan, and Uzbekistan—could achieve on an enduring basis reasonable living standards, equivalent, say, to the level of Spain in the late 1980s;[19] this progress could permit consolidation of democratic institutions and also of reasonably strong political values among a significant portion of the population. While theoretically possible, an economic transformation of this magnitude would depend on a smooth transition to free-market mechanisms, on relatively smooth relations among the larger successor states, and on provision of large amounts of Western capital, governmental and private, over a decade or more.

These conditions are unlikely to be met. Even optimistic experts believe that economic reform could take up to thirty years to bring Russia to the prosperity level of the European Community countries, and even then it would take very large sums of aid and investment from the outside each year during that period: an estimated $15–50 billion for infrastructure; $30–60 billion for energy production; $5–10 billion for agriculture; a like sum for unemployment benefits; $21–38 billion for balance-of-payments support, for a total of $71–158 billion a year. More modest proposals have been for $30 billion a year for five years or economist Jeffrey Sachs's suggestion that minimum aid amount to no less than $14 billion a year.[20]

Advocates argued that aid even of the larger dimensions reported above, pooled from the industrialized states, would only amount to a fraction of the increased defense expenditures needed in the event democracy failed in Russia. Their logic is strong. But the economic consequences of ending the cold war—collapse of the huge defense industries and Germany's unification budget deficits—had brought recession and high unemployment in all Western countries. In February 1994, the Group of Seven finance ministers were still talking about outside help for a safety net for Russia's unemployed. However, the political reality is that Western economic aid to Russia has been limited and is likely to remain so. There is foreign investment in oil and natural gas production in Russia—even more so in some southern republics like Turkmenistan and Azerbaijan. However, total foreign investment is unimpressive, warned off by negative experience in joint ventures and direct investment thus far. The powerful showing of antireform parties in the December 1993 elections will not help Russia's case. The most likely prospect for Russia and its neighboring republics is for many years of individual privation in a depressed economy, with accompanying social and political instability.

These conditions will not be supportive of steady progress toward democracy. Democratic institutions in Russia are weak. The present system can be termed autocratic democracy. It depends on Boris Yeltsin, whose health is questionable. And it has already moved to the right. In future, efforts of the Russian government to maintain order and the distribution of food and energy supplies in the face of disorganization and manifestations of public discontent, to maintain itself in power against growing political opposition, and to implement its policies despite local resistance or lack of cooperation, could heighten the temptation to resort to authoritarian measures.

Almost instinctively, Western governments have sought to apply to Russia the policy of integration that was so successful with West Germany after World War II, through establishing a wide range of political, economic, and military links with Russia. As U.S. defense secretary William Perry put it, "I remain convinced that our best chance of influencing Russia in the direction we desire is to engage with them on many fronts and help move them fully into the community of nations."[21] With Russia, the policy of constructive engagement on all fronts is surely the right one. But links with Russia are far weaker than they were in the case of Germany. Russia is not an occupied country, even though it shows a classic defeat syndrome, and needs a respected leader like Konrad Adenauer or Charles de Gaulle to restore its own self-respect. Economic links are weaker than with postwar Germany. Germany's revitalization was key to restoring the European economy, and its military contribution was essential to NATO's effectiveness. Despite many references to partnership, Russia cannot make much contribution interesting to Western countries aside from its vote in the UN Security Council. Without a common enemy, military links among Russia and its would-be partners will remain much weaker than they were with Germany. And Russia is vast, with a hundred national minorities compared to small, socially homogeneous postwar Germany.

The dilemma for Western policy is to develop a policy toward Russia that is steadfast and has stamina, a policy that can hold up over a very long period, that avoids overreaction to adverse developments, and that does not give up prematurely on prospects for democracy. However, as excited Western reaction to the gains made by nationalists in the December 1993 elections showed, even limited moves in the direction of authoritarian government in Russia can cause serious difficulties for Western policy. Westerners want democracy in Russia to succeed; they correctly regard its future achievement as the best guarantee of productive relations and the most effective long-term insurance against security difficulties with Russia and the other states. At the same time, motivated by concerns about Russia's nuclear weapons and potential conventional military power, Western governments will seek to have good working relations with any government legally in power because this approach would still provide the best leverage for steering Moscow away from authoritarianism. Accordingly, the United States and other Western countries immediately declared their support for Boris Yeltsin when he unconstitutionally dissolved the Russian parliament.

But Western public opinion is not likely to take such a farsighted view. It is likely to recoil in disappointment if there is a pronounced rightward shift in Russia. Western governments might then feel compelled to show disapproval by visibly reducing close cooperation. This in turn could provoke a sharp reaction from the population and government of Russia, reinforcing ultranationalist sentiments. Western leaders need to make special efforts to clarify for their publics that support for functioning democracy in Russia will entail decades of continuous effort in often discouraging circumstances.

Western public reaction is especially prickly in situations of Russian military intervention in neighboring states. When conflict breaks out in neighboring republics, the costs for the Russian government associated both with intervention and with nonintervention are high. There is nothing especially noble about the governments of the republics where violence breaks out; most bear a good deal of responsibility themselves for the fighting. None of the republics is a model democracy or has strong claims for historic contributions to civilization. The tiny minorities seeking to assert themselves and contributing to the outbreak of fighting do not have an automatic right to independence. But on the left and the right of the Western political spectrum, champions of democracy and the underdog and those traditionally suspicious of Russia, have hurried to raise the charge of Russian imperialism. Although Russian actions in such places as Georgia and Azerbaijan have been self-serving, they have also put an end to fighting, which the participants were unable to stop, and have saved lives. It is not in Western interests to have these conflicts continue, yet the West is not willing to intervene with its own peacekeeping forces. As a partial solution, Western governments are trying to trade off Russia's desire to minimize foreign criticism of such activities for Russian acceptance of CSCE or UN standards in the tactics and aims of these interventions.

If an authoritarian strong-man regime, perhaps mainly military in character, should emerge in Russia, initially at least, it would probably focus its activities on domestic issues and deliberately seek to avoid the appearance of aggressive intent. But its existence would make neighboring states understandably nervous. As Russian Federation foreign minister Andrei Kozyrev forecast at the December 1992 Stockholm CSCE foreign ministers meeting, nationalist shifts in the Russian government could bring changes in Russian foreign policy, starting with the end of Russian cooperation to contain Serbia, the end of Russian cooperation at the UN on peacekeeping, the revocation of CSCE human rights and of arms control agreements, and Russian moves to force the other successor states to join a new alliance system.[22] Part of this forecast has already materialized. In a worst case, a politically gifted Russian nationalist leadership might seek to establish some sort of union among the Slavic states and, imitating Hitler and his lesser successor Slobodan Milosevic, call for incorporation in Russia of all territories with Russian populations.

Concerns of this kind prompted Czechoslovak president Vaclav Havel in his address to the U.S. Congress in February 1990 to say that the most important thing Western states could do for European security was "to help the Soviet Union on its irreversible but immensely complicated road to democracy." The appeal was heard and understood all through the Western world. For example, in his confirmation hearing before the U.S. Senate four years later, Secretary of Defense William Perry said, "No national security issue is more important to us and to our children than stable government in Russia dedicated to democracy."[23]

The dissolution of Soviet central power brought the end of Soviet global military power. The fragmentation of Soviet armed forces (cuts in readiness, training, draft calls, and budgets) has left even the portion of the former Soviet armed forces that remains under Russian control much weakened. Given the state of the Russian economy, it is improbable that this downward trend in defense resources will soon be reversed. Given the

weakness of the CIS structure and continuing insistence on national independence and complete separation from Russia by Ukraine and other
non-Russian successor states, it is doubtful, except in the most extreme
conditions, that the former forces will again be unified in a practical sense.
Russia is strong enough militarily to cause serious problems to its neighbors, including Ukraine, but not to the NATO states if they maintain a
healthy NATO.

Consequently, with one cardinal exception, Russia does not appear
a likely source of deliberate military aggression against its Western neighbors. The big exception arises from the possibility of a combination of
authoritarian trends with continued possession of a large long-range
nuclear arsenal whose weapons could reach the United States, Western
Europe, and Japan. Even a post-START arsenal of 3,000 deployed strategic-
range weapons, together with many thousands of stockpiled missiles, warheads, and fissile material, which provide the possibility of rapid force
expansion, is more than large enough for all-out nuclear war.

If it materialized, this combination of circumstances would represent a serious threat to Western security, possibly one with considerably
less predictability than at the peak of the cold war military confrontation.
A still unstable Russia under autocratic government, heavily engaged in
ethnic wars on its periphery, and disposing over a large stock of strategic
nuclear weapons would create an epicenter of nuclear instability for the
whole world, but especially for Europe. Many of the negative aspects of
cold war nuclear confrontation could reemerge. Fortunately, this situation
has not yet come about, and there is time to head it off by cooperative
means. However, despite this alarming possibility, the West's main problem with regard to Russia is steadfastly to maintain a constructive Western
policy throughout decades of developments of which many are likely to
be disappointing and negative. Russia has made a real beginning on the
road to an enduring, functioning democracy. But it will take a long time
for decisive good news on Russia to emerge. The bad news is already
with us, at least in part.

5

EASTERN EUROPE'S TROUBLED FUTURE

In the nineteenth and early twentieth centuries, caught between Germany and Russia, the Eastern European countries were the poor backyard of more prosperous Central and Western Europe.[1] Under Ottoman, Austro-Hungarian, Nazi, or Soviet domination, there was no chance for democratic development. In the short period between the two world wars, only Czechoslovakia had a functioning democratic government. All the other countries had authoritarian governments in one form or another. Poland's first modern democracy lasted only five years before it succumbed to military rule under Marshal Pilsudski.

Even after electoral shakeouts at the beginning of the 1990s that eliminated much residual communist influence (in Poland the reformed former Communist Party recently scored a comeback), most of the Eastern European states have weak and divided national governments. The Czech Republic may be the exception. These weak governments find it difficult to make the tough decisions required to put through economic reforms and to endure the impact of resulting public dissatisfaction. The economic problems of Eastern Europe are acute: In his New Year's speech to the Czechs and Slovaks in January 1991, Vaclav Havel commented, "What a year ago appeared to be a rundown house is in fact a house in ruins." His statement remains applicable today throughout most of Eastern Europe.

In all of the Eastern European countries, support for democratic institutions is weak. Low election participation is widespread. In parliamentary elections in Hungary in 1991, the voter turnout was less than 25 percent. Even in the hotly contested runoff for the Polish presidential elections of

1990, won by Lech Walesa, turnout was only about 50 percent. Public opinion polls taken in the summer of 1991 showed that the major institutions of the Polish liberation—Solidarity and the Catholic Church, and even national hero Walesa—had slipped badly in public esteem. The most trusted Polish institutions were the police and the army, the very instruments of earlier repression. To some degree, these results are a response to expanding criminality, endemic in Eastern Europe as well as the Soviet successor states.

State Department experts estimate that at least 25 percent of the adult population throughout Eastern Europe are disaffected from the democratic system in the sense of looking back to the communist past with nostalgia. (For understandable reasons, the figure in Russia is even higher.) Loyalty to democracy among senior military officers is uncertain, and there are few institutions for civilian control over the military. Communists still control seven of Poland's eight major trade unions. Throughout Eastern Europe, former Communist Party officials remain in tight control of local government and enterprise management, including privatized enterprises in which they have persuaded workers to continue them as managers or where they have profited from insider knowledge to buy the firms at low prices. A recent survey indicates that former directors of socialist enterprises constitute half of the top managers of private enterprises.[2]

Social cohesion is weak; the economic gap between the relative few who are doing well from the shift to a market economy and the great majority of people who are facing great deprivation is widening in all countries.[3] Citizen self-confidence, the feeling of political and economic self-empowerment in the general population, is very low.

Public resentment over economic dislocation has fueled a further divisive phenomenon, the effort to retaliate against the agents and beneficiaries of the earlier communist systems. Although Eastern Europe avoided the bloody vigilante revenge of the French and Russian revolutions, throughout the area "decommunization" sentiment, strengthened by public access to secret police records, called for purging former communists from public office and for punishing them where possible. In Germany, the process led to a series of political resignations, including that of the deputy prime minister of the Federal Republic, Lothar de Maiziere, and the prime ministers of several eastern Länder. In Czechoslovakia, it took the form of a "lustration" or purification law banning senior Communist Party officials from government posts for five years. In Poland, President Lech Walesa fired Prime Minister Jan Olszewski in June 1992 after Olszewski's interior minister, an extreme nationalist intent on "purifying" Polish politics, released lists of former collaborators and police informers that included Walesa himself.[4]

The underlying problem is intractable. Many of those who had opposed the earlier communist governments in Eastern Europe were themselves party members, at least formally. Many nonparty people collaborated with communist regimes, as the Czechoslovak, Polish, and East German secret police records appeared to show. Moreover, without at least some implicit promise of amnesty or indulgent treatment, the communist regimes would have violently resisted the takeovers of 1989–90, as happened in Romania. Today, there is no majority in these countries either for the complete amnesty which Spain decided on in the post-Franco transition to democracy or for the fairly thorough process of denazification applied to the Germans by the Allies after World War II. There is no good solution to this problem of coming to terms with a tortured past; each country will be deeply riven by it for generations to come.

ECONOMIC HARDSHIP

The ranks of the dissatisfied in Eastern Europe have been recruited mainly from the casualties of transition to market economies. In East Germany, unemployment or part-time work covered close to 50 percent of the work force in 1992. Most other countries had unemployment rates of 15–20 percent, and unemployment in many localities was as high as in East Germany.

Gross national product and production levels were sinking. The United Nations Economic Commission for Europe estimated that, between 1990 and 1992, overall GNP in Eastern Europe went down by 25–30 percent from the 1988 level, in the same league as the disastrous 29 percent drop during America's depression of 1929–33. In Czechoslovakia, industrial production in 1992 was down by 40 percent from the 1989 level; in Hungary and Poland by 32 percent; in Romania and Bulgaria by 54 percent; in Albania by 58 percent. Inflation in 1991 spanned a range from 40 percent per month in Hungary to 400 percent in Bulgaria.[5] The World Bank was predicting that output per head might not again reach the 1989 level—the level when the area was still communist ruled—until 1996 or later. The Organization for Economic Cooperation and Development (OECD) predicted that it would take decades for Eastern Europe to catch up with Western living standards. All the countries in the area shared acute problems of environmental degradation far worse than anything Western Europe ever encountered.

In the early 1990s, most of the Eastern European governments freed prices and made their currency convertible, if not completely, then sufficiently for most business transactions. However, the Eastern European economies continued to show weakness in communications, banking, and business law, which inhibited joint ventures and investment by foreigners. As in Russia, slow privatization of larger state-owned concerns was a continuing bottleneck in the movement to a market economy, one whose stubborn nature threatened to prolong the process by many years. The main difficulties here included uncooperative bureaucrats, control of credit decisions by entrenched former communists, corruption, and an absence of profit-oriented banking. These circumstances perpetuated the influence of a "club" of communist managers. Without privatization of large industrial enterprises, the price pressures of the free economy sector were ignored, and plant managers were not subject to financial discipline. Instead, to stay in business, they obtained cheap loans from governments and from state banks and, in barter form, from other large concerns. Governments kept large firms going because they feared still more dramatic unemployment if the big firms collapsed.[6] These practices fueled inflation and government deficits and blocked the restructuring and expansion of more productive facilities. The indebtedness of the big concerns to banks held up privatization of banks because no one knew what should be done with their accumulated debts. Without banks and stock exchanges, there was no source of credit at market prices. Moreover, government deficits increased because there were large shortfalls in collection of revenue and taxes. The private economy was expanding but not paying taxes.

Underlying these problems was the same basic disagreement about the desirability of rapid movement toward privatization that prevailed in Russia, a disagreement caused by the desire to head off mass unemployment. But compare the 40 percent unemployment rate of some Eastern European countries in 1991 and 1992 with the 1.5 percent official rate in Russia. Eastern Europe may have reached the bottom without, thus far at least, the acute social disruption feared in Russia.[7]

Despite all these difficulties, by mid-1993, some economists were claiming that the most advanced Eastern European economies—those of the Czech Republic, Poland, and Hungary—had turned the corner. Swedish economist Anders Aslund argued that the Czech, Polish, and Hungarian economies hit their low point sometime during 1992 and were moving up. Foreign banks and businesses were investing somewhat more in Eastern Europe. Private direct foreign investment in Hungary reached a total of $4.8 billion by early 1993, with the Czech Republic at $2 billion and Poland at $1.5 billion. Characteristically, foreign investment in Romania, Bulgaria, Slovakia, and Albania was far lower. In 1993, the Polish gross domestic product grew 4 percent, and the Czech Republic and Hungary were not far behind. Annual budget deficits were stabilizing (down to 7–8 percent of GDP in Poland and Hungary) as was the inflation rate, which had dropped under 4 percent, except for Poland at 7 percent. Unemployment was relatively low—in Poland it was about 15 percent compared to Western Europe's 10 percent in the same period. The Czech Republic even had a tight labor market with only 2.5 percent unemployment. Privatization was moving ahead in these countries, if slowly—although scarcely at all in other countries of Eastern Europe. The private sector of the economy was growing fast. In Poland and Hungary, the private sector's share of production for 1993 was estimated at 40 percent of GDP.

However, there were plenty of negative indicators too. Poland's birthrate was the lowest in fifty years; its death rate was the highest in fifty years. One-third of the population were living below the official poverty level. A 1993 public opinion poll showed results similar to those in Russia: 20 percent of the population expressed confidence in parliamentary democracy; 50 percent considered the earlier communist system better.

These figures were reflected in the results of Polish parliamentary elections in September 1993. The center coalition of Prime Minister Hanna Suchocka was swept out of power by voters angry over the personal impact of free-market reforms. It was replaced by a coalition between the neocommunist Left Democratic Alliance and the Polish Peasants Party headed by Prime Minister Waldemar Pawlak of the Polish Peasants Party. The new government in Warsaw, though pledged to continue Poland's pro-Western foreign policy, went into the elections with a program of slowing economic reform and cushioning its harsh impact on individual Poles. Aleksander Kwasniewski, chairman of the Left Democrats, campaigned with the slogan that Poland should have "a market economy with a human face." The government's own doubts as to how to achieve this difficult goal became apparent as friction developed between the coalition parties, and the outlook for Polish economic policy and the government itself was uncertain. There was one clear gain from the elections—the number of parties in the Sejm was reduced from twenty-nine to seven. A similar political reversal in Hungary's elections, scheduled for May 1993, appeared probable.

Everyone agreed that the political and economic future of the Eastern European countries would be far more assured if they could join the European Community. Poland, Hungary, and Czechoslovakia concluded association agreements with the European Community in 1991, Romania and Bulgaria in 1993.[8] Trade with the European Community was already high. (For Poland, 55 percent of total exports in 1991; over 30 percent for Hungary, Czechoslovakia, and Romania.) The Eastern European countries were capable of exporting still more and wanted more rapid progress toward full membership in the Community.

The European Community formally agreed at its June 1993 summit meeting in Copenhagen that those Eastern European countries that so desired would in fact eventually be permitted to join the Community as full members. The EC Council defined the difficult conditions Eastern European countries would have to meet for membership: "Membership requires that the candidate country has achieved stability of institutions guaranteeing democracy, the rule of law, human rights and respect for and protection of minorities, the existence of a functioning market economy, as well as the capacity to cope with competitive pressures and market forces within the Union." Although the EC agreed to drop its tariffs on steel and textiles imported from Eastern Europe by 1998, it did not liberalize agricultural imports, which hurt Poland and the Balkan states particularly. In practice, it continued to place special quota restrictions on Czech steel and Hungarian textiles. The EC Council did not meet the desires of the three Central Eastern European countries to have a specific date for membership. Estimates of the possible dates ranged from the year 2000 to a decade or more later.[9] The most serious single problem of the Eastern European states with regard to EC membership was low per capita worker productivity. Unless this could be improved, EC membership would simply bankrupt Eastern European enterprises despite lower wages in the East.

Some observers believed that it would take some thirty-five years for Eastern European incomes to reach even half the average level of Western European incomes, although the Czech Republic, Poland, and Hungary might do somewhat better.[10] Other analysts forecast that, to achieve the EC average level of personal income by 2010, the countries of Eastern Europe would need $420 billion a year of investment, of which they were likely to receive $60 billion at most from foreign sources. The remainder would have to be generated from domestic investment, an improbable achievement. It is also doubtful that anything close to the $60 billion annual goal for foreign investment in Eastern Europe will be achieved, especially with recession in Western countries. In fact, at the end of 1993, total private direct foreign investment for the entire area totaled only $10 billion. The European Commission, which coordinates aid to Eastern Europe for all OECD countries, estimated that in 1990–91 it had pledged about $38 billion to Eastern Europe in credits and grants, but only about 10 percent of this in the form of outright grants.[11]

East European countries have some important economic strengths. Their populations are highly skilled, distances to major markets are not great, and transportation costs are low. Above all, their proximity, especially to Germany, combined with Western European nervousness over more migration from the East and the consequences of political instability there, means that there will be a flow of Western economic aid and investment—not enough to bring about rapid improvement, but likely to continue indefinitely. Unfortunately, this aid is likely to be distributed on a geographic basis, with the most westerly of the Eastern European countries receiving the most and the more distant ones receiving less.

EASTERN EUROPE'S DIVIDED PEOPLES

In the nineteenth and early twentieth centuries, Ottoman, Austro-Hungarian, and Russian repression generated intense nationalism and pressures for independence in Eastern Europe. The shots that started World War I, the June 1914 assassination of Archduke Franz Ferdinand of Austria-Hungary by the Bosnian Serb Gavrilo Princip, were part of a campaign for Bosnian independence. Deliberate government action to stir up patriotic nationalism was a central feature of interwar politics and also of wartime mobilization in World War II. These feelings welled up again once the communist grip was removed from Eastern Europe.

Nationalism is a complex phenomenon. There is continuing debate among historians and social scientists about the causes of the universal upsurge in the area of former communist control of nationalism and its twin sister, ethnic hostility. Among the factors that contributed to it are the removal of police state repression, enormous social upheaval and loss of status through introduction of the market economy, and repudiation of old elites and of the official ideology. After the humiliating collapse of officially sanctioned orientation, millions took refuge in the only other known orientation, the only remaining source of personal pride, the national tradition, often highly mythicized. The German sociologist Max Horkheimer believed extreme nationalism expresses "the collective confidence of individuals whose self-confidence has disappeared."[12] Whatever its genesis, everywhere from East Germany to Uzbekistan, fueled by self-questioning from unemployment and economic hardship, nationalism rushed in to fill the void in individual belief and value systems left by the collapse of the official ideology.

The nationalistic backlash extended all the way to Western Europe, where it found expression in xenophobic behavior, increase in the strength of nationalist anti-immigrant political parties, and also negative votes on the Maastricht Treaty for European Union. As the tragic war in former Yugoslavia erupted, and, along with it, fighting in the Soviet successor states, it became painfully evident that, next to nuclear weapons in the hands of unstable Russia and Ukraine, the most immediate and serious security problem of post-cold war Europe was ethnonationalism and ethnic conflict.

The accidents of historical migration and the fixing of borders have left many European ethnic groups as minorities inside national borders. As a result, ethnic tensions in Europe and elsewhere take two main forms: first, domestic tensions involving minority ethnic groups located wholly within a state; second, similar tensions, augmented by interstate tensions, when the territory occupied by an ethnic group crosses interstate borders.

The conflict in former Yugoslavia, to which we will turn in a moment, is by far the most fearsome case of the first type, tensions that erupted among ethnic groups within recognized borders. A second case of domestic ethnic tensions intense enough to break existing national structures was that between Czechs and Slovaks, whose union was dissolved without violence in January 1993.

The more frequent problem—and the greatest potential security problem in Eastern Europe today—is one of borders that divide ethnic groups and peoples. In Eastern Europe, leaving aside the tortured distribution of populations in the former Yugoslavia, there are at least nine ethnic groups divided by borders: Romanians, Hungarians, Poles, Byelorussians, Slovaks, Turks, Albanians, Greeks, and the unfortunate Roma, or gypsies. Unlike the others, the gypsies, who number up to 3 million, have no state that they control, so that they are solely victims of ethnic hostility rather than also inflicting it on others.[13]

There are also large German minorities of up to two and a half million in Russia—the Volga Germans—and smaller groups in Poland, Hungary, and Czechoslovakia. Because of Germany's cautious, conciliatory attitude toward the host countries, the activities of these minorities are not likely in the short run to lead to serious international frictions. Indeed, Germany's main aim today is to keep ethnic Germans where they are currently in order to avoid the social and economic impact of mass migration to Germany. Germany pays considerable sums for this purpose. But the German government cannot control the political activities of its own right-wingers or these minorities abroad. Those living in Poland have become especially assertive.

The classic European case of divided populations is that of Hungary, an ally of Germany in World War I, which after its defeat and a punitive peace treaty supposedly based on the principle of self-determination, lost about one-third of its population (the total number of Hungarians today is perhaps 15 million) to Czechoslovakia, the Soviet Union, Yugoslavia, and Romania. In the Transylvanian region of Romania there are as many as 2 million Hungarians.[14] In World War II, the Hungarians, once again allied to the Germans—largely for this irredentist reason—temporarily regained two-fifths of Transylvania from Romania. But, once again on the losing side, Hungary lost all of it to Romania in the 1947 peace treaty ending World War II.

Historically, actual or claimed mistreatment of minorities wholly contained within the borders of a single state has often been a cause of domestic conflict and even civil war, and sometimes has provided grounds for foreign intervention. Actual or alleged mistreatment of minorities divided by borders has been a frequent cause of interstate wars. The typical dynamic in the latter case has been complaints by an ethnic minority that there is organized discrimination against it: decrees or laws preventing use of the minority language; the absence of schools to teach its children; suppression of publications in the minority language, or lack of equitable political representation. These complaints often lead to local unrest and then, in response, repression by the national government, followed by friction between that government and the neighboring government dominated by the same ethnic group as the original minority next door. The first government claims outside interference in its sovereign affairs, diplomatic relations are broken, and economic sanctions are applied. Armed clashes between border police or military units may take place—and sometimes culminate in war.

Hitler invaded Czechoslovakia to "protect" the ethnic Germans living in the Sudeten area; his justification for invading Poland was to protect the Danzig Germans. Political conflict between Greek and Turkish Cypriots, backed by their mainland governments, led in 1974 to a Greek military coup that displaced the independent Cypriot government. This led to Turkish military intervention on Cyprus on behalf of the Turkish Cypriot minority.

The important distinction between the earlier history of these divided peoples and the present, as is frequently pointed out, is that today the great power rivalry that made the Balkans the powder keg of Europe from the eighteenth century to the outbreak of World War I no longer exists—at least not in the same measure. The main rivalries are regional ones. Nonetheless, the danger that regional war may expand and involve others continues. At the present stage, aside from the former Yugoslavia, the problem of divided peoples in Eastern Europe is not yet one of efforts to change borders by force, although European governments are highly sensitive to this possibility. The use or threat of force to change borders is forbidden by a series of Conference on Security and Cooperation in Europe (CSCE) agreements, including the original 1975 Helsinki Accords and the 1990 Paris Declaration.

Instead, the Eastern European tensions caused by divided populations are today for the most part in a stage that historically has often preceded conflict—complaints by minorities over their treatment to their own and neighboring governments, resulting in friction between the two governments. The present level of such frictions is relatively low; all European governments are acutely aware of what is going on in Bosnia and of the past record of interstate conflict in the area. All are making a real effort to fend off conflict through CSCE mechanisms and other mechanisms of mediation and conflict prevention. However, the problem is compounded by the societal disorganization that is a byproduct of the move to free markets and by the inability of Eastern governments, weak and divided as they are, to withstand public pressure for demonstrative displays of nationalism.

WHERE WILL THE NEXT PROBLEMS ARISE?

The likelihood that a given state will move toward conflict with a neighboring state because of alleged or actual mistreatment of minorities there, or that it will use unjustified violence against a domestic minority may reflect the interaction of three factors: (1) the strength of democratic government in the state and its degree of willingness to seek nonviolent solutions; (2) the level of its economy and standard of living; and (3) the size and behavior of the domestic ethnic minorities inside its borders and of its own external ethnic minorities living in neighboring states. Using this standard, we can rank-order the Eastern European states as to their potential for ethnic conflict, starting with the least likely and moving to the most likely.

THE CZECH REPUBLIC AND POLAND

Applying this approach, the Czech Republic and Poland both rank low in probability of ethnic conflict. The Czech Republic ranks high among Eastern European states both as regards democratic institutions and economic level. It has a domestic minority of over 300,000 Slovaks, but no external minorities.

Poland is also low on the scale of probable involvement. Poland ranks quite high in democratic institutions and economy. Ethnically, it is one of the most homogeneous of the Eastern European countries; it has domestic minorities of about 300,000 Germans and 200,000 Byelorussians. But its external minorities are large: nearly 1.2 million Poles live in the former Soviet Union (Lithuania, 258,000; Belarus, 600,000; Ukraine, 300,000).

Lithuania, which has a historically conditioned inferiority complex toward Poland, suspended the autonomous local administrations in the Polish areas around Vilnius in a panic reaction to the August 1991 putsch in Moscow.[15] Lithuania, Belarus, and Ukraine are all adopting laws and regulations on citizenship and use of majority languages in schools, courts, elections, and official transactions that discriminate against Polish and other minorities. Tensions over these states' treatment of Polish minorities are probable, but the likelihood of conflict between them and Poland is low. Because of Poland's greater relative economic well-being, Poland has the quite different concern, more typical for Western Europe, that political and economic unrest in these three states could result in efforts by hundreds of thousands of economic refugees to cross their borders. The ethnic Poles in those countries have some moral right to claim refuge in Poland if there is real deterioration in their living conditions; most of them live within the pre-World War II borders of Poland.

HUNGARY

Hungary is somewhat more at risk of involvement in ethnic conflict. It ranks relatively high economically, with $3,446 estimated GDP per person estimated for 1992, higher than the Czech Republic ($2,550) or Poland ($1,895). However, although it has a successful parliamentary system, Hungary ranks higher than the Czech Republic or Poland as regards potential for conflict over minorities. Hungary's former president Jozsef Antall, who died in late 1993, often and demonstratively stated that he was president of all 15 million Hungarians, the 10 million in Hungary and the 5 million who live beyond its borders. Although Hungary has signed the CSCE pledge not to seek to change existing borders by force or threat of force, prior to the May 1994 elections which brought a coalition of socialists (former communists) and Free Democrats to power with a more conciliatory policy, the Hungarian government several times declined to undertake explicit guarantees for the borders of neighboring states.

Hungary also has several extreme nationalistic political parties, fortunately still small in size. The nationalist Istvan Csurka, who advocates the ingathering of territories occupied by Hungarians abroad, failed in his January 1993 bid at the national convention of the governing Democratic Forum party to unseat President Antall as chairman of the party, but then founded a party of his own. A World Federation of Hungarians, partly financed by the Hungarian government, is actively beginning to foster Hungarian autonomy movements in neighboring countries. The Free Democrats now in government have also advocated a greater Hungary.

Hungary has domestic minorities of 500,000 gypsies and 200,000 Slovaks. But it also has external minorities of up to 2 million Hungarians in Romania, where there is a historic record of their mistreatment by the Romanian authorities; 600,000 in Slovakia; 500,000 in the Vojvodina province of Serbia; and 200,000 in Ukraine.[16] The issue of Hungarian minorities in neighboring states has remained at a low boil, but it is unpleasant to think of what might happen on this issue if the Hungarian economy encounters real difficulties and there is wide public dissatisfaction, or, on the other hand, if the living standard in the areas occupied by Hungarian minorities continues low as compared with Hungary's.

One factor of moderation arises from the fact that Hungary's armed forces, limited by the Conventional Forces in Europe (CFE) Treaty, are small and do not have regional military superiority as Serbia has within Yugoslavia. Moreover, well aware of the potential consequences of these frictions, the Hungarian and Romanian governments in February 1992 concluded the first bilateral Open Skies agreement to permit aerial observation of each other's military activities to warn of possible preparation for surprise attack and prevent miscalculation of the other country's actions. Since it permits each country only four three-hour flights a year, this measure is only a modest beginning.

SLOVAKIA

The Slovak Republic is less developed than Hungary both as regards its economy and its political system. Until April 1994, the Slovak government was headed by a group of nationalistic ex-communists that remains politically strong. Slovakia has sizable external minorities in the Czech Republic (308,000) and Hungary (200,000) as well as small ones of about 25,000 each in Poland and Ukraine. But Slovakia also has even more important domestic minorities: about 600,000 Hungarians, now 11 percent of the population of Slovakia, as well as 200,000 gypsies. The Slovak Hungarians tried at the time of separation of Slovakia from the Czech Republic to insert a clause in the new Slovak constitution assuring protection for minorities, but their proposal was voted down. Instead, the new constitution is based explicitly on the ethnic concept of the "Slovak nation."[17] Slovakia is already engaged in a bitter dispute with Hungary because Slovakia has diverted a segment of the Danube River, which runs between the two countries, for a power dam project. In a more positive development, the new CSCE high commissioner for minorities has succeeded in bringing Slovakia and Hungary to agree on a set of rules for protecting their respective minorities.

BULGARIA

Bulgaria comes next on a scale of mounting potential for ethnic clashes. It ranks below Slovakia on the scale of GNP per head ($815) and also ranks low as regards democratic government. In the first general elections (June 1990), the Socialist Party (the renamed communists) held onto power. The opposition pushed for new elections. In those elections, held in October 1991, the opposition's Reformist Union of Democratic Forces with 34 percent of the vote came in only 1 percent ahead of the Socialist Party. Political gridlock ensued until December 1992, when Lyuben Berov was nominated as prime minister by the Movement for Rights and Freedoms, the party of the Turkish minority in Bulgaria. Since then, Berov, who has become seriously ill, has governed unsteadily with support of the Reformist Union and of the Movement. Anti-Turkish sentiment is mounting among a large part of the Bulgarian population who identify the country's economic problems with the "new Ottoman rule" of the Turkish minority or with the machinations of Turkey itself.

As a relic of the Ottomans, Bulgaria has domestic minorities of about 1 million Turks; it also has over 570,000 gypsies. About 350,000 Turkish Bulgarians were expelled to Turkey in the last days of the communist regime. Bulgaria chronically fears intervention by Turkey. (Turkey, of course, has its own serious minority problem; its Kurdish population of about 12 million, about 20 percent of Turkey's 60 million population, has long been repressed and fighting between the Turkish government and the extremist Kurdistan Workers Party continues.)

Together with Greece and Serbia, Bulgaria has historical claims on Macedonia. Macedonia belonged to the Bulgarian empire until the Ottoman conquest, and again to Bulgaria after the Russo-Turkish War of 1878 until 1913, when it was cut into three segments by Bulgaria, Serbia, and Greece. In both world wars, Bulgaria temporarily reconquered all of Macedonia. In August 1991, Bulgarian president Zhelyu Zhelev, an anticommunist intellectual, opined that an independent Macedonia was only an "invention of the Comintern." Many political groups in Bulgaria are calling for union with Macedonia republic.[18]

ROMANIA

Romania, with an estimated GDP per person for 1993 of only $1,000, real wages at 50 percent of 1989, and in its third year of 200 percent inflation, still has a largely communist government. In May 1990 the forces composing the National Salvation Front, which had deposed and executed communist dictator Nicolae Ceausescu, won the general elections with 63 percent of the vote cast. The Front's chairman, former communist leader Ion Iliescu, was elected president of Romania. The Front, since renamed the Party of Social Democracy in Romania, is a party headed by former Communist Party functionaries, army and secret police officers; their main point of difference with former dictator Ceausescu was that he had fired them or sent them into domestic political exile. In September–October 1992, reform elements forced new presidential and parliamentary elections in Romania. Iliescu was reelected president in the second runoff ballot. However, his Party of Social Democracy received only 27 percent of votes in the parliamentary election, although it emerged the strongest single party. Extreme nationalist groups increased their cumulative strength to 12 percent of the vote. Iliescu formed a shaky coalition composed of the Party of Social Democracy and these extreme nationalist groups, the same combination of nationalists and old-line communists that has formed the main opposition to Russia's Boris Yeltsin. As late as 1993, voting in the Romanian Chamber of Deputies was secret, as was the Chamber's agenda.[19]

Romania has about 470,000 gypsies but its 2 million Hungarian citizens are the principal minority. In the period of communist rule, there was repeated friction between Transylvanian Hungarians and the Romanian government and smoldering resentment between the two governments. Ceausescu's hated program of razing peasant villages in Romania and creating high-rise agricultural cities in their stead was directed in large part toward destroying settlements occupied by the Hungarian minority. After Ceausescu was deposed and executed, the situation improved somewhat, although there was rioting in March 1990 between Hungarians and Romanians. At present, Hungarians living in Romania have declared that they want to work within the Romanian system. But what will their attitude be if the Romanian government mishandles minority relations, or, as is probable, if Hungary makes markedly more economic progress than Romania? In April 1993, the Romanian government agreed to a series of protective measures for the Hungarian minority creating a National Minorities Consultative Commission to advise the government, providing for training of more Hungarians as teachers, for some Hungarian language schools, and for street and public signs to be in Hungarian; also a modest beginning.[20]

Romanians in the republic of Moldova, about 2.7 million of a total population of 4.3 million, and in Ukraine, are Romania's largest external minority and the largest contiguous group in Eastern Europe split by national borders. (The more numerous Hungarian minorities are dispersed in four countries around Hungary's periphery.) Almost the entire territory of Moldova was once part of the Romanian principality of the same name. A large part of that principality, the regions of Bessarabia and Bukovina, opted to join Romania after World War I, but they were taken over by the USSR under the 1939 Molotov-Ribbentrop Pact. After World War II, Joseph Stalin divided these territories between the Moldovan Soviet Socialist Republic and the Ukrainian Soviet Socialist Republic. Romania also lost the territory of Dobrudja to Bulgaria in 1940, and this loss also still rankles.

Romania has high potential for ethnic conflict both with regard to its domestic Hungarian minority and with regard to its lost territories in Moldova and in Ukraine. Both the Romanian and Moldovan governments acknowledge that there is strong public sentiment for unification in both countries but state that the subject of political unification is too sensitive for discussion now. Nonetheless, the two governments emphasize their special ties and are aiming at the economic integration of what President Iliescu calls "the two Romanian states" and at the creation of "a common cultural and spiritual space" of all Romanians.[21]

ALBANIA

It is widely considered that, because of its large external minorities in Serbia and Macedonia, Albania is in the most exposed position of the Eastern European states with regard to possible participation in ethnic conflict. Albania ranks low with regard to democratic government. Its first free elections in 1990 brought a large majority for the Socialist (former communist) Party. In March 1992, the Democratic Party led by medical doctor Sali Berisha, a former communist official, was able to win by nearly 70 percent of the popular vote, while the former communists went down to 20 percent. Since then, the Berisha government has condemned the leaders of the Socialist Party in a show trial and clapped controls on the public media, domestic and foreign.[22]

Albania is Europe's poorest country by far, with GDP per person of only a few hundred dollars a year. Domestic minorities are small in this tiny country of only 3 million inhabitants—some gypsies and Macedonians, and also a Greek minority, estimated by Tirana at under 100,000, and by Athens at 200,000. Athens has charged mistreatment of these Greeks by Albanian authorities. The latter claim some members of the Greek minority are agitating to add their border territory to Greece. About 200,000 Albanians work in Greece.[23] The big problem is Albania's external minorities in Serbia and Macedonia. These are estimated at up to 2 million in Kosovo province of Serbia where, although Albanians comprise up to 90 percent of the population, they have been systematically deprived of their rights by the ruling Serbs. An estimated 450,000 Albanians, at least 20 percent of the total population, live in Macedonia, which, like Kosovo, is contiguous to Albania; there are dangerous ethnic frictions between the Albanians and Macedonians.

Landlocked Macedonia was blockaded by Greece in February 1994 contrary to EC rules, because of the still-unresolved dispute about Macedonia's official name and state symbols that Greece considers as implying claims on parts of historic Macedonia within Greek borders.

The quarrel reflects extreme nationalism on both sides, but the resulting economic misery in Macedonia, with annual per capita income down to $700, has much increased the possibility of clashes between Macedonians and Albanians. There are smaller Albanian minorities in Montenegro and southern Serbia.

All political groupings in Albania make territorial unification of all Albanians part of their program. For their part, all of the political groups composing the Democratic Alliance, which represents the great majority of Albanians in Kosovo, also advocate territorial union with Albania.[24] The Albanian Kosovars have, with great determination, thus far maintained a policy of nonviolent resistance to the Serbs. Kosovo and Macedonia are probably the two most inflammable areas of Eastern Europe.

To summarize, of the twenty-four minority issues described in this chapter, Bulgaria, Romania, and Albania have the most troublesome ones, by and large the weakest democratic structures, and the weakest economies (including the lowest prospects for Western economic aid and investment), and, in terms of the present analysis, the highest potentiality for eruption of ethnic violence.

EASTERN EUROPE'S "SECURITY VACUUM"

The most eloquent representative of the Eastern European states, President Vaclav Havel, now president of the Czech Republic, said in a speech to the NATO Council in March 1991, "When the totalitarian systems collapsed in Central and Eastern Europe and democracy won, everything seemed clear and simple—the North Atlantic Alliance would start speedily transforming itself into an entirely new security system covering the whole of Europe." But, Havel continued, the building of democracy and a free-market economic system turned out to be much more difficult than anticipated. "Our countries are threatened with political and social shakeups, material poverty, criminality, the growth of social helplessness, and hence even the danger of populism—nationalism, xenophobia, and national intolerance." Moreover, there was continuing turbulence in the Soviet Union, economic complications relating to the concurrent Persian Gulf crisis, and the Western countries were reluctant to provide adequate economic aid. "The effect of all these factors," Havel said, "is that our countries are dangerously sliding into a certain political, economic, and security vacuum."[25]

The security vacuum President Havel described is a generic term covering several specific security concerns of the Eastern European governments. First among these is the absence of a trusted alliance commitment and dependable defense support from the Western countries, especially the

United States, whether in the form of an expanded NATO, or a strengthened Western European Union (WEU), or of a strengthened Conference on Security and Cooperation in Europe (CSCE) backed by a treaty commitment from the Western countries. The Eastern European states, all of them militarily weak, find themselves in a situation of domestic political and economic turmoil, frightened by the collapse of Yugoslavia and by the prospect of other ethnic conflicts in their own and neighboring countries, and still caught between a powerful if now peacefully inclined Germany and a large increasingly nationalistic Russia and a new, highly nationalistic Ukraine. The Eastern Europeans are without the certainty, however stifling, once provided by Soviet domination and membership in the Warsaw Pact. The situation makes them understandably nervous and fuels a powerful need for reassurance.

The main fears of the Eastern European governments are not so much specific ones, such as fear of outright aggression by Russia or Ukraine, although this possibility is not excluded, but rather a general reaction to the negative possibilities in their environment. They fear nuclear-armed political instability in Russia and Ukraine. They fear cross-border involvement in ethnic conflict in Moldova or Ukraine or from disputes between Russia and Ukraine. They are concerned over possible trends toward authoritarian government, especially in Russia and in neighboring Ukraine, Belarus, and Moldova. They fear waves of refugees fleeing to their territories driven by economic or political breakdown in the successor states. Those Eastern European states that are direct neighbors of Yugoslavia—Hungary, Bulgaria, and Albania—are also threatened by more immediate risks of instability and violence.

Given these fears, the most immediate security aim of the Eastern European states after regaining their independence, especially of Czechoslovakia, Poland, and Hungary, was to join NATO and the European Community governments. All Eastern European states, even that of distant Albania, officially stated interest in doing so. Yet the explicit security guarantees they wanted from the United States and other NATO countries were not forthcoming. At the outset, while the Soviet Union still existed, the NATO allies wished to avoid creating a dangerous impression that the West was ganging up on it, seeking to profit from Soviet weakness through recruiting the Eastern European states, and moving the Eastern boundary of NATO right up to the borders of the westernmost Soviet republics. The Two-Plus-Four agreement on German unification between the Western allies and the Soviet Union was based on an implicit understanding that, if the united Germany did become a member of NATO, NATO territory would stop at the former border of West Germany and would not expand into East Germany. This understanding was reflected in the inclusion in the treaty of a commitment not to station NATO forces on the territory of the former German Democratic Republic.

Even after the Soviet Union was gone, this consideration remained valid for Western states concerned over developments in the still-powerful, nuclear-armed Russian Federation and in Ukraine. Germany in particular has not wanted to offend Russia while some former Red Army troops remained on its own territory. The Bush administration did not want to guarantee the security of unstable Eastern European governments that could develop into populist-authoritarian regimes and was sure that the Senate would not ratify such agreements. The administration also argued that its NATO allies should not extend bilateral or WEU security guarantees to Eastern European countries because these guarantees would indirectly commit NATO and the United States.

The NATO allies did do something to meet these repeated Eastern European demands. In June 1991, the North Atlantic Council in ministerial session stated that the security situation of the Eastern European states was "of direct and material concern" to the NATO alliance, a clear political commitment that NATO would become involved if the security of these states was threatened. NATO set up a network of bilateral arrangements with the former Warsaw Pact states and, at its Rome Summit of November 1991, established the North Atlantic Cooperation Council (NACC) with membership of the NATO states and all former Warsaw Pact governments, including those of the Soviet successor states. Since Russia and Ukraine were also members of the new organization, they could not object to membership of the Eastern Europeans.

Nearly all the Eastern European countries have bilateral friendship treaties with Germany (in the case of Poland and Czechoslovakia, guaranteeing their borders), France, the United Kingdom, and other Western European states. They are also members of the CSCE. The Conventional Forces in Europe Treaty, concluded in November 1990 and ratified by the Soviet successor states, contains a provision (Article IV), that forbids stationing foreign forces on the territory of a signatory state without its express agreement. This provision provides a contractual basis for objection and possible action by NATO states in the event of military actions by Soviet successor states or others that might seek to coerce individual Eastern European countries to accept their forces. After Boris Yeltsin's use of armed force in dissolving the Russian parliament and the gains in nationalist strength in the December 1993 Russian elections increased Eastern European anxieties, NATO in early 1994 added a new program of bilateral cooperation with them, the Partnership for Peace, and the European Union also began to develop new forms of association short of full membership. But these actions too did not fully satisfy the perceived security needs of the Eastern European governments.

REGIONAL GROUPINGS

Partly motivated by their security apprehensions, the Eastern European countries actively engaged in establishing various regional groupings of mainly economic significance, but with some security content. These included the "Pentagonale" proposed by Italy in 1989 and originally including Austria, Czechoslovakia, Hungary, and Yugoslavia. Poland joined later, creating a "hexagonale." After the breakup of Yugoslavia, Slovenia and Croatia joined the organization, which has been renamed the Central European Initiative. The organization's areas of interest include cooperation in economics, environment, transport, and culture. An "Alpen-Adria" economic grouping was founded in 1978 including Bavaria, Slovenia, Croatia, parts of Austria and Hungary, and Northern Italy. In May 1990, Austria and Bavaria launched the "Donaulaender Group," consisting of states bordering the Danube River from its source in Bavaria to its mouth in the Black Sea. A coordinating organization for states bordering the Black Sea was established in 1992.

In February 1991, representatives of Czechoslovakia, Poland, and Hungary met at Visegrad, Hungary, for the purposes of jointly promoting their aspirations for membership in the European Community, presenting a common position in economic dealings with the Soviet successor states, and cooperating in security matters. From the viewpoint of geography, such cooperation is logical, but in fact all three countries have had rather cool relations with one another, in part for historic reasons, in part because they compete for Western economic aid and investment. Despite this, since Visegrad, the three countries have carried out an active program of meetings among their heads of government, foreign ministers, ministers of foreign trade, and defense ministers, which makes the "Visegrad Group" the most active of the regional groups. The Visegrad troika became a foursome with the division of Czechoslovakia into the Czech Republic and Slovakia.

Motivated by its confrontation with Russia, Ukraine too has been seeking to organize a new Central-Eastern European security grouping, as yet without marked success. Later, we suggest how these Ukrainian desires might be met through establishing a regional center of the Conference for Security and Cooperation in Europe based in Kiev.

All of these regional groupings remain weak and can make only a limited contribution to meeting the security preoccupations of the Eastern European states. For the very long term, the possible answers to these preoccupations include full membership in an expanded NATO, full membership in a prosperous European Community that has its own functioning defense arm, or membership in a treaty-based expansion of CSCE with its own armed forces. But current prospects of any of these developments are distant. For the midterm, the best hope for the Eastern Europeans—and for the Soviet successor states—lies in a functioning NATO and NACC, in the network of confidence-building measures and force limits that has been agreed in Europe, and in a Conference on Security and Cooperation in Europe that grows in competence and authority.

SOME CONCLUSIONS ABOUT EASTERN EUROPE

The main problems of the Eastern European states for the next two decades are likely to be a poisonous combination of economic problems and ethnic tensions, the first often leading to the second. Although a few experts are more optimistic, prospects for rapid economic progress in Eastern Europe are not good. There is little prospect of full European Community membership for Czechoslovakia, Poland, and Hungary before the end of the decade. It is unclear whether the other four Eastern European states or the Yugoslav successor states will ever be admitted to full EC membership. We have described the reasons why Bulgaria, Romania, and Albania are at considerable risk with regard to their potential involvement in ethnic conflict.

Against this background, it seems probable from the viewpoint of economic development that for the next decade or more, Eastern Europe will remain a relatively depressed area, with some economic progress, but with the rate of progress falling short of public expectations and with economic performance declining as one moves from West to East. Pressures for at least partial retention of the command economy will be high, as will pressures to move toward populist, authoritarian solutions.

It is extremely difficult to progress toward participatory democracy while at the same time seeking to insulate difficult government decisions on economic issues from popular pressures. Singapore leader Lee Kuan Yew, when asked to explain the economic success of the Asian "tigers"— his own Singapore, and Hong Kong, Taiwan, and South Korea—replied that, in the early stages of industrial growth at least, democracy was not conducive to success because too many unpopular decisions had to be taken. When the economy has become more complex, he believed, voluntary participation of trained experts becomes more essential and democracy is furthered.[26] Eastern European economies now find themselves in the early stage of this process.

Other circumstances may blunt the effects of these negative trends. Among these are the fearful, deterring example of violence in the former Yugoslavia, the dependence of the Eastern European states on the continuation of Western economic help, continuing Western efforts to defuse perilous situations, and also the weakness of Russia and the other Soviet successor states. If the Western governments ultimately make a success of postconflict peacekeeping in Bosnia, if they have in fact learned from the lessons of the former Yugoslavia, and are prepared in future cases to act on these lessons, then it may be possible to prevent interstate war or new civil wars of the Yugoslav type in Eastern Europe. In any event, the war in the former Yugoslavia, horrible as it has been, may prove to have been the worst outbreak of violence in Eastern Europe in the post-cold war aftermath.

If the continuing risk of ethnic violence can be controlled, the main trend in Eastern Europe over the next two decades may be for slow, halting progress. Internal political pressures and inadequate capital will probably slow moves toward functioning free-market economies. Recurrent reverses to the democratic process are likely. But, overall, the prospect is for maintenance of weak positive trends.

6

SARAJEVO IS BURNING

W hen the heads of state or government of the (then thirty-five) member states of the Conference on Security and Cooperation in Europe (CSCE) met in Paris in November 1990 to solemnly mark the end of the cold war, they expressed pride and confidence in the broad array of institutions and agreements established to keep the peace in Europe and to prevent renewal of the conflicts that had shattered the continent in two world wars. Yet an underlying weakness of all these institutions and agreements—NATO, the Western European Union (WEU), the CSCE, the Conventional Forces in Europe (CFE) Treaty, and an impressive regime of CSCE confidence-building measures—was that they had been designed to prevent interstate conflict between member countries. NATO was designed to deter war through its formidable defensive capacity; the CFE Treaty limited the size of national forces; the regime of confidence-building measures was designed to improve mutual knowledge of military activities of rival states and thus to make surprise attack or conflict through miscalculation more difficult; the CSCE conflict-prevention institutions were designed to head off interstate conflict through mediation or clarification of incidents between the military forces of member states.

None of these institutions or agreements was designed to cope with organized military action by a state against its own citizens, or with a situation where a government was too weak to prevent civil war among ethnic groups. And this happened in Yugoslavia when already-dominant Serbian communists swept aside the multiethnic superstructure of the Yugoslav state and completely took over the apparatus of the state, including its armed forces, and used these forces against the other republics, fomenting or aiding uprisings of Serbs in Croatia and Bosnia against their governments.

YUGOSLAVIA DISSOLVES

In the late 1980s, Western leaders increasingly feared the violent breakup of the Yugoslav Federation, which had been slowly crumbling since the death in May 1980 of Marshal Josip Tito. The process of dissolution had accelerated since Mikhail Gorbachev had introduced his more cooperative policy toward the West, severing the last major bond that held together the six disparate Yugoslav republics—the constant fear, since Tito's 1948 break with Stalin, of Soviet dominion.[1] Western governments were apprehensive that Yugoslavia could fall apart in civil war, possibly drawing neighboring European states, many with territorial claims on Yugoslav territory, into its quarrels. They were well aware of the centuries-old festering hatred between Serbs and Croats, which had resulted in a series of reciprocal massacres in the Balkan wars early in the century and during and after World War II. (In the World War II period, according to one conservative calculation, Serbs suffered nearly 500,000 dead, the Croats 200,000, mostly civilians, at each other's hands.)[2] Yugoslavia's neighbors—Italy, Austria, Hungary, Romania, Bulgaria, Greece, and Albania—feared both a larger flow of Yugoslav refugees and cross-border military incursions. Ethnic resentments inside Yugoslavia were much intensified by economic decline—hyperinflation, mounting unemployment, and declining living standards throughout the 1980s.

The development that finally triggered long-nurtured independence plans of Croatia and Slovenia was a series of elections that took place between April and December 1990 in the six constituent Yugoslav republics. National, noncommunist governments were elected in Slovenia, Croatia, Bosnia, and Macedonia, but demagogic communist leader Slobodan Milosevic was reelected as president by a large majority in Serbia, the largest of the republics with a population exceeding 9 million. Montenegro, with a population of less than a million and usually subservient to Serbia, also voted communist.

In 1989, Milosevic had vetoed plans to introduce free-market reforms in the Yugoslav economy. In 1987, he nullified the autonomy of the Kosovo and Vojvodina provinces of Serbia guaranteed in Tito's 1974 constitution. Kosovo, the site of Serbia's defeat by the Turks in the fourteenth century, is a national shrine for Serbs, although over the years its population has become nearly 90 percent Albanian. Vojvodina has a large Hungarian minority. In March 1989, Milosevic ordered the arrest of the entire Albanian leadership in Kosovo. These repressive Serbian actions were followed by similar actions of the Croatian government against its Serb minority. In 1990, the government of the Croatian Republic issued new regulations defining its 600,000 Serb residents (about 12 percent of Croatia's 4.7 million population, most of them living along the border of Bosnia-Herzegovina), as a "minority" rather than as a "constituent nationality," with a requirement to take a loyalty oath to Croatia. Serbian police and some local Serbian officials were replaced by Croats.[3]

In 1990, it was revealed that Milosevic had stolen more than $1 billion of the Yugoslav Federation's funds to finance his own election campaign in Serbia. The following spring, as talk of leaving the federation became louder in Slovenia and Croatia, Milosevic explicitly threatened that, in the event of secession, Serbia would forcibly incorporate into a "greater Serbia" the territories occupied by Serbs living outside its borders. Unbelievably, a half-century after Hitler had set Europe in flames through his "Heim ins Reich" policy of incorporating into Germany areas occupied by Germans, Milosevic was proclaiming the same creed.

Efforts among the Yugoslav republics that spring to negotiate a looser federation failed. In May, Serbia blocked the scheduled rotation of the Croat representative to the chairmanship of the eight-man federal presidency. After many warnings that they would do so unless there were radical changes in the Yugoslav government, Slovenia and Croatia seceded in June 1991. Within days, fighting broke out in Slovenia as the Federation army, officered mainly by Serbs, tried to compel the Slovenes to revoke their decision to secede. This effort failed after only a few days of combat. The Federation army was poorly placed to continue the conflict, and there were few Serbs in Slovenia to support it. Serbia turned its troops toward gaining control over portions of Croatia inhabited by Serbs.

The United States, closely observing developments in Yugoslavia, had repeatedly warned its NATO allies that if Slovenia and Croatia attempted to secede from the Yugoslav Federation, Serbia would use force to prevent them and to gain possession of territories with Serb majorities. A U.S. National Intelligence Estimate completed in October 1990 predicted this very outcome.[4] All the NATO governments had been active in bilateral discussions with the constituent republics to prevent the breakup of Yugoslavia. They were concerned with the prospect of conflict, and, in the longer-range sense, with the possible emergence of a number of Balkan ministates too small to be economically viable, constantly feuding with one another and creating risks of widening conflict. At the time, Washington and some European capitals also feared that the fall of Yugoslavia might give impetus to the dissolution of the Soviet Union, with unpredictable consequences.

Consequently, Western governments continually urged the Yugoslav republics to stay together at all costs and peacefully renegotiate their relationship. The West threatened not to recognize or assist republics that did make good their threats to secede. This effort to hold Yugoslavia together at all costs was probably mistaken; Slovenes and Croats had no intention of remaining in a state structure dominated by Serbs, who moreover adhered to discredited communist tenets. A better approach might have been to convene early—before secession—a conference of the Yugoslav states under Western auspices of the kind that took place after the fighting was well under way. The Western governments could have stated they would back with economic aid and all other means any negotiated solution whatsoever—from federation to dissolution achieved without the use of force—and they could have sought to keep the conference in session until there was some outcome. One resolution might have been to adapt for the whole of Yugoslavia the concept of autonomous ethnic enclaves with representation in a loose central government later worked out in the Vance-Owen Plan for Bosnia. In any event, although they had made a realistic assessment of what might come, Western governments did not act decisively to block the outbreak of hostilities. With the United States holding back from involvement, they lacked the cohesion necessary to intervene in a preventive way, and they were inhibited by traditional restraints in their dealings with the "sovereign" Yugoslav central government.

When serious fighting broke out, the practical question for Western governments was, How could they act to end the conflict? They knew their publics would not tolerate total inaction on their part in the face of heavy civilian fatalities and masses of refugees intensively reported by Western media. Yugoslavia was not someplace remote. It was a part of the European community of nations, a fellow member of the CSCE, and bordered by two EC and NATO member states, Italy and Greece.

In a historically significant decision, NATO leaders quickly decided that the alliance should not play a direct role in the crisis. In retrospect, it appears plausible that prompt NATO military intervention could have been decisive in preventing full-scale war. A NATO naval blockade in the Adriatic and air intervention over Yugoslavia at the outset of fighting in Slovenia or even the rapid appearance of NATO's ACE mobile readiness brigade in Slovenia in the interest of an impartial cease-fire in place could have immobilized units of the Yugoslav federal ground, air, and naval forces and kept them from active involvement in Slovenia. The prospect of such NATO intervention might of itself have blocked Yugoslav Federal army intervention in Croatia on behalf of local Serbs.[5]

But NATO remained completely inactive at this time, not even passing a resolution supporting the subsequent involvement of the European

Community or providing logistical support for EC monitors. NATO's inaction might well damage its own future. Here was a situation in which limited use of armed forces at the outset of the fighting might have contained the conflict and avoided widespread killing. It was already evident that ethnic conflict—not only in the Yugoslav republics—was the most pressing security problem of post-cold war Europe. NATO had a practical monopoly over usable military force in Europe. If NATO, with its overwhelming military power, was not able to stop the bloodletting in Croatia, then what was its future value to Europe? As the fighting in the Yugoslav republics continued, the question was asked more insistently.

The United States was mainly responsible for NATO's categorical refusal to become involved in the conflict. The motivation of the Bush administration was complex. Secretary of State James Baker visited Belgrade in June 1991, urging the Yugoslav republics to stay together and stating that the United States would not recognize secessionist republics. In the Serbian capital, Baker was warned of the dangers of a long guerrilla war between Croats and Serbs in which NATO forces might become bogged down as the German forces had during World War II. The specter of Vietnam was invoked. Above all, the Bush team faced a presidential election campaign in which domestic issues would clearly predominate. It had scored an important victory in the Persian Gulf War earlier in the year. This was no time for another U.S. military involvement with the possibility of heavy casualties. The Yugoslav republics were a European problem; let the Europeans cope with it.

Yugoslavia was the first European security crisis in more than four decades in which the United States did not play a leadership role; the absence of unified leadership in the West played a fateful part in what followed. But the U.S. position was not the sole obstacle to early NATO involvement in the crisis. Public opinion in Germany, a major NATO ally, was massively opposed to any involvement of German armed forces outside its own borders, even in postconflict peacekeeping. For its part, the Soviet government had made clear in June 1991 that NATO involvement in Eastern Europe would elicit a hostile reaction, and it was a cardinal principle for the U.S. and other Western governments to maintain a cooperative relationship with a reforming Soviet Union. (In fact, the Soviet Union was only weeks away from the anti-Gorbachev coup of August 1991, when the main groups behind this negative position, the military and the KGB, would be discredited and the Soviet position on the former Yugoslavia would change considerably.)

Moreover, on what legal basis could NATO become involved in the disintegration of Yugoslavia? The country was outside the operational area of NATO, whose sphere of activity according to the traditional interpretation was confined to the territory of its member states. Beyond that, Yugoslavia was a sovereign state protected from outside intervention by all the rules of international law and by agreements in the Conference on Security and Cooperation in Europe. In fact, one set of CSCE rules—commitments to protect the human rights of individual citizens and minorities and to intervene at least politically when these rights were systematically violated in member states—was in conflict with a second set of international and CSCE rules. These rules, dating from the 1648 Peace of Westphalia that had ended the Thirty Years War, were designed to protect the sovereignty of states, especially small states, from outside intervention or pressure. Some justification could be found in resolutions of the UN Security Council authorizing outside intervention to prevent abuse of the Iraqi Kurds and Shiites and in the UN Security Council resolution of September 25, 1991, which imposed a ban on transfer of arms to Yugoslavia on the grounds that the Yugoslav civil war constituted a threat to international peace and security. Had it been desired, the latter resolution of itself might have provided a legal basis for intervention in Croatia by NATO or an ad hoc coalition of NATO members.

However, in place of armed intervention by NATO forces, Western governments mobilized the political institutions of the CSCE to cope with the problem. The day after heavy fighting broke out on June 29, 1991, Austria invoked the agreed-upon procedure for dealing with unusual military activities at the CSCE Conflict Prevention Center in Vienna, citing as justification the movement of Yugoslav forces into Slovenia and several incursions by them onto Austrian territory. A meeting of the CSCE Committee of Senior Officials was also summoned in Prague. The outcome of both sessions was in essence the same. Nearly all CSCE member states urged an immediate cease-fire in Yugoslavia. Representatives of the Yugoslav government, although cooperative on the surface, blocked efforts to send CSCE observers to conflict sites, stating that Yugoslavia's problems were domestic. There was no consensus because a single member had objected. Given its operating rules, the CSCE could take no action.

Yet the Western governments could not remain indifferent to continuing loss of life in a neighboring European state; after all, they had just overridden considerations of domestic sovereignty in Iraq in order to protect the Kurds. At the strong urging of the United States, the European Community engaged in the task. Community governments believed the EC had considerable leverage arising from Yugoslavia's desire for EC membership and from the EC's ability to control economic aid and trade with Yugoslavia. The Community had extended to Yugoslavia large credits, of which almost $1 billion remained unused. Although the EC, too, was a body that reached most decisions by consensus, it had the advantage in this case that neither Yugoslavia itself nor the Soviet Union were members.

But the EC greatly overestimated its leverage. EC influence was effective only with the weak and discredited Yugoslav Federation authorities, not with the leaders of individual republics inflamed with ethnic hatred and the desire for independence. Early in July 1991, the Community cut off arms sales by its member states to all republics of Yugoslavia. That action was backed by the UN Security Council in September; the UN embargo is the basis for the continuing embargo on arms transfers to Bosnia as well as to the other Yugoslav republics. The EC also suspended credits and offered to mediate between the Slovenes and the federal government in negotiations for a cease-fire. After Yugoslav Federation armed forces had been bested by the Slovenes in a few days of fighting, a truce for Slovenia was reached under EC auspices on the island of Brioni on July 8. Unarmed EC observers arrived a week later to supervise fulfillment of the terms of the cease-fire.

But the next task was far more difficult. By mid-July, intense fighting broke out between Croat and the Serb inhabitants of Croatia, the latter backed and supplied by Federation armed forces. The Serbs were trying to split off large chunks of Croatia, including the region known as Krajina, where most of the 600,000 Serbian inhabitants of Croatia lived, and attach them to Serbia. Partly because of the greater determination of the Serb-run Federation Army when the lives of fellow Serbs were at stake, partly because of help from local Serbs, and partly because the Croatian government had earlier complied with a Yugoslav-wide order to turn in to central authorities militia weapons stocked for possible Soviet invasion (Slovenia had not), the Federation armed forces and their local allies were far more successful against the Croats than Federation forces had been against the Slovenes. The fighting included a three-month bloody siege of the crucial Croat stronghold of Vukovar and a naval siege and bombardment of historic Dubrovnik. After retirement relieved him of the obligation of silence, General John Galvin, who had been NATO's senior commander at the time, told the House Armed Services Committee he believed that limited NATO naval intervention could have stopped the shelling of Dubrovnik and that ground intervention at Vukovar could have effectively damped down the fighting there.[6] NATO had missed a second chance for decisive intervention at low cost.

The combatants were slow to exhaust each other, although the Serb forces increasingly gained the upper hand in Serb-populated areas. A series of fourteen successive cease-fires arranged by a team of European Community mediators under Lord Peter Carrington were violated and collapsed. The United States, France, and some other Western governments suggested that the EC alone might not have enough weight and urged that the United Nations play a role in seeking an end to the fighting. In October, former secretary of state Cyrus Vance was appointed as UN mediator by Secretary-General Boutros Boutros-Ghali. With the cooperation of the United States, Canada, and European Community countries, Vance arranged a fifteenth and successful cease-fire in December 1991 in preparation for entry of a UN peacekeeping force into Croatia. In January 1992, Slovenia and Croatia were recognized by the EC, pushed by a German government under the pressure of runaway domestic public opinion.

An estimated 20,000 people died in the Croatian fighting, there were 600,000 refugees, and the entire Yugoslav economy was in shambles. As a result of these events, all of the European security institutions were to some extent discredited: NATO had stood inactive on the sidelines; the CSCE and the European Community had both intervened, but ineffectively. The Western European Union had at French instigation looked at the possibility of action by a WEU-organized coalition; but with Britain citing the unfortunate experience of British army action against Irish Republican Army (IRA) terrorists in Northern Ireland, the organization decided that the job was too big for it to tackle.

In March 1992, the first units of the 14,000-man UN Protective Force (UNPROFOR) entered four areas of Croatia with a mainly Serb population, but Serb militia units continued to strengthen their control in these localities, ignoring UN orders to store their heavy weapons under UN monitors. However, the Yugoslav civil war, as quietly forecast by some tough-minded Western leaders who opposed Western military intervention, had apparently been isolated and burned itself out.

This conclusion was sadly mistaken. The Yugoslav conflict flared up again, in adjoining Bosnia-Herzegovina. The government of Bosnia-Herzegovina had argued for continuation of the Yugoslav Federation in the unsuccessful interrepublic talks in the spring of 1991. But, when the European Community was in the process of recognizing Croatia and Slovenia, it also raised the possibility of recognition of Bosnia-Herzegovina as an independent state, dependent on the holding of a republic-wide referendum. The Bosnian government decided on such a referendum; it took place on February 29–March 1, 1992. The Bosnian Serbs, who had already announced that they would resist with armed force the independence of Bosnia and their own separation from Serbia,[7] boycotted the referendum. Of the 63 percent of eligible voters who participated in the referendum, 94 percent voted for independence. Muslims made up 43 percent of Bosnia-Herzegovina's 4.3 million population. Seventeen percent were Croats, and roughly a third were Serbs.

Two weeks after the referendum, Bosnian Croat, Serb, and Muslim leaders signed a plan formulated by EC mediators under Lord Carrington to divide Bosnia into three ethnic "cantons," linked in a loose confederation. Given what had already happened in Croatia, it was a logical solution. But only a few days later, Bosnian president Alija Izetbegovic, motivated at least in part by vociferous criticism of the canton scheme from the United States and Western Europe, repudiated his signature and called for a unified Bosnia in which ethnic groups would be integrated, not separated.[8] In early April, basing his action on the positive outcome of the March referendum, President Izetbegovic withdrew his republic from the Yugoslav Federation and proclaimed its independence. The Western governments rapidly recognized the new Bosnian state without raising the condition that the three main Bosnian ethnic groups must come to some political understanding before recognition took place. The fighting in Bosnia, as long predicted, began the next day.

Although they had all foreseen this second stage of the Yugoslav wars even more clearly than they had foreseen the first, the Western governments had not prepared any plan to head off the conflict in Bosnia or to cope with it if it occurred. A sizable UN or NATO peacekeeping force on the ground in Bosnia could have prevented widespread conflict. The force would have been invited in by the Bosnian republic government prior to independence and deployed in main population centers. Serbia, which still controlled the formal mechanism of the Yugoslav Federation government, would probably have objected, but without decisive effect. The failure to have considered this action in the light of what was already known at the time about ethnic fighting in Yugoslavia is perhaps the most serious Western error in Yugoslavia. Western officials also underestimated the Bosnian conflict's potential ferocity and duration, and Muslim determination to hold out. Many expected the conflict to "burn out" within six months, like the fighting between the Serbs and Croats in Croatia.

Bosnian Serbs made use of Yugoslav Federation armed forces and arms to help in seizing territories inhabited mainly by Serbs, as well as many areas inhabited by Muslims, preparatory to their later incorporation in a Greater Serbia. The Croat Republic despicably collaborated in the division of Bosnian territory in a small-scale version of the 1939 Molotov-Ribbentrop division of Poland. Well-armed Serb and Croat guerrilla groups repeatedly defeated less well-armed, less organized Bosnian Muslim forces. Thousands died in combat; thousands more were barbarously murdered and raped by Serbs who wanted to expel or eliminate non-Serb inhabitants of areas they wished to take over in order to create a belt of contiguous Serb-held territories from Serbia through Bosnia to Krajina in Croatia. The process became known as "ethnic cleansing." The Croats followed this grisly example. The Muslim Bosnian forces too carried out atrocities, although on a far smaller scale.

By 1993, estimates of the dead and missing in Bosnia were at least 150,000, with the Bosnian government claiming as many as 200,000. Together with the conflict in Croatia, the fighting left about 3.8 million displaced persons in former Yugoslavia and 600,000 persons with refugee status outside its borders, the biggest refugee flow since World War II.[9] The bulk of these displaced persons and refugees, about 2 million, were in camps in Croatia, Bosnia, and other Yugoslav states, about half a million in neighboring states, and about 400,000 in EC countries, where their presence contributed to sometimes murderous xenophobia. The nightmare of the Western Europeans about refugee swarms from the East had materialized.[10]

At last, the Bush administration began to see the consequences of its original refusal to engage this problem. At its urging, the UN Security Council declared an economic embargo of Serbia (May 1992). After presidential candidate Bill Clinton criticized President Bush in July 1992 for inadequate leadership on Bosnia, in August, the Bush administration pushed through Security Council Resolution 770. Resolution 770 called for all necessary measures, including the use of armed force, to ensure delivery of humanitarian shipments. After months of savage fighting in Bosnia, it was the right thing to do. But no action was ever taken under this resolution, then or later.

The United States also started to play a role in negotiations for a political solution in Bosnia. In September 1992, European countries including France and the United Kingdom, Ukraine, and others began to provide soldiers under an expanded UNPROFOR mandate to escort humanitarian shipments of food and medicine for distribution in Sarajevo and other towns in Bosnia. Despite UN and European pleas, the United States refused even symbolic participation in this effort. However, after its November 1992 presidential reelection defeat, the Bush administration, freed from domestic pressures, began to insist on enforcement of the UN economic sanctions against Serbia and on prosecution of Serbian leaders as war criminals. There was some evidence in the form of mounting inflation and unemployment and bank failures that the sanctions were having some effect in Serbia, but Milosevic did not appear to be facing serious popular resistance. The threat of trial as a war criminal may even have helped him to easy reelection as president of Serbia in December 1992.

President Bush wrote to Milosevic the same month warning him that if Serbian authorities violated the human rights of Albanians in Kosovo, the United States would respond with military force. Newly elected president Clinton repeated the warning in early 1993. The U.S. and other Western governments feared that if Serbia acted to repress the Albanians of Kosovo, it could result in military intervention by Albania, Bulgaria, and Greece. The United States was not willing to use its ground forces inside the former

Yugoslavia to stop the fighting there, but it was willing to threaten military intervention in Serbia or Macedonia in order to prevent the Bosnian conflict from spreading to other countries and placed a small trip-wire U.S. infantry force in Macedonia for this purpose. A mixed Scandinavian UN battalion was deployed in Macedonia in early 1993 to block the spread of the conflict and to damp down neighboring Kosovo. In July 1993, a U.S. ground-force contingent the size of an infantry company was also deployed in Macedonia, the fruit of a yearlong effort by State Department officials to gain political agreement to send a considerably larger force. A modest increase followed in 1994. In April, Macedonia was admitted to UN membership as "the former Yugoslav Republic of Macedonia," the conflict with Greece over its official name not yet resolved.

The success of the Western governments in helping to contain the fighting from spreading outside Croatia and Bosnia, and especially in preventing open conflict between Serbs and Albanians in Kosovo province and between Albanians and Macedonians in Macedonia, was a bright spot in the poor Western record in the former Yugoslavia. A second positive achievement was some improvement in the UN capability to conduct complex peacekeeping operations and, after some clumsy efforts to mesh, in peacekeeping cooperation between the UN and NATO. NATO and WEU finally began to enforce the UN-ordered naval blockade to enforce UN embargoes. Beginning in mid-1992, there was discussion of enforcement by NATO of the UN's existing ban on flights of military aircraft over Bosnia.

The subsequent handling of the flight-ban idea encapsulated the tragidrama and the complexity of the situation in the former Yugoslavia. The Bush administration pressed for rapid action in December 1992. However, Britain and France, fearful of Serb retaliation against their troops on the ground in Bosnia and resentful of U.S. refusal to provide any troops of its own, were cautious about timing and conditions. Russia, pressed by nationalists evoking traditional friendship with Serbia, also hung back in the Security Council. UN representatives in Bosnia feared repercussions on relief deliveries. For their part, UN negotiator Cyrus Vance and EC negotiator Lord David Owen argued against any use of force, including the flight ban, while negotiations among the combatant parties continued. Finally, under pressure from the new Clinton administration, the UN Security Council decided at the end of March 1993 to authorize NATO countries to shoot down planes violating its ban on flights over Serbia. The decision, circumscribed by many French, British, and Russian conditions, forbade pursuit of offending aircraft into Serbia or separate attacks on air bases. In mid-April 1993, NATO began its enforcement operation. It was the first NATO military action outside NATO's borders. In late February 1994, after hundreds of violations of the flight ban in the ensuing ten months, most of them lesser ones by transport helicopters, NATO aircraft destroyed four Serbian light combat aircraft engaged in bombing a Bosnian munitions plant. It had taken over twenty months from the time this useful idea had been raised for serious discussion to its implementation.

The domestic and international situation of the Clinton administration with regard to the Bosnian fighting was even more difficult than that of the Bush administration. During the election campaign, candidate Bill Clinton had criticized President George Bush for inaction on Bosnia. Once Clinton was elected, these statements incurred some obligation to act more energetically. However, the new administration had reached a firm decision soon after the inauguration to concentrate on domestic social and economic issues and to keep a low profile on foreign policy, with special caution regarding foreign military involvement. Administration leaders were haunted by the Vietnam experience, as were top military officers. They believed American public opinion shared this feeling and that a U.S. decision to intervene in the former Yugoslavia, especially with ground forces, would rip American opinion asunder. Richard Johnson, a former Yugoslav desk officer in the State Department, in a somewhat indiscreet repetition of a 1993 conversation with two top State Department officials, reported that they recognized the moral issue in Bosnia but believed that a failed U.S. intervention there could destroy the American presidency and the fragile liberal coalition it represented.[11]

In this conflicted situation, with increased pressure from the European allies to do more on Bosnia, but with even greater determination not to commit U.S. ground forces even stronger than that of the Bush administration, the Clinton administration decided to try to do more with air power. It also threw more support to the Bosnian Muslims, an action affected by resentment against Serbian aggression but also by concerns over the rise of Muslim fundamentalism elsewhere. Inaugurating its increased emphasis on air power, the administration introduced the idea of air-drops of food and supplies to beleaguered communities in Bosnia, most of them Muslim, and supported enforcement of the flight ban over Bosnia. The air-drop idea was disparaged by some journalists and European governments but nevertheless put into effect with some allied help. Secretary of State Warren Christopher reported at the CSCE foreign ministers meeting in late 1993 that in the eight months of its operation since February 1993, the U.S. component of the flights had air-dropped more than 10 million meals.

THE NEGOTIATION ROUTE

While Western governments wrestled with the problem of how to bring effective military pressure to bear on the Serbs and others to stop the civil war in Bosnia, they were also mediating and promoting negotiation among the three combatant groups. The first negotiating team, fielded by the EC and led by Lord Carrington, sought political solutions, but had given priority to bringing about a cease-fire in Bosnia. In August 1992, this effort, which was making only slow progress, was replaced by a more ambitious one based on cooperation between the UN, represented by Cyrus Vance, and the EC, represented by former U.K. foreign secretary Lord David Owen. The Vance-Owen approach, launched at a large-scale conference in London, was organized to cope with all aspects of the problem through applying the CSCE method of parallel negotiation on borders, economic aspects, and international recognition. In London there were nearly 200 participants organized in six working groups, each of them headed by an experienced UN or EC diplomat under the general guidance of the two principal negotiators.

After the talks shifted, partly to Geneva and partly to Sarajevo, considerable progress was made in the working groups. For example, from October to December 1992, the mixed military working group met quietly in Sarajevo seventeen times under the chairmanship of UN commander Lieutenant General Satish Nambiar. In early 1993 Vance and Owen decided to move the talks to the United Nations in New York to maximize pressure on participants to reach agreement and to engage the new Clinton administration more directly in the process. The result of their negotiations became known as the Vance-Owen Plan.

The nub of the plan was the establishment of ten provinces in Bosnia-Herzegovina, three each for the Muslims, Croats, and Serbs, plus Sarajevo, the capital, under mixed, but predominantly Muslim control. The plan would go into effect after an unconditional cease-fire took place. Guerrilla forces would be separated, disarmed, and returned to the various provinces. Bosnia-Herzegovina would be a decentralized state, with most governmental functions carried out by the provinces. A new government would result from elections under UN supervision. The new Bosnian government would be headed by a presidency of three representatives from each of the main ethnic groups. The new constitution could not be amended without the explicit agreement of all three groups. Disagreements over the operation of the settlement would be heard by a constitutional court. Significantly, jurists from outside the former Yugoslavia would constitute a majority of the court's members. The provinces could not enter agreements with foreign states. Serbian control would be reduced in the new provinces to 43 percent of the area of Bosnia instead of the 70 percent or more the Serbs held in early 1993. (The Serbs, mostly farmers, held more than 60 percent before the civil war). Some of the Muslim-dominated provinces would be along the border of Serbia, preventing the establishment of a contiguous Greater Serbia going down into Krajina.[12]

The Bosnian Croats signed the Vance-Owen Plan. Initially the Clinton administration expressed strong doubts as to whether the Vance-Owen

Plan took sufficient account of Muslim interests, but weakly endorsed it in February 1993 with an implied commitment to contribute U.S. forces, including a ground-force contingent, to a peacekeeping force in Bosnia if all parties accepted the plan and after an effective cease-fire was in effect.[13] In late March, Bosnian president Izetbegovic, after dramatic trips to Washington to consult, also signed the plan.[14] Izetbegovic indicated that his final decision was based on the willingness of the United States to contribute ground troops to a peacekeeping force and on a UN commitment that peacekeepers would actively remove heavy weapons from Serb groups if they failed to relinquish them voluntarily in accordance with the planned settlement.

But in early April, the Bosnian Serb assembly, as had been predicted, rejected the plan.[15] In fact, by this time, refugee flight and expulsion of populations on all sides from most of the provinces, compounded by the probable reluctance of most refugees to return to their original homes, probably meant the plan was unworkable. Nonetheless, it was estimated that if the Vance-Owen Plan were implemented, it would take from 30,000 to 60,000 UN peacekeeping troops to prevent further violence in the new Bosnia. The potential size of the peacekeeping operation brought NATO into the picture as a possible agent of the UN acting under the general guidance of the Security Council. NATO staff planners began drawing up contingency plans But neither the U.S. nor other NATO governments showed any inclination for imposing the plan on the Bosnian Serbs through NATO ground-force intervention if the Serbs did not agree to it. Instead, they hoped that air interdiction and additional economic sanctions might cause both Slobodan Milosevic and Bosnian Serb leader Radovan Karadzic to reconsider the Bosnian Serb rejection of the Vance-Owen Plan.

Following its course of placing greater emphasis on air power, the Clinton administration, after extended policy review, decided in April on a two-pronged policy of lifting the UN embargo on the import of arms by the Bosnian Muslims and of using NATO combat aircraft, already enforcing the flight ban over Bosnia, to support UNPROFOR if it encountered Serb or Croat resistance in making humanitarian deliveries in Bosnia. While NATO would not support the Bosnian forces as such, the rationale of the approach was that it might create time for the Muslims to receive arms and training, ultimately positioning them to defend a viable Bosnian state.

At the beginning of May, Secretary of State Christopher went to Europe to explain the plan and gain European acceptance of it. But in a rare show of NATO resistance to U.S. proposals, Christopher was rebuffed, apparently at least in part because his presentation of the idea was indecisive and tentative. European leaders indicated that they would agree that NATO combat aircraft could be used to protect safe areas for the Bosnian Muslims if U.S. ground forces joined the Europeans and shared the increased risks of any Serbian response to NATO air attacks. They also vigorously rejected the idea of lifting the ban on arms deliveries. That idea, supported only by five nonaligned members of the Security Council and the United States, was formally voted down in the UN Security Council at the end of June.

Meanwhile, Serb and Croat forces were closing in on the remaining strongholds of the Bosnian government. By the spring of 1993, Bosnian forces held only 10 percent of the state's territory. Several of the safe havens the UN approved had already fallen to Serbs or Croats. In May, now under pressure from President Milosevic, who was at last feeling the pinch of economic sanctions, and of Greek prime minister Konstantin Mitsotakis, Bosnian Serb leader Radovan Karadzic finally signed the Vance-Owen Plan. But it was again repudiated by the Bosnian Serb assembly a few days later and then once more by 96 percent of 1.2 million participants in a popular vote of Bosnian Serbs and Croats arranged by Karadzic and his colleagues.

Following this setback, EC negotiator Lord Owen changed tack. He dropped the Vance-Owen Plan and urged the Bosnian government to adopt the latest version of the less generous confederation plan proposed by the Serbs and Croats.[16] Slobodan Milosevic and Franjo Tudjman had resurrected the EC-sponsored framework approach put forward in March 1992 before Bosnia's declaration of independence. According to Radovan Karadzic, the new version of the plan offered 30 percent of Bosnian territory to the Muslims, including the best industry and mines, and would also provide internationally supervised human rights guarantees. However, the proposal would confine the Muslims to two separate landlocked areas around Sarajevo and around Bihac in the northwest, with uncertain arrangements for a free port on the Adriatic.[17] The Bosnian government rejected the new EC-UN approach, now called the Owen-Stoltenberg Plan (Thorvald Stoltenberg of Norway had replaced Cyrus Vance as the UN's special negotiator), but agreed to put it to a vote in the Bosnian parliament.

By July 1993, Sarajevo seemed on the verge of falling. If this catastrophic development occurred, it would not only be a tragedy for the Bosnians, but it would expose Western governments to acute embarrassment for their ineffectiveness. Picking up its once rejected proposal, the United States again urged air action against Serb positions surrounding the city. In August, NATO finally agreed on this course, but under restrictive conditions. As if to demonstrate the elusiveness of consensus, the UNPROFOR commander and his chief of staff publicly criticized the concept and said that resort to it would block the ongoing negotiations in Geneva, perhaps permanently.

In September 1993, Bosnia's Muslim-dominated parliament formally rejected the Owen-Stoltenberg proposal for division of Bosnia into
three ethnic components. The Bosnians complained that they would not
receive enough territory under the scheme—specifically, they wanted
control of a string of formerly Muslim-majority towns throughout Bosnia—
and that it did not provide assured access to the Adriatic Sea or ironclad
assurances that compliance would be guaranteed by U.S. forces on the
ground. Lord Owen subsequently claimed that the United States had
killed the plan through its refusal in advance to commit itself to provide
ground-force peacekeepers. Meeting in late November, the EC foreign
ministers sought to make the Owen-Stoltenberg approach more acceptable
to the Bosnians. They indicated that they would consider relaxing economic sanctions against Serbia if the latter would influence the Bosnian
Serbs to make additional territorial concessions. The United States gave
this idea lukewarm support. But when the Geneva talks among the
Bosnian Muslims, Serbs, and Croats resumed in mid-January 1994, they
promptly collapsed.

Part of the reason for this negative outcome was that the Bosnian
Muslims were stiffening their position. Hard-line factions had gained more
influence, and the military situation improved as the Muslims received
more money as well as more volunteers and smuggled arms from Muslim
countries abroad. Aside from repeated atrocities against civilians that
were committed by all sides, most of the fighting in the second half of
1993 focused on Muslim efforts to recover pockets of land held by Croat
forces in central Bosnia. But the Bosnians could not realistically hope for
victory no matter how much their arms supplies improved; at most, they
might improve their negotiating position at great cost in terms of human
lives and physical destruction.[18]

Meanwhile, owing to French insistence, Western leaders at the
NATO Summit on January 10–11, 1994, rather reluctantly confirmed
the NATO decisions of six months earlier "to carry out air strikes in
order to prevent the strangulation of Sarajevo, the safe areas, and other
threatened areas in Bosnia-Herzegovina." French political opinion was
turning against the cost and continued risk of France's 6,000 peacekeeping troops in Bosnia (twenty-one had been killed), in a situation
that had no apparent end. The French and British governments had been
talking openly about withdrawing their peacekeepers from Bosnia. This
talk was intended mainly to move refractory Bosnian Croat and Serb
negotiators toward agreement on a peace plan, but unfortunately, the
French public seemed to like it. At the same time, the French government had finally become convinced it could not move the Clinton government to send ground troops, but France still wished a more rapid
solution in Bosnia. Considerations of this kind led to an important shift

in the French position from determined opposition to air strikes in Bosnia to supporting them.[19]

But the NATO Summit did not settle Western differences over Bosnia. To the contrary, the argument among Western governments over air strikes became more vehement and more public, with Secretary of State Warren Christopher accusing France of trying to muscle the Bosnian Muslims into accepting an inequitable agreement and French foreign minister Alain Juppé coming close to accusing the Clinton administration of cowardice. An intemperate public statement by a Canadian expert typified the private comments of many alliance officials: "You Americans were run out of Haiti by a gang of thugs on the dock because you didn't want to soil your hands. You were run out of Somalia because you took casualties and couldn't stand the heat. Now you want to bomb Bosnia to the last Canadian, British, and French peacekeeper."[20]

Actually, France was arguing not only for a more robust U.S. military policy in Bosnia but also for more active U.S. support of a political solution. Claiming that, unless the United States engaged its political prestige, no solution would be found, France urged the Americans to back the latest European Union (EU) effort to gain acceptance of the Owen-Stoltenberg Plan through combining the carrot of lifting of sanctions against Serbia with the stick of imposition of sanctions against Croatia if it did not cooperate in reaching a settlement. In the face of problems with French officers and other peacekeeping commanders in Bosnia and the shift in the position of the French and ultimately the British government on air strikes, UN secretary-general Boutros Boutros-Ghali too shifted his ground. In a letter to the Security Council at the end of January, he said he had given UN officials on the ground in Bosnia permission to call on NATO for air strikes to help open the way for relief shipments to Tuzla and Srebrenica, two Bosnian towns under Serbian siege. To avoid further friction with France and other European NATO countries, Washington reluctantly agreed to air strikes in these two cases—if needed.

Nonetheless, NATO's internal dissent and inactivity might have continued indefinitely, except that some Serb gunners near Sarajevo took matters into their own hands. On February 5, 1994, they fired a mortar shell into the Sarajevo central market that killed sixty-eight people and wounded nearly two hundred more. There was wide television coverage of this biggest single bloodletting in the siege of Sarajevo. There was no longer any valid excuse for NATO inaction. On February 9, the NATO Council gave an ultimatum to Serb forces surrounding Sarajevo to withdraw their heavy artillery twelve miles from the center of Sarajevo or face air strikes. NATO had, through a French proposal, finally found a formula for applying its overwhelming air strength toward specific objectives in the Bosnian war.

After a period of confusion in which UN and NATO officials interpreted the ultimatum terms differently, the Serbs largely complied with the
ultimatum. They were helped to do so by a sudden decision by President
Boris Yeltsin to respond to the UN appeal for more peacekeepers in Bosnia
by sending 800 additional Russian soldiers. Russia claimed that it had not
been informed of NATO's February decision on air strikes and opposed it,
and Russia gave the impression that its peacekeepers would protect the
Serbs from NATO action. In any event, the Russian action provided a face-
saving excuse for Serb compliance with NATO's order to withdraw the
artillery or to hand it over to UN peacekeepers, and a pattern of sometimes
disharmonious U.S.-Russian diplomatic collaboration began to emerge.

Following on this successful threat of NATO military action, once
again ill-considered Serb action led to NATO military intervention. On
February 28, U.S. fighter jets implementing NATO's enforcement of the UN
flight ban over Bosnia shot down four Serb aircraft flying from the Bosnia
Serb airbase at Banja Luka that had been caught bombing an arms facto-
ry operated by Bosnian Muslim forces. It was the first use of force by NATO
in its forty-five-year history. Serbian reaction, to continue to fall back in the
face of NATO's new resolve or to contest it, would be decisive.[21] Pulling
back from earlier Russian statements opposing air attacks on Serb positions around Sarajevo, Foreign Minister Andrei Kozyrev explicitly approved
the NATO action. The Russian government also successfully pressed
Bosnian Serb leader Radovan Karadzic to agree to open the Tuzla airbase
to UN relief flights if Russian peacekeeping troops were on hand to assure
that flights were not ferrying military supplies to the Muslim defenders.

In agreeing to the French proposal to use air strikes to defend
Sarajevo, Secretary of State Christopher also yielded to the insistent French
request for greater U.S. involvement in the negotiation process. In an
impressive display of diplomatic agility, the United States, acting through
special envoy Charles Redman, brought together Bosnian and Croat negotiators to sign an outline agreement in Washington on March 1, 1994—
nearly two years to the day from the outset of fighting in
Bosnia—providing for a confederation between the Bosnian state and
Croatia and for a federal system of autonomous ethnic cantons within
Bosnia. The Croats had apparently relinquished their claim to a separate
state within Bosnia. The new confederation was to be admitted quickly to
NATO's Partnership for Peace program and placed in a favored position
for eventual membership in the EU. The Bosnian Serbs, who had not been
consulted, rejected the outcome as one imposed by the United States,
but they could not prevent at least portions of the scheme from eventually going into operation. They would be invited to participate in later negotiations in which they would be asked to surrender a large portion of the

territory they now held. The Croatian Serbs in Krajina also initially criticized the proposal, but dropped their overt disagreement and instead signed an agreement with the Croatian government brokered by Russia providing for disengagement of Croat and Serb forces in the Krajina area with a long-term prospect for negotiation and regional autonomy.[22] The Bosnian-Croat confederation would probably have the support of NATO, the European Union, and the UN. By shifting the negotiations out of the European Union-United Nations framework to a new forum which it dominated, the Clinton administration had, as France and others had sought, taken on more responsibility for assuring some outcome in Bosnia.

Apparent progress toward a settlement was blocked, at least for a time, following two NATO bombings of Serb positions in the vicinity of the Muslim-held town of Gorazde southeast of Sarajevo, one of the towns designated by the UN as safe havens. This was followed by renewed Serb attack on Gorazde, sporadic Serb shelling at various locations and by the Serb capture as hostages of about 200 UN peacekeepers. President Yeltsin again vehemently objected that he had not been consulted before the actions by NATO aircraft, but sent Deputy Foreign Minister Vitaly Churkin to negotiate with the Serbs. The latter returned to Moscow infuriated by what he claimed was Serbian duplicity in failing to make good an agreement to pull back from Gorazde. The United States, NATO, and the UN backed off from further air operations around Gorazde after a NATO plane was downed, but their reputation and credibility were once more on the line. Whether there would be escalation or new negotiation depended on the Bosnian Serbs, yet the options of both sides had narrowed.

With the United States, the EU countries, and Russia at last uniting behind a specific negotiating approach for Bosnia, and with Serbia and Croatia also apparently joining them, the prospects were for a slowly subsiding conflict.

NATO and the United States had partially redeemed themselves from the discredit into which they had fallen over the former Yugoslavia; they would do so further if a political settlement was reached and they carried out peacekeeping functions.[23] Whether or not the latest negotiating approach succeeded in stopping the killing in Bosnia, that tragic country seemed headed toward an eventual weary peace based on some form of ethnic segregation.

Some Consequences

One persistent question about Bosnia is whether the Western powers decided correctly in supporting the predominantly Muslim Bosnian government's insistence on multiethnic statehood with an ethnically mixed population throughout Bosnia rather than separating the ethnic groups in largely homogeneous cantons. The Bosnian Serbs and Croats had overwhelmingly rejected this form of integration, and it had already broken down in Croatia. Western support for multiethnic tolerance and democratic ideals was wholly understandable. Nonetheless, Western governments chose a fatal combination of policies in Bosnia. They supported the Izetbegovic government in its multiethnic approach, prolonging its opposition to other solutions. They maintained the arms embargo against all the Yugoslav republics, including Bosnia. But they also provided extensive humanitarian supplies, many of which fell into the hands of combat troops of all sides, enabling them to continue fighting. At the same time, they refused to intervene with enough military force to bring the fight in Bosnia to a stop. The net effect of Western policies was to protract the fighting in Bosnia and to bring an outcome less favorable for the Bosnian government than the EC-sponsored confederation plan that Izetbegovic had signed in March 1992 before the fighting began. However, European refusal to follow American advice to lift the embargo and arm the Bosnian Muslims seems justified. At best, the result would have been intensified and prolonged killing. Lifting the embargo would have required withdrawal of the UN peacekeeping and humanitarian presence and explicit admission of total failure of the UN mission, with the United States in effect entering the war on the side of the Bosnian Muslims.

Throughout 1992 and 1993, despite their overwhelming military power, the Western states were determined to avoid serious military involvement in the Bosnian "quagmire" through large-scale involvement of their ground forces. The fighting in Bosnia did not threaten the territorial security of any NATO or EC country, nor did it imperil access to any vital natural resource. Nonetheless, above and beyond humanitarian interests, the long-term security interests of the Western states were in fact directly involved: the discrediting of European security institutions and of the United Nations for failure to resolve the problem; the resultant resentment on the part of Muslim countries everywhere; the possibility that Serbs and Croats would resume fighting in Croatia; the possibility that fighting would spread to Kosovo and Macedonia, most likely bringing in Albania, Bulgaria, Greece, and even Turkey; and the continuing long-term costs of relief and rehabilitation for millions of displaced persons. It was clear that the inability of the world's main security institutions to cope with the problem would give free rein to ethnic conflict elsewhere, and it would discourage supporters of multilateral security worldwide.

Considerations like these caused former British prime minister Margaret Thatcher, former president Ronald Reagan, former secretary of state George Shultz, four State Department desk officers who resigned in protest over U.S. policy, and several of the successive UN commanders in

Sarajevo all to argue for the decisive use of military force. But none of the NATO governments dared to incur the domestic political criticism that would come in reaction to televised casualties among their peacekeeping forces. Senior American officers, traumatized by the Vietnam experience, were open in their hesitation to support committing U.S. ground forces without advance assurances from the administration that sufficient force would be used to do the job properly, and that the political goals of any involvement be clear. The British government kept looking over its shoulder at Northern Ireland, where a classic ethnic conflict had tied down 18,000 British troops for years. Germany was paralyzed by domestic political dissent over use of German military forces abroad and in any event barred from participation by brutal German World War II occupation of Yugoslavia.

Yet it is necessary to maintain some perspective in analyzing the Yugoslav tragedy. Yugoslavia was a tragedy of avoidable deaths and destruction and a serious blow to hopes for constructing a more effective regional and global peace system after the end of the cold war. At the same time, if conflict in Yugoslavia had posed an immediate threat to the security of Western European countries, they would almost certainly have intervened, as would the United States, which explicitly threatened to do so if the war spread. The fighting in Yugoslavia did pose a long-term threat to Western security in the sense that the collective reluctance of the major Western allies to commit themselves on the ground revealed serious weaknesses in the concept of multilateral peacemaking. At the same time, it is already clear that the Yugoslav ethnic conflicts are far from finally over and that, in one form or another, they will long remain a festering problem of European security.

7

UNIFIED GERMANY—
RESURGENT OR SELF-PREOCCUPIED?

A fter more than a century of restless and sometimes catastrophically destructive efforts to bring about unity among the German states and to find an accepted place for Germany in Europe and the world, unification on October 3, 1990, found Germany in an enviable domestic and international position.

The western part of the country was prosperous beyond the imagination of any German or any outsider looking at the ruins of 1945. It had a functioning democratic system. The Federal Republic of Germany (this designation now applies to united Germany) was firmly integrated in NATO, the European Community, and the new structure of permanent Conference on Security and Cooperation in Europe (CSCE) institutions. It had a respected position in the United Nations, an organization originally founded to ensure against a repetition of German and Japanese aggression, and was even moving toward a seat on the Security Council. Ernst Weidenfeld of the University of Mainz says with telling insight that, below the surface, many Germans considered the division of Germany a punishment for the crimes of the Hitler period, a punishment for which East Germans had to pay most. From this perspective, the crime was expiated and the punishment ended with German unification. The rapidity and the near-effortlessness of the unification process encouraged the belief among many Germans, unfortunately short-lived, that a new age had dawned.

Are there risks, inherent in the institutions of the new Germany or in the deep-seated attitudes of its government and people, now or as they may plausibly develop in the next decades, of antidemocratic development, of an overly assertive trend in Germany's international relationships, of negative complications in German relations with Western countries or with the East European and Soviet successor states? In short, is there any appreciable risk that the new Germany will break out of the web of cooperative arrangements established over the years since the defeat of the Third Reich and once more play a destructive, autonomous, maverick role in European politics?

In seeking answers to these questions, we should bear in mind that, in the 1920s, many careful observers concluded that Germans had learned from defeat in World War I and that the democratic institutions of the Weimar Republic would prevent any repetition of earlier aggressive behavior. In fact, given the record of Germany's unification by force of arms against Austria and France in the 1860s, the central German role in World War I, and the horrors of the Nazi regime, it is nearly certain that the apprehensions of Germany's neighbors and the gloomy reflections of Germans on their own history will endure for many decades, if not for centuries. As a consequence, German behavior will be analyzed and reviewed with a hypercritical intensity accorded few other countries. Tiny incidents passed over elsewhere without the slightest interest will be viewed as significant.

Nonetheless, any simple repetition of Germany's past is extremely improbable. German national feeling is on the rise, but from a very low starting level of self-denigration. The authoritarian and militaristic values of the old Germany have for the most part dissolved. Prussia has disappeared, the concepts of *Lebensraum* and prosperity through conquest of territory have been discredited in Germany. Germany has no official territorial claims on others although it has lost up to 30 percent of its pre-Hitler territory. German minorities still exist outside the country, but today they are regarded by Germans as a burden and an obligation and definitely not as an asset or as grounds for incorporating territory into Germany as in Nazi times (as they still are by the Serbs). Germany's armed forces are under tight civilian control and are limited to a low level by treaty and integrated in the NATO alliance, Germany has little capacity for independent military initiative. It has renounced production or possession of nuclear weapons and is flanked by nuclear weapons states that have every interest in ensuring that this prohibition is maintained.

Aggressive German behavior on past lines seems wholly excluded for the short term. Is there any appreciable risk that it could reappear in the long term? That is the question we shall evaluate here.

A Bad Hangover

German unification brought with it a towering edifice of domestic and foreign expectations about the future performance of the new unified Germany that no normal state could possibly fulfill: East Germans expected rapid improvement of their living standard to the level of West Germany. West Germans expected that this process would be costless and painless to them. Although it knew better, the Kohl government allowed this euphoria to continue too long. The united Germany was also expected to continue to welcome with attractive subsidies and citizenship rights everyone with the most distant claims to German ethnic origin and also to maintain its policy of open political asylum, the most generous among the larger nations of the world.

Beyond this, Germans in East and West expected that the outside world would leave them alone to enjoy their glowing vision of reunification. For its part, the outside world expected that the united Germany would take over and continue West Germany's deserved reputation for a foreign policy of dependability, predictability, rejection of nationalism, and principled emphasis on internationalism and the multilateral approach. United Germany was expected to be the main dynamic force for building the institutions of the European Community and a motor for world economic growth under conditions of price and currency stability, while lowering interest rates and increasing its imports of foreign products as well. It was to be the economic savior of Eastern Europe and the Soviet successor states (but without gaining undue influence over these countries). Germany was expected to be the closest partner of France, but at the same time a worldwide partner of the United States, supporting the U.S. position in the General Agreement on Tariffs and Trade negotiations and persuading France to reduce its agricultural subsidies, protecting NATO against French efforts to undermine it, and acting like a still bigger United Kingdom in giving loyal political and military support to U.S. policy worldwide.

In the sober light of the morning-after following the exhilaration of reunification, each of these expectations was in fact disappointed to some extent. But the fact that a country has disappointed many unrealistic expectations does not make that country a potential source of serious international security problems. We have to look more closely at Germany's institutions and policy to answer recurrent questions about Germany's long-term future.

COULD A UNITED GERMANY GO BROKE?

At the end of 1988, before unification, West Germany ranked third in the world in gross domestic product and third or fourth in adjusted living standard. It had foreign currency reserves of $60 billion, second only to Japan and the United States. East Germany, although one of the most prosperous states of the Warsaw Pact, ranked only twenty-sixth in total GDP, and its GDP per head was only about one-quarter of that in West Germany.[1] This huge economic gap describes the main practical problem of unification, although it leaves out of the calculus the unexpected total collapse of the East German economy that took place after unification.

The single most important factor in German unification was the intense desire of the East German population to have access to the West German way of life, combining a high level of economic well-being and a high standard of personal freedom. Before the first all-German election of December 1990, in which Helmut Kohl won a solid victory, especially in the East German states, Chancellor Kohl forecast that the East German economy would be at the West German level within two or three years. Against the urgent advice of the Bundesbank, he added to inflationary pressures by accepting a one-for-one exchange of the high-value West German mark for the worthless East German mark. Like candidate George Bush's promise not to raise taxes in the 1988 U.S. presidential election campaign, Chancellor Kohl also promised before the election that the transformation of the East German economy could be achieved without raising taxes in West Germany.

But the disparity between the two economies was far too great. As experience in other former Warsaw Pact countries shows, the task of converting socialist economies to a free-market system is far too difficult a process to be painless or rapid. In fact, the costs for West Germany associated with German unification and the collapse of the Soviet system are enormous and will continue enormous. In 1990, Germany spent DM 50 billion (equivalent to $29 billion at the rate of 1.70 to the dollar) for the reconstruction of the former German Democratic Republic (GDR) and twice that, DM 100 billion, in 1991. In further outlays linked with unification, Germany by the spring of 1993 had made available a total of DM 85 billion to Russia and other successor states; this sum includes the costs of Soviet troop withdrawals from Germany and other loans and credits. These payments to the former Soviet Union compare with DM 15 billion from the United States and DM 5 billion from Japan in the same period.[2] By mid-1993, unification had cost Germany over DM 500 billion.

In 1992–93, the economic situation in East Germany continued to deteriorate sharply despite Chancellor Kohl's promises to rapidly close the gap between the two economies. Taking together the figures for 1990, 1991, and 1992, gross national product in East Germany declined 50 percent from the preunification level. Industrial output shrank by roughly 70 percent. Total employment in East Germany dropped from 10 million before unification to a little more than 5 million in 1992. Official unemployment reached 30 percent during 1992, 45 percent if early retirees are included. In 1991, real GDP per person in East Germany was 30 percent of that in West Germany, only a small improvement in the wide gap before unification. In 1993, inflation rates in East Germany were at 12–14 percent; the nationwide rate was 6 percent. Meanwhile, the unemployment rate in West Germany, over 10 percent before unification, went down to 7.5 percent in 1993. Despite all the difficulties, West Germany was better off after unification while the East German economy and living standard was far below the preunification level. Not unnaturally, this rankled in the East.

To cope with this situation, Chancellor Kohl had to renounce his campaign pledge of unification without tax increases. In mid-1991, income taxes for individuals and corporations were increased by 7.5 percent for a one-year period. Taxes on gasoline, heating oil, and tobacco were sharply increased. The government also increased value-added taxes (VAT) by 14 percent in January 1993. The increase in the federal German budget deficit to pay the costs associated with unification was calculated at over DM 100 billion a year, raising the overall German budgetary deficit to 7 percent of GNP, twice as large as the peak rate of the U.S. deficit.[3]

In Group of Seven (G–7) meetings in 1991 and 1992, the Bundesbank rejected urgings of the United States and its EC partners to lower German interest rates in order to stimulate the economy of the United States and other G–7 countries. To the contrary, in December 1991, it raised its discount rate still further to its highest level since World War II in order to counter inflation. In addition to inflationary effects of deficit payments to East Germany, the Bundesbank was trying to cope with the inflationary impact of average West German wage increases of over 7 percent in 1991 as well as much increased outlays by the German Länder, or states.[4] In early 1992, the German steelworkers got a wage increase of 6.5 percent, well over the 5 percent limit that the Bundesbank and the German government said was the maximum allowable to avoid inflation, a recession, and large-scale unemployment.

Chancellor Kohl belatedly tried to get across the point that all Germans, and not only the East Germans, would have to pay the huge costs of German unification. On these grounds the government refused to meet demands in April 1992 of a wage increase of 5.4 percent (arbitrated down from an original demand of nearly 10 percent) by the Union of Public Service and Transport Workers. The union declared a nationwide strike in public transportation, postal services, medical services, and trash collection. The Frankfurt airport, Europe's main air traffic hub, was closed down when its fire department joined the strike. It was the most widespread strike in West Germany in over thirty-five years. The government finally conceded to the 5.4 percent increase it had originally rejected. The country barely escaped a round of strikes in the private sector. Other strikes followed in East Germany. West German workers were now making more than $25 an hour, the world's highest wages.[5]

In 1992, a total of DM 218 billion in public funds was transferred from West to East Germany. The estimated figure for 1993 was DM 112 billion, or 5 percent of GNP. The important thing is that three-quarters of these expenditures were not for investment, but for payments to individuals in the form of unemployment benefits, family allowances, pensions, and job retraining expenses. Future costs of unification could be well over DM 100 billion a year for the rest of the decade. This includes costs for moving the capital of Germany to Berlin, debts of the Treuhandanstalt, the agency charged with privatizing former state-owned businesses in the East, which has taken over an estimated DM 300 billion worth of debts of bankrupt former East German companies, subsidies to the budgets of the East German Länder, or states, and modernizing East German telecommunications.

In addition to continuing unemployment benefits and pensions, very large sums will also have to be found to compensate former owners of property in East Germany and to clean up a disastrous environmental legacy. The Federal Association of German Industry, the recognized spokesman for German business, warned in October 1991 that rebuilding the infrastructure of East Germany—roads, bridges, canals—would require investments of close to DM 500 billion by the year 2000, including DM 127 billion for roads and transportation, and DM 40 billion for energy.[6]

The challenge—and the political requirement—for the German government is to create roughly the same standard of living in all of Germany. According to one calculation, to achieve this, the economy of East Germany would have to grow by 17 percent per year until the year 2000. One German economic institute calculated that it would in fact take twenty years before the living standards in East Germany converged with those in the West.[7]

It is generally expected that in the long run there will be a tremendous boom in the German economy as the rewards from all this investment materialize and East German salaries and consumption levels approach those of West Germany and as the East German industrial plant, which will be the most modern in all of Europe, goes into high gear. But what would happen if these hopes did not materialize and the entire German economy slowed into enduring recession?

The effects could be momentous: still-worse unemployment and collapse of businesses in both parts of Germany, more East German migration to the West, and a serious breach of the Bundesbank discipline that has been at the core of European Community prosperity. For a considerable time at least, Germany could no longer be the motor of economic growth in the European Community and one of the motors of the world economy. Tied in practice to German interest rates, economic activity in the rest of the European Community would slide into recession. The capacity of the most reliable and important donor of economic support to Eastern Europe and the Soviet successor states would be reduced at the time of the recipients' greatest need and of the greatest potential effect on prospects for democracy. Slower growth would increase protectionist tendencies in the European Community and encourage an existing trend in Europe toward national self-preoccupation, to the detriment of multilateral cooperation and actions to cope with a worsening economic and environmental situation in Third World countries. "Europe could become a much more fractious and unhappy place," predicted economist Robert Samuelson in early 1992. "It could be so obsessed with its own problems that it could hardly help with anyone else's."[8]

During 1993, it looked as though precisely this condition had in fact set in. German GNP growth slowed to less than 1 percent in 1992. In November 1992, Germany's five leading economic institutes projected zero GNP growth for Germany in 1993 or even a decline of as much as 1.5 percent. The figures for 1992 showed that German manufacturing output had declined for the first time in a decade.

The economies of the European Community stalled as the German economy slowed. EC unemployment reached over 10 percent; credit had been throttled for over two years as member country national banks were obliged to follow the Bundesbank in its high interest rates in order to avoid heavy capital movement to Germany. Europe was in its worst recession for over ten years.[9] In September 1992, the United Kingdom, Portugal and Ireland were obliged to drop out of the European exchange rate mechanism and in practice devalue their currency.

In August 1993, the economic consequences of German unification—big government budget deficits, rising government debt, and determined action by the German Bundesbank to hold down German interest rates—took further victims. This time, high German interest rates meant that France, now with 11.5 percent unemployment and only 2 percent inflation, could not cut its own interest rates to infuse some new life into its economy. The failure of the Bundesbank to make an expected limited reduction in interest rates led to heavy speculation against the French franc. In a hurried decision, the EC banks broadened the band of permitted deviation from the value of the D mark in the exchange rate mechanism from about 2 percent to over 15 percent, preserving the mechanism on paper and permitting the franc to come down without the humiliation of explicit devaluation. This development, triggered by the economic consequences of German unification, was a real blow to prospects of a single European currency under the Maastricht Treaty, whose original objective had been to tie a unified Germany even closer to the European Community.[10]

In the fall of 1992, a worried Chancellor Kohl proposed a "solidarity pact" of self-restraint among government and opposition employers and trade unions. His objective was to reduce the deficit incurred through financing the recovery of East Germany through achieving cuts in spending from the federal government and the state governments, themselves a major source of the mounting deficit, through self-restraint from the trade unions in wage demands and through increased private investment in East Germany. The attempt at voluntary restraint was only modestly successful, but the federal government bit the bullet and decided to incorporate the solidarity pact cuts in spending for social services and unemployment benefits into the 1994 budget. West Germans were called on to pay still more taxes for German unification, including a renewed 7.5 percent income tax surcharge to begin in 1995. The cuts included a 3 percent reduction in unemployment benefits, a two-year freeze in the level of social security payments, and reduction of child-care benefits.[11]

Finance Minister Theodor Waigel claimed in the summer of 1993 that the German recession had hit its low point. The claim was disputed by some experts. In part the recovery of the German economy depended on the government's capacity to maintain its determination to cut public spending in the face of political pressures expected both from elections in most German states and from nationwide general elections in 1994.[12] It seemed clear that the costs of unification would depress the German and European economies for several years. Indeed, some experts believe that the European economy with Germany at its center is incapable—because of economic and social rigidities, including high wages and social welfare costs—of successfully competing with the more flexible Asian and North American economies. They conclude that for a long time to come, Europe will fall further behind, with continuing recession and high unemployment rates, bringing increased protectionism and economic nationalism in the EC countries. Majority opinion is only somewhat more optimistic.

Strains in the German Polity

After reunification, East Germans wanted to live like their countrymen in the West. West Germans wanted to live as before and to let the East Germans do the job of building a new society on their own. Neither got their wish. Instead, in the early 1990s, with close to 40 percent out of work, unemployed East Germans received only 60 percent of the benefits paid to unemployed workers in West Germany, while East Germans with jobs received only 70 percent of the pay of West Germans. For their part, West Germans now paid about 10 percent more taxes, both direct and indirect, for a total of about 45 percent of their income, to meet the costs of bringing up the East German living standard. In these circumstances, it is not surprising that, in a poll in the spring of 1990, 75 percent of East Germans said they felt like second-class citizens; or that, a year later, the figure had risen to close to 90 percent, with sharp growth in mutual resentment between West and East Germans.[13] Germany is unified, but far from united.

Because all East Germans under age sixty have lived only under Nazi and then communist dictatorships, it is not surprising that many are confused and lack personal initiative, with low self-esteem and a low sense of empowerment. These feelings have been intensified by West German domination of East German society. West Germans came over to East Germany and organized East German political parties, elections, state and local governments, businesses, department stores, and banks. West Germany sent 18,000 officials to run both local and state government in East Germany; most of them paid considerably more than East German counterparts. Because unification took place through extending federal German laws and institutions to East Germany, East Germans have no institutions of their own to be proud of; most older East Germans believe they have totally wasted their lives working for a communist regime.

These resentments and disappointments arose rapidly: To the shock of most West Germans, Chancellor Kohl, an authentic hero of German unification, was bombarded by tomatoes and raw eggs during a May 1991 visit to the East German city of Halle only six months after unification and four months after his impressive victory in the December 1990 elections, especially strong in East Germany.

For their part, many West Germans consider East Germans as lazy, ineffective, and ungrateful free-loaders. As the 1990s wore on, this mutual hostility appeared to be hardening into a permanent feature of German politics, something like the rancor between North and South in the United States a generation ago. One result is likely to be a continuing trend toward protest voting and support for political extremes, including the Right, Greens, and the former communists. It is too early to discern what other political effects this enduring animosity will have, but it seems sure to have important ones.

There are many other significant differences in attitude between West and East Germans. A poll published in the *Frankfurter Allgemeine Zeitung* in 1992 showed that 80 percent of West German respondents considered democracy the best form of government, while only 32 percent of Eastern respondents thought so.[14] East Germans continue to show far greater respect for state authority, police, and discipline in the schools than their West German countrymen.[15] East Germans are more national-minded, West Germans more international. West Germans are far more positive than East Germans toward the European Community and toward NATO. Asked in early 1992 whether they still considered NATO essential for German security, 64 percent of West German respondents said yes, but only 35 percent of East German respondents did so.[16]

Given the continuation of hierarchical views among the East German population, strong feelings that they are being discriminated against, and the economic pressures they face, an increase in extremist political attitudes in East Germany is possible. But this development has not yet crystallized. If extremist politics nonetheless do make headway in East Germany, based on the specific conditions of East German social and economic life, this gain is not likely to be strong enough to decisively affect the all-German political system.

CONFRONTING THE COMMUNIST PAST

Political cohesion in East Germany has also been severely strained by the effort to come to terms with the communist past, a moral, political, and juridical problem that is likely to last for decades. The problem has three aspects: first, bringing to justice those who were responsible for specific crimes of the East German police state; second, the problem of the very large group of East Germans not guilty of specific crimes whose democratic credentials are undermined by some role in the communist state, most often as informants of the secret police, known as STASI; third, the problem of the former communist elite, officials, and managers who retain positions of influence within East German society, especially in the economy. Their power is maintained by interpersonal links of common interest and mutual support, informal mutual aid groups that Germans call *seilschaften*, a term used by mountain-climbing teams whose survival often depends on the single rope that links them together.

All Eastern European states have the problem of cliques of former communists in positions of influence. The potential negative political effects of this phenomenon are less serious in East Germany than elsewhere because of the continuing stake of the West German polity in minimizing the influence of this group. Former communists may regain political influence in East Germany, but they will not gain control of the government of all of Germany, as they have in Poland.

On the other hand, the issue of coming to terms with the past, of retribution and retaliation, is being pursued with more follow-through, determination, and also more vindictiveness in East Germany than in other former Warsaw Pact states. This is not only a result of traditional German thoroughness. The problem is more acute in East Germany than elsewhere because those in East Germany who are demanding that specific individuals be brought to justice or that former high party officials not be permitted to serve as officials or judges of the new democratic state are not simply a minority on their own like similar people in the East European states, who are forced to compromise on this issue. Instead, those who raise the issue in East Germany can rely on strong support from political parties and media in West Germany.

Nonetheless, early efforts to bring senior officials of the former Socialist Unity Party (SED) regime to trial for specific misdeeds while holding high office were not successful. In September 1991, four former East German border guards were brought to trial for shooting an East German citizen, Chris Gueffroy, as he tried to escape over the Berlin Wall from East Germany in February 1989. Gueffroy was the last of up to 600 East Germans killed trying to escape since August 1961, when the East German regime walled itself off from West Germany in an effort to block the mass defection of its citizens. After a five-month trial, two of the four border guards, who had all claimed that they were not responsible but had acted on higher orders, were sentenced and two acquitted.[17]

This action was the first to decide that West German criminal law could be applied to events that took place in East Germany under communist rule. It opened the way for prosecution of about 300 former East German officials accused of wrongdoing, including the inconclusive trial of SED boss Erich Honecker and five colleagues in his repressive regime that brought the release on health grounds of Honecker himself and two colleagues and the sentencing in September 1993 of the three remaining defendants to short prison terms.[18]

An even more festering aspect of the communist past and a grim reminder of the tragedy and moral waste of daily life under totalitarian dictatorship is the question of what to do about those who had some relationship with the East German secret police (the STASI) either as officials or as informants. The STASI kept files on 6 million of East Germany's 16 million people and used an estimated 500,000 informants to keep track of them. Beginning in 1992, East Germans could see their own

STASI file from the 120 miles of files still preserved and learn the names of these informants. Already, either because of information in those files or because of allegations from former STASI personnel and others, a large number of East German political leaders have been implicated as former STASI informants.

This divisive issue could eliminate from public service an entire group of people some of whom courageously engaged and argued with the old East German leadership in the interest of more rights for individuals or for the whole country. Given the small size of the democratically inclined East German elite and the limited number of East Germans who have the interest and ability to enter public office, the push for purification eliminates from political life a large part of the age group over thirty and increases the influence of West German "carpetbaggers" over East German politics. Despite sensible calls for reconciliation among all Germans, controversy over this tragic and divisive issue will continue to reduce the cohesion of the East German electorate as well as those of the Eastern European countries.[19] But because of the large size and power of West Germany and its institutions, it is doubtful whether the strains and tensions in East Germany described here will seriously endanger German democracy.

THE FOREIGNERS

Clearly, Easterners were not the only Germans dissatisfied by the process of unification. As soon as it became evident with the fall of the Berlin Wall in November 1989 that East Germany would be an economic burden, many West Germans reacted adversely. Coming at a time of continuing high unemployment (then 10 percent) in West Germany, the idea that hundreds of thousands of East Germans should come to the West and receive generous start-up grants and then that West Germans should pay monumental sums to keep the East Germans in East Germany and to improve their living standard was too much for many West Germans. The feeling was so widespread that Oskar Lafontaine, unsuccessful candidate of the Social Democrats in the December 1990 general elections, tried to capitalize on it by making slowdown of the expensive reunification process the main plank of his election platform. But a majority of West Germans felt it was not morally right to harbor such resentments against fellow Germans. Instead, resentful Germans in both East and West unhappy over the costs and difficulty of unification and a gathering economic recession found a more acceptable scapegoat: foreigners in Germany.

Three categories of people are involved: "ethnic Germans" from Eastern Europe and the former Soviet Union; "asylum seekers"; and "guest workers." As regards the first two categories, the authors of the 1949 Basic Law or constitution of the Federal Republic wished to make amends for the actions of the Nazi regime and also for the consequences of the collapse of the Third Reich for ordinary Germans left behind in foreign countries as often harshly treated minorities after World War II. They included in the Basic Law two open-ended commitments. One commitment, Article 16, was to political refugees. It stated categorically, "Persons persecuted on political grounds shall enjoy the right of asylum." The second, Article 116, entitles people of German ethnic origin living in countries from which Germans were expelled or had to flee after World War II to automatic German citizenship.

These were noble aims. Both were honored in the forty years between establishment of the Federal Republic and collapse of the Soviet system in Eastern Europe. Then both contributed to political catastrophe. Under Mikhail Gorbachev's reforms, whose effects spread to Eastern Europe, emigration of ethnic Germans became easier. After the collapse of communist government in Eastern Europe and of police-state controls over passports and borders, there was real freedom of movement to prosperous Germany from the East for the first time since the mid-1930s. This freedom was used by hundreds of thousands of people.

As regards ethnic Germans in the East, relaxation of controls in the Soviet Union under Gorbachev brought 202,000 ethnic Germans in 1988, nearly 400,000 both in 1989 and in 1990, and 220,000 in 1991, when a requirement went into effect that German consulates abroad should review evidence of German ethnicity on the spot rather than automatically issue visas. The figure for 1992 was again about 200,000, with more than 3 million interested ethnic Germans still in the former Soviet Union and a backlog of 700,000 applications. The total entering Germany since 1988 was over 2 million. In addition, about 300,000 East Germans moved to West Germany in 1991 and a like number in 1992, probably a million in all since the Berlin Wall came down in late 1989, so by 1993, there were over 3 million new German residents in Western Germany.

As for asylum seekers, Germany received 100,000 in 1989, over 200,000 in 1990, over 256,000 in 1991 (when the United States took 75,000 in a similar category), and about 440,000 in 1992. These figures do not include the approximately 250,000 refugees from former Yugoslavia that Germany took in a separate category. As a result of these migrations, in 1991, West Germany had to find housing and jobs for 670,000 new foreign residents and hard-pressed East Germany for 100,000.[20] The equivalent for the immigration-friendly United States, with a population four times larger than West Germany's 60 million, would have been an influx of nearly 3 million people, four times the actual annual rate of about

800,000 legal immigrants in the 1980s and 1990s. Most of the large increase in German asylum seekers was made up of Eastern Europeans, especially gypsies. A large majority seemed to be motivated by economic considerations rather than political ones, although many of the gypsies had been harshly treated even after the end of communism, especially in Romania.

Part of the problem with asylum seekers was that German authorities were committed to accept and support them until they had a hearing to prove the genuineness of their claims of political persecution. In the earlier years, owing partly to trade union pressure to protect already employed German workers, asylum seekers, then a far smaller number (the figure for 1972 was only 5,000) were not permitted to work but were given free housing and a cash allowance for food until their hearings. These costs often reached DM 10,000 a year per person. As in the United States where there is a similar problem of coping with asylum seekers, the immigration staff assigned to hear asylum cases in Germany is far too small. In 1992, there was a backlog of more than 400,000 cases. The hearing process sometimes takes up to four years, and even when the result is negative (as it has been in 95 percent of cases), persons scheduled for deportation have disappeared into the general population.

The influx of asylum seekers fed the main "security" preoccupation of most Germans, a fear found throughout Europe—that political and economic breakdown in Eastern Europe and in the former Soviet Union would send an unstoppable wave of hundreds of thousands of starving refugees who would have to be taken in and who would consume the substance of German postwar prosperity like a biblical plague of locusts. These worries intensified already strong antiforeigner feelings in the country.

The third category of foreigners in Germany is the more than 4 million Turks, Yugoslavs, Greeks, Italians, Spaniards, and Portuguese who had come as "guest workers," mainly to Western Germany, for jobs in road and building construction, industry, and municipal trash collection and street cleaning, jobs that now-prosperous West Germans were no longer willing to do. The situation was complicated by the fact that, unlike France, which has given citizenship automatically to those born on French soil, Germany has no systematized immigration quota or citizenship procedures. Its citizenship law, passed in 1913, is based mainly on German ethnicity: The child of a German father or German mother can receive citizenship. The result is that second- and third-generation Turks and Yugoslavs living in Germany are still legally foreigners, cannot vote, and have negligible influence on the political process, either locally or nationwide. Taking together guest workers, refugees from the former Yugoslavia, and asylum seekers, Germany had 6.8 million foreign residents in the spring of 1993, most of them in West Germany, where they formed over 10 percent of the population.

Although there was some resentment against immigrant ethnic Germans, many of whom did not speak German and had only a very distant connection with German culture, public resentment focused on non-German asylum seekers and on foreigners in general. Many Germans asked why West Germany should pay huge sums and credits to the Soviet Union, Poland, and other Eastern European states to restore their economies and then open its doors to Eastern Europeans seeking economic prosperity under the guise of political asylum. Or for that matter, why should united Germany permit millions of Turks, Yugoslavs, Italians, Greeks, and Portuguese to live in Western Germany and take jobs away from thousands of unemployed Germans?

The hostility elicited by migration is a serious and increasing problem for all Western states and has led to racial incidents in nearly all European countries. But in Germany, a state that lacks either immigration quotas or accessible procedures for giving foreigners citizenship, and that has taken in by far the largest numbers in Europe, the pressure was greatest and the outcome was worst.

The first result was beatings and muggings of Polish migrants and small traders in East Germany, then in 1990 an outburst of beatings, firebombings, and threats against foreigners throughout Germany. Incidents of racial violence rapidly multiplied after neo-Nazi "skinheads" in September 1991 surrounded an apartment complex for foreign workers and asylum seekers in Hoyerswerda, East Germany. The "siege" lasted for a week, while police and curiosity seekers looked on. Town authorities were finally forced to take the foreigners out by bus and truck. Although until the mid-1980s such offenses averaged fewer than 100 per year, in 1991 the Federal German Criminal Office registered over 1,500 criminal offenses against foreigners. In a copy-cat effect, there were 900 incidents in October 1991 alone, the month after the Hoyerswerda events seemed to show that the German authorities would merely look on. There was also one death in 1991, a classic lynching of an Angolan streetcar rider in Frankfurt/Oder. But in 1992, even worse outbursts of right-wing antiforeigner feeling resulted in nearly 2,285 incidents of racial hatred throughout Germany, including seventeen killings and numerous cases of arson.

Most of these statistics focus only on violence against foreigners by persons believed to have right-wing connections. Using a different method of evaluation that takes no special account of the nationality of victims, Chancellor Kohl reported to the Bundestag in mid-June that federal legal authorities had in 1992 investigated more than 12,000 reported cases of right-wing extremism or xenophobic actions; 10,000 cases were tried in the courts.[21]

The 1992 race incidents included three days of uninterrupted rioting, again under the eyes of a complaisant citizenry and police, in front of a migrant hostel in Rostock, East Germany, in August, and a firebombing with deaths of a Turkish woman, her granddaughter, and a second little girl in Moelln near Hamburg in West Germany in November. Just when there was some hope the worst was over, a horrifying firebombing in Solingen in the industrial Ruhr area of West Germany in May 1993 killed five Turkish women.[22]

In 1990, Chancellor Kohl's Christian Democrats began pressing vigorously for restrictions in German asylum law, which, as we have seen, is anchored in the German constitution. A change in the German constitution requires a two-thirds vote in the German Bundestag; in practice, votes from all major parties. But for two years, the Social Democrats and Free Democrats opposed a change in the constitution and insisted on maintaining the open-ended right of asylum.

Finally, after the incidents in Rostock and Moelln, the Social Democrats and the Free Democrats shifted ground and agreed to amend the Basic Law. In late May 1993, the Bundestag voted by a large majority for an amendment. The new wording, Article 16a, repeats the original language that "Persons persecuted on political grounds shall enjoy the right of asylum," but then goes on to bar persons coming from countries where there is no widespread political persecution.

It was a difficult decision up to the last moment. Many Bundestag members had to be helicoptered in for the deciding vote; the Bundestag was surrounded by over 10,000 determined demonstrators who refused to let anyone through for the vote. To the bitter end, the German left showed the generosity and moral responsibility that motivated the original federal German approach to political asylum. But it had long been evident that the political costs of this approach to the German polity had become so high that it was no longer affordable.[23]

Germany has now adopted the general practice of the EC countries on asylum cases. Arrangements have been made for accelerated hearings within a few days of arrival, partly in fenced-in areas at the Frankfurt/Main Airport and at the Frankfurt/Oder crossing point from Poland, and for the immediate expulsion of the overwhelming majority back to the country they had been in most recently before reaching Germany, on the grounds that asylum requests should have been dealt with by the authorities of those countries. Germany has enlarged this standard EC practice to include the Eastern European states. It has concluded agreements with Poland, Czechoslovakia, Romania, and Bulgaria to accept backlogged asylum cases against payment of processing costs by Germany. The new more restrictive approach went into effect in July

1993. The immediate result was a reduction in asylum applications from 31,123 in June 1993 to 14,521 in August, 1993.[24] Poland, Hungary, and the Czech Republic in turn heavily reinforced their own eastern borders with police and soldiers, and demanded visas from many countries to their south and east. In the first five months of 1993, Hungary turned back over 320,000 would-be migrants.[25]

In June 1993, Chancellor Kohl promised that a new citizenship law replacing the 1913 statute would be passed by the end of 1994. He also announced easing of regulations based on the present law in order to permit citizenship after residence of fifteen years, eight years for those under age twenty-three. But the Chancellor also worried about growing political extremism, both ethnic and Islamic fundamentalist, among Turks and Kurds in Germany.[26]

Among the political costs that caused the German Free Democrats and Social Democrats to change their position on the asylum issue were the state elections in Bremen in September 1991. Together, two right-wing extremist groups, the German Peoples Union and the Republican Party, won 8 percent of the vote in elections where the Social Democrats also lost their long-standing majority. Both extremist parties focused their campaigns on the theme that Germany was being overrun by foreigners. The German Peoples Union nearly doubled its vote from the previous elections and gained representation in the Bremen parliament. In state elections in Schleswig-Holstein in early April 1992, the German Peoples Union received 6.3 percent of the votes and became the third strongest party in the state parliament. At the same time, in state elections in solid-ly Catholic, prosperous Baden-Württemberg, the Christian Democrats lost their majority for the first time since 1946, largely because the Republican Party got 10.9 percent of the vote and fifteen seats in the state parliament.

A public opinion poll in the weekly news magazine *Der Spiegel* at the end of April 1992 showed public support for the Christian Democratic Union (CDU) down to a low 37 percent and the Republican Party topping 5 percent of the population nationwide. The two developments were directly related. Most of the right-wing gains had come from Chancellor Kohl's Christian Democratic Union and its sister party, the Christian Social Union (CSU). According to the poll, the single most important issue for West German voters according to the poll was cutting back the flow of asylum seekers.

Starting as a byproduct of voter dissatisfaction over reunification, the foreigner-asylum seeker issue has revived right-wing extremism in Germany to an extent that probably ensured the representation of the far right in the German Bundestag in the 1994 general elections. For decades, the far right has not been able to muster the minimum 5 percent of popular vote needed for representation in the Bundestag.[27] Equally disquieting was a report of the Federal Criminal Office German Bundeskriminalamt of June 1993 that the great majority of known and suspected offenders in cases of antiforeigner violence were not members of marginal skinhead or right-wing extremist groups, but were from middle-class homes. For example, more than 90 of 152 suspects pursued by German police in April 1993 were from middle-class homes with no criminal record. Only 10 percent were associated with skinhead groups and 13 percent with rightist extremists. This evidence is especially depressing because it suggests that the transfer of values to these young men from their parents and the older generation includes a strong component of racial intolerance.[28] In an individual instance that caused much concern, papers found after his death in the fall of 1993 revealed that Professor Theodor Maunz, one of federal Germany's most respected authorities on constitutional law, had for decades been a clandestine close adviser of the right-wing German Peoples Union.[29]

Deliberately, federal chancellor Helmut Kohl followed the same unpopular course with regard to neo-Nazi attacks on foreigners in Germany as he had earlier with regard to the issues of definitive German recognition of the western borders of Poland and of hostile German public reaction to U.S. involvement in the Gulf War. He did little and said little. He even failed to attend a commemorative memorial service for the Solingen victims. Kohl's inaction was interpreted by friend and foe alike as condoning the antiforeigner sentiment of a majority of Germans. But the chancellor was fighting even now for his political survival in the federal elections of 1994. He was hoping that his behavior would keep most right-wing voters in the ranks of the Christian Democratic Union and the Christian Social Union.

The costs of the attacks on foreigners to the international reputation of the new Germany were high. As racial incidents developed in 1990 and 1991, they were not taken seriously by foreign opinion. As they continued and worsened in 1992, the sheer number and viciousness of the incidents unavoidably awakened memories of barbarous Nazi racism.

But aside from the tragic victims, the main costs of antiforeigner excesses was borne by the democratic institutions of Germany and of other prosperous Western states that face the asylum-immigration problem. In Germany, the costs of coping with antiforeigner feeling included tighter controls on all entry to the country. Germany's eastern border was increasingly policed and fortified like the southern border of the United States, and for similar reasons; a perceptive journalist commented that Germany's eastern border with Poland was becoming the "Rio Grande of Europe."[30] Post-cold war freedom of travel in Europe had been short-lived. Domestically, the steps undertaken by the German government against neo-Nazi groups, although justified, diminished political freedoms of speech, assembly, and organization for all Germans. These measures included the prohibition of at least six political groups; the publicly announced surveillance of a political party; restrictions on public statements by two rightist propagandists; banning of skinhead music with racist lyrics; restrictions on public display of party symbols or insignia; increases in prison sentences for assault convictions; weaker legal restrictions on imposing prison sentences; and finally a decree in December 1993 declaring that membership in the Republican Party, which was still legal, was grounds for firing federal officials. This politically astute move warned German voters that members of the Republican Party were considered political extremists without resorting to the more difficult move of proving the party illegal. But it also subjected federal officials to a new examination of political loyalty.[31] At the same time, the race riots and the controversy over asylum seekers have strengthened extremist opinion to the benefit of those right-wing political parties that remain legal. The economic costs of receiving, housing, and processing asylum seekers and then deporting them and of a tighter guard on Germany's borders are considerable, as are the additional costs of domestic public order.

At the end of 1992, democratic Germans showed, in part through public demonstrations of hundreds of thousands of people, that they realized the nature of the problem and intended to do something positive about it. Half a million demonstrated throughout the country on January 30, 1993.

New procedures and reduced numbers will reduce the inflammatory effects of the asylum problem. Three continuing issues remain: the problem of economic migration, German attitudes toward the nearly 7 million foreigners who live among them, and German citizenship. These developments have shown that Germany has an enduring race relations problem as do the United States, France, and Italy. Ultimately, Germany will have to become a practicing multiethnic society and establish some type of immigration quota with assured access to citizenship rights.

In the meanwhile, the German style of ethnic conflict and the abundant evidence of a continuing strain of right-wing extremism in German political opinion will continue to diminish Germany's international reputation and its capacity for international leadership. However, although the problem of race relations is serious, it seems plausible that both government authorities and individual Germans will gradually learn how to cope with it more constructively.

THE WEAKENING GERMAN POLITICAL SYSTEM

Even though this may be so, dissatisfaction from all political directions over the asylum issue and frustration with the inability of the German political system to deal with it—and with the related attacks on foreigners—

have combined with dissatisfactions arising from German unification and the economic recession in a process of alienation from the established political parties that is gravely weakening the vital center of the German polity to the benefit of extremes of both right and left and that could, if they continue, bring lack of trust in the democratic system as such.

The aftermath of reunification dealt heavy blows to Chancellor Kohl and his Christian Democrats. Kohl aimed for a visible upturn in the German economy by the summer of 1994 before the general elections that autumn. With an eye on that election, the German government paid Russia to advance the date of final departure of Russian soldiers from East Germany by six months so that the departure would take place, commemorated by appropriate, highly visible ceremonies, the summer before the 1994 elections. Beyond that, the chancellor was depending on the cautious "no experiments" attitude that had characterized the German electorate for many years.

But Chancellor Kohl faced an uphill fight. After twelve years in government, the accumulation of boredom and resentment against his Christian Democratic Union was high. Kohl also had to contend with the broad disaffection from established political parties that characterizes most of the world's democracies in the post-cold war period—a flood of pent-up demands and resentments previously held in check by the discipline and mobilization of the cold war confrontation that now batters established parties, whether in government or opposition, in nearly all industrialized countries—France, Italy, Britain, Japan, and the United States. In Germany, this alienation was intensified many times over by towering public dissatisfaction and disappointment with the major parties' handling of the unification and asylum issues as well as of a third highly divisive, emotional problem, the question of whether, under the historical shadow of Nazi military aggression, German armed forces should be deployed beyond the borders of Germany.

These dissatisfactions account not only for the rise of right-wing political parties at the expense of the Christian Democrats, but also for the decline of other established German political parties. Since Helmut Schmidt left office in 1981, the opposition Social Democrats have foundered with a succession of weak and unconvincing leaders unable to pull together the warring factions of the party. Many of the lost votes were picked up by the environmentalist Greens. Public opinion polls indicated that the Christian Social Union, the Bavarian sister party of the Christian Democrats, would for the first time in decades fall below 50 percent of the popular vote in the 1994 state elections. The Free Democrats had barely avoided political extinction for years and had lost Hans Dietrich Genscher, their most popular leader who rather suddenly resigned in April 1992.

The problem faced by all the established parties was powerfully illustrated in the Hamburg state elections of September 1993 where governing Christian Democrats and the opposition Social Democrats each lost about 10 percent of the vote they had gained in the elections two years before and the Free Democrats failed to get the required minimum of 5 percent of the vote and dropped out of the state legislature as a result. The Greens doubled their previous vote to about 14 percent. A protest party without any party platform called the Instead Party picked up 6 percent of the vote. The right-wing parties collectively got 8 percent of the vote. The November 1993 nationwide communal elections in Italy brought a strikingly similar result. There, the brief cause of alienation was corruption and crime rather than incompetence of the major parties as in Germany. But Italian voters turned out hundreds of local Christian Democratic and Socialist administrations in favor of the neo-Communists and neo-Fascists. In particular, the Christian Democrats lost nearly 35 percent of the vote they had in the last general elections. Back in Germany, communal elections in Brandenburg in December 1993 again brought a loss of about 10 percent for the Christian Democrats and a marked increase in extremist votes. This time, it was the Party of Democratic Socialism, the renamed former East German Communist Party, which was the main beneficiary of the protest vote, as in Poland and Russia.

Even if the German economy picks up, the disaffection of the German electorate with the established parties is very widespread, deep-seated, and enduring. On the national level, this probably means the end of the center-right Christian Democrat-Free Democrat coalition, which has ruled in West Germany through most of the postwar period and in united Germany since 1990. Disaffection with the established parties could open the possibility of a Christian Democratic Union-Social Democratic Party (SPD) coalition government, a coalition of all three established parties— CDU, SPD, and Free Democratic Party—or, though less likely, even a left-wing coalition of SPD and Greens, possibly with the Free Democrats. The backlash of disaffection seems very likely to increase both abstention from voting and protest votes for the political extremes, the Greens on the left and the right-wing Republicans. The latter could gain considerably more votes than the minimum needed to enter the Bundestag and could have opportunities for further expansion in an opposition role. The only time a CDU-SPD government was tried in Germany (1966–69), voter support for right-wing parties increased.

If it were a one-time phenomenon, an increased protest vote for the Republicans or for the Greens would not of itself have a decisive meaning. But it looks as though the phenomenon may be enduring. The result in that case may well be weak government in Germany, as well as an ongoing major realignment of political forces whose long-term direction remains unclear. However, there is a more serious underlying problem: In many individual voters, rejection of the main political parties as incompetent is not widely separated from the rejection of the institutions of democratic government as incompetent to solve the main problems of the time. This need not automatically lead back to authoritarian rule; it could lead forward to political innovation.

WORRIES ABOUT GERMAN DOMINATION

Outside worries that a more powerful Germany would seek to dominate the European Community and Eastern Europe have been a historically conditioned reflex reaction to German unification. They would have come almost without regard to circumstances. No matter what the Germans actually do, the worries will continue far into the future.

However, in an extreme situation, German porcelain-smashing in the European Community could lead to formation of an anti-German coalition of other members and paralyze the Community. This is the traditional fault line of the European Community; it means in practice that France becomes alienated from Germany and leads a coalition against it inside the EC, which paralyzes all EC decisionmaking. Former chancellor Helmut Schmidt gloomily predicts, for example, that unless the Deutsche Mark is in fact replaced by a single European currency open to broader political control by other EC states, a strong mark will make Germany the "masters" of the European Community and inevitably lead to formation of an anti-German coalition.[32] For the short term, however, although German relations with EC countries and Eastern Europe will have their ups and downs, there is little possibility of this kind of outright confrontation as long as a self-preoccupied, politically divided Germany continues to struggle with the economic and social consequences of unification.

Perhaps in five or six years, after the East German economy has been renovated, German behavior could conceivably lead to more serious frictions with Germany's neighbors. But it is equally plausible that divided domestic opinion over issues like the role of German armed forces abroad and public resentment of the Germans over exploitation of Germany as the rich man of Europe will at least for a time cause Germans to shrink from a leadership role in the European Community, in peacekeeping, and in financing the economic recovery of Eastern European and Soviet successor states.

Indeed, in the early 1990s, Germany's failure to meet the often excessive expectations of many outsiders as to Germany's postunification economic and foreign policy performance ultimately led to widespread concerns abroad over German self-preoccupation, concerns intensified by evidence of antimilitarism so deep-seated that Germany, like Japan, has thus far been unable to engage in UN peacekeeping except on a very limited scale.

In the light of frequently voiced fears that Germany may become too assertive and seek to dominate Europe, these concerns are paradoxical. Similar concerns about excessive self-preoccupation have been raised about Japan and about the United States, concerns that these countries will instead preoccupy themselves with domestic concerns and make only a less than maximum contribution to multilateral efforts to solve world problems. The vision that all three countries, each with great leadership capability, could turn inward to deal with their own problems leaving the international community rudderless, is a recurrent apprehension of the new era. Public opinion the world over argues that their own countries should do less, but that other large countries must do more.

We have traveled a long way from the highly mobilized pattern of cold war global East-West confrontation to these concerns over insufficient international involvement of the most powerful "Western" states. As some visualize the problem, Germans want Germany to be permitted to be an "ordinary" country without extraordinary demands placed on it and without an extraordinary past.

As a facet of the self-absorption of Germans in problems of unification, the level of German interest in European unity has visibly slackened since 1990. But, reflecting postwar Germany's desire to work its way back into the community of nations, the level of German public interest in European integration has since the outset been higher than in other European countries. A diminution in this level is not evidence of hypernationalism.

When German unification became imminent at the end of 1989, French leaders thought, almost by reflex, of gaining a still tighter grip on a larger Germany. Chancellor Kohl acted to overcome French reservations over unification by rapidly agreeing with President François Mitterrand to move toward European monetary and political union. After only two years of negotiation in the European Community, the steps leading to this objective were agreed at the summit meeting of Community leaders at Maastricht in December 1991. Yet German public opinion, too, recoiled from the far-reaching draft treaties agreed in Maastricht as the process of ratifying these treaties began in each of the EC member states. Public opinion polls indicated that most Germans wanted to retain their own D mark and were apprehensive about relinquishing it for a common European currency. In the same vein, they were also chary about diluting the strict control over money and credit of their own Bundesbank, which had maintained a stringent anti-inflationary policy throughout the postwar years, even though the new European Community monetary and banking system defined in the Maastricht Treaties had been modeled on the Bundesbank.

Ironically, these German reservations about European integration were coming at a time when the Bundesbank itself had been forced to relax its standards to permit mounting deficits, high (for Germany) inflation at 4.3 percent, and record-high interest rates. Pro-Community feeling in Germany was still strong enough to overcome these second thoughts,[33] and in December 1992, the Bundestag ratified the Maastricht Treaty with a high majority. In October 1993, the German Constitutional Court rejected claims that the Maastricht Treaties would progressively arrogate German sovereignty, and the way was open for entry into force of the treaties, which took place on November 1, 1993. However, there were many signs that pro-European sentiment in Germany had passed its peak, and was in serious decline in a period of increasing national feeling, both healthy and xenophobic. According to public opinion polls in the fall of 1993, fewer than 20 percent of German respondents saw any advantage in German membership in the EC, and the conservative Bavarian Christian Social Union party, facing serious losses to the nationalistic extreme right in the 1994 state elections, began deliberately to distance itself from Chancellor Kohl and from further European integration. In the style of Charles de Gaulle's "Europe des patries," the newly elected chairman of the Bavarian Christian Social Union insisted that there should be an end to euphoria over a united Europe and that the European Community could not and should not develop beyond the stage of a confederation of states.[34]

European worries about increased German assertiveness were triggered when Germany struck out on its own in the fall of 1991 on the issue of granting diplomatic recognition to Slovenia and Croatia following their secession from the Yugoslav Federation. Although the German Foreign Office had earlier recommended against recognition in early August while fighting in Croatia had been under way only for a month, Chancellor Kohl had raised the possibility of outside recognition of the independence of Slovenia and Croatia if the Yugoslav Federation armed forces did not disengage and return to their barracks. In September, Foreign Minister Hans Dietrich Genscher raised the idea of recognition of Slovenia and Croatia in the EC Council of Ministers but did not receive support for this action. In October, with uncustomary emphasis, Genscher threatened unilateral German action if the EC did not act collectively. In a ten-hour meeting of EC foreign ministers in Paris in mid-December, Minister Genscher again threatened to recognize the two republics unilaterally by Christmas if the EC did not act. In the interest of avoiding an open break with Germany, the council agreed with reluctance that EC states would recognize the two states by January 15. The EC also urged member states to make recognition dependent on the ability of the two states to meet agreed criteria on democratic institutions and human rights, but this requirement was not compulsory.

German insistence that the European Community recognize the independence of the seceding Yugoslav republics of Slovenia and Croatia ran against the conviction of most EC governments, as well as of the Bush administration and UN secretary general Javier Pérez de Cuellar, that diplomatic recognition of Slovenia and Croatia would lead to more military action by the Serbs and worsen the situation in Yugoslavia. In fact, diplomatic recognition of Croatia and then of Bosnia-Herzegovina did intensify Serbian efforts to gain control of more territory in both. Ironically, the aim of Germany and other Western countries in recognizing Slovenia, Croatia, and Bosnia was to decrease the hold of the Serb-dominated authorities over these republics. But this was only one of many questionable Western decisions in the former Yugoslavia.

In retrospect, the German push for Croat and Slovene recognition does not appear to have been the precursor of a pattern of German assertiveness. Instead, it seems to have been an instance, rare in postwar German history, in which German public opinion, the German political parties acting unanimously, and the media stampeded the German government into acting against its original inclinations. At least part of the popular motivation arose from the belief that German unification had come about through years of West German insistence on the right of self-determination, a right finally exercised by the East German electorate that should be open to others. This sentiment caused Germany to press early for the independence of the Baltic states from Soviet domination. The actions of the German government were also influenced by pressures from the 700,000 Yugoslav guest workers in the Federal Republic, the majority of them Croats.

During the years following the founding of the Federal Republic, there was a good deal of worry inside and outside Germany over the possibility of right-wing developments among German refugees and expellees from territories in the East. Yet, almost unnoticed in the clamor over neo-Nazi skinheads, the formal end of the political crusade of the 12 million expellee Germans, a large group that once had its own influential political party and a separate cabinet post, came with a whimper, and not a political explosion. In the Bundestag ratification in May 1992 of the German Treaty with Poland accepting as definitive Poland's western border at the Oder-Neisse line, only thirteen deputies of the Christian Democratic Union and its sister party, the Christian Social Union, voted against the treaty, and ten abstained. All were representatives of refugee or expellee groups. The West German political and economic system—

and not least the German political parties, especially the Christian Democrats—had done a remarkable job in integrating this group into German society and in providing it political representation while restraining it from political extremism.[35] The passage of time had also thinned the ranks of the expellee organizations.

Despite this constructive outcome, does the issue of Germany's eastern borders represent a threat for the future, an irredentist issue that could be exploited to aid the emergence of an extremist government in Germany or even lead to conflict between Germany and Poland, Russia, Lithuania, or the Czech Republic, all of which incorporate in their borders territories earlier belonging to the Reich? The German right-wing parties, given a powerful boost by the social tensions connected with German unification and the immigration issue, will in future almost certainly also pick up the border issue in the effort to attract voters from refugee and expelled groups. However, this problem seems as definitively settled as anything can be in international politics, with treaties protected by a range of mediation, human rights, and conflict resolution institutions of the CSCE. Extremists will not have much success in making the issue a major one unless there is prior serious economic and political collapse in Germany.

In fact, the question of German domination over Eastern Europe appears to have been superseded by history: Today, Poland and Czechoslovakia are as fortunate to be neighbors of the new Germany as they were unfortunate to be neighbors of the old Germany. To the extent of German capability, enlightened self-interest will maintain German support and economic help for the political stability and economic progress of these adjoining countries. More distant Romania, Bulgaria, and Albania will receive less help. Fears of excessive German political ties with Russia are academic as long as Russia remains an economic and political morass, as may be the case for decades. Germany will not trade off close relations with the West for a closer relationship with a disintegrated Russia. Here, too, the opposite fear, that Germany will not be able to do enough to help Russia, is far more plausible.

The more fundamental reply to the question of whether Germany will attempt to use its economic and political power to dominate the European Community or the East is that the answer depends most directly on the internal health of German democracy. That health is good even though now showing some strain from unification.

THE FUTURE ROLE OF GERMAN ARMED FORCES

One of the strongest positive developments in postwar West Germany was the establishment of a new officer corps with positive views toward democracy and of successful institutions of civilian control of the military. There have been several cases of corruption by civilian officials in armament procurement, but in the nearly forty years of its existence since 1955, the Federal German Bundeswehr has not raised a single major question as to its democratic orientation. This record seems likely to continue. The Two-Plus-Four Treaty of 1990 limits German active-duty military personnel to a total of 370,000 men, down from the combined total of West and East German forces of 660,000 active-duty personnel in 1989. The treaty forbids Germany to have nuclear, chemical, or biological weapons. The Conventional Forces in Europe (CFE) Treaty, which went into effect in November 1992, limits the heavy equipment of the German armed forces to about 4,000 tanks, 3,500 armored combat vehicles, 2,700 artillery pieces, 900 combat aircraft, and 300 attack helicopters, still the largest armed forces in Europe next to those of the Soviet successor states. However, together the latter are allowed five times as much as the German total.

In February 1992, the German cabinet adopted a plan to cut the Bundeswehr from its present strength of 454,000 to the treaty figure of 370,000 (almost all East German military personnel have been discharged with the exception of some younger officers placed on probationary status for possible takeover into the Bundeswehr). As presented by then Defense Minister Gerhard Stoltenberg, the new Bundeswehr would consist of eight instead of twelve divisions, organized into twenty-eight brigades (twenty brigades will be disbanded); there will be a rapid reaction force of seven brigades with air and navy support. Two of the eight divisions will continue to be stationed in East Germany. The German navy will be reduced from 180 to 90 vessels. Savings from the spending level of DM 52 billion for 1992 were expected to amount to about DM 4 billion a year over the next decade, a decrease of about 7 percent annually. Germany planned a reserve structure with the capacity to expand to 900,000 men under full mobilization (as contrasted with the earlier full mobilization total of 1.3 million for the West German forces alone).[36] However, by February 1993, only a year later, under the impact of recession and the continuing impact of unification costs, it became evident that the government intended to cut German forces still further to a level of only 300,000 active-duty personnel.[37]

Unless some future German government broke out of the Two-Plus-Four Treaty and the CFE Treaty, the country could not build its armed forces to a size sufficient to be a serious threat to European security. Of all possible security problems that could arise with regard to the unified Germany, this is one of the most implausible—except in one particular set of circumstances to which we will return at the end of this chapter.

Indeed, as the Gulf War confrontation with Iraq reached the combat stage in the late winter of 1991, Germany's NATO allies, above all the United States, received an unpleasant surprise. As it assembled its military forces for the Gulf, the United States received rapid, effective help from the German military in moving the U.S. Seventh Corps to embarkation points. Without this help, the move of U.S. troops to the Gulf would have taken much longer. The nearly 4,000 trucks and large amounts of artillery ammunition provided by the Germans to coalition forces in the Gulf were an important component of the coalition's military victory.

However, there was not even a modest German military role in the Gulf. It was fairly clear from earlier German statements that there would be domestic political difficulty in contributing German armed forces to the Gulf coalition. But what was not expected was the near total silence of the German political leadership on the issue. This meant that the only German voice heard was that of the German peace movement, with its rejection of the use of military force against Iraq and overtones of criticism of the United States. Polls showed that 80 percent of the German public supported sanctions, but not war. The German political parties wrangled over whether Germany should send German aircraft as part of NATO's air-mobile force to Turkey, a NATO member, to protect Turkish territory against possible Iraqi reprisals for the use of Turkish air bases for U.S. aircraft bombing Iraq. Opponents argued that such reprisals would be in response to provocation and were not a clear case of purely aggressive attack against the territory of a NATO member state. In the end, the German aircraft went, with some ground-based air defenses in the bargain. Germany also released some of its own Patriot batteries to be sent to Israel, where they were operated by U.S. personnel. But the German objections left a bad taste.

German opposition to involvement of German armed forces in the Gulf War reflected more than near-total absorption in the immediate problems of German unification. Inevitably, German attitudes toward the use of force are shaped by memories of the past. Despite the conclusion of many outsiders that Germany after unification was now a major world power, most Germans did not want this outcome. In the *Infratest* poll published by the *Sueddeutsche Zeitung* on January 30, 1990, 75 percent of the German respondents said that unified Germany should keep out of future international conflicts. A large majority thought Germany should model itself on the role of neutral Switzerland. For many Germans, now that the cold war was over, there was no more need for armed forces. There is a fundamental revulsion among the German people toward the use of military force, a feeling based on the experience of World War II, which caused the death of millions of Germans, and the cold war confrontation, which divided Germany and threatened its extinction by nuclear arms. West Germany's new model army was the best in Europe, but this had been at best an unpleasant defensive duty. There were no more Prussians in jackboots.

Germany's Western allies should have been delighted at this convincing evidence of the German population's conversion from aggressive militarism, similar to Sweden's change from being the terror of eighteenth-century Europe to its modern peace-seeking role. (Modern Sweden, too, is a favored role model for contemporary Germans, along with Switzerland.) Instead, the allies were deeply upset over Germany's inability to carry its part of the burden of international peacemaking and peacekeeping. The French government, which had spent the past century wishing Germany were weaker militarily, now feared it was too weak. Americans who had seen in Germany a second, larger Great Britain to give loyal aid and endorsement to the United States were even more disappointed. Instead of the second Britain it had hoped for, Robert Gerald Livingston observes, the United States had a second France, fractious and self-centered.[38]

In the debate over this issue, triggered by the wars in the Gulf and in the former Yugoslavia, most center-right Germans thought German military participation in multilateral coalitions for peacekeeping and peace enforcement was desirable and necessary. Center-left Germans were strongly opposed to an outside military role.

The division of German opinion over military involvement found expression in extended debate over amendment of the German Basic Law. The Basic Law (Article 26) prohibits German participation in wars of aggression, but permits participation in a system of collective security (Article 24). Article 87a, an amendment passed in 1956 to permit establishment of the new Bundeswehr, permits the federal German government to establish armed forces for defensive purposes, but to use the armed forces only as explicitly permitted by the Basic Law itself. The article then specifies use of troops in civil emergencies; peacekeeping or peace enforcement is not mentioned.

To win over German public opinion in the bitter debates of the post-war period over whether recently defeated Germany should establish new German armed forces, then-Chancellor Konrad Adenauer and his Christian Democratic supporters had emphasized time and again that the new German forces would be democratically organized and would participate only in defense of their own territory; there would be no repetition of German military imperialism abroad and no more Hitlerite military adventures for Germany. Many German experts, including onetime defense minister Rupprecht Stolz, himself a constitutional lawyer, insisted that no change of the Basic Law was necessary to permit German participation in multilateral peacekeeping. However, given the past emphasis by the Christian Democrats on using the Bundeswehr only to defend Germany's borders and the strong opposition to departure from this position, Chancellor Kohl pledged himself to clarification of the situation through a constitutional amendment, requiring a two-thirds vote in the Bundestag, including the votes of at least some opposition Social Democrats.

But the Social Democratic grassroots supporters had become so anti-military in the course of the cold war that the party leadership repeated-ly failed in its efforts in party meetings to obtain endorsement of German participation limited to peacekeeping forces organized and approved by the UN Security Council. Later, the Social Democrats seemed prepared to accept a constitutional amendment permitting German participation in UN peacekeeping, but not in UN peace enforcement and not in other multilateral contexts like the Western European Union or the CSCE. Finally, Chancellor Kohl slowly moved away from the concept that German military involvement abroad would require prior amendment of the constitution and began instead to establish a record of de facto involvement. He sent German naval units to the Adriatic as part of the Western European Union (WEU) and NATO naval observer forces mon-itoring sanctions in the former Yugoslavia. He sent German personnel to serve in the AWACS aircraft flying over Bosnia to adopt the UN's ban against aircraft flights by the Serbs and other combatants. In December 1992, he announced that 1,600 German troops would be sent to Somalia. The Social Democrats challenged all three developments in the German Constitutional Court, which upheld the government.

It is a welcome development, not a negative one, that Germany did not spring into military action at the first postunification bugle call. It is nat-ural that Germans hesitate to relinquish their postunification hopes of a better world to become active in the very area of national life that their his-tory has made most negative to them. Nonetheless, some German military participation in multilateral peacekeeping and also peace enforcement will ultimately be needed, especially in a UN framework. The United States moved in the summer of 1993 to formally propose membership of Germany and Japan in an expanded UN Security Council, and Germany has indicated interest in becoming a member. Germany cannot isolate itself from UN peacekeeping operations, or support them only economi-cally, without eliciting resentment and estrangement. Germans will have to find some consensus of their own on the narrow middle way between too little and too much military activity. German participation is espe-cially necessary for operating the institutions contributing to European security—the European Community, the CSCE, and the WEU, as well as

NATO. Germany is a major player in these organizations, and they cannot operate effectively without full German participation. Germany will ultimately come out of internal debate over use of German soldiers outside national borders. It will ultimately gain a permanent seat on the United Nations Security Council. But Germany will long retain a useful sensitivity to agreeing to military intervention.

German attitudes will be critical to the future of NATO, both as regards acceptance by the German public of continued deployment of U.S. forces in Germany and as regards a positive German contribution to the political as well as military operations of NATO. Both the United States and France continually try to get Germany to take their side in the political competition between the Western European Union, backed by France, and NATO, supported by the United States. Many American experts consider it a mistake to try to oblige the German government, which wants both, to make a choice between NATO and WEU. They fear that, if obliged to make a definitive choice, Germany may feel compelled to choose European over Atlantic solidarity. In a survey taken at the end of December 1991, 49 percent of West German respondents said all U.S. troops should be withdrawn from Germany; 84 percent of East Germans expressed this view, resulting in an overall national figure of 57 percent supporting total withdrawal. The German government continues to support the U.S. presence, but it has to walk carefully.

SOME CONCLUSIONS ABOUT GERMANY

The end result of this survey of security issues connected with postunification Germany is to eliminate Germany from the list of major potential problems for European security. Only if the multilateral institutions dealing with European security consistently fail in their task of controlling the dangers of ex-Soviet nuclear weapons for Europe and of holding down the level of organized violence in the European region will Germany be motivated to renationalize its defense and to take greater charge of its own security.

Repeatedly, in meetings between Chancellor Helmut Kohl and East German leader Erich Honecker in the second half of the 1980s, the two pledged that, "never again would war spring from German soil." Although Honecker represented East German opinion in little else, these solemn pledges did capture the fundamental determination of the German people not to contribute to conflict through actions of their own, evidenced in the intense antimilitary sentiment of Germans.

A logical consequence of these values is that Germany has become the biggest European consumer of security services from multilateral security institutions like the EC itself, NATO, CSCE, and WEU. In 1990, John

Mearsheimer of the University of Chicago caused an academic uproar when he asserted that, because all states seek to increase their individual security in an insecure world, Germany might ultimately decide to develop nuclear weapons on its own, and that the most rational course the United States could take to reduce the resultant political friction would be to facilitate this development.[39]

There is nothing further from the German mind today than going it alone, an "Alleingang" to develop nuclear weapons. Modern Germany is perhaps the world's most active supporter of the multilateral approach to security, expending ceaseless efforts to strengthen NATO and to expand the CSCE into a pan-European security system, with new permanent institutions for conciliation, mediation, and conflict prevention. Despite serious concerns that Ukraine as well as Kazakhstan will emerge as nuclear weapon states, Germany did not react to these developments as Japan did to the threatened withdrawal of North Korea from the Non-Proliferation Treaty with publicly expressed doubts about the advisability of indefinite renewal of the treaty. Instead, Germany immediately subscribed to the call for indefinite renewal adopted by the NATO Council in its July 1993 meeting in Athens.

But what will happen if these multilateral institutions are not successful over the long term in keeping the peace and providing adequate security for Germany? Up to now, the multilateral institutions in which Germans place so much faith have not done well. For one thing, the European Community, the CSCE, NATO, and the United Nations failed completely to halt the war in the former Yugoslavia despite many, many months of effort.

For Germany, the most important potential security threat is Russia—the possibility of autocratic government there, the possibility that nuclear weapons may play a negative role in Russian foreign policy, the dark possibilities arising from Russian frictions with neighboring states, especially Ukraine, and even the possibility of utter anarchic collapse of Russian society. This fear is the major reason why Germany holds onto its close security relationship with the United States.

But the United States is having great difficulty in resolving the dangerous nuclear logjam in Ukraine. The European security institutions in which Germans have placed so much confidence—the EC, the CSCE, and NATO—have also not been able to contain the killing and tensions in the former Soviet Union—in Nagorno-Karabakh, which threatens outright war between Azerbaijan and Armenia and the possible involvement of Iran and Turkey on one side and of Russia on the other; in Moldova, which from the outset has had the potential of interstate war between Romania, Ukraine, Russia, and Moldova itself; or to resolve the smoldering feud between Ukraine and Russia over control of nuclear weapons and the Crimea.

Among potential negative long-term European security developments are the decline of NATO and the withdrawal of most U.S. forces from Europe in an atmosphere of mutual recrimination; the possible development of autocratic government in Poland, Russia, or Ukraine; continued interstate conflict in Eastern Europe and in the Soviet successor states; an outright war between Russia and Ukraine; and the complete breakdown of the START regime for control of the nuclear weapons of the former USSR, a breakdown that could increase nuclear dangers both to Europe and the United States from Russia, Ukraine, and from Belarus and Kazakhstan as well.

If threats to its security appear greater, Germany would surely make energetic efforts to improve and activate European peacekeeping institutions. But if it is not successful in doing so and the negative developments are protracted, then, in a situation of enduring disappointment and frustration with the multilateral cooperative security approach, German political leaders may begin to think there is a need for more decisive actions of self-protection. They will not formally withdraw from multilateral institutions, but they will think more of the need for autonomous German action. Even in the face of good reason for discussing more independent German action and in the absence of implementing actions, evidence of an ongoing change in fundamental German attitudes on multilateral defense will elicit all the old worries about Germany for its partners. Mutual alienation may well set in. As a result, European multilateral security institutions could become still weaker and ineffective.

But it is vital to realize that Germany's actions in a potential future situation of this kind will not be solo actions. They will not be associated with some specifically German militancy. To the contrary, all the European countries will be doing the same thing in a general collapse of European security institutions; Germany would probably be among the last to give up on multilateral institutions.

We will return to this disturbing possibility after we have reviewed some further security risks in the new Europe and have more closely evaluated the capability of NATO, the CSCE, and other European security institutions to cope with these problems.

8

The Sword of Islam, the Dagger of Migration

We have reviewed the spectrum of potential threats to European security, including those arising from the nuclear weapons of the ex-Soviet Union, political instability in Russia, and from continuing ethnic conflicts in the Yugoslav republics and in the Soviet successor states. In the eyes of many Europeans, there are at least two further major threats to European security. First, the possibility of uncontrollable migration from the east, from the East European and Soviet successor states, and from the south, the North African states. Second, the flow of North African immigrants is connected in European perceptions with a still more menacing possibility—the possible consolidation of the Islamic states in a hostile alliance against Western Europe comprising a vast arc ranging from Central Asia through the Middle East and its vital oil reserves and on across North Africa all the way to Morocco.

The Immigration Threat

The increasing flow of migrants throughout the world to the richer industrial countries from less-developed ones is already a major social and political problem for the industrialized countries, one that will become far more difficult in the coming decades of intensifying population and resource pressures. Modern communications have brought graphic evidence of Western prosperity to the eyes of millions of Third World people. Air travel has become cheaper and more widespread.

The end of the cold war eased travel restrictions globally. The United Nations Population Fund estimates that in 1992, 80 million people moved across borders to seek better economic opportunities, the majority in Africa and Asia, but 15 million of them in North America and 15 million in Western Europe.[1]

In the United States, the flow of illegal migrants from Mexico, Central America, and the Caribbean, including the desperate Haitian boat people, is an enormously complex and difficult problem that has contributed to the social and economic problems of America's cities. The United States as a country composed of immigrants is more accustomed than Europe to the problem of people knocking on its doors or trying to get around or under these doors. Even so, state governments in California, Texas, and Florida have sought emergency federal aid to pay the expanding social services costs for illegal migrants from Mexico and Haiti. The clandestine arrival of shiploads of illegal would-be immigrants from as far away as China caused the Clinton administration in July 1993 to announce new restrictions on asylum seekers to cope with problems similar to those of Germany.

As cold war restrictions in Eastern Europe relaxed and the war in former Yugoslavia displaced hundreds of thousands of people, immigration to Western Europe from North Africa and Eastern Europe (including legal immigrants, illegal immigrants, asylum seekers, refugees, and ethnic Germans) increased from a level of about 1 million in 1985 to 3 million in 1992. Regular immigrants in 1992 doubled from 700,000 to 1.3 million; asylum seekers quadrupled from 170,000 to 690,000; estimated illegal entrants went up from 50,000 to 400,000. Germany got the majority of asylum seekers (438,000) and roughly half the Yugoslav refugees (250,000), plus 200,000 ethnic Germans from the East. The costs to European Community states to cope with asylum cases alone ballooned from $2.1 billion in 1988 to $8.3 billion in 1992.[2]

We have already described the dismaying outcome in Germany. Antiforeigner violence and support for xenophobic political parties increased in nearly every European country, not merely in Germany. The negative public reaction was magnified by expectations of even far greater uncontrolled migration. As the communist system in Eastern Europe and in the Soviet Union itself began to totter, governments in Western Europe steeled themselves to repel an onslaught of starving men, women, and children. Countries on the periphery of the Soviet Union—Finland, Poland, Czechoslovakia, Hungary, and Austria—developed contingency plans, organized camps, and moved police and military units to their eastern borders to cope with the anticipated flood of refugees. The fear of this peaceful invasion became a near obsession because it was felt that, owing to humanitarian considerations, such refugees could not be rejected. They would have to be accepted, and they would in their huge numbers consume the substance of Western European prosperity.

At the end of 1990, Western Europeans believed that as many as 3 million Russians and Ukrainians would try to get into Eastern and then Western Europe that winter. Poland alone expected more than a million ethnic Poles from Ukraine and Belarus, left behind when Stalin moved Poland's boundaries west at the end of World War II. Some estimated that Western Europe's 12 million registered immigrants would quadruple to 50 million by the end of the 1990s. Each successive political convulsion in Ukraine and Russia renewed these fears.

The refugees and asylum seekers from the east did not come in their expected millions, but they did come in their hundreds of thousands. For example, when the communist regime in Albania began to crack in 1991, an estimated 100,000 Albanians fled by sea and land. Forty thousand of them landed—temporarily—in Italy, 20,000 in March 1991, and 18,000 in a second wave in August of that year. Using forbiddingly rough treatment, the Italian government congregated most of the Albanian refugees in inhospitable collection centers and shipped them back to Albania, stepping up Italian naval patrols in the Adriatic to stop these new boat people, but also sensibly stepping up emergency food deliveries and economic aid to Albania itself.

Actual and feared migration brought a marked increase in racially motivated attacks and right-wing extremism throughout Western Europe. The trend has been pronounced, not only in Germany, but in Austria, Belgium, and Spain. Even tolerant Sweden was affected. A few racially motivated killings have taken place there; the New Democracy party, a populist party with some anti-immigration points in its program, suddenly gained twenty-five seats and the balance of power in the new Swedish parliament (September 1991). In French regional elections in March 1992, the anti-immigrant National Front got close to 14 percent of the vote nationwide, up from about 10 percent four years previously.

But the costs of heavy migration are found not only in increased antiforeigner sentiment and heightened support for extremist political parties. The efforts of European governments to close their borders and to tighten asylum regulations are bringing new entry restrictions with tougher police controls. This is taking place not only in the Western European countries but also those to the east, like Poland and Hungary. The tightening of controls extends to domestic regulation of foreigners. Although Germany has relaxed its restrictive citizenship laws, most European countries are moving to tighten theirs. Finally, efforts to control antiforeigner attacks are leading in Germany and other countries to pro-hibitions on political groups and legal restrictions on the right of free speech. These measures are aimed at racial extremists, but they entail an evident if thus far limited restriction of individual rights for all.

In France as well as Germany, the problem is especially acute. The bulk of France's recent immigrants have come from former French colonies in North Africa—Algeria, Tunisia, and Morocco. Of the 3.6 million foreigners living in France in 1993, 60 percent are Arabs and Africans. In 1975 alone, 2.3 million immigrants came to France from the former North African colonies; during the 1980s, the average figure was 1.3 million a year. In contrast to Germany, in France it has been relatively easy for immigrants to acquire citizenship. Like U.S. law, French law has provided that children born in France automatically become citizens (in France, at age eighteen). One-quarter of the French population is composed of people who are immigrants or who have an immigrant parent or grandparent. Illegal immigration, estimated at 100,000 per year, is increasing.

Even before the economic recession of the early 1990s, evidence of racism in France was increasing. In public opinion polls, more than 70 percent of respondents complained that there were too many Arabs in France. Racial incidents were on the increase. Jean-Marie Le Pen's National Front party gained up to 30 percent of the votes in districts with a large number of North Africans. It has a strong potential for fur-ther increase in strength through voters drawn away from other conser-vative parties.

The conservative government of Edouard Balladur, which gained power in France in the spring of 1993, was well aware of this electoral threat. In May 1993, its interior minister, Charles Pasqua, announced a goal of "zero immigration." He introduced three draft laws that would permit the police freely to make identity checks even when there is no suspicion of crime; ease deportation of illegal immigrants; deny them public health care; preclude immigrant workers from bringing their families to France for two years or preclude foreign students from bring-ing their families at all; and require children born in France to foreign-ers to declare their desire to become citizens between the ages of six-teen and twenty-one, at which point a police record could provide grounds for refusal. The constitutionality of some of these measures was questioned, but Pasqua's personal popularity rating went up 25 percent after introduction of the bills.[3]

Immigration and the refugee flow have been perceived by some European political leaders as a security problem. Immigration is clearly a security problem in the general sense of the term because what is perceived as excessive immigration can undermine vital democratic institutions and the mutual tolerance on which democracy is based. The degree of that damage seems controllable for the foreseeable future. Immigration is not yet a security problem as it is defined in this book, a problem that can lead to widespread armed conflict. Moreover, with Western Europe's low birthrate and aging population, new migrants willing to do the dirty jobs of industrial civilization will be needed.

The long-term prospect for European Community countries may be similar to that in the United States—an uneasy and ineffective mix of intensified border policing, restricted legal migration, and continuing illegal migration helped by businesses interested in cheap labor. The long-term answer, far easier said than done, is promoting economic development and creating jobs in the sending countries through trade, investment, and aid. The European Community is moving toward a free-trade agreement with the Northern African countries as well as increasing its economic aid to these countries.[4]

THE "SWORD OF ISLAM"

To many citizens of the EC countries, especially those bordering on the Mediterranean like France, Italy, and Spain, migration from the south has even more negative connotations than migration from the east.

The geographic location of these European countries makes their focus on North Africa understandable. Americans would be equally disturbed by the prospect of mounting instability in neighboring Mexico. However, the difference in emphasis does not merely arise from geographic location. The fear of rising population and rising unemployment in North Africa with unstoppable waves of illegal immigrants landing on the soft, unprotected underbelly of southern Europe has intermingled with other fears: fear of Islamic fundamentalism; of nuclear weapons in the hands of fanatical Third World governments calling for retribution for colonialism and for parceling out the wealth of the industrialized states; and fear of a renewed threat to the oil reserves of the Persian Gulf and North Africa on which Europe remains painfully dependent.

In the thoughts of many Europeans, all these dark visions have been fused into a single awesome threat to Europe, the nightmare that all the Islamic states in a giant crescent extending from Turkmenistan to Morocco could some day be united under the green banner of a new Saladin or al-Mahdi riding out of the desert to take historic vengeance for the victory of Charles Martel over the Arabs at Poitiers, for the Crusades, for the expulsion of the Moors from Spain, for European colonial domination of Islamic countries, and for Western support of Israel. "Let Australians worry about the Yellow Peril, and Americans about Hispanic wetbacks or drug barons. Europe's private nightmare is the sword of Islam," writes Edward Mortimer, foreign policy commentator of the London *Financial Times*. Michel Debré, formerly defense minister of France, wrote in a fiery article in the Paris press, "The threat is from the South. . . . The Islamic movement that has just triumphed in Algeria's local elections carries within itself a threat to France. . . . We must never underestimate the adversary. Let us realize that Islam is now the adversary of Europe and, primarily, of France."[5] These fears have some outside encouragement. President Hosni Mubarak of Egypt, under increasing pressure from Islamic extremists at home, and Israel's Prime Minister Yitzhak Rabin, under pressure of terrorist activity from Hamas, the radical organization of Palestinian Arabs, repeatedly warn the West that its most serious enemy is Muslim extremism.

The vision is a fearsome one. It has been seized on and embellished by defense analysts in Europe. Here is a new enemy nearly as shadowy, as universal, and as menacing as Soviet communism. In the case of the cold war, a genuine threat to Western countries underlay the sometimes exaggerated Soviet threat, although often it was a difficult task for the Western governments to find exactly the right terms to describe the nature of that threat without hyperbole. Does a real threat underlie the exaggerations of this new nightmare of Islamic extremism?

True, Islamic fundamentalism is spreading, in some places quite rapidly. Takeover of individual countries by fundamentalist groups is possible; it has already happened in Iran and Sudan. The most important endangered country is Egypt, with its large (55 million), rapidly increasing population, limited resources of water and agricultural land, faltering economy, and growing social discontent. If the Egyptian government came under fundamentalist control, it could destroy Arab-Israel reconciliation, endanger the flow of Mideast oil, and affect the political orientation of the remaining countries of North Africa.

In many Muslim countries, the increasing power of fundamentalism is causing very serious domestic political problems, including a mounting number of cases of intimidation and assassination of modernizing intellectuals who oppose fundamentalism. Although there have been some divergent minority traditions, the underlying difficulty is that, from its outset, even mainstream Islam has been theocratic in its insistence that the state and civil society should be conducted in conformity with religious principles in all aspects of life, much as the medieval Catholic Church or John Calvin's Geneva so insisted. Where this theocratic insistence has been tempered by secular modernism, fundamentalist Islam is determined that its rule be restored. This insistence was set aside by secular leaders like Egypt's Gamal Abdel Nasser, Tunisia's Habib Bourguiba, and later, Iraq's Saddam Hussein. Radical Islamists joined these leaders in the national liberation movement against European colonial powers but were suppressed when they caused problems for the new secular rulers. Today's Islamists represent a third generation. They relentlessly criticize the modern state and its adherents for materialism, impiety, abandonment of core Islamic values, imitation of Western secularism, and failure to take a sufficiently militant position against Israel and its Western supporters. The Islamists often take on social welfare tasks inefficiently performed by governments. Organizations like Hezbollah "Party of God" in Lebanon, the Islamic Salvation Front in Algeria, and the Muslim Brotherhood in Egypt run schools, hospitals, and clinics and provide cheap housing and food.

Some have engaged in terrorist acts directed against their governments.[6] In Algeria, the problem is increasingly serious. The fundamentalist Islamic Salvation Front Movement was legalized in 1989. It was a time when the ruling National Liberation Front, composed mainly of secular modernizing nationalists who led the country to independence from France in 1962 after fierce fighting, had lost its inspiration and also its popularity because of its inability to cope with extended economic decline. The Islamic Salvation Front won 55 percent of the vote in regional elections in 1989 and 49 percent of the vote in December 1991 nationwide elections, winning 188 parliamentary seats to the Liberation Front's fifteen seats in the first of two voting rounds. The Algerian army took over from the National Liberation Front government in January 1992 in order to prevent the runoff elections and a victory by the Islamic Salvation Front that would have brought control of the Algerian government. The military junta banned the Islamic Salvation Front.

Forced underground, the fundamentalists began a campaign of ambush and assassination against Algerian leaders. In June 1992, its extremists assassinated Mohamed Boudiaf, Algeria's president. By the end of 1993, according to the government's low official estimates, over 3,000 people had been killed. In the fall of 1993, the extremists adopted a still more dangerous version than that of the Egyptian fundamentalist attacks on foreign tourists: They threatened all foreigners who had not left Algeria by the beginning of December with death. By mid-December, twenty-three foreigners had been killed, and the United States, Canada, Russia, and France had warned their nationals not to travel to Algeria. The United States and several other countries also urged all of their nationals in Algeria to leave the country, but France, whose 75,000 citizens

(50,000 of them also have Algerian citizenship) play a vital role in Algerian economic life, held out, but acted the next spring. France feared that economic chaos, accompanied by a flood of French and Algerian refugees to France, might result if it withdrew all its citizens.[7]

In Tunisia, the government banned the fundamentalist Islamic Renaissance party, which was gaining considerable popularity in June 1991. Surprisingly, even in Libya, where to outsiders, with deliberate help from supreme leader Muammar Qaddafi himself, Qaddafi appears the prototype of the stern ascetic tribal leader riding in from the desert, the regime is under pressure from fundamentalist groups that have engaged in raids and organized violence.

Although sternly repressed by the Mubarak government, fundamentalist groups have been gaining considerable strength in Egypt, where there has been an increasing number of acts of violence, including bold assassination attempts on the Egyptian interior minister in August 1993 and on the prime minister in November of that year. Over 200 extremists were executed during 1993 after summary trial by military courts in a context of increasing social misery. In Sudan, which the United States in August 1993 declared to be a state supporting terrorism, the ruling military junta is dominated by a fundamentalist party, the Nationalist Islamic Front, which receives support both from Iran and Saudi Arabia. Although friendly to the West, Saudi Arabia, itself governed under strict Islamic principles, is engaged in supporting Islam as a religion from the Sudan to Lebanon to the Central Asian republics. Turkey, predominantly modernist, secular, and Europe-oriented, is feeling continuing pressure from fundamentalist groups that, however, still represent fewer than 20 percent of the electorate. Iran, with a fundamentalist government, is supporting similar groups in Lebanon, Jordan, Sudan, Algeria, and the Central Asian republics. Afghanistan is in the hands of competing fundamentalist guerrilla groups after the unseating of pro-Soviet president Najibullah in May 1992.

Sparked by the anti-Gorbachev coup of August 1991, the predominantly Muslim republics of Kazakhstan, Azerbaijan, Turkmenistan, Uzbekistan, Kyrgyzstan, and Tajikistan, also the poorest republics of the old USSR, threw off what many regarded as the Russian colonial yoke and proclaimed their independence. The new states, liberated but destitute, took up links with Iran, Turkey, and Saudi Arabia, all of which are competing for influence in this area, where Muslim influence dominated until its takeover by czarist Russia or Stalin's Soviet Union. Within two years, the number of mosques in these states, which had been held down by Soviet policy, increased from 160 to 5,000. The number of Islamic seminaries increased from one to nine. Islamic fundamentalist parties were established in several of the republics in September 1991 and have been growing in strength despite repression in some of them. We have described how, in 1992, fundamentalists joined with anti-communists in Tajikistan in an unsuccessful effort to overthrow the old-line regime of Rakmon Nabiyev. In Pakistan, the Islamic Democratic Alliance won a majority in the October 1990 election. Although some of the parties composing the alliance are more moderate, the most influential single party is the fundamentalist Jamat-i-Islami. However, the alliance lost the October 1993 national elections to Benazir Bhutto's Peoples Party; the extremist wing of the alliance, which campaigned on its own, did even more poorly. In the Jordan elections of November 1993, the Islamists lost a number of seats, in part because of a change of the election law.

Despite these setbacks, there is no doubt that Islamic fundamentalism is gaining strength along the entire arc from the Central Asian republics to Morocco. Experts argue over the political significance of this phenomenon. Many believe that wherever Islamic fundamentalists gain the upper hand, they establish authoritarian, antidemocratic, and antiforeign governments, dedicated to use of organized violence against the Western states as exemplified by the government of Iran under the Ayatollah Ruhollah Khomeini.[8]

The concerns of European observers over the political effects of rapid increase of population in the Muslim crescent combined with economic stagnation are also understandable. Of the nineteen Muslim countries between Iran and Morocco, fifteen have populations growing at a more rapid rate than their economies. In seventeen of the nineteen countries, more than one-half of the population is under twenty-five years of age. Fairly typical for the whole area, in Algeria nearly 75 percent of people under age twenty-five are unemployed. In Western Europe north of the Mediterranean, the population has leveled off or is declining. But some experts expect the population of North Africa, now about one-half that of the European Community, to exceed that of the EC countries at some point during the first three decades of the next century; 349 million in North Africa versus 326 million in the EC.[9] This high rate of population increase is also found in the Muslim states of the former Soviet Union, which have the lowest per capita GNP of all the Soviet successor states.

A principal component of Europe's recurring Islamic nightmare is the fear that instability in the Persian Gulf could cut off European access to the world's largest oil reserves. Iraq sought to move into a dominant position in the region through its 1990 invasion of Kuwait. Next time, Europeans fear, it could be anti-Western Iran that seeks hegemony in the Gulf. Or radical Muslim fundamentalists could displace the conservative Saudi royal house. In the 1980s, a group of Islamic militants under the command of a Saudi colonel made a nearly successful effort to capture and hold the holy places of Mecca. Some senior American officers believe that ultimate military confrontation between Iran and the United States and other Western countries is inevitable. One of the objectives of NATO's new strategy approved at Rome in November 1991 is to cope with renewed war in the Persian Gulf.

Much of Europe's uneasiness arises from realization that European forces on their own would not have been capable of prosecuting the Gulf War against Iraq; Europe was dependent on U.S. military power for the victory against Saddam Hussein. Even small-scale European interventions in former colonies in Africa, like French interventions in Chad in the 1970s and 1980s, and Franco-Belgian interventions in Zaire in the 1970s and again in 1991, have been dependent on U.S. air lifts and satellite intelligence. For some Europeans, this fact has confirmed the value of close alliance with the United States. For France and some other European states, the conclusion has been that Europe should take steps to increase its own military capabilities.

It has been calculated that, in order to cope with renewed serious conflict in the Persian Gulf, a Western coalition military force might need six ground-force divisions, three to four carrier groups, a strong amphibious landing force of one to two divisions, and several wings of fighters and fighter bombers to establish air supremacy and carry out an initial attack. It will be a long time before Europe will be in a position to mount a coalition force of these dimensions, although it is not beyond the bounds of the possible. However, because its own economic well-being depends on preventing major oil price increases, it is doubtful that the United States would remain inactive in the event of a renewed serious threat to Mideast oil, even if Europeans were unable to assemble an intervention force on their own.

The most worrisome aspect of fears that Europe might be confronted by a bloc of hostile Muslim states is the concern that one or more of these states would develop nuclear weapons of their own, thus neutralizing Europe's greater economic and conventional military strength. Libya provided a foretaste of these fears with the illicit development of chemical weapons at its Rabta plant and its apparently deliberate missile attack in 1986 against a U.S. installation on the Italian island of Lampedusa. Even more, these fears were activated by Iraqi Scud attacks on Israel, Kuwait, and Saudi Arabia during the Gulf War, by Baghdad's possession and use of chemical weapons, and by discovery of its efforts to develop nuclear weapons. Many Europeans fear that if radical

Muslim states did obtain nuclear weapons, their leaders might not be deterred, as were the leaders of the Soviet Union, from using these weapons by rational considerations about the damage that Western retaliation could do to their own countries. Instead, some Western experts think, authoritarian leaders in the grip of fanatical religion would be far more interested in destroying Western societies than in protecting their own populations; deterrence based on previous theories would no longer work. Some even argue that developments are moving inexorably toward a new world war where the sword of unified Islam would be a nuclear one.[10] In the West, fear of an Islamic bomb is by no means confined to anti-Muslim groups. It is the main single motive underlying the nuclear nonproliferation policies of Western governments. Fear of the Islamic bomb dominates Western policy toward Muslim countries.

Today, most of these worries focus on Iran, which is building up its armed forces with expenditures topping over $2 billion a year for new weapons and which is believed to be engaged in a vigorous secret effort to develop missile-delivered nuclear weapons. Robert Gates, director of the Central Intelligence Agency, forecast in early 1992 that Iran might be able to develop nuclear weapons by the end of the decade and that it could have missile-delivered chemical weapons much earlier. Iran took delivery of several submarines from Russia in 1992. Since Iran is in a position to make a bid for control over Persian Gulf oil supplies and continues to demonstrate fervor in supporting extremist Muslim groups elsewhere, it is a source of particular concern not only to Europeans, but to the United States, still smarting under the humiliation of the 1979 capture of its embassy in Teheran. To dispel these suspicions, Iran has opened itself to anywhere, anytime inspections by the International Atomic Energy Agency (IAEA). The IAEA carried out several inspections of Iran's nuclear facilities in 1992–93 and failed to find evidence of a nuclear weapons program.

A new nuclear weapons scare arose in early 1992 in connection with Algeria, when it was reported that Iraq had sent some of its nuclear scientists and a quantity of illegally enriched uranium to the Algerian reactor at Ain Oussera, ninety miles south of Algiers. The reactor, under construction since 1986 with Chinese help, had some suspicious characteristics: It was larger than it had to be for its announced fifteen-megawatt capability, and no evidence could be found that power lines were being built to take away electricity for distribution. The reactor was guarded by several nearby surface-to-air missile installations. Under pressure of Western suspicions, Algeria, not a signatory of the Nuclear Non-Proliferation Treaty, announced that it would in the future become a signatory and that the new reactor would be placed under IAEA inspection when completed.[11]

SOME DOUBTS

Not all Muslim fundamentalists are militant radicals vowing to extirpate secularism, women's rights, and Western influence. Some stay strictly out of politics. Other have participated in parliamentary elections in Turkey, Pakistan, Egypt, and Jordan. It is argued by some experts, notably Graham Fuller of the Rand Corporation, that Muslim fundamentalism has been fueled by social protest. Consequently, when the fundamentalists are repressed as they were in Iran in the 1960s and 1970s, and as they have been in Egypt and Algeria, they become the main voice of opposition. But, it is argued, when they are admitted to the political mainstream, they lose much of their fire. When they join in the election process or participate in government, as in Iran, their zeal is blunted by confrontation with practical problems, or at least they can be more easily controlled by less extreme leaders.[12] The debate over whether politically extreme fundamentalists can be "tamed" continues, largely because there have been so few cases of participation in government by Islamic fundamentalists and because the orientation of Iran, the major country where they are in power, remains extremist.

However, although the confrontation between the West and Islam may last longer than the cold war, it will not achieve cold war dimensions. The possibility that Islam will unify is very slim. And, even if unified, Islam would be no military match for the West.

Although nothing is wholly excluded in the realm of politics, the possibility of a single unified leadership of the Muslim countries forming an "arc of Islam" is extremely remote. Sunni and Shiah Muslims have been bitterly divided for more than a thousand years. Their enmity contributed to the 1980s war between Iran, a Shiah country, and Iraq, where the population is mainly Sunni, although the government is dominated by the secular Baath party. The Shiah-Sunni hostility emerged once again in the Iraqi government's slaughter and persecution of Shiahs in the south of Iraq after the Gulf War. There are wide cultural differences between the Arabs of Morocco or Jordan and the Turkic inhabitants of Central Asia. Even among Mideast Arabs, differences can run deep. Gamal Abdel Nasser was the most widely respected Arab leader of modern times. Yet he failed repeatedly in efforts to bring about a union of only Egypt, Syria, and Libya. The Maghreb countries of North Africa have made several ineffective efforts at union. As yet the fundamentalists themselves have no important common cross-border organization. Even inside countries where there is strong fundamentalist activity, like Egypt, the groups involved are numerous, divided and hostile toward one another. There is no unified front of Muslim countries against Western countries. Turkey, a secular Muslim country, is a member of NATO; Turkey, Bosnia, and the Central Asian republics are members of the Conference on Security and Cooperation in Europe; Saudi Arabia is pro-Western.

New regional groupings are possible. However, even if Sunni-Shiah differences can be overcome, it is questionable whether the shared values of the Muslim countries both in terms of religion and in terms of resentment against Western countries are sufficiently strong to provide an effective bond of unity among all the Muslim peoples. Up to now, national feeling in individual countries has been a stronger bond than cross-border Islamic ties. A perceptive Pakistani observer, Pervez Hoodbhoy, points out that if a further Muslim country does develop a nuclear weapon, it will be a national weapon, not an Islamic one, just as Pakistan's nuclear capability has been in actual practice.[13]

In any event, the European countries are not powerless in this matter, condemned to wait immobilized by fear until the worst happens. France, Italy, and Spain, the main states of southern Europe, are seeking a structured dialogue with the countries of the Maghreb that would combine economic, social, human rights, cultural, dispute settlement, and defense issues into a single framework as has been done in the Conference on Security and Cooperation in Europe (CSCE). Italy and Spain put forward a formal proposal for a Conference on Security and Cooperation in the Mediterranean in September 1990. The plan has had difficulties, among them whether or how to include Israel and the Near East Arab states. However, the underlying concept is a useful one and the establishment of some such organization seems quite possible. The European Community's plans for a free-trade area with North Africa would combine trade concessions with agreements to limit migration to Europe. The Community already has an ongoing program for Mediterranean development of about $6 billion in grants and loans for the 1992–96 period, and the World Bank is making important loans to the area.[14] Beyond this, some carefully thought out mediation moves, perhaps by the European Community, would be useful in Algeria—to bring the army command and the Islamic Salvation Front into a serious dialogue—and also perhaps in Egypt.

Relations between European and Islamic states may worsen in coming years, but they will not soon culminate in the organized armed conflict of one culture against another, a new crusade, or jihad. Rather than war, increasing terrorism by Muslims and increasing anti-Muslim violence by Europeans is the real problem. Terrorism is a favored weapon of weak governments and weak groups against stronger governments, especially stronger democratic governments restrained by their own values and public opinion from violent retaliation. Radical Islam has already brought serious acts of terrorism to the more distant United States in the February 1993 bombing of the World Trade Center in New York City; plans to bomb the United Nations and other sites were frustrated by arrests of the would-be participants in June 1993. In southern Europe, as the result of continued migration pressures, there will probably be increasing numbers of ethnic incidents and demonstrations, even race riots. Lynching and ethnically inspired terrorism against Muslims may become more frequent, as well as both spontaneous and state-supported terrorism by Muslims. Xenophobic extremist political parties in Western Europe will become larger, perhaps much larger, to match the growing influence of increasingly xenophobic Islamic fundamentalists in the Muslim countries. Antagonism between the governments of southern Europe and those of North Africa will probably intensify.

However, even on a worst-case basis, this antagonism seems likely to fall short of outright military conflict. Even if Egypt becomes hostile and even with increasing population in all the North African states, these countries will not be able to mount military forces that can be a serious challenge to those of Europe, especially if the Europeans cooperate to limit arms sales to Arab states.

True, southern Europe is within range of nuclear-armed missiles from North Africa. But an active multilateral nonproliferation policy will keep these risks to a minimum. In an extreme situation, collective action against suspected proliferation under the aegis of the UN Security Council should be possible. Iraqi use of Scud missiles during the Gulf War has caused some European governments to think with more favor of missile defense systems. In the fall of 1993, the Clinton administration suggested amending the U.S.-Russian Anti-Ballistic Missile Treaty limiting antimissile defenses in order to cooperate with the NATO allies in developing a new and more effective system of defenses against tactical-range ballistic missiles. However, such systems are expensive and of limited value. An active nonproliferation policy directed both at nuclear weapons and missiles, backed by collective military force in extreme situations, is a more effective approach to the problem.

North African supplies of oil and natural gas are important to southern Europe, but there are substitutes for these sources if they are cut off. To cope with serious threats to oil supplies in the Persian Gulf, the European Community will have to develop other possibilities that we will discuss in a later chapter.

To sum up, a potentially very serious issue underlies the lurid vocabulary of Western commentators on the "Islamic threat": Their repeated forecasts of a final clash between Islam and the West and parallel statements by Muslim extremists do have some potential over the long term to become a self-fulfilling prophecy, creating an ideological and cultural confrontation similar to the cold war ideological clash, minus its military dimension. A development of this kind could unloose a cycle, not of organized warfare but of terrorism and counterterrorism, with high economic costs and high political costs in restrictions of democratic freedoms in the Western states. This particular Islamic bomb has dangerous potential; Western states should undertake concerted action to defuse it.

Among many possible ways of deflating this deadly phantasm, they should draw on top-flight philosophers and theologians of the kind who made the dialogue of reconciliation between Christians and Jews so successful over the past half century and attempt to structure a similar dialogue between the best Western thinkers, both Christian and secular, with those of Islam. Western and Islamic thinkers should seek out the alternative Islamic tradition which leads away from theocratic insistence on governing the state by religious principles and use it to help bring about an accelerated version of the process in which majority Christian churches in the West relinquished this same insistence and carved out a separate spiritual sphere for themselves.

PART III

THE NEW EUROPEAN SECURITY INSTITUTIONS

9

THE CONFERENCE ON SECURITY
AND COOPERATION IN EUROPE—
CAN IT DO THE JOB?

U nsurprisingly, the main security problem that has emerged in Europe
after the collapse of the Soviet Union is that of an unstable, nuclear-
armed Russia, which has already moved toward greater nationalism and
which could move further toward authoritarian government. Russia elicited fears of resurgent imperialism as it intervened in the mainly ethnic
quarrels of neighboring republics. It remained on dangerously bad terms
with its largest western neighbor, Ukraine. The huge arsenal of nuclear
weapons in Russia and Ukraine, as well as Belarus and Kazakhstan, made the
area the world's most serious proliferation risk. In Yugoslavia, the other main
problem area, European security institutions had failed to damp down the
continuing fighting in Bosnia, which had the potentiality of spreading and of
becoming outright war between Croatia and Serbia, as well as involving
Macedonia, Albania, Bulgaria, Greece, and even Turkey in expanding conflict.

The capacity of European security institutions to cope with these
problems—or the lack of that capacity—is the key to the future of
European security. The failure of these institutions—NATO, the Western
European Union (WEU) and the Conference on Security and Cooperation
in Europe (CSCE), and also the UN itself—could result in the gradual
alienation of their major supporters, the United States, Germany, and also
Russia, and in gradual movement toward greater reliance on national military capabilities. The multilateral European security system, as we pointed

out at the beginning of this book, is on trial for its long-term existence. In the following chapters, we discuss the European security system as it has emerged since the end of the cold war, evaluate its adequacy, and describe improvements that should be made in it.

THE CSCE

In its own words, the Conference on Security and Cooperation in Europe "is a forum for dialogue, negotiation, and cooperation, providing direction and giving impulse to the shaping of the new Europe."[1] The CSCE has come a long way from hesitant beginnings at its first 1975 conference in Helsinki as a loose consultative process between the governments of East and West aimed at mitigating the cold war division of Europe. Today, CSCE is an increasingly structured organization dedicated to preventing conflict and to keeping the peace in Europe, although based on a network of intergovernmental political understandings rather than the treaty obligations that underpin the European Union and NATO.[2]

Of the major institutions concerned with European security, including the European Union, NATO, and the WEU, the CSCE is the most comprehensive in terms of membership and functions. Can it perform its mission of helping to keep the peace in Europe in the face of continuing, bloody conflict in the Yugoslav republics and the Soviet successor states? Officials in all the member governments are asking this same question with mixed hope and doubt. They all want the CSCE to succeed; many have nurtured the new permanent CSCE institutions with deep personal engagement. For them and for all, the CSCE's success or failure will be an important test, perhaps the decisive test, of the viability of multilateral security institutions in the post-cold war period.

At the CSCE "summit" meeting of heads of participating governments in Helsinki in July 1992 (Helsinki 92 for short), the CSCE had fifty-two member states: the United States, Canada, and the fourteen European NATO member states; eleven European neutral states; the five former Warsaw Pact states of Eastern Europe (Czechoslovakia separated into the Czech Republic and Slovakia in January 1993); Albania; the three Baltic states; Russia and the other eleven members of the Commonwealth of Independent States; plus Slovenia, Croatia, Bosnia-Herzegovina, and the rump Yugoslav government (Serbia and Montenegro).[3] The Yugoslav government was suspended from CSCE membership just before the Helsinki summit owing to its role in the war, but Serbia and Montenegro continue to participate in many CSCE activities. Of the European states, only Macedonia, its acceptance contested by Greece, has been omitted from CSCE membership, but it has observer status.

The main function of the CSCE is to assure fulfillment of the central commitment of CSCE members dating from the original Helsinki conference to renounce the use of force and violence in interstate relations—and, increasingly, in relations between governments and their citizens. The activities of the CSCE extend from promoting democratic institutions and protection of minorities, to mediation, dispute settlement, and conflict resolution, confidence building and transparency, and arms control. They also include cooperation in economics, environmental problems, science, and cultural exchange. In practical terms, European experts see the CSCE as having four principal functions in the 1990s: (1) The CSCE's main job is to contribute to the integration of Russia and other former Warsaw Pact countries in a democratically oriented European system. (2) The CSCE conducts political dialogue on the political, security, and economic policies of member governments. This dialogue describes, clarifies, and on occasion criticizes government policy. (3) It carries out conflict prevention and crisis management activities. (4) It negotiates and coordinates the implementation of arms control, transparency, and confidence-building measures.

The Helsinki 92 Summit was only the third meeting of heads of government of CSCE member states (officially, "participating states") after the original Helsinki Summit of August 1975 and the Paris Summit of November 1990. CSCE Summits will now become a regular occurrence; it was agreed at the Paris meeting to hold these sessions every two years. The fourth summit was scheduled for Budapest in December 1994.

At Helsinki 92, government leaders, motivated by the eruption of ethnic wars in former Yugoslavia and in the former Soviet Union and by the painful realization that the CSCE was not equipped to deal with them, decided that the organization should assume responsibility for organizing peacekeeping operations. For future peacekeeping missions, the CSCE can either organize its own operation, relying directly on forces of member states, or, more likely, it can call on the help of Europe's two main military security organizations, NATO and the WEU, and also on the Commonwealth of Independent States. Helsinki 92 also decided that CSCE should become a regional organization of the United Nations under Article 52 of the UN Charter. This action, implemented by a simple notification to the secretary general of the UN, enables the Security Council to request the CSCE to carry out missions of regional peacekeeping in Europe under council authority.

More functions and structure will probably be added in future. However, the CSCE's array of mechanisms and measures is now fairly complete. After the decisions made at Helsinki 92, the CSCE was in a position to act on the full spectrum of security problems, from investigating a minor ethnic clash to mounting a peacekeeping operation. Today, the question is whether the CSCE can make these measures work, whether it can in time develop into an effective multilateral peace-securing institution, or whether it will fade away into ignominy like the League of Nations (an organization also in practice focused on European security issues despite its wider membership).

As regards crisis management, CSCE has thus far been a relative failure. Its initial efforts in the former Yugoslavia were ineffectual and brushed aside. Its first halting attempts to find a role in the crises in Moldova and Nagorno-Karabakh came to little. However, the story is not ended. CSCE has performed valuable backup work for the European Community and the UN in the Yugoslav states. It has also done innovative work in preventive diplomacy. It provided teams of diplomats and military officers in Serbia and Macedonia to damp down frictions in advance of arrival of peacekeeping troops—or in their absence. It is developing a useful role in ethnic conflicts in the Soviet successor states, monitoring, mediating, and reducing the incidence of military abuses and oppression.

It is highly doubtful whether CSCE will ever function as a military alliance organizing large-scale military intervention outside Europe—for example, in a second Gulf War. It is also doubtful whether CSCE could serve as an organization of collective defense to defend other members against aggression by major states; for example, a resurgent, nationalistic Russia. CSCE will not become a second NATO.

But there is a vitally important security role for CSCE in Europe short of these roles. Even if it takes a long time to reach this point, CSCE must ultimately be able to keep its own house in order when confronted by lesser military challenges like those of the early 1990s in the former Yugoslavia, Moldova, and Nagorno-Karabakh, preventing them where possible, containing them when they occur, if necessary through multilateral peacekeeping and peace enforcement forces, and preventing them from developing into interstate war among CSCE's own member states. In the extreme case, CSCE should ultimately have the capacity to bring to a fairly rapid end "small" interstate wars through a mix of mediation, economic sanctions, use of military force to enforce sanctions or to isolate the conflict area, and postconflict peacemaking activities.

Harsh circumstances oblige the CSCE to become the policeman of Europe as well as its chief institution for prevention of conflict. Unless CSCE, or some equivalent, with the help of organizations like NATO, is able to take on this policing role effectively, current ethnic conflicts will continue and new ones will erupt, leaving a wake of bloodshed, economic destruction, and swarms of refugees. Some of these conflicts could expand to interstate war. Even where this does not happen, they will cause the discrepancy between CSCE's pretensions and its actual performance to become more and more evident, discrediting CSCE, depriving it of support from member governments and publics, and sharply reducing its authority, power, and effectiveness to head off or deal with future conflicts, and leading its member states to rely increasingly on their own resources for their security.

CSCE's BEGINNINGS

The CSCE has gone through three distinct periods of development; the first two were determined mainly by changes in Soviet policy, the third by the outbreak of ethnic violence in Europe. The first phase, from 1975 to 1985 (the Brezhnev era), was characterized by considerable improvement in East-West intergovernmental relations. This period was defined mainly by Soviet efforts to gain Western acceptance of the political status quo in Eastern Europe and by Western efforts to gain pledges of broader domestic freedoms and better human rights performance from Eastern governments. The second phase, from 1986 to 1990, during Gorbachev's rule, emphasized agreements on human rights and security issues and the establishment of institutions for conflict prevention. The current phase, characterized by armed violence in the former Yugoslavia and Soviet Union, has emphasized new CSCE institutions and measures for conflict prevention, crisis management, and peacekeeping.

EARLY DAYS

The origins of CSCE are often traced back to a Soviet proposal of 1954, made in one of the series of foreign ministers' meetings over how to deal with conquered Germany that were held in the first decade of the cold war. Over the years, all the main participants except the United States came to support holding an all-European conference. The United States was still the odd man out at the founding of CSCE. In many ways, despite its vital role throughout the CSCE process, it remains an outsider.

In April 1969, Finland, flag-bearer for the neutral and nonaligned countries of Europe, extended an invitation to meet in Helsinki for a preparatory conference. In October of that year, the Warsaw Pact suggested that the agenda for this conference might cover security issues, inviolability of frontiers, recognition of the existence of two separate German states, and renunciation of nuclear weapons. This selection of topics reflected basic Soviet interests. In December, NATO suggested in response that the conference agenda should include prior notification of maneuvers and freer movement of people and ideas. The latter topics were to become the core of future CSCE achievements. The Soviet Union was anxious to restore its international reputation after its August 1968 invasion of Czechoslovakia. Consequently, it agreed to include NATO's proposals in the conference agenda. It also agreed as a Western precondition for holding a first CSCE meeting to a Four-Power Agreement on Berlin (1971) which after decades of confrontation finally ensured German civilians access to the city.

As would become the pattern for CSCE meetings at senior level, the leaders attending the first Helsinki CSCE summit meeting in August 1975 put the finishing touches on documents that had been negotiated in long preparatory sessions by working groups of diplomats under guidance of their foreign ministries. The preparatory sessions for Helsinki lasted two and a half years, from November 1972 to July 1975. At Helsinki and for the next decade or more, the negotiators were organized in three informal caucuses, one for NATO, one for Warsaw Pact members, and a third group for neutrals and "nonaligned," a term that referred to Yugoslavia, a founding member of the nonaligned movement of the 1960s. The Yugoslav government together with the European neutral states made an energetic and valuable contribution to progress in CSCE in suggesting compromises between NATO and Warsaw Pact positions.

Because CSCE was continually breaking new ground, the role of senior on-site negotiators became even more important than in most multilateral negotiations, where the constantly evolving mix of views can be evaluated better at the negotiating scene than at capitals. Despite lack of interest in the CSCE project by political leaders in Washington during most of the period from 1972 to 1990, the United States's role in the talks was highly important, especially from the point of view of developing specific proposals.

Two important, lasting characteristics of the CSCE approach emerged early in the preparatory talks for Helsinki: First, there was the decision to include in the conference agenda all the major items advanced by the three negotiating groups, rather than to dispute endlessly over the merits of each. Second, there was the decision to negotiate on these topics not in sequence, one after another—a process that might never have brought results—but in parallel working groups, in three main categories or "baskets." (The term goes back to a British diplomat who told fellow negotiators how his mother sorted balls of wool into different baskets according to their color.)

This approach of accepting for discussion the main interests of each group made possible the political deal that underlay the 1975 Helsinki Accords: Soviet acceptance of Western human rights norms—at first only pro forma acceptance, but with increasing seriousness over time—in return for Western acceptance of the division of Germany through official dealings with the German Democratic Republic and Western acceptance of the postwar borders in the East as inviolable. It was also agreed at Helsinki, however, that borders would be open to change by "peaceful means and by agreement." This amendment was insisted on by West

German officials in order to reassure aroused German public opinion that they were protecting a unification option that most then considered utopian.

The 1975 Helsinki Accords consist of three main documents. The first document (Basket I) contains ten principles governing relations among CSCE states. The main principles are respect for sovereignty and for the political independence of member states, refraining from the use or threat of force, territorial integrity and inviolability of existing frontiers, nonintervention in domestic affairs, and peaceful settlement of disputes.

The principles include a detailed paragraph on respect for human rights and the fundamental freedoms of individuals. The first document closes with a statement of the need to decrease the risks of conflict through misunderstanding or miscalculation of military activities of participating states through providing clear and timely information on these activities. It provides for voluntary prenotification of military maneuvers exceeding 25,000 troops in an area extending from the Atlantic in the West to border areas of the USSR (later extended to the Ural Mountains). Most of the subsequent activity of CSCE grew out of these two points.

Basket II covered cooperation in the field of economics, including fostering of trade, exchange of scientific and technical information, and protection of the environment. Basket III covered "cooperation in humanitarian and other fields," including cultural and educational exchanges, contacts between peoples, and the "solution of humanitarian problems," interpreted by Western participants to mean issuance of visas to Soviet and Eastern European dissidents and freedom to travel.

An essential aspect of the Helsinki approach was the concept of an ongoing, neverending dialogue, taking the form of a series of expert meetings on specific topics in the three baskets and of periodic "follow-up meetings" to review progress. Each follow-up meeting scheduled subsequent experts sessions for specific dates and places and did not leave them, as is often the case in diplomatic practice, to the uncertain outcome of later consultations. The continual convening of member-state officials for discussion on the agreed topics even if earlier meetings were not productive created the concept of the "Helsinki Process," which characterizes this first phase of CSCE development. Counting preparatory conferences, follow-up meetings, and experts meetings, more than thirty separate CSCE sessions were held between 1972 and 1991.[4]

THE GORBACHEV PHASE

Shortly after his designation as general secretary of the Communist Party of the Soviet Union (CPSU), Mikhail Gorbachev's influence became apparent in the human rights and security fields and in establishing

permanent CSCE institutions. Gorbachev began in 1986 to release political prisoners and permit unification of Soviet family members with their
relatives outside the USSR. The concluding document of the Vienna
Follow-Up Meeting (September 1986–January 1989) contains some
remarkable human rights commitments by the Soviet Union and other
Warsaw Pact participants. This was followed by three expert Conferences
on the Human Dimension, a heading that combined human rights,
family contacts, and other humanitarian issues into a single subject
(Paris, June 1989; Copenhagen, June 1990; and Moscow, September–
October 1991).

The Copenhagen concluding "Document," as the agreed products of
CSCE meetings are termed, was adopted just as the communist system in
Eastern Europe was beginning to collapse. It contains an exemplary comprehensive program of agreed principles for the functioning of pluralistic
democracies and the rule of law. The program includes rules for conducting free elections leading to representative government. It also stress-
es equal rights of all before the law, the right of representation for accused
persons, who will be presumed innocent until proven guilty, and freedom to establish political parties. Elections in all CSCE countries are to be
open to observers from member states.

The Copenhagen Document represents the essence of Western
democratic practice. Formulating it and gaining consensus on it represents a high point of CSCE achievement. Actual practice, especially in
some Soviet successor states, lags considerably behind, although many
Copenhagen principles have been incorporated into new constitutions in
the Eastern states. The 1991 Moscow meeting on the Human Dimension,
held in the brief interregnum after failure of the anti-Gorbachev coup and
before the collapse of the Soviet Union, added human rights coverage
for women and disabled persons.

The CSCE Documents now contain an encyclopedic compilation of
individual rights and democratic practices supported by all participants.
The issue for the future no longer is the willingness of member governments to formally subscribe to these principles, as it was during the first
CSCE period, but the capacity of governments actually to fulfill the principles. In the long run, these democratic codes will provide useful guides
for domestic institutions as well as barriers to possible authoritarian practices in Eastern European and Soviet successor states.

Participants in the September 1991 Human Dimension Conference
in Moscow also adopted trail-blazing procedures to enable fact-finding
missions from other CSCE states to investigate human rights complaints in
a participating state. A fact-finding commission can do a great deal of
good in some situations by publicizing its findings, highlighting negative

practices by governments, and providing public media with details of non-compliant behavior. It can also advance and promote proposals for improving the situation. The underlying idea, fundamental for the CSCE concept, is that if a member state is singled out and its practices publicly criticized, this isolation in itself can ultimately have remedial effects on its behavior.

CSCE AND THE MEDITERRANEAN

Driven in part by the concerns of southern European states—France, Italy, and Spain—over developments in North Africa described in earlier chapters, the CSCE has sponsored four subregional meetings on Mediterranean issues: The meeting at Valetta, Malta (1979), focused on economic and environmental cooperation; the meeting at Venice (1984), with participation of Egypt and Israel, focused on water and air pollution problems; and the meeting at Palma de Mallorca (1990), with representatives of eight nonmember Mediterranean states, focused on environmental protection and economic cooperation. In 1993, a further CSCE Mediterranean seminar took place on environment, demographic trends, and economic cooperation. Because these seminars deliberately seek to attract participation by as many non-CSCE Mediterranean states as possible, their outcome does not take the form of a Document of agreed conclusions binding on all CSCE members.

France, Spain, and Italy have also sponsored meetings investigating the possibility of establishing a separate regional CSCE for the Mediterranean that would cover security as well as economic issues. The United States has been reserved about this project, believing it might complicate Mideast peace efforts. But the concerns of the southern European states about the nations on the other side of the narrow Mediterranean are strong, and these efforts are likely to continue.

CSCE ACTIVITIES IN THE MILITARY SECURITY FIELD

The second major CSCE advance in the Gorbachev period was in the security field. Not long before his death in November 1982, Leonid Brezhnev agreed that the "area of application" for the new, intensive round of CSCE talks on confidence building in Stockholm could expand beyond the border area of the western USSR covered in the Helsinki Accords to include the large segment of Soviet territory extending eastward to the Ural Mountains.

The Stockholm negotiations ended in November 1986 with agreement on many important confidence-building measures (officially, "confidence- and security-building measures," or CSBMs). The Soviet

Union agreed for the first time to on-site inspection of Soviet territory: under provisions of the CSCE Stockholm Document, inspectors from other CSCE countries have been drawing on a limited quota of inspections to observe whether military activities inside the former Soviet Union are large enough to have required prenotification. The Stockholm Document also introduced a far-reaching, coherent program of improving the access of member states to information on one another's day-to-day military activities, the so-called transparency measures. Building on the Stockholm Document, two further rounds of negotiation on confidence building in Vienna (1990 and 1992) incorporated many of the ideas developed by historians of war and peace researchers to reduce the risks of inadvertent conflict arising from activities of armed forces in peacetime and to provide warning of deliberate preparation for conflict.

One of the most innovative CSCE confidence-building measures is the procedure on unusual military activities. Under this procedure, a member state can summon a second state to send officials to the CSCE Conflict Prevention Center (CPC) in Vienna to account for unusual military activities on its part. Its sponsors believed that this measure would be a useful device to place the floodlight of international attention on sudden troop concentrations or other military actions intended to intimidate. However, its initial use in the former Yugoslavia was disappointing.

CSCE confidence-building measures also provide for exchange and discussion of information on the size, armament, and organization of armed forces and on defense budgets, for advance notice of deployment of new models of tanks, artillery, and aircraft, and for some verification of these obligations. In the future, the CSCE information exchange will include production of armaments, an important expansion of its coverage. The measure on force-planning adopted at Helsinki 92 provides an opportunity to question critically advance-planning on budgets, structure, and deployment of the armed forces of any member state.

The Conventional Forces in Europe (CFE) Treaty, which was signed in November 1990 and provisionally entered into force in July 1992 after the Soviet successor states had agreed with difficulty on dividing among themselves the conventional arms of the former Soviet Union, was negotiated under the auspices of the CSCE. The "mandate" or agenda of the CFE negotiations formed part of the Document of the Vienna Follow-Up Meeting (1986–89).

The CSCE process of negotiations on confidence building and arms control is ongoing. The July 1992 Helsinki Summit established a Forum for Security Cooperation, a new negotiating arena for both confidence-building and arms control measures. The forum coordinates information exchange and the operation of confidence-building measures. It is trying to develop a standard set of force limitations, provisions for information exchange, and a code of military behavior that would apply to all CSCE states, including the European neutrals not covered by the CFE Treaty.

The CFE Treaty's force limits and the CSCE confidence-building measures have not been rendered obsolete by the end of the cold war and the collapse of the Soviet Union. To the contrary, these measures are needed more than ever given the uneasy, violence-ridden nationalism of the present period. Without the network of practical assurances obtainable through these measures, concerns and suspicions about military activities, especially those of the larger member states, would make European cooperation on political and economic issues very difficult if not impossible. Since Helsinki 92, CSCE cooperation also extends to two further areas related to security, combating terrorism and the drug trade. Up to now, activities in both areas have largely taken the form of exchange of information.

CSCE INSTITUTIONS AND MEASURES FOR CONFLICT PREVENTION

The third major aspect of CSCE expansion in the Gorbachev period was the development of institutions and procedures for crisis management and conflict prevention.

During the cold war, most participants considered a minimum of structure and formality advantageous for CSCE deliberations. The CSCE was then a series of specialized seminars punctuated by sessions of review by foreign ministers. With the advent of the Gorbachev regime, negotiation became more serious in the areas of human rights and military security. But beyond that, as it became apparent during 1989 that Germany would be unified, the communist regimes of Eastern Europe abolished, and Soviet forces withdrawn from Europe, the mission of CSCE shifted from mitigating the effects of an ongoing political confrontation of apparently indefinite duration to consolidating the sudden peace and to preventing another world war or cold war in Europe. The old CSCE methods of ongoing dialogue and persuasion were thought by most member governments to be inadequate to the new task. This conclusion brought many proposals to establish permanent institutions for CSCE. The pressure to do so was intensified by the knowledge that preparatory talks were getting under way for a CSCE Summit that would take place in Paris during 1990, and would celebrate the end of the cold war.

The spectrum of views on establishing new institutions for the CSCE was wide. German Social Democratic leader Egon Bahr proposed converting CSCE by treaty into a supranational institution with integrated military forces. This organization for collective security could if need be decide by majority vote to undertake joint economic sanctions or military action against offending states, whether members or not.[5] Another German expert, Harald Müller, urged establishing a United States of Europe and North America with its own armed forces, a logical idea in many ways, but one that overlooked American ambivalence over the idea of total immersion in Europe.[6] Richard Ullman suggested establishing a European Security Organization, or ESO, building both on the CSCE and the Western European Union, and combining both collective security and arms control functions.[7] Charles and Clifford Kupchan suggested topping off the CSCE as it now stands with an additional great power "security group" or security council (United States, Russia, France, United Kingdom, and Germany), modeled on the post-Napoleonic concert of Europe.[8]

Many of these proposals, especially those advanced in the glowing optimism of liberation and revolution in 1989 and 1990, suggested the abolition of NATO. Those making such suggestions believed there might well be conflicts in the new Europe, but that they would be small ones that European institutions could handle themselves.

The United States, with some support from the United Kingdom, found itself at the other, more restrictive end of this spectrum. Rather late in the game, the United States had become a convert to the original European vision of the CSCE as a community of values based on consensus, operating through periodic conferences and Documents that fixed that consensus, but without permanent institutions. But in the meantime, the European governments had almost without exception moved on from that original view to support institutionalization.

In Washington, the State Department finally prevailed over General Brent Scowcroft's National Security Council (NSC) staff in a lengthy dispute over whether CSCE and NATO should be considered organizations that complemented each other rather than competing. The idea that CSCE and NATO were complementary was contained in a Berlin speech by Secretary of State James Baker in April 1990. However, skepticism toward permanent CSCE institutions persisted in Washington, perhaps not completely without ground, given proposals like those by Egon Bahr and many others to dissolve both NATO and the Warsaw Pact. Proposals of that kind dropped out of sight rapidly as problems like ethnic unrest in Bosnia and nuclear succession in the USSR emerged, only to reemerge in different form as NATO proved unable to cope with these problems. Up to the time of Secretary Baker's statement, the United States opposed all standing institutions for the CSCE and gave this concept only grudging minimalist agreement for some time thereafter.

The problem kept coming up. Even the heads of government meeting at the 1990 Paris Summit could not resolve the difficulty that the CSCE, which foresaw that its Council of Foreign Ministers would meet only once a year, had no agreed procedure to convene the council for emergency purposes. The United States opposed such a procedure; the NSC staff took the view that NATO was the right organization for managing crises in Europe, not CSCE. It took six months more, until the CSCE foreign ministers meeting at Berlin in June 1991, before a procedure could be agreed to convene on an emergency basis the governing council of an organization whose mission was to preserve the peace in Europe. As agreed at Berlin, the Committee of Senior Officials, the next layer down from the foreign ministers, can now be convened within seventy-two hours in a crisis situation, but even then, the request must be backed by an ungainly total of thirteen member states. It took two years more before the CSCE foreign ministers meeting in Rome in late 1993 established a committee of senior officials in Vienna that would be in permanent session, convening at an hour's notice like the North Atlantic Council.

To be fair, the United States was not the only CSCE member state to make difficulties on this issue; the large number of cosponsors for the procedure to summon the Council of Foreign Ministers to emergency session was a requirement of the Soviet Union, whose foreign minister Alexander Bessmertnykh and deputy foreign minister Yuri Kvitsinsky (both soon to be dismissed in connection with the anti-Gorbachev coup), held out during the June 1991 Berlin foreign ministers session for applying the unanimity rule and succeeded in inserting in the text of this measure that emergency sessions must not intervene in internal affairs of a member state.

The desire to preserve NATO was not the only consideration motivating the United States in resisting institutionalization of the CSCE. There is a built-in tension between the role of the United States as a powerful non-European country strongly interested in maintaining the security of Europe, and the position of the European states, which though they cannot always agree on details, are nearly all of the view that the CSCE should be built up further in the direction of supranational authority. The determination to deepen CSCE institutions still further is perhaps strongest in France and Germany, the guiding powers of the European Community, and among the states located close to the former Soviet Union, like Finland, Sweden, the Czech Republic, Poland, and Hungary, which continue to worry over a security vacuum in Eastern Europe. For unified Germany, CSCE is a near-perfect reflection of its security interests: to calm fears over German unification, to influence in a positive way developments in Eastern Europe and the Soviet successor states, and to link the United States to European security.

The fact that the CSCE is not a treaty-based organization but is based on executive agreements among member governments deprives it of some authority, but also gives it considerable flexibility, as ministers and senior officials can often commit their governments on the spot. This capability is shown in the steady although not yet complete improvement of CSCE decisionmaking, with the establishment and building up of the Committee of Senior Officials, establishment of the Office of a Secretary General, and establishment of the Permanent Council.

CSCE EXPANDS TO CRISIS MANAGEMENT

Despite divergent viewpoints about the desirability of institutionalizing the CSCE, at the Paris Summit of November 1990, the participating states agreed on an impressive range of standing institutions; their main focus was on mediation of disputes and the prevention of interstate conflict.

Even as the Paris Summit took place, however, events were in the making that obliged the CSCE to expand its institutions from preventing interstate conflict to cover crisis management and, finally, peacekeeping. A number of armed conflicts had broken out in Europe before CSCE or any of the European security institutions was organized to cope with them. The police states of the Soviet Union and of Eastern Europe, which had ruthlessly suppressed all public disputes within their borders, were no more. The fear of escalation to nuclear war, which had placed iron constraints on conflict with conventional weapons, had also dissolved with the end of the East-West confrontation. Speaking at the Helsinki Summit in July 1992, President Vaclav Havel of Czechoslovakia argued that the new situation in Europe was more dangerous than the cold war.

Two major events precipitated the expansion of CSCE into crisis management and peacekeeping: the outbreak of war in former Yugoslavia in mid-1991 and the entry of the Soviet successor states into CSCE.

When the CSCE Council of Foreign Ministers at its second meeting in Prague (January 1992) acted to accept the Soviet successor states as CSCE members, the ministers did not have much time to think of the implications of their action; the Soviet Union had collapsed only six weeks before, in early December 1991, with the Russo-Ukrainian agreement to withdraw from it.

But the entry of the Soviet successor states into CSCE (the Baltic states had already become members; Georgia did so later) had two important consequences: It extended the CSCE writ into Central Asia, a fact reflected in an extension of the area of application for CSCE confidence-building measures to the territory of states like Kazakhstan and Uzbekistan. Of greater immediate importance, the entry of the successor states into CSCE meant that they were bringing with them their existing quarrels—in

Nagorno-Karabakh, Moldova, and Georgia—and that CSCE was assuming some degree of corporate responsibility for dealing with these problems. Even if these consequences had weighed more heavily with Western governments, the imperatives of including these new states in the CSCE regime of human rights, in conventional and nuclear arms control, and in the regime of confidence-building and transparency measures overrode worries about other effects of their membership in CSCE. Moreover, membership of Russia and the Western successor states was considered essential and there were no equitable criteria for excluding the others.

The outbreak of fighting in the Yugoslav Federation, a charter member, also confronted the CSCE with serious problems. Now, facing the eruption of several conflicts on member-state territory, the CSCE had to move beyond preventing interstate conflict toward coping with actual conflicts and to crisis management, the third stage of its development to date. By this time, at least, the United States had finally shed most of its reluctance about institution building in CSCE.

The shift to crisis management, which requires rapid, effective decisionmaking, highlighted CSCE's major internal problem, the rule that all decisions be by consensus among member governments. The new CSCE institutions had been developed to head off possible conflict between member states, not inside them. Accordingly, the rule that member states were sovereign and secure from outside interference was the primary, founding principle of CSCE, dating from the days when a major interest of most member governments was to protect the independence of the Western European states, the neutrals, and to the extent possible, the Eastern European states, from Soviet encroachment. As a result of this emphasis on sovereignty and of its own early history as a loose organization linking states based on widely different political systems, the CSCE was based on consensus, unlike the UN, which has provision for majority voting in both the General Assembly and the Security Council. In CSCE, the disagreement of a single member state could nullify any projected decision. As the CSCE became involved in the Yugoslav conflict, this rule was modified. But before turning to evaluate CSCE's performance in the former Yugoslavia, we should review CSCE's current structure and institutions.

CURRENT INSTITUTIONS OF THE CSCE

The organizational structure of CSCE, formed through decisions taken at the Paris Summit of November 1990, the Helsinki Summit of July 1992 and in four meetings of the Council of Ministers for Foreign Affairs (Berlin, June 1991; Prague, January 1992; Stockholm, December 1992; Rome, 1993), now includes the following institutions (see chart on page 218) :

INSTITUTIONS OF THE CSCE

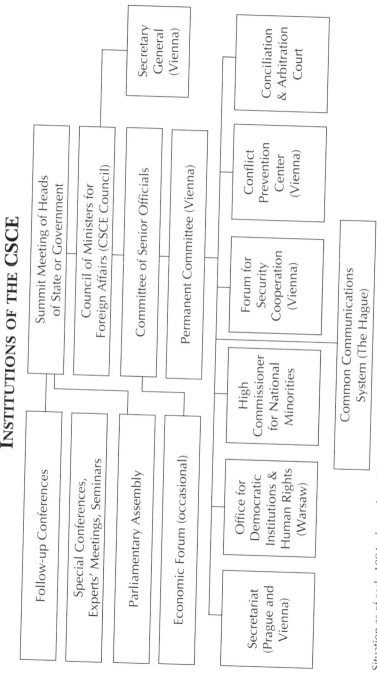

Situation as of early 1994; chart adapted from Norbert Ropers and Peter Schlotter, *The CSCE*, Study no. 14, Foundation Development and Peace, Bonn, 1993, p. 11.

REGULAR SUMMITS. Heads of member state governments meet every two years to review CSCE activities. This practice ensures at least periodic high-level political attention to CSCE activities by member-state governments.

THE COUNCIL OF MINISTERS FOR FOREIGN AFFAIRS. The council is the principal decision-making institution of CSCE. Its "chairman in office," which has been rotated each year on the basis of the capital selected to host the annual meeting of the council, is in formal charge of day-to-day business and of the activities of the Committee of Senior Officials. The council meets at least once a year, but as we have seen, can do so more often.

THE COMMITTEE OF SENIOR OFFICIALS (CSO). The committee is also a nonpermanent organization, consisting of senior officials who travel to its meetings from member-state foreign ministries. It is the executive organ of CSCE. Presided over by a "chairman in office" representing the foreign minister chairing the Council of Ministers, the CSO prepares meetings of the Council of Ministers and carries out its decisions and makes decisions of its own in representation of the council. The CSO has specific responsibilities for early warning, for fact-finding missions, preventive diplomacy, crisis management, and peacekeeping. The CSO, which can meet at short notice, has held most of its meetings at Prague, the site of the CSCE Permanent Secretariat. However, as the CSCE became more and more involved in the crises in the former Yugoslavia and the Soviet successor states, the workload and the tempo of CSO meetings became too much to handle. The Council of Ministers in its December 1992 Stockholm meeting established the Vienna Group, a group of officials of CSCE countries permanently stationed in Vienna and able to meet frequently and if need be at short notice. The December 1993 Rome meeting of the council converted this institution into the Permanent Committee of the CSCE.

THE PERMANENT COMMITTEE OF THE CSCE. The Permanent Committee, consisting of representatives stationed in Vienna (many are at the same time bilateral representatives to the Austrian government or to the International Atomic Energy Agency or other UN bodies in Vienna) has functions similar to those of the NATO Council in Brussels. The main function of the Permanent Committee is to be available at short notice for decisionmaking on day-to-day operational tasks of the CSCE. When the CSO is not in session, the Permanent Committee takes decisions on all CSCE issues. It prepares sessions of the Committee of Senior Officials, runs the procedure on unusual military activities, and operates fact-finding missions on human rights under the Human Dimension program. The committee manages the now numerous CSCE preventive diplomacy and mediating missions in former Yugoslavia and the Soviet successor states.

The establishment of the Permanent Committee should help in CSCE decisionmaking; it probably means that meetings of the Committee of Senior Officials, the next higher level, will become less frequent. However, because of the fact that the CSCE can depart from consensus only in a few specified cases and because of its large (fifty-two members) size, the CSCE is still far from the level of competence of the North Atlantic Council in preparing and reaching decisions. The original decision to disperse permanent CSCE activities at three sites in Vienna, Prague, and Warsaw, taken to tie in Czechoslovakia and Poland even more tightly to CSCE activities, is proving increasingly impractical. Vienna, with better communications and facilities, seems the natural center of gravity for the CSCE.

THE SECRETARY GENERAL OF THE CSCE. The 1992 Stockholm meeting of the Council of Foreign Ministers decided to establish the position of secretary general of the CSCE, a position to which an experienced German diplomat, Wilhelm Hoeynck, was appointed in June 1993. The United States, ever suspicious of CSCE moves toward supranationality, opposed the creation of this position, but the CSCE's structure and finances had become so complex that there was clearly a real need for it. The secretary general's duties include management of CSCE organs, preparing CSCE meetings, and acting as the CSCE's chief administrative officer with responsibility for finances and efficient operations. The secretary general is charged with overseeing the work of the still very small (under twenty in 1993) permanent CSCE staff, civil servants detailed by their governments to work for extended periods in CSCE units, including the personnel of the CSCE Secretariat, the Conflict Prevention Center, and the Office for Democratic Institutions and Practices. Ambassador Hoeynck has located his office in Vienna.

There is some potential for overlap between the secretary general, who is formally responsible directly to the rotating chairman-in-office of the Council of Foreign Ministers, and the Committee of Senior Officials and the Permanent Committee, whose presiding officials also represent the chairman-in-office: However, this will probably be straightened out in time.

THE PERMANENT SECRETARIAT. The small Secretariat is divided into two branches. The branch in Vienna supports the Permanent Council and the secretary general. The branch in Prague has the function of providing administrative support for meetings of the Council of Foreign Ministers and the Committee of Senior Officials. The Prague Secretariat consists of only two officials and a few administrative personnel and is also charged with maintaining CSCE archives and with the public information function of answering outside inquiries about the CSCE.

The Office for Democratic Institutions and Human Rights (ODIHR). An Office of Free Elections established at the 1990 Paris Summit was expanded in 1992 to the Office of Democratic Institutions and Human Rights, after most of the new Eastern member states of CSCE rapidly carried out reasonably democratic elections. Consisting of a director and one additional official, the office's mission is to serve the new Eastern democracies as a center for information and advice on elections and democratic structures, the rule of law, and human rights. It holds seminars and conferences on related issues like migration, treatment of national minorities, and independent news media.

The Office of Democratic Institutions and Human Rights also is responsible for handling claims of violation of human rights under the Human Dimension Mechanism of the CSCE. The agreed procedure for such claims commits member-state governments to respond within four weeks to complaints on human rights of individuals or groups, to meet within three weeks bilaterally with the representatives of the complaining government, to bring these cases to the attention of other member states, and to bring them to the attention of the ongoing Conference on the Human Dimension or the Follow-Up Meetings. The procedure also provides for voluntary requests by a member state to invite monitors and observers on human rights issues from other member governments to assist it in dealing with human rights problems.

In a second procedure, agreed at the Moscow meeting of the Conference on the Human Dimension (October 1991), a member state can request a good offices panel of experts to investigate a human rights problem in a second member state. If the receiving state refuses to invite the panel to observe the problem, that state may be obliged to receive a fact-finding mission within two weeks if six member states request it or to do so immediately if requested by ten member states. Two such missions had been sent by the end of 1993: to Croatia and to Estonia. Under some conditions, this monitoring mission can be extended in time. The Office of Democratic Institutions and Human Rights maintains a list of experts and operates this procedure. With the agreement of the newly established democracies of Eastern Europe and the Soviet successor states, the office is the watchdog of the actual practice of democratic concepts in these states and an important channel for transmitting Western democratic experience.

The procedure permitting the CSCE to send a human rights fact-finding mission to the territory of a member state that is obligated to receive it and to facilitate its work is a limited restriction on state sovereignty. The fact-finding mission remains an informational one; it cannot order officials or citizens of the target state to take actions outside the scope of its enquiries. However, the Helsinki 92 Document (Paragraph 8) emphasizes in language agreed to by all member states that "the commitments undertaken in the field of the human dimension of the CSCE are matters of direct and legitimate concern to all participating states and do not belong exclusively to the internal affairs of the state concerned." This is a precedent-setting statement of the legitimacy of outside interest in how a government treats its own citizens and a justification of at least some degree of outside intervention even if contrary to the desires of that government. It should be kept in mind that compliance with human rights and other CSCE procedures is in effect voluntary. Nonetheless, this measure, like UN intervention on behalf of the Iraqi Kurds and in Somalia, pushes forward the frontier of legitimated intervention by the international community when a state structure is incapable of maintaining minimum public order or minimum welfare and rights of its citizens and the situation does not permit establishing a new government by elections.

In the human rights field, the CSCE works fairly closely with the older Council of Europe, which has been promoting better practices on human rights since its establishment in 1949 to promote the unification of Europe. The council immediately took the initiative on human rights by drafting the European Convention on Human Rights (1950) and establishing the European Court of Human Rights at Strasbourg, which hears cases brought by member states or individuals against states considered to have violated rights specified in the covenant.

In October 1993, a first summit meeting of heads of government of Council of Europe member states convening in Vienna agreed to make the Court of Human Rights a court in permanent session, to accelerate hearings of individual complaints of human rights violations (which now take up to five years), and to draft a framework convention containing principles for protection of national minorities. Efforts to launch a full-scale draft treaty on the latter subject broke down in the face of opposition from Turkey, France, and Great Britain, all countries with difficult minority problems.[9]

It would have been logical from one viewpoint for CSCE to request the Council of Europe to take over responsibility for its work in the human rights field. The council has admitted Poland, Hungary, and the Czech Republic as candidate members. But the council's membership does not include all members of CSCE. Neither the United States nor Canada as non-European countries are members and several Eastern European and Soviet successor states including Russia have not yet met the council's own human rights standards for membership. Moreover, the council has thus far focused on individual cases rather than on institutional change. Nonetheless, there is some overlap and competitive friction between CSCE activities on human rights and the Council of Europe.

THE HIGH COMMISSIONER FOR NATIONAL MINORITIES.

In an important decision taken under the impact of fighting in the former Yugoslavia and the Soviet successor states, the Helsinki 92 Summit established the position of a high commissioner on national minorities to be a troubleshooter in heading off ethnic conflicts. The Stockholm meeting of the Council of Foreign Ministers designated Max van der Stoel, a distinguished former foreign minister of the Netherlands, for this job.

Under guidance from the Committee of Senior Officials, the high commissioner is to act to prevent ethnic conflict at the earliest possible stage, providing early warning of pending conflicts and suggesting early action to defuse confrontation. Working together with the Office for Democratic Institutions and Human Rights, the commissioner is to collect information on possible ethnic frictions from any government or group within the CSCE area, and to promote dialogue through direct consultation with the affected parties.

As one of his first activities, Commissioner van der Stoel brokered an agreement between the Slovak and Hungarian governments on fair treatment for the large Hungarian minority in Slovakia and for the Slovak minority in Hungary. As we have seen, treatment of the Hungarian minority in Slovakia is one of the most troublesome ethnic minority issues in Eastern Europe. The commissioner has also done useful work in Macedonia with regard to treatment of the Albanian minority there. He has undertaken missions to the Baltic states and Romania and presented suggestions to improve minority relations there as well as to improve the situation of European gypsies.

The United States acceded to the proposal to establish the new high commissioner position because nearly all European states wanted it. But the question of how minority issues should be handled has long been disputed between the United States, often with support from the United Kingdom and France (which claims there are no national minorities in France because all are French citizens), and most continental European members of the CSCE. In the U.S. view, human rights are held by the individual. According special rights to groups could undermine equal treatment before the law; the ultimate objective should be to absorb minorities and amalgamate them in the general population, as the United States has historically done. The European experience has been a different one: Numerous, clearly identifiable minorities have existed inside national boundaries for hundreds, even thousands of years. In the

European view, the important thing is to secure fair treatment of these groups by ensuring their use of their own religious practices, language, schools, and so on. In the United States, there has been preferred treatment for minorities in the still-contested affirmative action program. However, the objective of that program is not to perpetuate separate minorities but to place all on an equal footing.

The problem is complicated by the fact that there are two types of minorities in Europe: individuals dispersed through the general population, like North Africans in France, Turks in Germany, and gypsies throughout Europe—people without any territorial claim—and, second, culturally homogeneous groups that have long occupied the same territory, like the Basques or Corsicans. In the first case, general standards of human rights are applicable. In the second case, ethnic minorities usually aspire to a greater degree of autonomy or even independence, often leading to conflict with central authorities, as in Slovenia, Croatia, Abkhazia, and Ossetia.

For decades, the same U.S.-European difference over this issue has prevented agreement in the UN on minority rights. Some progress was made through establishment of the office of a UN High Commissioner for Human Rights in early 1994. In CSCE, this topic was treated without agreement at a meeting on minority issues in Geneva (July 1991) and at the CSCE Moscow Human Dimension meeting (September–October 1991). One specific problem for the United States is that, because CSCE human rights obligations extend to U.S. territory, even though as political agreements rather than as treaties, the federal government might at some future point be faced by local minority initiatives to establish ethnic enclaves on its territory, each with its own language, schools, and laws.

Both the United States and the European Community countries are right for their own spheres, the United States that European procedures are not suitable for application in the United States, and the Europeans that long-standing national minorities in Europe should receive the most sensitive and careful treatment as an important aspect of conflict prevention. In this sense, the decision to establish the Office of a CSCE High Commissioner for National Minorities is fully justified.

The secession of Slovenia, Croatia, and Bosnia from Yugoslavia raised another related problem, that of self-determination of minority groups living inside a larger state. In the abstract, the principle of self-determination is a good thing; in practice, it often leads to bloody conflict or the establishment of ministates without economic viability. With hundreds of national minorities in Europe, encouraging self-determination through secession could lead to chaos. In the Council of Europe's October 1993 Vienna Summit, Czech president Vaclav Havel warned the other heads of government engaged in the effort to formulate a code of protection for

European minorities not to let in the "demon" of ethnic nationalism "through a seemingly innocent emphasis on the rights of minorities and on their right to self-determination."[10]

President Havel was right. Self-determination and national sovereignty would be ridiculous for most of the small, dissatisfied ethnic minorities in Europe. But no one can repudiate the right of national self-determination, which is at the basis of the existence of many CSCE states, among them the Soviet successor states, the United States, and unified Germany, whose East German population voted to exercise self-determination in joining West Germany. The best CSCE leaders have been able to do to clarify the issue was expressed by United States delegate Max Kampelman at the 1991 Moscow meeting on the Human Dimension when he pointed out that no decision on self-determination should be taken unilaterally or in isolation without full consultation with the affected state or states, or implemented by violence.[11] We return to this troubling issue at the end of the book.

THE FORUM FOR SECURITY COOPERATION. The forum, located in Vienna, is CSCE's arms control segment. This committee of member-state officials is charged with standardizing existing arms control agreements covering Europe, operating confidence-building measures, organizing exchange of information on armed forces and their activities and operating procedures for clarifying that information, devising further arms control and confidence-building measures, and preparing seminars and conducting a dialogue on future defense budgets, force structure, equipment, and documents. Current activities of the forum are described later in the book.

THE CONFLICT PREVENTION CENTER (CPC). The Conflict Prevention Center is the stepchild of the CSCE system. With a staff of three officials, it has the multiple functions of providing support for implementation of confidence-building measures, organizing the annual exchange of military information and an annual meeting to assess the operation of confidence-building measures, and supporting mediation, political fact-finding, and peacekeeping missions.

Earlier, the German government had wanted to place a senior official in charge of the Conflict Prevention Center and to give him considerable autonomy to raise warnings of threatening new situations and to take early action to deal with them on his own initiative. Some experts suggested that the center have its own aircraft for observation, or even satellite capability. The United States and some other CSCE participants strongly resisted the possibility that a CSCE institution could develop its own supranational competence without government instruction and gave this executive authority to the Committee of Senior Officials and the Permanent Committee acting under direct instructions from member governments.

THE COMMON COMMUNICATIONS SYSTEM. Authorized in 1990, this system was still not fully operational at the time of the Helsinki Summit two years later, largely because of high hook-up costs arising from obsolete communications systems in Eastern Europe and the Soviet successor states. By November 1992, only twenty-five of fifty-two member states were linked by the system.

THE CONCILIATION AND ARBITRATION COURT "WITHIN THE CSCE." The December 1992 Stockholm foreign ministers' meeting approved the text of a Convention on Arbitration and Conciliation establishing a Court of Conciliation and Arbitration "within the CSCE." The latter phrase is intended to indicate that this institution is not supported by all CSCE members. France, Germany, Switzerland, and some other CSCE members have long pressed for a treaty providing for obligatory arbitration, a principle rejected by the United States and United Kingdom, both reluctant to accept development of the CSCE toward supranational authority. A compromise was reached permitting establishment of such a tribunal by those CSCE states that wish to subscribe to it. The court will be established when twelve CSCE member states have ratified the convention; by early 1994, only about a third of CSCE's fifty-three members had indicated willingness to do so. The United States and United Kingdom have declared that they would not join. Under the convention, the CSCE Council of Foreign Ministers is to be informed if a party to a dispute does not accept a settlement proposed by a conciliation commission of the court. The council can then presumably take some further action. Acceptance of the findings of an arbitration tribunal of the court is obligatory. In setting up the court, the CSCE has thus shown useful flexibility in acting on the desire of some members to engage in a particular project while permitting others to opt out.

The CSCE has three other agreed procedures for peaceful settlement of disputes between members states:

1. The "Valetta mechanism" permits a member state to insist on appointment of a panel of arbitrators to resolve an ongoing interstate dispute. There is provision for selection of the panel even if one of the parties disagrees on its composition. The findings of the panel are not binding, but the issue can be referred to the Committee of Senior Officials if it endangers peace, security, or stability in Europe.

2. The 1992 Stockholm foreign ministers' meeting adopted a conciliation procedure that is available to any two or more member states on an ad hoc basis on a given issue, or if they desire, on a reciprocal basis for all disputes. In practice, this measure will cover those states that do not wish to sign the Convention on Conciliation.

3. In an unusual departure, the Stockholm foreign ministers' meeting conferred on the Committee of Senior Officials authority to direct any two member states, with or without their agreement, to seek settlement through a conciliation panel of disputes that they have not been able to resolve within a reasonable time. However, this procedure cannot be invoked if a party to the dispute considers that the dispute involves issues of its territorial integrity, sovereignty over its territory, or national defense. This restriction was originally introduced by Turkey and Greece, motivated by their quarrel over sovereignty over areas of the Aegean Sea, some of them believed to be oil-rich, and by the United Kingdom, which wished to avoid a new opening for Spanish claims over Gibraltar.[12]

The CSCE thus has at its disposal a wide range of agreed procedures for conciliation and arbitration between member states, but few if any have yet been invoked.

THE PARLIAMENTARY ASSEMBLY. In response to a U.S. suggestion, a group of legislators from CSCE member states held a preparatory meeting in Madrid in May 1989, a first plenary session in Budapest in early July 1992 and a second in Helsinki in July 1993, and sent a delegation to monitor the December 1993 Russian elections. The assembly is designed primarily to bolster parliamentary practices in the newly established democracies; its resolutions are passed to the Council of Foreign Ministers for possible action.

THE ECONOMIC FORUM. The Prague meeting of the Council of Foreign Ministers (January 1992) established a CSCE Economic Forum to be operated by the Committee of Senior Officials. The forum, also the result of a U.S. initiative, is not a permanent institution but a procedure for convening conferences on specific problems of economic cooperation—the first was held in March 1993 in Prague and the second a year later in the same city. The forum provides the CSCE a vehicle for activity in a field that on a day-to-day basis is dominated by the activities of the European Union, Organization for Economic Cooperation and Development, and the UN Economic Commission for Europe. The forum is intended to spotlight specific economic topics calling for intergovernmental attention.

NONGOVERNMENTAL ORGANIZATIONS. Owing to membership in it of many European governments with strong peace movements, the CSCE is exceptional among intergovernmental conferences in making a sustained effort, mandated by the Paris Summit, to inform nongovernmental organizations (NGOs) on CSCE activities and to encourage their attendance and participation at many of these events. The Office for Democratic Institutions and Human Rights and the High Commissioner for National Minorities depend on a flow of information from NGOs. The United States Commission on Security and Cooperation in Europe, an unusual mixed commission with participation by the executive branch and Congress, is active in this area, and several European countries like Austria and Finland have very active NGO organizations.

CSCE MOVES INTO PEACEKEEPING

As part of its move into crisis management, the Helsinki 92 Summit decided that the CSCE could undertake peacekeeping operations (but not peace enforcement, which is thus far specifically excluded) and that, for such services, it could call on NATO, the Western European Union, or on the Commonwealth of Independent States, the rudimentary organization hastily cobbled together after the collapse of the Soviet Union. According to the Helsinki 92 Document, CSCE peacekeeping operations can take place only with the "consent of the parties directly concerned," and only after "an effective and durable cease-fire" has been established; they "will not entail enforcement actions."[13]

These moves were made with U.S. support, indeed at U.S. initiative. By the time the preparations for the Helsinki Summit began in March 1992, the United States was energetically supporting the crisis management role for CSCE that it had opposed at the Paris Summit of November 1990. In effect, the agreement that NATO and CSCE should cooperate on peacekeeping meant the end of the lingering American tendency to see CSCE as competing with NATO. Now the two organizations were seen as fully complementary. In fact, CSCE was a potential lifeline for NATO at a time when the latter's future was in doubt—the new arrangement created the possibility of new practical uses for NATO forces.

Giving CSCE a peacekeeping mission and placing NATO troops at its disposal for that purpose was an imaginative move, but it left some practical problems. Among them was the continuing U.S. vendetta with France over organizing European security. France wants a continued guarantee of U.S. military protection for Europe—from a distance—while otherwise allowing European governments to make their own decisions. Consequently, France objected to the establishment of the North Atlantic Cooperation Council and came out against the proposed new peace-making arrangement between NATO and CSCE. It argued that NATO should stick to its sole task of providing insurance against backsliding in Russian policy and should leave peacekeeping to the Western European Union. To this end, in a meeting at Bonn two weeks before the Helsinki Summit, France mounted a parallel peacekeeping offer to the CSCE from the WEU.

To meet French objections, a complicated set of CSCE procedures for calling on outside forces for peacekeeping had to be devised: Military personnel for peacekeeping are to be supplied by individual CSCE participating states (that is, not by NATO as an organization); decisions to seek the support of NATO, WEU, or Commonwealth of Independent States will be on a case-by-case basis (that is, NATO will not become the habitual peacekeeping agent for CSCE); and any action must be preceded by consultations with the individual members of NATO, WEU, or the CIS, rather than with the leadership of these organizations as such.[14] Because France retains a veto both in NATO and in the CSCE, these provisions entail a real possibility of gridlock and inaction. Moreover, given the painful difficulties of UN peacekeeping in Croatia and Bosnia and NATO's travails in making a peacekeeping contribution there since both NATO and CSCE decided to go into peacekeeping in the summer of 1992, CSCE governments have been very cautious about undertaking actual peacekeeping missions.

The Actual Record

The CSCE now has a wide repertory of permanent institutions and agreed procedures in the security field. What has CSCE actually done since its first institutions and procedures were established at the end of 1990?

As the war in former Yugoslavia erupted in the summer of 1991, the CSCE went into action rapidly—but without great effect. The Committee of Senior Officials was convened on an emergency basis in July 1991 and has remained seized with the Yugoslav problem. The procedures of the unusual military activities confidence-building measure, for which great hopes had been held, were invoked at the Conflict Prevention Center in Vienna in early July 1991 by Austria and Italy with complaints about violation of their air space by Yugoslav military aircraft. Yugoslav officials appeared in Vienna as required by the measure. A chairman's report calling on parties to stop all fighting and recall all armed forces to barracks was unanimously adopted, but Yugoslavia denied the border incursion and refused to accept CSCE observers. (The June 1992 foreign ministers meeting agreed that the center should have the right to send fact-finding observers of its own in future cases.) In September 1991, Hungary invoked the unusual military activities procedure to raise concerns in a bilateral meeting with Yugoslavia about Yugoslav military activities on the Hungarian border. This led to a joint report, but no further action was taken. Yugoslavia itself used the measure in the spring of 1992 to request information from Hungary about an alleged violation.

The unusual military activities procedure also could not be used for conflict inside the borders of a state like the fighting that then broke out in Croatia. Consequently, the procedure faded into the background. The main day-to-day responsibility within CSCE for action on Yugoslavia shifted to the Committee of Senior Officials. The Council of Foreign Ministers meeting in Prague issued the first of several declarations calling on the combatants to stop fighting and to resolve their differences in negotiation, offering to mediate. The language was anodyne because of the need under the consensus procedure to secure the vote of the Yugoslav government.

As the crisis continued and the European Community became involved in mediation and in monitoring the fighting, the CSCE played a supporting role. The Committee of Senior Officials passed resolutions supporting the European Community (EC) intervention and calling for an embargo on arms for the combatants. It sent some monitors of its own, including some from Sweden and Canada, to supplement those of the European Community on the scene.

But the CSCE was largely powerless to take more useful action on its own. Part of the problem was the CSCE's rule of taking decisions by consensus; many decisions were blocked by the Yugoslav delegation or abandoned because of the probability of a Yugoslav veto. Finally, in May 1992, the Committee of Senior Officials, then engaged in preparing the Helsinki 92 Summit, made experimental use of a new "consensus-minus-one" procedure approved at the Prague foreign ministers meeting. The committee excluded the Yugoslav rump government (by now representing only Serbia and Montenegro) from discussion of Yugoslav issues for a month. The United States wanted to exclude the two Yugoslav republics from CSCE membership indefinitely, but Russia, which has traditional ties of friendship with Serbia, objected to the severity of this action. In July 1992, to avoid the embarrassment of having a Yugoslav delegation possibly headed by Serbian strongman Slobodan Milosevic appear at the Helsinki summit, the Committee of Senior Officials suspended the rump government of Yugoslavia from CSCE membership for one hundred days, later extended.

Once again, the United States and a few other member states pressed for expulsion, but once again, Russia said no.

The consensus-minus-one procedure permits CSCE decisions to be made even if a member state opposes, but only if that state is deemed to have engaged in gross violations of CSCE principles and commitments. Moreover, action against the offender is limited to actions outside the borders, like political statements of disapproval and suspension of membership, and does not entail any right to infringe the sovereignty of the offending member state through any form of intervention inside its borders. The measure at least allows the CSCE to speak with a clear voice, as was not possible earlier. However, the limitations of this device were illustrated by repeated Russian intervention in favor of Serbia, causing some CSCE negotiators to quip that the measure ought to be recast as "consensus-minus-two."

The Committee of Senior Officials also sent several fact-finding missions to Yugoslavia in 1991. But the fighting continued unabated. The gap between CSCE's pretensions to keep the peace in Europe and what it could actually achieve on the ground was large and painfully evident. The CSCE was learning the lesson of the League of Nations: that institutions and resolutions are insufficient to meet bullets.

However, during 1992, CSCE activities in former Yugoslavia increased as the organization began to develop a distinctive and useful role of its own. The Committee of Senior Officials sent fact-finding missions to Croatia, Bosnia, Kosovo, and Belgrade (the latter to observe elections). Gradually, it began to send small resident teams of monitors (a total of twenty diplomats, officially, "Missions of Long Duration") to three regions of Serbia that have large ethnic minority groups and where there was risk of mistreatment by the Serb authorities, with an ensuing possibility of the spread of armed conflict. These were Kosovo (with a very large Albanian population), Sandjak (Muslims), and Vojvodina (Hungarians). These monitors operated on their own locally, seeking to mediate and resolve local ethnic tensions before they built up further.[15] These missions were useful. However, in July 1993, because of CSCE's continued formal suspension of Yugoslavia from membership, the Serbian authorities refused to renew the agreement on which the missions were based and withdrew the monitors' visas.

There was a resident CSCE monitor team in Macedonia, where there was also considerable risk of expansion of ethnic conflict, particularly between Macedonians and the large Albanian minority. The eighteen-man CSCE team, mainly diplomats detached from their home ministries, monitored the situation on the border with Serbia—the Albanian enclave of Kosovo is right across the border. A small UN force including a U.S.

infantry company was deployed in the same area. The CSCE mission also maintained a continual dialogue with the Macedonian government and political parties, warning and advising for conflict prevention and reducing ethnic frictions. The mission had no aid to distribute, only the prestige of the CSCE and of sending governments, but these factors gave it some weight.

The CSCE sent Sanctions Assistance Missions (a total of 150 persons) to Romania, Hungary, and other countries bordering Serbia and Montenegro to monitor and coordinate UN sanctions against these two republics. An Italian diplomat was appointed as sanctions coordinator, and an experts meeting was held in early 1994 on how to equalize the burden of economic sanctions. However, the CSCE was unable to carry out a request from the UN secretary general in July 1992 that it provide a mechanism for supervising heavy weapons in Bosnia-Herzegovina. This mission had to be carried out, although only partially, by the UN itself through United Nations Protection Forces (UNPROFOR) in Croatia and Bosnia.[16]

CSCE ACTIVITIES IN THE SOVIET SUCCESSOR STATES

The CSCE is playing a growing role in mediation and observer activity in the Soviet successor states. This activity too started on a small scale. Beginning in 1992, the chairman-in-office of the CSCE Council (in 1992–93, the Swedish foreign minister), appointed "Personal Representatives" to monitor ethnic conflicts and peacekeeping operations in Moldova (July 1992 and March 1993) and Georgia (November 1992) to advise participants in the conflict and report back on progress. In Georgia, a six-man CSCE team monitored the activities of the 1,800-man Russian, Ossetian, and Georgian peacekeeping force.

By 1994 the CSCE had missions in Moldova, Georgia, Nagorno-Karabakh, Estonia, Latvia, and Tajikistan. Short visits gave way to resident missions of four to eight diplomats and experts. Typically, the objective was to discuss with parties to the conflict, to identify sources of tension, to make suggestions on their elimination, to raise with local commanders cease-fire questions, to collect information on the military situation, and to assist in the creation of a political framework for a political solution.

In Estonia and Latvia the job of the CSCE mission is a different one, to improve relations between national and local governments and the Russian minorities. The mission works with government authorities responsible for citizenship, migration, language, social services, and employment, and with local groups to facilitate dialogue between Russian and national communities. The mission to Tajikistan started only in 1994 and at the outset focused on observing local conditions, lending its weight to recommendations of the already present UN observer, and on trying to define functions the CSCE could usefully perform on its own.[17]

In Nagorno-Karabakh, the CSCE involvement has been broader and more ambitious. Since 1991, the CSCE has repeatedly sent observer missions to Nagorno-Karabakh in the effort to bring about a monitored ceasefire. During 1992–93, an ad hoc committee of eleven CSCE states, including the United States and Russia, was able to convene representatives of Armenia and Azerbaijan and of Nagorno-Karabakh to a series of meetings in Rome (the Azeris of Nagorno-Karabakh attended all, the Armenians of Nagorno-Karabakh only a few) designed to lead to a more formal conference in Minsk to approve a CSCE monitoring presence with the mission of ensuring safe passage of food and relief supplies into Nagorno-Karabakh and exclusion of further weapons. The Minsk meeting was repeatedly postponed because of lack of substantive agreement among the main parties. Among other problems, Azerbaijan objected that establishing safe access from Karabakh to the nearby Armenian border in order to facilitate transport of food and medicine would prejudice Azeri sovereignty over the corridor area.

In spring 1993, CSCE was on the verge of deploying a hundred-man unarmed monitor mission under a Swedish general in Karabakh when fighting intensified as the Armenians went on the offensive. The Committee of Senior Officials sent another mission to Karabakh in June 1993 to arrange for deployment of a larger group of up to 600 monitors.[18] Although the UN too has sent fact-finding missions to Karabakh, by mutual agreement, it has thus far left this conflict to the CSCE, endorsing the work of the CSCE in Security Council resolutions. A mediator from the Russian Foreign Ministry is active in the area. Since Western countries are not willing to send peacekeeping troops to trouble spots in the former Soviet Union like Karabakh, the only feasible peacekeeping force there, if fighting is finally stopped through Russian economic pressures on the combatants, is a combined Russian-Armenian-Azerbaijan force. This could be monitored by the CSCE. The CSCE could also authorize the peacekeeping operation and participate in the formulation of its rules and goals.

This possibility points to a wider objective. During 1992 and 1993, the United States, Russia, Germany, and other Western CSCE members cooperated in an effort to take a more general approach to the problems of peacekeeping in the former Soviet Union. These problems arose when conflicts erupted, when Russia appealed for peacekeeping help from the UN and CSCE, when the Western countries declined to send peacekeeping troops to this Eastern morass, and when Russia then intervened with its own forces, leading to foreign criticism that Russian imperialism was again on the rise. The objective of the Western countries was to delegate the peacekeeping role in the former Soviet Union to Russia and the Commonwealth of Independent States, as provided for in the Helsinki 92 CSCE decision to go into peacekeeping. In return for CSCE endorsement of the operation, Russia would accept some degree of CSCE guidance in defining the aims and rules of engagement of the peacekeeping operation and even its tactics.

This approach was ingenious but risky. CSCE influence could never be certain or decisive, and the whole idea was open to accusations that CSCE was condoning and whitewashing acts of old-fashioned Russian expansionism. Of course, it was Foreign Minister Kozyrev's desire to avoid these charges that provided the Russian motivation for the scheme, while CSCE with minimal investment of its own would be able to kibitz and influence Russian decisions. There was no discussion as yet of a CSCE role in financing these operations. But at least it would be a CSCE contribution to several dangerous situations.

An effort to gain approval of the CSCE Council of Foreign Ministers in their December 1993 meeting for a general CSCE peacekeeping code to be applied in cases of this kind failed when Estonia and others criticized it as an effort by Moscow to obtain international support for questionable military activities. As a compromise, the council agreed that CSCE could on a case-by-case ad hoc basis consider setting up CSCE cooperative arrangements in order to ensure that the role and functions of a third-party military force in a conflict area would be consistent with CSCE principles and objectives. The council instructed the Committee of Senior Officials and the Permanent Committee to develop conditions and principles for possible CSCE arrangements of this type, to include: respect for sovereignty and territorial integrity; consent of the parties; impartiality; multinational character; a clear mandate; transparency; integral link to a political process for conflict resolution; and a plan for orderly withdrawal.[19] The outcome fell short of the blanket CSCE endorsement Russia had been seeking and also of a standard CSCE procedure for influencing specific Russian peacekeeping operations, but it came close to the latter and it was clear this effort would be pressed further. At the same time, it was unclear how far the concept would get if Russian policy toward neighboring republics hardened under the influence of nationalist gains in the 1993 Russian elections.

THE CSCE AS AN EXAMPLE

Despite its problems, the CSCE, especially its highly developed repertory of confidence-building measures, has had considerable impact on other parts of the globe. The CSCE has been used as an informal model for parallel discussion of political, economic, and security issues in the round of Mideast talks between the Arab states and Israel launched by the United States in October 1991 at Madrid. It has been used as a model by the two Korean states in organizing their own security dialogue and by the Association of Southeast Asian Nations (ASEAN) states in promoting confidence building. CSCE experience has been drawn on for agreed confidence-building measures between India and Pakistan and between India and China.

The Helsinki 92 Summit approved liaison arrangements between CSCE and the European Community, Council of Europe, NATO, WEU, and the United Nations. The summit agreed to a Japanese request for association with the CSCE, which has allowed Japan to attend meetings of the Council of Foreign Ministers and Committee of Senior Officials and other specialized bodies in which it has an interest. One difficulty in developing this desirable relationship is that enhancing Japan's status might have to be accompanied by similar treatment for North African Arab states, a prospect less attractive to some CSCE states. However, if the relationship with Japan does develop further, then the CSCE, whose boast is that it extends from Vancouver to Vladivostok, could be on its way to becoming a security organization that covers most of the Northern Hemisphere.

CURRENT AND FUTURE PROBLEMS

The costs of CSCE's traditional conference activities were absorbed without great difficulty by member governments. But, with a quite large expansion of crisis management activities in the former Yugoslavia and the former Soviet Union, finances became a serious problem for the CSCE. Individual monitoring or conflict-prevention activities have been financed through ad hoc levies on members according to the plan of graduated annual contributions established by the Helsinki Summit. But as of early 1993, 50 percent of designated contributions were in arrears, especially from the Soviet successor states. CSCE's ordinary budget for 1991 was only $3 million, and for 1992, $4 million. But if the CSCE took on monitoring a cease-fire in Nagorno-Karabakh, estimates of the ensuing costs alone ranged from $10 million to $30 million per year. The extension of CSCE membership to the Central Asian republics was probably unavoidable in the circumstances of the time. Yet it represents an overextension of CSCE's financial and human resources.

Despite improvements, there is still too much overlap between CSCE and other organizations. The CSCE is to some extent involved in institutional competition with the Council of Europe on human rights, with the

EC on activities in former Yugoslavia, and, to a considerable extent, with the North Atlantic Cooperation Council (NACC) and WEU with regard to both organizing military dialogue with officers and defense officials of Eastern Europe and Soviet successor states. On the other hand, CSCE should really have organized the conference held by the European Union in April 1994 at the initiative of France's prime minister, Edouard Balladur, to draw up a "Stability Pact" designed to guarantee rights of minorities and consolidate frontiers in Europe. This French initiative, motivated by the European Union's inability to cope with the Yugoslav tragedy, is designed to head off similar outbreaks in Eastern European states that are candidates for membership in the European Union; it does not extend to the former Soviet Union. The plan was that the opening conference would be followed by bilateral negotiations between Eastern European states on good neighborly relations and by a windup conference in 1995 or 1996.[20]

Although there is plenty to do in the peacekeeping field in Europe, there is also proliferation and overlap in the activities of various agencies—UN, NATO, NACC, EC, WEU, and CSCE itself—in various trouble spots like Moldova and Georgia, and a need to coordinate better and to give priority to one organization in a specific area or activity. In 1993, the heads of the UN and CSCE missions in Georgia were reported not to be on speaking terms. The CSCE Council of Foreign Ministers in December 1993 appealed to the UN to agree to a common UN-CSCE mission in Georgia. In such cases the CSCE, with a more restricted mandate, is obliged to subordinate itself to the EC and above all to the UN.

CSCE does not have a military organization of its own or a tried means of assembling military contributions from member states and is unlikely to do so for some time to come. Existing organizations including NATO and WEU are too small in terms of membership and are competitive with one another. Even the North Atlantic Cooperation Council, which does include all members of NATO, the Eastern European and Baltic states, and the Soviet successor states, does not include the European neutrals. And the big gap in European peacekeeping remains Germany, with its inability to resolve its internal controversies about sending German armed forces beyond its borders. The CSCE is still waiting for a breakthrough to a possible cease-fire in Nagorno-Karabakh and a real test there of its capacity to perform at least traditional peacekeeping functions.

Conflict prevention and mediation are the most important areas of CSCE strength. Here, the CSCE is clearly ahead of the UN both as regards developing institutions of mediation and procedures for application on the territory of member states. This is the logical area for future CSCE development. But CSCE conflict prevention institutions and procedures remain directed mainly toward coping with the possibility of interstate war, and they are not sufficiently oriented toward heading off domestic ethnic conflicts. The potential CSCE deal with Russia on peacekeeping remains a gamble, although a brilliant one.

CSCE will also have to find productive ways of maintaining the important support and contribution of the United States without obliging the United States to accept moves toward pan-European supranationalism. The flexibility the CSCE has shown in establishing a Court of Conciliation and Arbitration for some member states while setting up less formal conciliation procedures for use by the United States and other participants that did not wish to sign the treaty establishing the court is a useful precedent.

In recent years, several proposals have been made to convert CSCE obligations into treaty form from their present status as political understandings among member governments. France proposed during the preparations for the Helsinki 92 Summit and at the summit itself that CSCE security obligations at least be converted into treaty form. The United States opposed the project. It does not want to be confronted by a choice between accepting treaty obligations overriding United States domestic law or rejecting CSCE obligations it has already accepted. As one U.S. official put it informally, a CSCE treaty based on European concepts of minority rights might someday lead to efforts to establish a separate Hispanic republic in the American Southwest. But this objection does not apply to some codification of CSCE obligations in the security field. That could have some positive benefits. The idea of a CSCE security treaty is far from dead, but it would represent a quantum jump for which most member states are not yet ready. This possibility is further described at the end of the book.

The United States's dilemma is reflected in another issue, the extent of the CSCE area of application. Some CSCE agreements, like those on human rights and exchange of data on military forces, defense budgets, and production, extend to the entire territory of all CSCE member states. Other CSCE agreements, like the confidence-building measures, have an "area of application" that covers the territory of all member states in Europe—except Russia, which, unfortunately, is only partially included. Russia would accept inclusion of all its territory in these measures if U.S. territory were included. But, owing to U.S. opposition to accepting constraints on military activities on its home territory, these measures also omit the entire territory of the United States and Canada. Here again, the United States is partway in the CSCE and partway out.

The architects of CSCE have already incorporated into it an unprecedented number of devices for confidence building and conciliation. The CSCE does not need more new machinery, but rather the willingness and determination to use existing machinery. There are four possible exceptions: With regard to conflict prevention, the CSCE has as yet no capacity either to penalize by imposing economic sanctions or to reward through economic incentives. The first problem, sanctions, should be easier to settle than the second, incentives. The Council of Foreign Ministers can simply give itself this capacity by deciding to impose sanctions in a specific case that affects a member state, if necessary applying to the UN to broaden application of the sanctions to countries outside the CSCE area. Moreover, arranging a package of grants, loans, and credits as the European Community is doing on behalf of the Organization for Economic Cooperation and Development (OECD) countries should also be feasible. Second, the CSCE also needs to develop a code for national minorities, providing a prescribed, nonviolent path to autonomy within national borders for those minorities willing to pay the price; we discuss this possibility in our final chapter. Third, CSCE has shown flexibility in adding human rights and minority rights experts to its resident missions. But it needs to go further and to establish permanent conciliation and confidence-building centers in critical areas that include senior officials of the host state and neighboring governments, plus officials from Western states not involved in the quarrel. Two obvious candidates for such CSCE regional centers are Ukraine and Macedonia. A CSCE regional center for Ukraine with a permanent office in Kiev, with members consisting of Ukraine and all its neighbors including Russia, and some outside CSCE members like the United States and Germany, could discuss Ukraine's security problems on a continuing basis, help to keep down the temperature of Russian-Ukrainian relations, and, if needed, develop and apply confidence-building measures tailored for the Ukraine situation.

Finally, with fifty-two equally sovereign members, the CSCE is unwieldy. If it ever undertakes major responsibility for handling a crisis, its decisionmaking will need to be streamlined, especially as regards its conflict prevention and mediation operations. Establishment of the Office of Secretary General, of the Committee of Senior Officials and the Permanent Committee are moves in the right direction but not enough in view of the large size of CSCE membership. Large organizations need some device, whether in the form of a designated head or an informal steering group of more powerful members, before they can take effective action. The latter approach is incorporated in the mechanism of the Permanent Five members of the UN Security Council and is also found in the informal grouping of four or five member governments—most often, the United States, United Kingdom, France, and Germany—that has made many of NATO's decisions.

Czechoslovakia's Vaclav Havel and several others have suggested establishment of a CSCE Security Council similar to that of the UN. The CSCE Council of Foreign Ministers has a chairman with service for a year. Although both Czechoslovakia and Sweden provided energetic chairpersons, there was somewhat less energy from their Italian successor. More important, the chairman does not have clear additional responsibilities that go much beyond administration of agreed CSCE procedures. The Helsinki Document endorses the idea, taken from the European Community, of using a "troika" of past, present, and future CSCE chairmen for day-to-day administrative decisions. But, because the CSCE's practice of rotation of the chairmanship could cause the troika to be composed of the representatives of three small states—for example, Latvia, Liechtenstein, and Lithuania, or Malta, Moldova, and Monaco—this form of leadership does not appeal to the larger countries as a basis for substantive decisions affecting all members. The Helsinki 92 Document does foresee establishment of ad hoc steering groups for individual peacekeeping operations, but so far, it has not been possible to reach agreement on how members of these steering groups would be chosen.

One logical solution of the leadership dilemma would be to establish a CSCE Security Council based on the scale of contributions for CSCE member states established by Helsinki 92, with the six largest members (France, Germany, Italy, Russia, the United Kingdom, and the United States) as permanent members, but without a veto—this is, after all, a steering committee for an organization that still does not envisage binding its members through treaty obligations—and with other member governments serving in rotation.

No matter how this specific issue is resolved, and no matter how many limited divergences from consensus the CSCE agrees on, the CSCE would probably be wholly paralyzed by serious disputes between its larger members, say, Germany and Russia or Russia and the United States. The reluctance of Russia to cooperate on CSCE decisions like those designed to pressure Serbia sends a dangerous signal, particularly in the light of Russia's potential for movement toward more autocratic government.

CSCE's record in its earliest phases, while the Soviet Union still existed, is one of solid achievement. It remains a valuable vehicle for arranging systematic dialogue in all spheres between the Western states and the states of Eastern Europe and the former Soviet Union, and an important vehicle for continuing U.S. engagement in security issues in Europe.

However, CSCE's record in the first few years of operating its new function of crisis prevention and crisis management has been mixed, with many worthwhile day-to-day results. On one hand, CSCE has been an international trailblazer in conflict prevention and conflict resolution. It has gone further than any other multilateral international organization in legitimizing multilateral intervention when national authorities do not meet minimum standards of human rights. On the other hand, together with other European security institutions, the CSCE, however understandably, failed the test of conflict prevention and peacemaking in former Yugoslavia.

CSCE's next and possibly decisive tests are whether it can contribute materially to preventing new ethnic conflicts in Eastern Europe and the Soviet successor states, while coping with the existing ethnic conflicts that have been slowly burning away in the Balkans and the Soviet successor states, like brush fires moving toward full-scale forest fires. Civil servants and diplomats have given the CSCE the widest array of conflict-prevention measures ever agreed by governments. The main question remains whether CSCE can marshall enough backing from member governments and can bring enough resources to bear to have a decisive effect on at least some of the many problems it is dealing with or whether its impact will remain secondary even though useful.

10

NATO'S NEW ROLE—
AND NEW PROBLEMS

Since its formation in 1949, the North Atlantic Treaty Organization has achieved two magnificent results. First, as senior U.S. officers like to put it, NATO won the cold war without firing a shot. Although this claim overlooks bloody conflicts in Korea and Vietnam, NATO was the most important aspect of a Western policy of containment of Soviet expansion that culminated in the collapse of the Soviet Union and of the communist-dominated governments of Eastern Europe. And it is true that, when the Soviet army withdrew from most of Eastern Europe without violence, NATO accomplished its containment task peacefully. Second, NATO provided the necessary security assurance for the economic and political integration of Europe following World War II, which brought European Community institutions strong enough to rule out war among European states that had been fighting one another for a millennium.

It is nearly certain that future historians will confirm this assessment. But does achieving such unparalleled success mean that NATO's work has been done? Should it give way, perhaps to a strengthened Western European Union (WEU), the defense arm of the European Union, or to some more highly organized version of the Conference on Security and Cooperation in Europe (CSCE) equipped with its own security council and armed forces?

Outcomes like these are possible in the long term, and we will discuss them further. But after reviewing the security issues of post-cold war Europe and the institutions now available to cope with them, the

conclusion seems unavoidable that an active NATO with a sizable contingent of U.S. troops will be needed over the coming decades to provide
the assurance necessary for continued European integration and for a sustained Western effort to help in building democracy in Russia and other
Soviet successor states and in Eastern Europe. No other security organization existing or on the horizon can perform as effectively NATO's main
functions of serving as insurance against the possibility of a resurgent
Russia and at the same time as a major vehicle for integration of Russia
into the Western system.

To say that an "active" NATO will be needed in coming decades is
to make the point that NATO as an organization is almost certain to survive over the next two decades and quite possibly even longer. But there
is a world of difference between an active NATO and a pro forma organization of diplomats going through the motions of administering unsolved
problems. The distinction is like that between the active UN Security
Council of today and its relatively ineffectual cold war precursor.

Unfortunately, there is no assurance that NATO will maintain the
vitality to perform its tasks effectively. Among the obstacles to NATO's
continuing effectiveness are the diminishing willingness of the U.S.
Congress to pay the costs of a large U.S. troop presence in Europe; conflict between NATO's role of insuring against a resurgent Russia and its
role of integrating Russia in a broader European community, and the
unwillingness of nearly all NATO governments to pay the political,
human, and economic costs of peacekeeping in Eastern Europe.

As a result, the tasks that an active NATO might best fulfill may be
performed inadequately or not at all. If things develop in this way, the current strong emphasis in Europe on multilateral approaches and integration
in security matters may in time yield to a trend toward individual autonomy and greater self-reliance on the part of member governments, what
in NATO parlance is called the "renationalization" of defense.

CONTINUING BENEFITS FROM NATO

NATO's most important continuing function is to provide general
assurance about the security of Europe. NATO insulates Europe against
negative developments in Russia or in united Germany, and against any
form of coercive hegemony over Europe. Without the confidence provided by a functioning NATO, the European integration effort could fal-
ter, and Western help for the democratization process in Russia and
Eastern Europe would be sharply curtailed. Instead, European leaders and
publics would be spending much of their time and energy worrying about
the Russians or the Germans. NATO itself also provides a vehicle for

supporting development toward functioning democracy in Eastern Europe, Russia, Ukraine, and other successor states. Not only Europe benefits. From the viewpoint of the United States, the decline of the European Union states into quarrelsome disunity or the rise of aggressive right-wing government in Russia would be major disasters.

Could these functions be carried out by a less active NATO, one in which the NATO organization was dissolved or led a ritualistic existence, in which, as some recommend, all U.S. combat forces had been withdrawn from Europe but the North Atlantic Treaty still continued in effect with its commitment by the United States to come to the aid of European NATO members if they were attacked? Probably not. Under such conditions, it is doubtful that American political leaders would have the ongoing active interest in European developments or that European political leaders and publics would have a degree of confidence in U.S. support which would create nearly as much assurance as the present setup.

The possibility of outright conflict between the NATO countries and a resurgent Russia was remote in the mid-1990s. Developments in this direction in Russia would probably give the alliance years of warning. Russia still has plenty of military personnel and equipment and above all a huge nuclear arsenal, but merely to reconstitute the logistics and reinforcements that would give a conventional attack the power to penetrate Western defenses would take several years. The existence of a strong, functioning NATO would make such a development unlikely from the outset. This is what is meant by saying that NATO's main role is to "balance" the Russian military potential.

In chapter 7, earlier, we pointed out why the possibility of serious friction between united Germany and its European partners is remote. Although they are under pressure from right-wing elements because of the immigration and refugee problems, German democratic institutions are strong and German foreign policy emphasizes a cooperative multilateral approach. However, a perceived German desire for domination, whether or not justified, could cause frictions between Germany and its European Union partners and slow down or paralyze decisionmaking in the union. As long as the general assurance provided by NATO continues, circumstances like these if they occur would not be magnified into a security crisis, and it should be easier to deal with their sources.

Let's look at the reasons for NATO's continuation by trying to visualize what might happen if there were no active NATO. Let's posit that U.S. forces had been withdrawn from Europe, that NATO had degenerated to a formalistic existence, with low confidence in its capabilities from European governments and publics, and that it had not been replaced by some more vital security organization. In these circumstances, if East-West relations worsened and the Russian government moved toward outright hostility toward the West, its capacity to intimidate the countries of both Western and Eastern Europe could be considerable. In a situation in which the credibility of the U.S. nuclear guarantee was attenuated by nearly complete withdrawal of U.S. forces from Europe and in which Western Europe was dependent on British and French nuclear forces far weaker than those of Russia, political incidents between East and West could develop into a dangerous crisis. In more immediately plausible circumstances of conflict or a nuclear weapon incident in Ukraine, in Russia, or between the two, the absence of a strong NATO could have similar effects. If NATO had been dissolved by the time the anti-Gorbachev coup took place in the Soviet Union, as many were urging in 1989 and 1990, the European countries might have hesitated and wavered before condemning the coup instigators. As things were, President Boris Yeltsin was on the telephone to the NATO secretary general urging him to continue NATO's categorical condemnation of the coup and its leaders.

What if the new European security system—of which NATO, the CSCE, the European Union, and the WEU are the principal components—although still in existence, was also still failing to cope with new security challenges of the kind that have emerged since the end of the cold war, and these security challenges worsened at the same time? For example, the process of reducing and controlling the nuclear potential of the Soviet successor states might break down, leaving three or four new nuclear powers with large arsenals in the hands of unstable governments. Organized violence in Eastern Europe and in the ex-Soviet states might continue and spread, resulting in a series of limited interstate wars.

In not implausible circumstances like these, European political leaders might feel compelled to devote more resources to their national armed forces and, however reluctantly, to consider the need to use them autonomously. If chaotic conditions continued for a long time, some European governments might ultimately consider developing nuclear weapons, the ultimate renationalization of defense forces and policy. It would be unfair to imply that, of the European countries, only Germany would feel these pressures. All of them would. But a functioning NATO, backed by the deterrent power of U.S. nuclear weapons, should make it unnecessary for European leaders to think in these terms.

NATO's INTEGRATIVE FUNCTION

In addition to providing long-term insurance against the possibility of an aggressive Russia, NATO also deals in a more positive sense with Russia and the other Soviet successor states. It is the most important device available for avoiding the military isolation of Russia and drawing it into systematized military cooperation with the Western states. NATO's adjunct body, the North Atlantic Cooperation Council (NACC), to which all Eastern European states and the Soviet successor states belong together with NATO's original members, provides a framework for the beginnings of joint training and common doctrine on peacekeeping that could be the seed of later development to an integrated security organization for all of Europe. These efforts have been expanded by the Partnership for Peace proposed at the NATO Summit of January 1994. The Partnership for Peace, developed to meet security concerns of the Eastern European states, offers the possibility of a more intensive bilateral relationship between NATO and individual Eastern European countries, Russia, and also European neutral states than has been possible in the NACC.

OTHER NATO FUNCTIONS

NATO also provides some degree of protection against escalation of ethnic conflicts in Eastern Europe into interstate wars. For example, the possibility that NATO forces could intervene in one way or another reduces the possibility of violence between Lithuania and Poland, Ukraine and Poland, Romania and Hungary, and Russia and the Baltic states. The possibility of NATO intervention has already reduced the possibility of internationalization of Yugoslav ethnic conflicts although it has not eliminated this possibility. Warnings by the Bush and Clinton administrations to leaders of the Serb republic that mistreatment of the Albanian population of Kosovo would bring U.S. or NATO intervention and the preventive deployment of a U.S. battalion in Macedonia have at least played some role in preventing spread of the Bosnian conflict and may have been decisive in that regard. If NATO is used to the extent of its capabilities, it can provide the most effective means available of organizing the peacekeeping and preventive intervention force that will ultimately be necessary in Bosnia.

NATO will continue to provide an assurance of U.S. support in guarding the oil supplies of the Persian Gulf, vital for the Europeans, from hostile interruption. Their own experiences in the Gulf War against Iraq convinced the countries of Western Europe that they were far from having the capability to mount such an operation on their own.

Because the U.S. role in the Gulf War and NATO itself represent a U.S. contribution to European security—although in the national interest of the United States as well—it is not unreasonable for the United States to expect some political and economic cooperation from the European NATO states in other areas of the world. That cooperation was forthcoming on innumerable occasions during the cold war period.

More recently, it has been demonstrated in the UN Security Council, with regard to Cambodia, Iraq, Somalia, and North Korea. Without the willingness of Western Europe to cooperate when a good case for doing so is made, it would not be possible for the present world security system, however fragmentary, to operate through the UN Security Council, and it would not be possible to hope for the future expansion and improvement of that system. European readiness to help the United States in dealing with threats to peace around the globe will be influenced by the continuation of NATO.

NATO ADJUSTS TO NEW CIRCUMSTANCES

As a sixteen-nation organization operating by consensus, although with a strong tradition of reaching compromise on disputed issues, NATO moved with remarkable rapidity to meet each of the revolutionary changes of the 1989–91 period: German unification (October 1990); dissolution of the Warsaw Pact (April 1991); outbreak of war in the Yugoslav Federation (June 1991); and collapse of the Soviet Union (December 1991). It succeeded in all but the Yugoslav case.[1]

These dramatic changes left NATO with a new role. No longer was its main role to prevent possible Warsaw Pact attack and to manage the huge NATO-Warsaw Pact military confrontation in order to reduce its risks and dangers. The new role was to protect and ensure an existing peace among the states of Europe—and, as became increasingly necessary, to contain violence inside those states to prevent it from developing into interstate war.

NATO took four main actions to this end. First, as the Warsaw Pact melted away in Eastern Europe, NATO moved rapidly to establish a more positive relationship with Gorbachev's Soviet Union in order to support the constructive direction of Soviet policy. By doing so, NATO won the important advantage of inclusion of the united Germany in NATO. At NATO's London Summit meeting of July 1990, alliance leaders extended a hand of friendship to the Soviet Union and other Warsaw Pact states and declared that nuclear weapons would be "weapons of last resort."

NATO also adopted a new strategy and a new force structure. The Defense Planning Committee of NATO defense ministers established a new rapid-reaction corps in May 1991. The Rome NATO Summit (November 1991) dropped the concept of forward defense of the German border and adopted a new strategy focused on readiness to defend "points of concentration" without specifying an enemy. In addition, as the Soviet Union itself collapsed and was replaced by Russia and eleven other republics, NATO introduced an increasingly important program of outreach to Eastern Europe and the ex-Soviet states. At the Rome Summit, it established a new organization, the North Atlantic Cooperation Council (NACC), to expand contacts with the former pact states, including Russia. This action was complemented by establishment of the Partnership for Peace at the January 1994 summit. Finally, NATO leaders decided at the Oslo Ministerial Meeting of June 1992 to add a peacekeeping function to the role of NATO and to place NATO forces at the disposal of the CSCE for that purpose; six months later, this decision was amplified to include peacekeeping missions undertaken for the United Nations as well.

The New NATO Strategy

The second of these major adjustments, NATO's new military strategy and organization, was formulated in the second half of 1990 and the first half of 1991, a period when NATO planners still thought they would face a reformed but intact Soviet Union as a potential future enemy. If the new strategy had been drawn up only six months later, there might have been still greater changes. As it is, the new strategy is a recipe for forces ready to go in any direction, like General Charles de Gaulle's earlier "tous azimuts," all-points-of-the-compass strategy.

In the unclassified but nearly complete version published in the communique of the Rome Summit, NATO's new MC 400 (Military Committee Memorandum number 400) is rather abstract and general.[2] Its wording is general because the new strategy is no longer an operational document like its predecessor, MC 14/3, which provided for forward defense at the German border and possible use of nuclear weapons in the face of a massive sudden Warsaw Pact attack. Now, with a serious Russian threat of land invasion only a theoretical possibility that would require a year or more of highly visible preparation even after emergence of a hostile government, NATO's strategy has become a contingency plan instead of operational guidance.

The new plan envisages three main potential threats to the security of NATO countries in Europe: renewal of a threat from Russia, conflict stemming from ethnic fighting in Eastern Europe, and conflict with Muslim countries of the Middle East or North Africa. The main tasks of the alliance are defined in the new strategy as to create a situation in which "no country" would be able "to intimidate or coerce any European nation or impose hegemony through the threat or use of force"; to serve as a transatlantic forum for consulting on issues affecting the security of member states; "to deter and defend against any threat of aggression against the territory of any NATO member state"; and "to preserve the strategic balance within Europe." (The country against which this balance should be preserved is not specified; Russia is meant.)[3]

The forces at NATO's disposal for the missions described in the new strategic concept are divided into three categories: immediate-reaction and rapid-reaction forces supposed to be ready for operational deployment with minimum delay; main defense forces, a mix of active-duty and reserve units deployed in Europe; and augmentation forces, mainly U.S. forces stationed at home. The rapid-reaction force, highly mobile and in an advanced state of readiness, is, as the name suggests, designed to be moved quickly to meet new threats at an early stage. NATO's main defense forces are focused on several "concentration points." Concentration points have a dual purpose: They are areas that a corps-sized formation could defend to block the main lines of approach of forces advancing from Russia; they are also designed as assembly areas in which forces can be gathered to move out in other directions.

The new strategy is reasonable as far as coping with possible aggression by Russia is concerned. But it does not help much with NATO's more immediate tasks. It provides few answers as regards possible NATO intervention in Eastern Europe or the Mediterranean. One reason for this is that when it was formulated, there was a difference of view within the alliance, to which it will return, over whether NATO should become involved in conflicts in Europe outside the borders of member states.

NEW NATO ORGANIZATION AND FORCES

The organizational structure approved by NATO to carry out this strategy was defined at the May 1991 meeting of the Defense Planning Committee. In addition, the defense ministers approved amalgamation of some subordinate commands and the elimination of some.

Reaction forces will consist of two elements. The first is immediately available, ready to move at short notice. This is the Allied Command Europe (ACE) mobile force, consisting of a multinational ground-force brigade and a multinational component of forty-two aircraft. ACE's air component was deployed for the first time in NATO history during the Gulf War, when aircraft were sent to Turkey to make the point to Iraq that the NATO alliance would respond in unison to attacks on Turkey.

The second component is a rapid-reaction corps of 50,000–65,000 men plus an air component. The corps is under command of a U.K. lieutenant general. Its multinational staff is backed by a Reaction Force Planning Staff at NATO military headquarters in Mons, Belgium. The rapid-reaction corps includes one British armored division deployed in Germany, one light division in Britain (the new organization probably preserves the pared-down British army from near extinction), and two multinational divisions, an air-mobile division with forces from Germany, Holland, and Belgium, and a second division under Italian command drawn from southern NATO states—Italy, Spain, Portugal, Greece, and Turkey. The rapid-reaction corps headquarters is located in Germany, along with its U.K. armored division and the German-Netherlands-Belgian airborne division. The corps will be fully operational in 1995. A rapid-reaction air corps is being formed, with about 400 combat and transport aircraft organized in thirty-eight squadrons.

The new NATO main defense force consists of five multinational corps staffed to a varying degree with active-duty personnel, but with a considerable number of personnel to come from reserves. Most will be deployed in Germany, where in practice they have the role of counterbalancing Russian forces. The concept of the multinational army corps is motivated mainly by the desire to make continued presence of foreign forces in Germany more acceptable to the German public. Many commentators have doubts about the military effectiveness of the idea, however. One of the corps to be stationed in former West Germany will have a German commander, a German division, and a U.S. division; a second German-commanded corps will have a German division and a Belgian-Netherlands division; the third, a German-led German-Danish corps, is stationed in the north of Germany. A fourth multinational corps, commanded by a U.S. general, will have one U.S. and one German division. The total NATO force in Germany will probably have about half of the twenty-odd divisions it had at the peak of the cold war.

NATO main defense forces will also include two Italian and one Spanish corps, plus several corps-sized Turkish and Greek formations. In a brave experiment to bring together hostile Greek and Turkish forces, a multinational division consisting of one Greek, one Turkish, and one Italian brigade, with probable headquarters in Thessaloniki, is to be established by early 1995. Greece withdrew from the NATO integrated command in 1974 because of the Cyprus dispute with Turkey, but will now return.[4] An agreement reached in late 1992 placed the Franco-German Eurocorps, which France had earlier been unwilling to subordinate to NATO, under NATO command in the event of a crisis.

How Strong Should NATO Be?

Under the impact of recession-boosted post-cold war cuts in defense forces, the level of NATO forces in Europe is declining from a 1990 level of about 3 million to an anticipated 2 million by 1997 or earlier.[5] NATO commanders are concerned about this downward plunge. Member governments agreed in 1991 to cut forces by 25 percent. But actual cuts have gone far beyond that: Germany, United Kingdom, and the Netherlands have cut forces by 50 percent; and Belgium by 60 percent. The German Bundeswehr, NATO's biggest force, will reduce from a level of about

500,000 (Federal Republic only) to 300,000 or below in the 1990s. Especially given Germany's unresolved problems about Bundeswehr service abroad, the problem now is to find enough European forces even for peacekeeping missions. In spring 1993, NATO force planners were in near desperation when they had to try to pull together a NATO ground force of 50,000 men for peacekeeping duty in Bosnia in the event that the original Vance-Owen plan had been implemented.

One problem faced by NATO force planners in the early stages was whether they should arm a central force dedicated to NATO's main role of balancing Russia while at the same time trying to field separate forces dedicated to peacekeeping or whether to settle for using the same force for multiple purposes. The second course will be followed for obvious economic reasons.[6]

What would be the lowest possible level of U.S. troop strength needed to maintain NATO's military vitality and an active U.S. role? General John Galvin, who retired as SHAPE commander in the summer of 1992, made a good case in arguing that a minimum U.S. force for Europe should be a corps headquarters and two divisions (down from two corps headquarters and four and two-thirds divisions in 1990), or about 70,000 army personnel, three air force wings with fighter bombers, reconnaissance, and air defense components (down from eight wings); 13,000 naval personnel mainly staffing the Sixth Fleet in the Mediterranean; plus personnel for multinational staff, intelligence, communications, and logistics functions, for a total of about 150,000 personnel (down from more than 300,000 in 1990).

The Defense Department supported a force this size and planned for it. But within months of formulation of these plans, they became casualties of a new administration dedicated to reducing the budget deficit and revitalizing the domestic economy. Congress mandated a reduction of U.S. forces in Europe to a ceiling of no more than 100,000 in Europe by the fall of 1995. Secretary of Defense Les Aspin accepted this figure.[7] The Clinton administration then committed itself in NATO to maintain this level. Even though the 100,000 figure is minimal considering NATO's tasks, it is clear that many groups in Congress will continue to press to further reduce the level of U.S. troops in Europe and that the administration will seek, at least for a time, to hold the line on this issue.

NATO's EASTERN OUTREACH PROGRAM

Together with possible peacekeeping functions, NATO's program of outreach to the states of Eastern Europe and the former Soviet Union is the most important growth area of the alliance. As the communist regimes of Eastern Europe began to collapse, NATO governments, led by the United

States and Germany, undertook rapid steps, while avoiding grounds for alarm to the declining Soviet Union, to deal with the desires of the new democratic governments of Eastern Europe for some degree of security assurance in a confusing new situation. Their objective was also to improve long-term chances for democratic government in the former Warsaw Pact states by transmitting to their armed forces and civilian leaders essential defense concepts from Western practice.

At the London Summit of July 1990, NATO leaders proposed conclusion of a joint "peace treaty" statement with Warsaw Pact governments declaring the cold war ended. The statement was issued officially at the CSCE Paris Summit in November. Alliance leaders invited Gorbachev to visit NATO headquarters in Brussels to address the North Atlantic Council, emphasized the desire of NATO countries for rapid completion of the Conventional Forces in Europe Treaty, and announced major changes in NATO force structure and strategy "making nuclear forces truly weapons of last resort."[8] These actions made it politically possible for Gorbachev to agree to NATO membership for a united Germany ten days later in the decisive meeting with Chancellor Helmut Kohl at Stavropol.

NATO's July 1990 London declaration was followed by a broad program of visits to NATO by Gorbachev, leaders of Eastern European and of Soviet successor states, as well as of senior Soviet and Eastern European military leaders; and by tours of NATO Secretary General Manfred Wörner to Moscow and East European capitals. It was also followed by an extensive program of conferences of NATO and Eastern military officers on expediting the CFE Treaty, civil/military airspace coordination, defense conversion, promoting civilian scientific research, Western deliveries of medical aid and food to the successor states, by visits to military staff colleges in East and West, and by invitations for officers from former Warsaw Pact states to attend special courses at the NATO Defense College and other NATO training courses.

Chapter 5 describes why many Eastern European governments expressed concern about finding themselves in a security vacuum after the collapse of the Warsaw Treaty Organization and urged some form of membership in NATO. NATO leaders were especially sensitive at this stage to the possibility that the Soviet government would react negatively to eastward expansion of NATO territory to abut on the Soviet Union itself. Consequently, NATO officials then discouraged the idea of direct membership in NATO of former members of the Warsaw Pact. But NATO did take some action to meet the security concerns of the Eastern European states. At the Copenhagen ministerial meeting of June 1991, NATO foreign ministers issued a special statement on "Partnership with the Countries of Central and Eastern Europe," declaring, "Our own security is inseparably linked with that of all other states in Europe. The consolidation and preservation throughout the continent of democratic societies and their freedom from any form of coercion or intimidation are therefore of direct and material concern to us."[9]

This statement sets forth in the classic language of defining "vital interests" that NATO would react to attempts to intimidate the East European states or to threats to their territorial integrity. At the Oslo meeting of NATO foreign ministers (June 1992), Lawrence Eagleburger, then deputy U.S. secretary of state, kept open the possibility of membership expansion in carefully chosen general terms. "Indeed, even the very composition of the Alliance may need to expand, at the appropriate time, taking full account of our rigorous democratic standards and the need to preserve the strong fiber of common defense."[10] There the matter stood until the election of a new U.S. administration, intensification of the Russo-Ukrainian vendetta, evidence of political instability in Russia itself, and the approach of a new NATO summit meeting with a new U.S. president combined to intensify debate on this subject and resulted in the Partnership for Peace, discussed in more detail later in the book.

NATO officials were already worried at this time over the effects on the viability of the organization of its apparent lack of day-to-day responsibilities. In a stroke of creative ingenuity, they conceived of a way of addressing this whole range of new problems—NATO's longevity, Eastern European security worries, and concerns about the future of democracy in the USSR in the wake of the unsuccessful anti-Gorbachev coup of August 1991—through founding a new organization, the North Atlantic Cooperation Council (NACC), to which all former members of the Warsaw Treaty could belong along with NATO members.

This new organization would address the question of NATO's future by giving its liaison activities with the East an enduring, organized form. It would provide for more formal association of the Eastern European states with NATO without affronting the Soviet Union, which could also join, and it would provide a more effective vehicle for NATO's efforts to transmit its experience in the security field to all the states of the former Warsaw Pact. In short, the new organization would provide a framework for the effort, inspired by the success of the postwar experience with Germany, to integrate the former Soviet enemy by imbedding it in a network of useful associations and commitments. Through establishing this new organization, NATO could vault over Anglo-American disputes with France over the organization of Western defense, and with one stroke, become a pan-European security organization.

French officials nonetheless objected that NATO should stick to its central function of counterbalancing Soviet military power, arguing that close contacts and liaison with the Soviets would blur its prime focus. Moreover, French officials objected, the new organization would compete with the CSCE by duplicating many of its activities. But in the end France acceded. The establishment of the North Atlantic Cooperation Council was announced at the 1991 Rome Summit.[11] By June 1992, when the NACC met in Oslo in conjunction with the summer meeting of NATO foreign ministers, it included all Eastern European states, Russia and the other Soviet successor states, and the Baltic states, plus Albania. Finland has observer status. After the January 1993 split-up of Czechoslovakia into the Czech Republic and the Slovak Republic, NACC membership totaled 38 states.

Establishment of the North Atlantic Cooperation Council was a worthwhile move toward securing NATO's future by formalizing new links with the East. But agreement with France on this subject did not come without considerable stress. At the November 1991 Rome Summit meeting where the issue was decided, President François Mitterrand sourly remarked that, after all, NATO was "not a Holy Alliance" like that established by European governments after Napoleon's defeat at Waterloo, meaning that it could be changed or dropped. President George Bush angrily commented in response that, if the ultimate aim of European NATO states was "to provide individually for their own defense" and to dispense with the United States' help, "the time to tell us is now."[12] But the benefits that could arise from the new NACC organization became apparent only a month later as the Soviet Union collapsed into its component republics. The North Atlantic Cooperation Council almost immediately took on the role of liaison with (often wholly inexperienced) officials of the successor republics, passing on Western views and know-how in the military field and arms control.

At the inaugural meeting of the North Atlantic Cooperation Council on December 20, 1991, participants agreed "to develop a more institutional relationship of consultation on political and security issues," including annual meetings with the NATO Council at foreign minister level, bimonthly meetings with the NATO Council at the level of NATO permanent representatives, regular meetings with NATO subordinate committees, including the Military Committee and other military commands, as well as with NATO's committee of national policy planners, the Atlantic Policy Advisory Group.

Consultation and cooperation in the NACC were to focus on security and related issues like defense planning, conceptual approaches to arms control, democratic concepts of civil-military relations, and conversion of military production, as well as participation in NATO's environmental programs. The Eastern member states agreed to help NATO disseminate information about its activities in their countries.[13]

By the time of the NACC's second meeting in Brussels in March 1992, all the Soviet successor states had become members. Council members adopted a detailed "work plan" or agenda containing five pages of activities and meetings at regular intervals on defense policy issues, defense conversion, policy planning consultation, and air-traffic management. The latter is an area of widespread concern calling for confidence-building measures; domination of this activity in the former pact states by military authorities created the theoretical possibility of unannounced large-scale aerial attack partly concealed under the guise of civilian air activity.

A first meeting of the defense ministers of the states of the North Atlantic Cooperation Council convened in Brussels in April 1992 adopted a supplemental work plan covering such matters as military strategies, defense management, the legal and constitutional framework for military forces, harmonization of defense planning and arms control, exercises and training, defense education, reserve forces, search and rescue, a military contribution to humanitarian aid, and military medicine. The participants could not agree on another logical area for military cooperation— catastrophic disaster relief—because France wanted this activity to be covered in the CSCE with its broader membership. Finally, the issue was resolved in a way when NATO placed its expertise on civil, national, and environmental disasters at the disposal of the CSCE, while WEU announced a plan of cooperation with the armed forces of the Eastern European states to cope with natural disasters.

Like the CSCE, the NACC is a useful device for coordinating the policy of member states on specific issues, a device that proved particularly useful in bringing the Soviet successor states to assume obligations incurred by the Soviet Union on arms control and related issues. A series of NACC meetings adopted common positions calling for full implementation and early ratification of the CFE and START treaties, an active policy toward nuclear nonproliferation issues featuring early signature of the NPT by the Soviet successor states, reliable control over nuclear weapons, prohibition of unauthorized experiments with nuclear components, and also agreement on manpower limits in the CFE follow-on negotiations.

The French claim that the NACC duplicates some CSCE activities is valid. However, NACC has the considerable advantage of being able to call on a well-trained NATO international staff to prepare specialist conferences, and it enjoys high prestige among military officers of the Eastern countries. It is doubtful whether CSCE could have transmitted the Western message about arms control ratification and compliance with the same effectiveness. However, the NACC was hamstrung in its future development because it had no permanent staff or budget of its own.

NATO Goes into Peacekeeping

The second half of 1991 brought increasingly damaging demonstrations of the incapacity of the CSCE and even the European Community to cope with the continued bloodletting in Croatia. As the fighting went on, NATO's inactivity became more obvious and more harmful to NATO's prestige. After all, with the fall of the Soviet Union, NATO had a practical monopoly on military force in Europe. For a time at least, the collapse of the Soviet Union removed an earlier, important obstacle to NATO activity in the Yugoslav Federation: Far from objecting to NATO activity in the East, Russian foreign minister Andrei Kozyrev told the press during the March 1992 NACC meeting that NATO involvement even in Nagorno-Karabakh on Russia's borders would be welcome.[14]

In February 1992, Secretary General Wörner made a "personal" suggestion that NATO place its forces at the disposal of CSCE for peacekeeping purposes. CSCE itself was preparing for its July Helsinki 92 Summit, in which it was clear that the organization would agree to undertake peacekeeping operations. At the March 1992 NACC meeting, Secretary of State James Baker endorsed a proposal from the Dutch foreign minister calling on NATO to place its forces at the disposal of the CSCE for peacekeeping; he also urged NATO involvement in a peacekeeping role in Nagorno-Karabakh.[15]

By the time of NATO's foreign minister meeting at Oslo in June 1992, the preparatory work had been done. At Oslo, the NATO Council declared its concern over fighting in former Yugoslavia and Nagorno-Karabakh and its readiness to support peacekeeping activities under CSCE responsibility, making alliance resources and expertise available to CSCE on a case-by-case basis. (Not to be outdone, the Council of the WEU, meeting near Bonn two weeks later, made a parallel offer to the CSCE.) Deputy Secretary Lawrence Eagleburger stated that the United States was "prepared to make essential contributions such as lift and logistics to peacekeeping operations. We also do not exclude providing ground contingents on the same basis as other nations; like members of the Alliance, we would take such a decision on a case-by-case basis."[16]

Subsequently, administration spokesmen and President Bush himself at the CSCE Helsinki Summit indicated that the United States would be willing, in cooperation with other NATO countries, to provide air cover to UN humanitarian food deliveries in Sarajevo but not to ground troops. The Bush administration had consistently shown great reluctance to become involved in Yugoslavia since Secretary Baker's visit to Belgrade in June 1991, and the administration had provided the American public with a wide range of reasons why U.S. involvement was not needed and was undesirable. The trouble was that most of the same political inhibitions pertained in other NATO countries. Nonetheless, the December 1992 meeting of NATO foreign ministers also made NATO available to the UN for peacekeeping under the same terms it had offered CSCE.

In making its offer to participate in peacekeeping operations in Eastern Europe, NATO had silently crossed the "out-of-area" limit that had been so much debated within the alliance, the issue of whether it was permissible under the terms of the North Atlantic Treaty for forces organized and led by NATO to intervene militarily outside the territory of its member states.

During the cold war, in order to emphasize in a situation of massive military confrontation that NATO's posture was wholly defensive, NATO officials had emphasized that the wording of the North Atlantic Treaty precluded "out-of-area" activities. As the cold war wound down, NATO officials continued to stress this theme, this time in order to explain why NATO could not immediately offer membership to the Eastern European states and to reduce the possibility of Soviet or Russian hostility while negotiations on the NATO membership of a united Germany proceeded.

There were further reasons for the traditional restriction against NATO out-of-area activities: the fear of European alliance members that U.S. involvement in conflicts with the Soviet Union elsewhere could trigger a conflict in Europe, and the resistance of some European allies to being drawn into cold war conflicts abroad. The latter concern continued in the post-cold war period when the United States became involved in conflicts like that in Panama, which to many Europeans had a taint of traditional American "colonial" intervention.

Ironically, in the light of European concerns about being dragged into American quarrels outside the continent, the "out-of-area" restriction had originated in the United States. It went back to the formative days of NATO, when influential members of the Senate and House of Representatives wanted to ensure that the United States would not become involved in the colonial conflicts of European allies like Britain, France, Belgium, and Portugal. For that reason, the area of application of the collective defense commitment contained in Article 5 of the North Atlantic Treaty was limited by Article 6 to the home territory of the allies in Europe and to the North Atlantic area. But this limitation does not apply to decisions by any or all of the NATO allies to conduct military operations other than as a direct response to attack. This possibility is not covered by the treaty text, although implicitly it could come under the authority of Article 4, which provides for consultation by NATO members whenever in the opinion of any ally their "territorial integrity, political independence, or security" is threatened.[17]

By the summer of 1993, NATO had in fact crossed the out-of-area line; it was involved in peacekeeping in the former Yugoslavia. A combined NATO-WEU flotilla under NATO command was enforcing economic sanctions against Serbia. NATO aircraft based in Italy were enforcing a ban on military flights over Bosnia and were readied to intervene against Serbian units to protect the ground-force personnel of UNPROFOR or to assure the survival of Sarajevo. NATO planners had done the advance planning for a large ground-force presence in Bosnia if a dependable cease-fire could be negotiated.

In the shadow of the deepening Yugoslav crisis and the increasing possibility that some large-scale Western intervention might be needed, France was moving toward closer cooperation with NATO. In September 1992, French defense minister Pierre Joxe urged closer discussion between France and NATO countries. In December 1992 the French government, which in 1966 had withdrawn from NATO's integrated command and the NATO Military Committee, requested that its observer on the Military Committee, General Jean-Paul Pelisson, participate in deliberations of the committee when they concerned the former Yugoslavia. In June 1993, the new government of Edouard Balladur, which favored greater cooperation between France and NATO, indicated that the French observer in the Military Committee would participate actively in decisions on all peacekeeping missions involving French forces. French officials hinted that France might also send representatives to the international military staff, the same integrated staff from which France had withdrawn years before.[18]

As evidence mounted that prospects for further progress on European integration were clouded, French zeal for pushing the potential of the Western European Union as the preferred vehicle for peacekeeping in Europe also declined. France withdrew its insistence that NACC work in peacekeeping be restricted to "conceptual cooperation." The result was agreement in the NACC's June and December 1993 meetings on an impressive program of East-West cooperation on peacekeeping. Two successive reports of the NACC ad hoc group on cooperation in peacekeeping[19] described NACC preparations and studies on a common satellite-radio communications system, joint exercises, and agreements on cost sharing, command arrangements, personnel exchanges, common doctrine, procedures and terminology, and logistics for peacekeeping. To provide coordination with CSCE, Sweden, in the CSCE chair for 1993, sent a liaison official to the ad hoc group. Finland attended as an observer. The ad hoc group's report urged that participation in NACC cooperation on peacekeeping should be open to the European neutrals like Sweden and Austria. As Russian foreign minister Andrei Kozyrev put it during the June 1993 NACC meeting, the focus of the future "should be on converting NACC to an effective peacekeeping instrument." The foreign ministers at this meeting addressed themselves not only to Bosnia, but also to all the trouble spots of the former Soviet Union, including Nagorno-Karabakh, Abkhazia and Ossetia in Georgia, the Transdniester fracas in Moldova, and the conflict in Tajikistan.

If command arrangements with the UN were worked out, the NACC structure might be used to coordinate activities of peacekeepers from NATO and former Warsaw Pact countries in Bosnia—and clearly also in other peacekeeping situations under UN or CSCE auspices. Cooperation on peacekeeping, which involves a high degree of coordination from command staff down to the small unit, is at the same time a serious move toward overall military integration of the type that NATO exemplifies. Theoretically at least, some long-term solutions to Europe's security problems were beginning to appear.

At the same time, the NACC overlaps seriously with CSCE activities in many areas like military liaison, economic conversion, and more seriously as regards the ongoing dialogue on defense planning on strategy which is a major function of the CSCE Forum on Security Cooperation. More serious, it is not clear to what extent NACC's potential for peacekeeping will flourish or wither away after agreement on the Partnership for Peace program at the January 1994 NATO Summit and the decision at the same meeting to establish a special NATO staff to organize military interventions by ad hoc coalitions of European states.

NATO's Nuclear Problems

The issue of U.S. nuclear weapons on European soil, the catalyst in the 1980s for German antimilitary sentiment, although quiescent in the early 1990s, remains a problem. It is quite possible that German antinuclear sentiment will in the future become focused on U.S. nuclear sites in Germany or on the nuclear role of Bundeswehr aircraft. If remaining U.S. air-delivered nuclear weapons are at some point pushed out of Germany by political pressure, it is unlikely that a place can be found for them elsewhere in Europe. The United Kingdom has nuclear weapons of its own, but strong feelings in the British public against nuclear arms makes it unlikely that the country could provide a deployment site for U.S. weapons pushed off the continent.

NATO leaders at the November 1991 Rome Summit endorsed President Bush's exchange of proposals with Mikhail Gorbachev of that September to withdraw all nuclear artillery charges and nuclear warheads for surface-to-surface missiles and for tactical nuclear weapons on naval vessels, as well as the proposal of the NATO Nuclear Planning Group to reduce the number of U.S. air-delivered nuclear weapons deployed in

Europe. Taken together, these decisions leave only about 700 nuclear aerial weapons available to NATO commanders. (A small number of these belong to the United Kingdom, which participates with its assets in NATO nuclear planning. France, which has its own aircraft-delivered nuclear weapons, does not.)

The document on "The Alliance's New Strategic Concept" issued at the Rome Summit pointed out that, given changes under way in the USSR, NATO's capacity to mount a purely conventional defense had increased. Consequently, the threshold for using nuclear weapons had become "even more remote." The communique drafters emphasized, however, that nuclear weapons "continue to fulfill an essential role of ensuring uncertainty in the minds of any aggressor about the nature of the Allies' response."[20] Because of this desire to maintain uncertainty about the point at which nuclear weapons would be used, the document on the new strategy does not repeat the concept of the London Communique a year earlier that nuclear weapons would be a weapon of "last resort"—a last-ditch response to successful aggression. NATO leaders continued for the same rather unconvincing reason to reject the idea of an East-West commitment not to make first use of nuclear weapons. Unfortunately, the weakening of Russia's conventional military forces and the unstable political situation in Russia and other successor states with nuclear arms heighten the temptation for early use of nuclear weapons in the event these governments become involved in serious conflict.

In practice, the new situation meant that the alliance had dropped earlier plans for a "limited" strike using U.S.-based long-range missiles against the Soviet Union in order to back up an unsuccessful "warning" use of tactical-range nuclear weapons against advancing Warsaw Pact troops. Instead, it will draw up contingency plans for a range of possibilities focusing on striking military targets of high value to an aggressor on his own territory.

The United States is insistent that the responsibility for deciding to use these weapons and for delivering them must be shared with other allies, and that the risk of nuclear retaliation if the weapons are ever used should not be directed at the United States alone, but should also be shared among the NATO allies. "Risk-sharing" is regarded as a central element of NATO cohesion. In the past, some American leaders also argued that deployment in Europe of tactical nuclear weapons was needed as a nuclear shield for U.S. troops deployed there and that the removal of the shield must entail withdrawal of the troops. Most remaining nuclear weapons are in Germany, but they are also deployed in Belgium, Holland, Italy, Greece, and Turkey. All of these countries have air force units organized and equipped for delivery of U.S. nuclear weapons.

Many proposals have been made to eliminate all tactical-range nuclear weapons from Europe. In a crisis, air-delivered U.S. nuclear weapons could rapidly return to Europe. But in a crisis situation, their return may not be politically feasible. If all U.S. nuclear weapons are at some point removed from Europe, an important transatlantic linkage will have been severed. Politically, their removal would make Europe and the United States more remote from each other. In the military sense, aircraft-delivered weapons deployed in Europe are a more limited, more plausible means of U.S. nuclear backup for Europe than strategic-range missiles for the United States. Given the large continuing stocks of nuclear weapons in former Soviet successor states, especially Russia, and the probability that political instability there will long continue, retention of some U.S. air-delivered nuclear weapons in Europe seems a reasonable contribution to containing potential panic in Western Europe over possible nuclear weapons incidents in the former Soviet Union or to deterring possible nuclear intimidation.

OTHER PROBLEMS

A further issue is the question of whether reduced production of conventional armaments in the United States and in Europe brought by the cold war's end will be managed competitively or cooperatively, both as regards sales to NATO armed forces and exports to Third World countries. There have been moves in both directions amid continuing sharp decline in total worldwide arms transfers. The European Union is in the process of adopting a common position on arms production and sales. The United States and other European countries formally agreed at the Helsinki 92 CSCE Summit to exchange data on their production of major arms and also to control sales to unstable areas; a definition has been agreed in CSCE of situations or areas to which arms transfers should not take place.

The low level of standardization among NATO forces is one of several factors that raises questions about NATO's new multilateral corps. In 1992, the $38 billion European Fighter Aircraft (EFA) project, backed by a consortium of British, German, Italian, and Spanish aerospace companies, was suspended in its prior form and radically reorganized around a cheaper, less capable aircraft. This left France as the only Western European country building a modern fighter in the early 1990s. This is the Rafale, which was initially judged unsuitable for use by other European air forces. The decision to alter the EFA project may compel purchase or coproduction of U.S. aircraft or a decision to build a lighter aircraft in partial competition with the Rafale. There has been no serious evidence that Euro-American cooperation to produce or transfer a lesser number of arms will gain ground in the next several years over mounting competition in arms sales among the same countries. The net effect of this issue on transatlantic relations will probably be divisive.

How to Achieve a New Euro-American Consultative Relationship

Regardless of the specific outcome of the issues described here, the main fact of life for NATO is that its chief antagonist, the Soviet Union, is gone. In a short time, if developments in the ex-Soviet states do not take a dramatically negative turn, the U.S. military contribution to NATO will be less than one-third of the 300,000-plus personnel stationed in Europe in 1990. In circumstances like these, the U.S. influence in European security affairs cannot fail to decline. How far might this decline go? More generally, what should be the relationship between the United States and its European NATO partners in this new situation?

Senior U.S. officials and military officers have argued that U.S. forces in Europe cannot fall below some unspecified minimum if the United States is to maintain "a seat at the table of European security decisions." They believe that the only way for the United States to retain a reasonable degree of influence is with a militarily significant force commitment—at least a full army corps—in order to pay minimum dues for a "seat at the table." Otherwise, they argue, the United States will be a backbencher. Statements like these reveal U.S. insistence on having a say in European security decisions if the United States is going to retain some responsibility for defense of Europe and a recurrent U.S. fear of being "marginalized" in decisions on European security issues.

At the core of this fear is a persistent concern that European NATO members are not ready to act decisively on security issues by themselves without on-site American leadership and a concern that the United States could be called on yet again in adverse circumstances to bail out Europe. These problems are real ones. If the United States begins to fade out of NATO consultations and plays a more silent, low-profile role, its assurances of security support may then well appear less real to friends and potential foes alike. And, if the process of consultation in NATO declines toward rote and formalism, a U.S. administration could one day be suddenly confronted by a situation in which a NATO ally or allies had become embroiled in a conflict triggering the NATO commitment for collective defense.

Equally, in the light of the relatively uncoordinated European Community response to the emerging Gulf War with Iraq and its difficulties in handling the ethnic conflicts in the former Yugoslavia and the former

Soviet Union, the problem could be lack of capacity to reach decisions without some input of American leadership. The Yugoslav case provides a fairly good example of these concerns. Although from the start, the logical remedy was an early application of limited preventive military force by the Western countries, the total reluctance of the Bush administration to become involved, a reluctance reinforced, although not originated, by the onset of the 1992 presidential election campaign, left the European allies on their own to deal with the problem between 1990 and 1992. As the Clinton administration took essentially the same position through most of its first year in office, and thus disqualified itself from leadership of the Western coalition, the problem continued. With Germany, the other main NATO country, also out of the picture because of continuing domestic disagreement over use of German troops abroad, the remaining European countries lacked both will and resources to act.

The combination of lower salience of security issues and a much smaller U.S. troop presence in Europe will provide an unusually difficult challenge for American diplomacy. It will be tested for its ability to keep the alliance on course through brainpower instead of the weight of heavy battalions. U.S. diplomacy did show exceptional ingenuity in the 1990–93 period—in nuclear arms control, in German unification, and in a helpful, cooperative position during the collapse of Soviet power. For two decades, U.S. representatives to the CSCE have had remarkable success in influencing CSCE participants to accept U.S. suggestions. But to consistently achieve this kind of outcome, a different style of U.S. leadership will be needed, one that concedes more respect to the viewpoints of other allies than in the past—what General Klaus Naumann, the chief of staff of the German Bundeswehr, has repeatedly called a "mature" partnership, with real consultation.

The longstanding problem of consultation in NATO is not an issue of diplomatic point-scoring. Consultation is the vehicle by which the United States or the European allies most effectively bring their influence to bear. Early, seriously intended consultation enables participants to shape decisions while they are in their initial stages or to head off ideas believed to have damaging consequences. As discussed in the next chapter, realization of the importance of the consultative process caused the United States to seek de facto membership in the European Community's Political Cooperation program. It is the reason the United States has been so insistent that NATO, rather than the European Union, should be the primary venue for decisions on European security. In a period of declining influence in Europe, the United States, a superpower with an uneven record on quality of consultation, is constrained to approach this issue with new seriousness. As the EC decisions reached at Maastricht in December 1991 are carried out, WEU countries will as a matter of standard practice caucus before NATO Council meetings to reach common positions.

The issue now is how to make consultation work under changed circumstances. No matter how bureaucratic or out of place such an effort could appear at this late stage in NATO's existence, it might be desirable for NATO to consider adopting a formal Code of Consultation, a new set of ground rules for policy debate. Such an understanding would commit NATO governments to adopt only preliminary positions on major subjects, whether the positions are the result of caucusing among EC representatives or of decisions taken at the top national level in the United States, and to commit themselves to reevaluate their positions in the light of further discussion. (Possibly, the code might require reevaluation of an initial U.S. or EC position by all sixteen member states if at least two NATO members request it.) Such an understanding would slow down alliance decisionmaking. It would not help in every instance, but it could at least provide career officials with a means of coping with irate heads of government when the latter insist on maintaining their original positions.

The Outlook for NATO

In a short time, less than four years from the fall of the Berlin Wall, alliance governments implemented a series of creative decisions designed to prolong NATO's existence, among them establishment of the North Atlantic Cooperation Council and the Partnership for Peace and the decision to use NATO forces for peacekeeping. Despite this rapid adjustment to radically changed circumstances, NATO's long-term future remains uncertain. There is a strong case for continuing NATO in some form at least until the time, probably far off, when functioning democracy has taken root in Russia. But NATO has three main problems if it is to effectively meet its members' needs during this lengthy period and not fall into bureaucratic desiccation.

First, despite improvements described here and later on, NATO has not yet fully solved the difficult issue of its relationship to the Western European Union. Second, and more serious, NATO does not have a day-to-day function sufficiently compelling to elicit consistent long-term political support in either the United States or in Western Europe.

One of NATO's main missions, to discourage or cope with the revival of aggressive policy in Russia, could easily become more important in the event of negative developments in Russia or in other successor states, all of which remain highly unstable. But, in the early 1990s, danger from Russia appeared only a theoretical long-term possibility; the foreign policy of Russia and the other republics remained generally cooperative and positive even in the face of conservative nationalistic trends. NATO's second main role toward Russia, the effort to embed Russia, the other successor states, and Eastern Europe in a cooperative European framework, suffered both from lack of resources and a lack of plausibility in the face of such developments as the election success of Vladimir Zhirinovsky and Russia's questionable military intervention in Georgia. The integration approach is the right one, but conditions for its success are far weaker in the case of Russia than they were in postwar Germany, and Western governments have not yet fully articulated a version of this approach that takes account of the time span involved— the decades of effort required for its successful implementation.

Third, even more serious, neither NATO nor the other institutions concerned with European security—the EC, the WEU, the CSCE, or the UN—have been coping effectively with the most active issue of European security today, ethnic violence. Given the domestic problems of Russia, NATO continues to have a monopoly of usable military force in Europe, yet it has not been able to devise an effective way of applying that force in Bosnia or in a peacekeeping context in Ukraine, Moldova, Georgia, or Azerbaijan. However, NATO cannot wait for the big security problem of Russia to occur while remaining relatively inactive on lesser issues and expect to be around to cope with the big problem if it does develop. It cannot be like the fire department of a big city, daily pulling out and polishing its hook-and-ladder engines, adding auxiliary organizations like the NACC and the Partnership for Peace, and offering its fire-fighting services to the CSCE and the UN, while insisting that it will go into action only in the event of a major conflagration, and that it can do nothing about smaller fires that actually break out.

The contrast between NATO's huge, unengaged military capabilities and the daily bloodletting and atrocities in Bosnia has done serious damage to NATO's standing and future prospects. However unpopular the role, the situation in Europe calls for a police officer, not a single superpower police officer but a multilateral one. If NATO cannot find a more useful role in coping with the serious problems of organized violence in Europe, public support for it will diminish further. As a result, and in the absence of an alternate European institution with the capacity to take on the job, Europe might someday be left without effective protection if developments in Russia do take a serious negative turn.

11

Who Will Guard Europe— NATO or WEU?

A s NATO struggled to adapt itself to the new situation in Europe after the end of the cold war and the collapse of the Soviet Union, the hitherto shadowy Western European Union (WEU), a military alliance linking nine European NATO member states, was taking on new substance and moving to join the other institutions concerned with European security. The main question which arises from this development is whether WEU is an unnecessary duplication and hindrance to NATO as the main provider of security in Europe or itself the seed of Europe's future principal security system. Put another way, the question is whether the European Union (EU, as the European Community is now designated after entry into force of the Maastricht treaties on November 1, 1993) can develop a common defense policy and common defense forces strong and unified enough to make the Union, that is, Western and Central Europe, ultimately self-sustaining in defense.

Undistinguished Past, Potentially Important Future

The Western European Union is a byproduct of the Western decision after the outbreak of the Korean War to rearm West Germany. Its origin is in the five-power Brussels Treaty Organization, established in the wake of World War II by the United Kingdom, France, and the Benelux states through the 1948 Brussels Treaty of Economic, Social, and Cultural Collaboration and Collective Self-Defense.[1] The main commitment of the

Brussels Treaty (Article V) is the obligation of all member states to provide "all the military aid and assistance in their power" to any member government that is "the object of an armed attack in Europe," an obligation more explicit than that of Article 5 of the North Atlantic Treaty, which merely commits individual member governments to take "such action as it deems necessary" to assist a member who is attacked. As specified by its preamble, the Brussels Treaty's main aim was to protect against "renewal by Germany of a policy of aggression." Most of the defense functions of the Brussels Treaty were subsumed in the provisions of the North Atlantic Treaty of the following year, and the Brussels Treaty Organization became dormant.

As decisions on German rearmament grew closer, the United States gave heavy support to the French-authored draft treaty to construct a European Defense Community (EDC) composed of multinational units down to the division level, as a means of integrating the new West German forces and depriving them of the capability of independent action. The EDC was to be subordinated to NATO, but Germany would not be a direct member of the NATO alliance. The supporters of EDC, motivated by the urgency of mounting cold war confrontation with the numerically stronger Soviet Union, felt obliged to move early in the process of European integration to what logically should have been its last step.

This premature attempt at forcing the pace of European integration failed. The European Defense Community Treaty was rejected in the French parliament in 1954 by a combination of those who feared German rearmament so soon after the end of World War II and those who opposed relinquishing national control over French armed forces. The United States and other Western powers then moved as an alternative to EDC to fold West German forces into an integrated NATO command structure. The Brussels Treaty was recast in 1954 through a series of protocols to provide a range of controls over the new German forces. The Brussels Treaty Organization was at this time renamed the Western European Union, and Italy and the Federal Republic of Germany were admitted as members. The treaty's preamble was revised to drop the reference to possible German aggression, replacing it with a declaration that the objective of the treaty was "to promote the unity and to encourage the progressive integration of Europe." The protocols on force restrictions were worded in an even-handed way to apply to all WEU states, but in practice, they established a top limit of twelve divisions for German ground forces; prohibited German manufacture or possession of nuclear, chemical, or biological weapons; restricted by size and capability manufacture of specified armaments, including submarines; and established a verification agency, the Armaments Control Agency, to oversee implementation of these restrictions. The restrictions were finally dropped at the beginning of 1986; West Germany had long insisted they were anachronistic and incompatible with equal status.

For three decades, the WEU was largely neglected. In 1960, it transferred its social and cultural activities to the more active Council of Europe, whose parliamentary assembly and that of WEU were identical in membership. Aside from its implementation of armament restrictions on Germany, and from quarterly meetings to discuss political and economic issues with U.K. officials after France in 1963 rejected the U.K. application to join the European Common Market, the WEU was what its present secretary general, former Netherlands defense minister Willem van Eekelen, calls a "reserve institution."

In 1984, after European governments had been jolted by President Ronald Reagan's Strategic Defense Initiative (SDI) into fears of U.S. withdrawal behind an antimissile shield from its commitment to defend the NATO allies with nuclear weapons if necessary, the WEU was revived at the initiative of French president François Mitterrand. The WEU Council of Ministers, composed of both foreign and defense ministers of member states, was reactivated. However, an effort by the WEU to develop a common European position on SDI was torpedoed by the United States. In December 1984, Richard Burt, then assistant secretary for politico-military affairs in the State Department, sent a letter to WEU member governments, whose countries were also members of the NATO alliance, warning these governments against caucusing to form collective views on defense issues outside NATO. Such American warnings became frequent in the early 1990s as the WEU picked up momentum.[2]

President Reagan again gave unintentional impetus to the WEU with his November 1986 Reykjavik proposal to Mikhail Gorbachev to eliminate all long-range ballistic nuclear missiles and with his apparent agreement, later revoked, to Gorbachev's counterproposal that, instead, all nuclear weapons should be eliminated. This unnerving development raised the possibility of cancellation of the American nuclear protection for NATO Europe in even more dramatic form than President Reagan's SDI proposal. In response, French prime minister Jacques Chirac proposed that WEU members agree on a "European Security Charter" of their own. But this idea was watered down by more pro-NATO Britain and Italy to a declaration entitled "WEU Platform on European Security Interests" (October 1987). The declaration contained repeated references to the continued need for American nuclear protection. But its main point, significantly, was the statement that the member states were "convinced that the construction of an integrated Europe will remain incomplete as long as it does not include security and defense."[3] Much of the WEU platform has been overtaken by events, but it can be viewed as the point at which the concept of expanding the European Community into the defense field crystallized into political intent, leading four years later to the inclusion in the Maastricht Treaty of the concept of defense cooperation among member states.[4]

Early in 1987, in order to help ensure safe passage of oil transports during the end phase of the Iran-Iraq war, at the request of the United States, which lacked wooden-hulled minesweepers in its modern navy, the WEU organized a series of naval escort flotillas in the Persian Gulf with contingents from France, the United Kingdom, and Italy, as well as a joint Belgian-Dutch naval force. In 1990–91, during the Gulf War, the WEU operated thirty-nine naval vessels in the gulf enforcing UN economic sanctions against Iraq. This fleet was coordinated by the WEU Council and directed by a French admiral stationed in the Gulf. In April 1991, the European Community requested the WEU to coordinate air delivery of EC humanitarian aid to the embattled Iraqi Kurds.[5]

At French initiative, Spain and Portugal, which had joined the EC in 1986, were admitted to the WEU as full members in 1988, bringing its total membership to nine countries. Nevertheless, WEU activities were lamed by a characteristic dispute between Britain, which wanted to move WEU to Brussels to be close to NATO, and France, which wanted to concentrate all WEU offices in Paris. As a result, WEU headquarters stayed in London until 1993, when it finally moved to Brussels to be near both the European Community and NATO.

WEU institutions now include the WEU Council, still composed of foreign and defense ministers of member states—it meets twice a year and is presided over by foreign ministers in rotation; a parliamentary assembly, which predates that of NATO; and a Secretariat headed by Secretary-General Willem van Eekelen. The latter presides over meetings of the Permanent Council, whose members are also the member-state ambassadors to the EU or NATO. By mid-1993, six representatives to the WEU Permanent Council were also "double-hatted," as their countries' permanent representatives to the NATO Council. To develop policy positions, the WEU uses working groups of officials from member-state ministries of foreign affairs and defense ministries reporting to meetings of foreign ministry political directors. In 1990, it established an Institute for Security Studies in Paris. Prior to 1993, when the situation changed, WEU had no permanent military staff and no forces assigned to it. Article IV of the 1954 amendment of the Brussels Treaty says that it is undesirable for WEU to duplicate the military staffs of NATO and that WEU will rely on NATO for information and advice on military matters.

THE ROAD TO EUROPEAN POLITICAL UNION

The statesmen of the period after the end of World War II—among them Jean Monnet, Robert Schuman, Konrad Adenauer, Dean Acheson, and George Marshall—pondering the failure of the interwar era effort to hold down defeated Germany, had the brilliant insight that the best way to contain Germany was to embrace it rather than isolate it. The concept of cooperation, interdependence, and integration among the European Community states found expression in a succession of interlocking treaties among an expanding number of members. (In 1993, these were Belgium, Denmark, France, Germany, Greece, Ireland, Italy, Luxembourg, Netherlands, Portugal, Spain, and the United Kingdom.) The first of these agreements established the European Coal and Steel Community (effective July 1952) followed by the European Atomic Energy Community (January 1958) and the European Economic Community (March 1958). The institutions of the three European Communities were amalgamated into a single organization by treaty in July 1967.

Beginning in 1958, the European Economic Community began the long task of building a customs union among member states, eliminating interstate duties and setting a common tariff barrier against the outside world. A common agricultural market was devised in 1964; uniform agricultural price guarantees were put in place in 1967. After a ten-year argument with France, the United Kingdom, as well as Denmark and Ireland, joined the EC in 1973. Greece (1981) and Spain and Portugal (1986) followed.

With common prosperity rather than control of Germany now the dominant motivation of Community member states, the European Monetary System was initiated in 1978. The system includes a joint reserve fund to constrain currency fluctuations among members and a system of settling currency accounts through use of European currency units, or ECUs, whose value is based on a basket of member-state currencies. Following a recommendation from EC Commission president Jacques Delors for establishment by January 1, 1992, of a fully integrated European market with free movement of money and people on the basis of standardized laws and regulations, the European Community in February 1986 adopted the Single European Act. The act enshrined Delors's single-market objective and provided for majority voting instead of absolute consensus on most of the hundreds of individual issues that had to be resolved in order to get there.

On the basis of another powerful report by Commission president Delors from early 1989, well before the fall of the Berlin Wall, the top EC body, the European Council (heads of EC governments), meeting in

Strasbourg in December 1989, overcame objections from Britain's prime minister Margaret Thatcher and decided to convene an intergovernmental conference of EC members by the end of 1990 in order to draft a new treaty on Economic and Monetary Union.

Meanwhile, the victory of Chancellor Helmut Kohl's Christian Democrats and parties allied to them in the March 1990 East German elections made clear that the unification of Germany would be rapid and that it would come through extension of the Federal Republic's institutions to all of Germany. Thoroughly convinced by forty years of successful European integration that the best way to deal with concerns about a larger and more powerful Germany was to bind it more closely to its neighbors, Chancellor Kohl and President Mitterrand acted rapidly to move European integration into another dimension, that of political union. In a joint letter to their fellow EC heads of government in April, the two leaders urged a new Treaty on Political Union, which would make the EC more responsive to the European Parliament, make its institutions more efficient, and take steps toward a common foreign and security policy. They urged that a second intergovernmental conference be convened to work out a draft of this treaty, parallel with the intergovernmental conference which would negotiate the treaty on Economic and Monetary Union, and that both projects be completed in time to enter into force together at the beginning of 1993. The European Council agreed with this recommendation. Some critics, however, believed the decision was premature and its implementation rushed.

On December 11, 1990, just before the meeting of the European Council to inaugurate the two parallel intergovernmental conferences, President Mitterrand and Chancellor Kohl sent a second, even more significant letter to the other EC heads of government. The two leaders suggested that the European Council provide guidance for the intergovernmental conference on political union by identifying the priority foreign policy topics to be considered for "joint action," that is, a unified EC approach. The two suggested as desirable topics for unified action EC relations with Eastern Europe and the Soviet Union; the CSCE negotiations; arms control negotiations; and EC relations with countries of the Mediterranean. The letter urged that "political union should include a real security policy which would eventually lead to a common defense," and went on to suggest that the intergovernmental conference "should study how the Western European Union and the Political Union could establish a clear organic relationship and thus how the WEU, made more operational, could ultimately form part of the Political Union and draw up a common security policy for it."[6] This letter contained most of the elements about the EC role in defense and the WEU-EC relationship contained in the Maastricht

Treaty documents signed a year later. WEU had moved a long way from the shadows toward real substance.

In October 1991, as the intergovernmental conference on political union neared completion of its work, President Mitterrand and Chancellor Kohl addressed another important letter to the European Council. The letter contained the text of suggested language for the Treaty on Political Union, covering basic goals of the Political Union, security and defense, priority areas for joint action in common foreign policy, and a draft declaration of WEU member states on defense issues to be issued upon signature of the Maastricht Treaty on Political Union.

Kohl and Mitterrand did not take the position jointly recommended by the British and Italian governments and endorsed in the background by the United States, that WEU should have a dual role, working for both NATO and the EC, and that it should focus on out-of-area missions. Instead, they proposed that the WEU should be considered an integral component of the European integration process. As such, WEU should carry out decisions of the European Union on defense issues. Obligations of WEU member states under the North Atlantic Treaty would not be affected by this new relationship and would continue valid.[7]

In a postscript to their letter, the two leaders surprised allied governments, including that of the United States, by announcing that the integrated Franco-German brigade which had recently entered service, would be reinforced to become the nucleus of a European army corps that could include units of other WEU member states. "This new structure could thus act as a model for closer military cooperation among all member states of the WEU," and in practice be the core of a new Western European army. France and Germany were returning nearly forty years later to the European Defense Community concept of a European army composed of integrated units.

MAASTRICHT

The Maastricht Summit was a success for the Franco-German aim of deepening the EC. The Treaty on Economic and Monetary Union was signed. Under it, the EC states agreed to move forward in stages, with action to be completed by the end of the century, to a single European currency—the European currency unit, or ECU, now used only for accounting purposes—and to establish a European Central Bank, whose primary objective in controlling the supply of the new currency would be to maintain price stability.

The parallel Treaty on European Union (its designation was changed from the earlier Political Union) was also agreed at Maastricht. It established common European Union citizenship for all citizens of EC countries, with diplomatic and consular protection for EC citizens in nonmember countries. It introduced a right of veto for the European Parliament in economic and social affairs, and a right for the Parliament to confirm members of the European Commission in office. The treaty formulated rules for a common foreign and security policy, for judicial affairs and for social policy (though the United Kingdom opted out of the social charter).

With regard to foreign policy, the European Union Treaty obligates member states to uphold common positions in multilateral forums. The topics to be covered by this obligation to take "joint action" will be decided by the Council of Ministers on the basis of unanimity, with details to be implemented by a qualified majority. As regards defense, the treaty says, "The common foreign and security policy shall include all questions related to the security of the Union, including the eventual framing of a common defense policy which might in time lead to a common defence" (Title V, Article J.4, paragraph 1). This is a modest formulation of future aims. However, the following paragraph is more affirmative. "The Union requests the Western European Union (WEU), which is an integral part of the development of the Union, to elaborate and implement decisions and actions of the Union which have defense implications. The Council shall, in agreement with the institutions of the WEU, adopt the necessary practical arrangements." The text includes the proviso that actions taken under this article should not prejudice obligations of member states who are members of NATO. Together with other aspects of both Maastricht Treaties, the text of this article also provides for its review by the Council of Ministers in 1996.[8]

THE WEU DECLARATION

The participants in the Maastricht Summit took formal note of the Declaration of the Western European Union which responds to the request in the treaty text for WEU action. The declaration is published with the text of the Treaty on European Union and for practical purposes forms part of the treaty documents. The declaration says, "WEU member states agree to strengthen the role of WEU, in the longer term perspective of a common defence policy with the European Union which might in time lead to a common defence, compatible with that of the Atlantic Alliance."[9] Furthermore, "WEU will be developed as the defence component of the European Union and as a means to strengthen the European pillar of the Atlantic Alliance. To this end, it will formulate common European defence policy and carry forward its concrete implementation through the further development of its own operational role." The declaration specifies that "the objective is to build up the WEU in stages as the defence component of the European Union."

Thus, the declaration designates WEU as the defense component of the European Union. WEU is to act as the agent of the union in defense matters and to receive and carry out its orders. The WEU will also be "a means of strengthening" the European pillar of NATO, rather than itself being that pillar.

PRACTICAL SIGNIFICANCE OF THE MAASTRICHT DECISIONS FOR WEU

The WEU Declaration contains a number of practical instructions. To carry out its function as the defense component or agent of the European Union, WEU agrees to tighten its relations with Union institutions. In day-to-day terms, this means close liaison with the Secretariat of the European Council. The Secretariat executes council decisions and is the council's unofficial surrogate when not in session. The WEU has synchronized its schedule of meetings with those of the EU and engages in comprehensive information exchange on activities of both institutions. The chairmanship of the WEU Council (the presiding foreign minister) has been shifted so that it is identical with the presidency of the European Council, which rotates every six months.

The WEU Declaration specifies that WEU's relations with NATO will be "on the basis of the necessary transparency and complementarity between the emerging European security and defense identity and the Alliance. WEU will act in conformity with the positions adopted in the Atlantic Alliance."

NATO's primacy in decisionmaking on security issues, desired by American officials, is not assured by the declaration. As explained by a senior WEU official, in the event of a sudden new crisis, because of its established procedures and larger staff, NATO would "probably" be the first to discuss a given issue. This initial discussion would indicate whether the United States or other NATO members wished NATO to become involved. If not, then WEU would be informed and could decide to act. But, the official stated, there is no agreement to give priority in discussion to NATO or to accord NATO the final decision on military intervention. Indeed, since the declaration commits WEU members to adopt a common position in NATO, consultation in the WEU Council would logically have to precede NATO consultation.[10] In practice, this is done through oral or written statements presented by the NATO permanent representative of the country that holds the WEU presidency. However, the declaration directs WEU to enter into closer liaison with NATO and to establish close liaison between the offices of the secretaries-general of WEU and of NATO.

Initial application of the principles of transparency and openness was not promising. In late July 1992, the United States decided on its own to send navy ships to the Adriatic to observe implementation of UN sanctions against Serbia. Then the WEU acted on its own to send ships to the Adriatic for the same purpose without informing NATO. NATO as an organization was left to send a small flotilla of its own. It took a year to establish a single command-and-control arrangement for combined NATO-WEU operations, called "Sharp Guard," and then only under the combined authority of the councils of both organizations.[11]

WEU secretary-general van Eekelen believes that military action outside the NATO area of responsibility could be taken by NATO and WEU working in tandem, sometimes in coalitions under U.S. leadership as in the Gulf War, sometimes under European command, but with American political agreement and with American support in areas where the forces of EU countries are weak—logistics and intelligence among them. In his view, there might be some cases where the United States would want to take the lead, others where the United States would welcome a European lead. The critical issue for deciding whether WEU should take on a particular mission would be whether NATO was unable or unwilling to act. But there might also be circumstances where the European Union was not willing to act under U.S. leadership and used WEU instead.[12] In the early 1990s, France had argued again and again that WEU must be built up because American guarantees for the defense of Europe were no longer reliable. Unavoidably, the idea that the EU might have to act on its own took on increasing substance as two successive U.S. administrations demonstratively held back on any commitment of U.S. ground troops to secure the peace in Bosnia.

Thus, after many years of attempting to prevent formation of a caucus of European member states within NATO, the United States has been obliged to accept presentation of corporate views on behalf of WEU and even the continual operation of a WEU caucus within NATO on a day-to-day basis. Instead of being a forum for multilateral discussion between the United States and individual European members of NATO, NATO is in practice becoming a forum for U.S. consultations with the European Union on security issues. This is a reasonable development, but NATO consultations will unavoidably be more difficult on some occasions.

CURRENT WEU ACTIVITIES

After the 1993 move to Brussels, the WEU was still a small organization with only about 150 permanent staff. Its components included the Research Institute, still in Paris with about 15 people; the Secretariat, plus a "Planning Cell" of fewer than 50 officers headed by an Italian general, both in Brussels; and a group of about 40 operating the WEU's observation satellite program in Spain. As in CSCE, this small permanent staff is backed by a large number of committees and working groups where officials from national capitals or the Brussels missions of member states convene for meetings. These working groups include subgroups on Mediterranean issues and the former Yugoslavia; a defense representative's group; and a subgroup on space and operation of the Open Skies Treaty.

The WEU Planning Cell is really a small planning staff; the term *planning cell* is an attempt to get around the requirement in the 1954 revision of the Brussels Treaty that WEU must not duplicate the work of NATO staffs. Secretary-General van Eekelen argues that the decision in late 1992 to place the nascent Franco-German Eurocorps under NATO command in the event of general attack on the West has resolved the long, acrimonious argument between the French and U.S. governments in which the United States insisted that WEU should operate only outside the NATO area so as not to detract from NATO in collective defense and where France insisted that WEU as a European alliance must not be excluded from the defense of Europe. Therefore, van Eekelen points out, the WEU Planning Cell, headed at the outset by Italian air force major general Marcello Caltabiano, can focus on three other tasks: humanitarian and rescue tasks, peacekeeping, and crisis management.

Under these headings WEU planners are developing different scenarios that might call for WEU action, putting together force packages for these contingency missions, and making plans for transport, logistics, communications, and command and control.[13] The Planning Cell maintains a current listing of forces that might be assigned to WEU for specific operations. Command staffs for WEU operations will be assembled on an ad hoc basis from contributing governments. The scale of operations planning will not for a considerable time exceed two to three divisions. After 1994, when the Franco-German Eurocorps becomes operational, it will be at the disposal of WEU. Other WEU forces will be drawn from units already assigned to NATO's rapid-reaction forces, a development that places NATO and WEU in potential competition for the same soldiers.

The WEU has for many years specialized in verification activities, starting with monitoring limits on German forces. For verification of the Conventional Forces in Europe Treaty, WEU put together joint verification teams from smaller member countries. WEU plans to operate a fleet of four observation planes for use by smaller member states in carrying out inspection flights under the Open Skies Treaty. The WEU has been doing extensive work on establishment of a European observation satellite system, which it is hoped may be operational by 2005. Sensibly, the WEU decided to start with the more costly part of such a system, the ground element that analyzes the results of satellite observation, before making definitive decisions on what satellite system to use. In the spring of 1993, WEU opened a center for satellite data interpretation and training at Torrejon, Spain, with an annual budget of 38 million ECUs. It is also conducting serious study of a possible regional antimissile defense system for Europe.

In December 1992, it was decided to incorporate into the WEU the Independent European Program Group (IEPG) associated with NATO, which has sought since its establishment in 1976 by the EC states to coordinate weapons research, promote standardization, and defend the interests of European arms makers against those of U.S. producers. The WEU had a small program of its own in this field from 1955. WEU is also considering converting the WEU Institute into a training school for senior officers and defense officials somewhat like NATO's Defense College in Rome.

Following Maastricht, the WEU enlarged its membership to include Greece as its tenth full member, admitted antimilitaristic Denmark and neutral Ireland as observers, and Iceland, Norway, and Turkey as associate members. Associate members of WEU can participate in its deliberations but cannot block consensus with their vote. If Norway, Finland, Sweden, and Austria complete negotiations for membership in the EC and, as expected, become members by 1995 or 1996, they will probably become full members of WEU, bringing total membership to fourteen.

THE WEU ENTERS PEACEKEEPING

The WEU moved determindly in 1992 to head off a possible NATO monopoly on peacekeeping. Two weeks after NATO's announcement in its Oslo meeting of June 4–5, that it would place its forces at the disposal of CSCE for peacekeeping, on June 19, 1992, the WEU Council of foreign and defense ministers met at Petersberg outside of Bonn and declared its own willingness to participate in peacekeeping activities of the CSCE or the UN. On the same day, in a ceremonial session strongly reminiscent of the inaugural session of the North Atlantic Cooperation Council in Brussels six months earlier, the WEU Council of Ministers met with their counterparts from Eastern Europe and the Baltic states. The participants in this session, now called the WEU Forum of Consultation, decided to meet at the ministerial level at least once a year, and twice a year with the WEU Permanent Council in Brussels, and they planned a series of consultations and information exchanges between the WEU Institute for Security Studies and national institutes of foreign affairs.

It was decided at the Petersberg meeting that the chiefs of staff of WEU countries would meet regularly twice a year prior to semiannual council meetings, and that member-state delegations to the Permanent Council should have military advisers assigned to them. Member states were called on to earmark units for WEU service and to report their designations. The council also adopted more detailed rules on associate membership of WEU that make it possible for associate members to contribute military units to a WEU military mission—this is one point on which WEU is ahead of NATO. In listing the possible missions of WEU forces, the council included not only peacekeeping, but also "tasks of combat forces in crisis management, including peacemaking." In other words, WEU is in theory also prepared to take on "peace enforcement operations" (something that the CSCE is not yet ready to undertake).[14] It is interesting that the German government felt itself in a position to agree to this decision, given the unresolved debate in Germany over sending German forces abroad.

As regards actual contributions to peacekeeping, in addition to its Adriatic squadron under direction of the Italian navy for enforcement of sanctions against Serbia and Montenegro, WEU sent a squadron of eight river patrol boats with about 300 personnel from member countries (Germany, France, Italy, Spain, Netherlands, Luxembourg) to the Danube River to help Hungary, Bulgaria, and Romania enforce the sanctions. It has repeatedly reviewed the possibility of sending peacekeeping troops to Croatia and Bosnia as a WEU force but has not been able to reach agreement on this. In mid-1993, WEU was asked by the EC to prepare itself to police the city of Mostar in western Bosnia if a peace plan and cease-fire came into effect. (This was part of the Owen-Stoltenberg Plan, which provided for UN administration of Sarajevo and EU administration of Mostar.)

THE CASE FOR WEU

By mid-1992, the WEU had gone through a transition similar to that of CSCE and NATO in adapting to meet the most pressing challenges of Europe in the post-cold war period. Indeed, given WEU's exiguous existence before the revolutionary changes of 1989–91, it adjusted even faster than either NATO or the CSCE. In terms of institutional status, WEU had moved to near equality with NATO, although remaining far behind NATO in capability.

There is a strong theoretical case for developing a more or less autonomous European military capability. In 1992, even before contemplated expansion to include Norway, Finland, Sweden, and Austria, the EC states had a population of 345 million compared to 253 million for the United States, a gross domestic product of $6.9 trillion, $1 trillion more than the United States, exports of $565 billion compared to U.S. exports of $448 billion, and armed forces of 2.2 million compared to 1.9 million for the United States.[15]

Logically, an organization tying together such sizable and prosperous countries should have the capability of self-defense and should not be indefinitely dependent on U.S. military support; there is no intrinsic reason why Europeans should not protect European terrain themselves. The danger of major war in Europe has receded. In theory, Europe's armed forces are a match for a resurgent Russia except as regards nuclear weapons. Current problems that might require use of military force short of that appear within Europe's current capabilities. Driven by political and economic considerations, the United States will probably carry out further reductions of its forces in Europe. European defense cooperation could theoretically provide adequate military insurance less subject than NATO to shifts in U.S. domestic politics.

Most European governments want greater independence from sometimes heavy-handed U.S. hegemony. This is true not only of France, but also of Germany, which has been subject to unremitting U.S. pressures from the occupation period to the present. Part of the shock of the Gulf War for Europeans—and a further impetus for European defense integration—was the realization that the end of the cold war did not mean the end of U.S. dominance in defense. As some European experts on security issues argued, Europeans felt like second-rate citizens, with U.S. generals and arms controllers calling the shots; they concluded that if Europe did not have separate military power of its own, it would also not have a real say on policy.

Feelings like this have resulted in the emergence among European political and economic elites of a kind of "Euronationalism," or "Europatriotism," a kind of national feeling transmuted to a European level, a desire to play a role in the world commensurate with European capabilities, sometimes augmented by resentment over the influence exercised by the United States. Ian Davidson, an influential expert on European politics for the London *Financial Times* argues, "NATO cannot be the forum for a Euro-American strategy because Europe will not give it that task. The twelve EC members are committed to work on a common foreign policy; they will not subordinate it to U.S. domination in NATO."[16] In political terms, the existence of this attitude requires a more equal balanced relationship, articulated in terms of institutional equality between NATO and WEU, if there is to be continuing cooperation between the United States and European states on defense issues.

WEU supporters argue that a strengthened WEU would be helpful for improved sharing of burdens and responsibilities with the United States. They believe that, in the longer term, despite serious setbacks since the Maastricht treaties were agreed, it is probable that the European Community will ultimately emerge as the primary security agency of Europe after full economic and political union are achieved, even if this goal is delayed from the present schedule of 1999. In this view, the European Union will someday become a superpower, the reliable and powerful if not automatically supportive partner in world affairs the United States has sought since the end of World War II possessing the autonomous capabilities required for genuine partnership. Therefore, it is in the United States' interest to support the military development of the European Union.

Some European experts also argue that the European integration process cannot continue or survive indefinitely without a defense component, that cooperative defense is a necessary articulation and support of a common foreign policy.[17] Advocates of the WEU submit that there are and will be European security problems where NATO or the United States will be unwilling or unable to intervene. They point out, correctly, that the case for almost any out-of-area military intervention is harder to make to electorates than the case for defense of home territory against aggression. They claim that the EC will have an easier time than NATO members in making this case because WEU intervention would be based on common foreign policy aims shared among EU members but not necessarily with the United States. This is a tenuous argument, but WEU supporters can cite the continuing reluctance of the United States to become involved in the conflicts in the former Yugoslavia.

WEU has a record in its two Gulf involvements and in its Adriatic involvement of permitting a self-selected group of its members to operate under its name and aegis, to opt in or out. Against this background, supporters claim that WEU is the best vehicle for organizing a "two-speed" or "variable geometry" European Union, where new members like Sweden may not be ready to plunge immediately into defense collaboration. These new members are very unlikely to join NATO. It is argued that it is better to grant them associate or observer status in WEU than to see them wholly unintegrated for defense purposes.

Proponents argue that, in coping with the difficult task of finding budgetary support for armed forces in a period of relative peace, WEU can draw on public support for European unity; NATO does not have this asset.[18] Moreover, there is obvious need for more cooperation among smaller countries that cannot field the whole range of armed forces. It is argued that smaller countries will pool their resources more readily in a contractual framework like the Brussels Treaty, which offers automatic assistance in the event of attack, rather than in a situation where they are dependent on an uncertain American political decision as in NATO.[19]

WEU supporters believe that in a period of lower budgets and higher equipment costs, there should be more European collaboration in defense procurement, with Germany buying French aircraft and France buying German tanks. They accurately claim that the United States has proved unreliable in establishing a two-way flow for arms procurement. Supporters assert that the French commitment in the Franco-German Eurocorps and in WEU marks the definitive French move away from defense autonomy and toward defense integration and that French acceptance of the WEU Declaration places French forces more unequivocally than heretofore under NATO command in the event of external attack against the territory of NATO states. It is also argued that, given continuing antimilitary sentiment in the German public and the negative identification of NATO with the cold war by many Germans, especially East Germans, the most effective way to gain support from the German public for continued German defense integration with the West is via German support for the European Community and for its defense arm, the WEU.[20]

WEU's Problems

On the basis of considerations like these, it is probable that the review of progress toward common foreign and defense policies already provided for 1996 in the Treaty on European Union will confirm the WEU as the defense component of the EC. But the WEU is not without problems.

The WEU's potential for growth is directly tied to the prospects for the European Union itself. However, the future of the European Union has become problematical. Rejection of the Maastricht Treaties by a narrow margin in the Danish referendum of April 1992 (even though a repeat referendum a year later reversed this outcome) and the bare 2 percent majority for the treaties in the hard-fought French referendum of September 1992 were real danger signals. The collapse of the exchange-rate mechanism (ERM) for maintaining currency stability among member states in September 1992 in a wave of foreign currency trading, culminating in the devaluation of the Italian lira, the U.K. pound, and Spanish peseta, intensified the dissatisfaction of EC governments with weaker economies with the rigid discipline of a system tied to the high interest rates imposed by the German Bundesbank in order to contain the inflationary effects of Germany's $100-billion-a-year outlays to revive the East German economy. In August 1993, the ERM's link with high German interest rates, compelling other members of the system either to devalue—a politically difficult step—or to maintain high interest rates of their own, which acted as a brake on economic expansion, brought the near collapse of the French franc and a further crisis of the exchange-rate mechanism.

This lockstep of economic and fiscal policies would be perpetuated and much tightened in the economic and monetary union agreed at Maastricht. Consequently, many experts believed that economic and monetary union would at best have to await successful completion of efforts to bring the East German economy up to the West German level. Others believed that the requirements established by the Treaty for Economic Union were so stringent that they could never be implemented even by the German officials who had proposed them. In mid-1993, only Luxembourg came close to meeting the requirements for monetary union. Public support for the European Union and for further steps of integration decreased still further as the Bundesbank's high interest rates led EU economies into their worst recession and highest unemployment since the end of World War II.

These developments also brought a backlash of national feeling in most EC countries against the European Commission and the prospect of rule by anonymous Eurocrats in Brussels. The political difficulty was greatest in the U.K., where Prime Minister John Major faced strong negative opinion, causing him to speak of a revised approach to further integration and repeatedly to postpone British ratification of the Maastricht Treaty, finally achieved in July 1993. Negative sentiment was also increasing in the German public, once the strongest of all in its support of European integration. There were growing public concerns in Germany that Economic Union could dilute strict Bundesbank controls against inflation. Some outside commentators believed EU members might ultimately be faced by a choice between accepting German economic hegemony or forming an anti-German coalition. As a result of this slowdown of the general integration process, some European analysts considered that, at best, it would take two to three decades for the Community to achieve a functional degree of defense unity.

Because the WEU was still a separate institution, the slowdown in the EU might not automatically affect the WEU. But it would affect the EU's effort to develop common foreign and defense policies, and therefore the impetus for further growth of the WEU, as well as the policy guidance received by the WEU from the European Union. The WEU's new link with the EU via the Maastricht Treaty could mean in practical terms that possible military intervention by WEU would from now on require prior legitimation through a formal EU decision and that the WEU would consequently no longer have the broad latitude to decide on its own, as it had in undertaking activities in the Persian Gulf in 1987 and 1990–91 and even as it had in sanctions enforcement in the Adriatic in August 1992.

But the WEU faced more specific problems than these. WEU is weak in the organizational sense. Even after its planning staff was fully assembled, the WEU had no command or operation staff. There were serious questions whether a command structure rapidly assembled on an ad hoc basis for a specific operation could perform smoothly and effectively. For larger operations involving combining forces of different nationalities, integrated command, with frequently exercised group decisionmaking, is highly desirable. The WEU had no airlift capability, no independent intelligence collection or surveillance capability, limited combat air force capability, command, and control, and no troops trained for rapid intervention. In the view of most senior European military officers, it would take years to develop such capabilities. As demonstrated in the small-scale WEU activities in the former Yugoslavia, WEU's capacity to conduct operations independently from NATO and U.S. forces was limited to small operations. One problem here will be the availability of money for expensive new equipment. WEU might eventually have satellite imaging capability, but it would take many years to raise the money for a complete system. One possible answer would be use by WEU of NATO's extensive physical infrastructure and the logistic and intelligence capabilities of NATO staffs, many of them drawing directly on U.S. national capabilities. But would the United States go along with this?

WEU has other problems. It was unclear whether France's agreement at Maastricht to the Political Union Treaty really meant that France is finally willing to throw in its lot with a European military grouping. France has rejected the idea of an integrated military staff for WEU and for the Eurocorps. Questions about the wholeheartedness of French support merge into more general questions about whether the European countries are capable at the present stage of development of generating sufficient cohesion to take joint decisions on difficult foreign affairs or security issues. They did not do well in coalescing around on a single position during the Gulf War. Britain disputed tactics with France, which went its own way in offering a last-minute deal to Saddam Hussein. Belgium refused to sell ammunition to its British ally. Germany was immobilized by indecision at the top and by strong antimilitary sentiments. Some German political leaders denied that there was any NATO obligation to defend Turkey if it were attacked by Iraq. Some experts believe that if procedures for EC common foreign policy had already existed at the time of the Gulf War and a majority of EC members had sought to enforce a do-nothing approach, this would have caused Britain to withdraw from the Community.[21]

In the Yugoslav conflict, the record of EC decisionmaking was if anything worse. Early in the war, France appeared to support Serbia, and Germany Croatia, culminating in the preemptory German demand in the council session of December 1991 that the EC must recognize the independence of Croatia and Slovenia. In mid-1992, President Mitterrand undermined Lord Carrington's mediation efforts for the EC by publicly insisting they were ineffective.

As EU membership increases in 1995 or 1996 with the probable membership of the European neutrals, joint decisionmaking on all issues including defense will probably become even more difficult. Sweden is one of the EU candidate members. The Swedish Parliament recently insisted that Sweden should remain neutral in peacetime and join no alliances in war. Nevertheless, the European Commission has asked Sweden to provide specific and binding assurances that it would accept the eventual framing of a common defense policy and the ultimate establishment of a common defense. Sweden's prime minister Carl Bildt objected that not even EC members have yet had to produce specific and binding assurances of this kind.[22] The special procedures agreed by the EC Council in order to encourage the favorable outcome of the second Danish referendum on the Maastricht treaties would permit Denmark to opt out of a common defense policy.

The biggest difficulty with regard to joint decisionmaking on defense and security issues faced by WEU is the same problem that has weakened NATO's stance on peacekeeping—the unresolved stalemate within Germany over deploying German troops outside national borders, or at least outside the territory of NATO states. The controversy is completely understandable, but the result is like trying to stage a band concert without the brass instruments. France often has a desire to exercise leadership but sometimes does not carry enough weight. The Franco-German duo that brought about the Maastricht Treaties and that has provided the main decisionmaking capacity of the EC does well when the leaders of the two countries agree, but it has nearly been inoperative as regards security issues because of divided opinion in Germany over use of German forces abroad. Although German opinion on this topic is slowly evolving, German internal decision-making on this topic is likely to continue difficult for decades. The main problem area is the unwillingness of the Social Democrats to agree to deployment of German troops abroad for any purpose other than peacekeeping operations run by the UN. This position precludes German participation in other multilateral activities, including those of the WEU as well as of NATO.

OPPOSITION FROM THE UNITED STATES

Among WEU's greatest difficulties during its 1990–92 period of expansion was U.S. hostility to the entire project. However, the advent of the Clinton administration, with its emphasis on domestic reform within the United States rather than on foreign policy and its less possessive attitude toward NATO, considerably improved the situation.

From the end of World War II, the United States supported the concept of European integration. The United States insisted on economic cooperation among the European states as a prerequisite for receiving Marshall Plan aid. It supported the establishment of the European Coal and Steel Community and Euratom. In the security field, it fully backed the European Defense Community project and later supported a second failed effort at integration in the nuclear weapons field, the Multilateral Force project. In 1990, Secretary of State Baker took the initiative to establish new formal links with the European Community.

On paper, the Bush administration supported WEU. For example, the Rome "Declaration on Peace and Cooperation" issued in November 1991 just after President Bush and other NATO leaders were taken aback by the Kohl-Mitterrand announcement of the establishment of a Franco-German Eurocorps outside NATO, contains a lengthy endorsement of the development of a European security identity and defense role and the steps to strengthen the WEU "both as the defense component of the process of European unification and as a means of strengthening the European pillar of the Alliance."

But U.S. support for European integration has been ambivalent, especially as regards defense matters. Günther van Well, the insightful former German ambassador to the United States, pointed out in one of his last writings that the United States has always followed a two-track policy that combines principled support for European unity with insistence that the military and economic position of the United States in Europe must remain so strong that its influence would not diminish in the face of further practical steps toward European integration. For example, in 1973–74, the United States welcomed the initiation of European Political Cooperation, the network of policy coordination among senior officials of EC member state foreign ministries, which was the precursor of the concept of a common foreign policy set forth in the Political Union Treaty. But at the same time, President Richard Nixon warned the EC states against "ganging up" against the United States by caucusing and developing common EC positions before consultation and negotiations; Secretary of State Henry Kissinger then proposed direct participation for the United States in the European Political Cooperation program and when that did not work, asked for "an organic consultative relationship" that would ensure that the United States would be consulted before the EC took definitive positions.

Despite its statements of support for European defense integration, the Bush administration remained deeply worried that actions to strengthen WEU would undermine NATO and with it, U.S. influence in Europe. Throughout 1990, 1991, and 1992, senior U.S. officials made repeated representations to European capitals warning that pending WEU actions could undermine NATO. For example, in spring 1992, just before a key meeting between Chancellor Kohl and President Mitterrand in France, U.S. ambassador to NATO William Howard Taft IV warned that "undermining the Alliance's integrated military structure in the uncertain process of developing a European security identity would be the height of folly."[23] After Kohl and Mitterrand had issued details of the new Franco-German European Corps from La Rochelle, National Security Adviser Brent Scowcroft sent a letter to both governments expressing concern over the negative effects of this development. A spokesperson of the French government reacted that the Scowcroft letter was evidence of a U.S. desire to block European integration.

Putting together the elements of the repeated American complaints, they were: NATO must be the first to decide. NATO, and with it the United States, must have the first right of refusal for military operations because NATO could later be caught up in operations that did not go well. If the United States is not involved in decisions before a war starts in Europe, it may have to be there afterward to pick up the pieces, but without having had any say in the decisions that led up to the conflict. If the United States was to maintain a serious defense commitment to Europe, U.S. political opinion would not support a residual role for the United States in European security decisions, only to be brought in to redress European mistakes. If East European states ultimately entered the EU, this would mean an involuntary alliance guarantee by the United States to Eastern Europe.

These statements were all advanced by senior American officials or military officers during the controversy. They reveal a pervasively low opinion of European judgment and leadership.

France and its allies fought back against these U.S. arguments all along the line. In most of the arguments, France made a strong effort to gain agreement on its own position, but if this was not possible, accepted the American one, often in a watered-down version. France accepted U.S. command in the Gulf War and in the Somalia relief operation; it ultimately went along on most U.S. proposals for UN Security Council resolutions on the Yugoslav states. It rejoined the NATO Military Committee for discussion concerning issues of peacekeeping. But French officials were also good negotiators.

As the dispute wore on, the United States focused on the need for the primacy of NATO consultation. In the U.S. view, if European states have views on security issues, they should bring them to NATO to develop. These views can be initiated in NATO, WEU, or the EC. But they must be brought to NATO for decision. Then they can go to CSCE or other organizations for implementation. Future military operations might be NATO operations or they might be WEU operations. But this choice must be made in advance in each case, and it must be made by NATO. NATO must be the primary forum for decisions on European security. At one point in the second half of 1991, U.S. officials were almost pleading for serious consultations among equals in terms that European governments long had been addressing to the U.S. government regarding its own failure to consult in advance on many important policy decisions.

The United States lost on many of these points because it was on the weaker side. Its adversary was not only France but all the other core members of continental Europe: Italy, the Netherlands, and, in particular, Germany. In all these governments, the drive to build Europe and the drive to achieve more equal status with the United States prevailed over fears of alienating the United States and distancing it from Europe.

Germany is the strongest single member of the WEU and the strongest European member of NATO. German acceptance of continued stationing of U.S. forces on German territory is crucial to the continuation of U.S. ground and air combat forces in Europe. Without this acceptance, U.S. forces could be squeezed out of Europe, just as U.S. officials fear. Flowing from those factors, Germany's role in the WEU-NATO controversy was paramount. Both the United States and France continually appealed to Germany to throw its weight on their side of the NATO-WEU controversy, both on the big issues of WEU's relationship with NATO and the EC, the Franco-German corps, and the establishment of the North Atlantic Cooperation Council and on the thousand day-to-day details of the arrangement. Germany found this balancing role highly uncomfortable and often sought to avoid it.[24] Yet, despite often painful embarrassment and frictions, the role of balancer nonetheless gave Germany influence and a deciding voice on individual issues. In practice, as documented in the series of Kohl-Mitterrand initiatives to build the defense dimension of the EC and the EC-WEU connection, in recent years, Germany has more frequently made the choice of European integration than the Atlanticist choice. Instead of becoming a second loyal ally like the United Kingdom as U.S. officials had hoped, the united Germany has in the NATO-WEU context become a second France. With these forces arrayed against it, it was no mystery why the United States had lost out in its effort to keep the WEU down.

This sterile debate between a France dedicated to resisting U.S. dominance in security decisions whether in NATO or at the UN and a United States apprehensive about retaining its influence in European security issues in a situation of decreased military threat might have been ameliorated or even resolved by discussion between Presidents Mitterrand and Bush. Unfortunately, this high-level discussion in depth never took place.

Nonetheless, by the spring of 1993, the worst of the battle over principles and institutions appeared over. Neither WEU nor NATO had succeeded in subordinating the other. In the future, the relationship between NATO and WEU would be characterized either by competition on the practical level of individual cases rather than on issues of principle, or by cooperation and "complementarity." There had been a change of governments in both the United States and France to administrations less inclined to argue over this issue. France had made moves toward NATO, including an acceptable solution to the issue of command authority over the Eurocorps. Under the pressure of economic recession, the Clinton administration had made much deeper cuts in U.S. forces in Europe than foreseen in the Bush administration, reducing to some extent the degree of influence it could aspire to. At the same time, the manifest problems of the European Community clearly meant that the WEU could no longer expect to develop at the rate that appeared possible at the time the Maastricht Treaty was concluded. In particular, the EC's weak performance in Yugoslavia demonstrated its limitations in the security field.

As documented here, the WEU has come from far behind to win the right of equal treatment with NATO as an institution. But we have not yet been able to answer our question at the beginning of this chapter as to whether or not autonomous European defense can be achieved in the reasonably near-term future. It is still unclear whether the European Union with the WEU as its agent will develop as the primary security institution of Europe, combining economic strength with political unity and military capability from the Atlantic to the border of Ukraine. What is clear is that such an outcome if it does come will not be a rapid one. The resistance of the Bush and Clinton administrations to involve U.S. ground forces in Croatia or Bosnia has increased the motivation of the European Union states to move toward military autonomy, but it is quite uncertain whether this development will be accompanied by European willingness to make the greatly increased political, economic, and military investment. WEU will need to fill that role.

12

CONTROLLING EUROPE'S ARMED FORCES

R eaching far back into prehistory, men have believed that the only feasible way to defend their families, tribes, or nations is reliance on their own armed strength together with that of allies. Flavius Vegetius Renatus, a Roman officer of the fourth century A.D. who wrote a comprehensive treatise on the Roman army, formulated the concept that has dominated thinking on armed forces for thousands of years: "If you wish peace, then prepare for war." This central axiom about having enough armed strength to discourage attack or defeat an opponent is the basis of self-defense. It has in fact prevented many wars.

But this concept has also led to many wars, serving as the justification for arms races, preemptive attack, and wars of conquest, especially as it mutated in the Western countries into the idea of having enough armed strength to inflict decisive defeat on the armed forces of the enemy on his own territory.[1] The immense cold war military confrontation was a dangerous and costly monument to the latter version. To escape from the ambiguous consequences of preserving peace through preparing for war, some have envisaged a world without any armies. But this categorical step requires a degree of trust and confidence in the potential adversary that is psychologically impossible for most people, who find it more reassuring to rely on capabilities within their own control.

Finally, the tragic losses of two world wars and the pressures of the massive cold war military confrontation brought an intellectual resolution to the clash between the view that peace could be preserved only by arming and the view that peace was possible only through cooperation with the potential adversary and disarming. The logical answer is to combine the two basic views in some mix of one's own armed forces and of cooperative measures with the potential adversary. This combination of armed forces for self-defense and of arms control and confidence building is often called common security because it contains an element absent from the concept of unilateral self-defense: at least some degree of empathy for the situation of the other side. In a world where armed forces and nationalism will exist for the foreseeable future even if multinational peacekeeping can make real progress, combining national armed forces with arms control measures is the rational approach for defense.

Obviously, the combination of national armed forces and arms control is more reassuring for most people than complete disarmament and exclusive reliance on arms control. But the combination of national armed forces with arms control measures can also provide more security at lower cost than reliance on national forces alone. The combination of armed forces and arms control is cheaper than sole reliance on armed forces, despite costs of verification, because it requires fewer armed forces and inhibits arms race competition. The combination is more secure than reliance on national armed forces alone because, properly applied, arms control and transparency measures can effectively reduce the risk of surprise attack, miscalculation, and error by the military commands of either side and prevent crisis escalation and pressures for preemptive attack. The arms control component makes possible greater knowledge of the armed forces, deployment, and force activities of the potential adversary than is possible in a situation of tight adversarial secrecy about armed forces. It also reduces the risks of surprise attack, miscalculation, and preemption through establishing restrictions on the size, armaments, activities, and deployments of armed forces. Violation of these restrictions gives early warning to the defender. Their existence requires the attacker to use additional valuable time after warning is given to prepare his forces for attack.

Now that the cold war has ended, have these benefits of arms control been superseded? There are two answers to this question, both negative. The first is that arms control in Europe has not been superseded because it continues to provide a necessary foundation for cooperation among European states on political, economic, and security issues. Without treaties governing its nuclear and conventional forces, worries about an increasingly nationalistic Russia would probably freeze all East-West cooperation.

The more general answer is that arms control is an essential component of a wider range of activities we can call peacemaking, whose common objective is to prevent conflict, to minimize its effects if it takes place, to bring it to an end, and to prevent its recurrence. This spectrum includes armed forces for national defense, confidence-building and transparency measures, restrictions on deployment and activities of armed forces, negotiated force reductions and limitations, control over weapons production and proliferation, and also conflict prevention, mediation, conflict resolution, multilateral peacekeeping, and peace enforcement.[2] Together with the multilateral security institutions that apply them, these peacemaking measures are the main tools in the effort to lower the incidence of organized armed violence in Europe. New arms control measures will be needed in most of the current hot spots of Europe where military conflict already exists or threatens, including former Yugoslavia and the Soviet successor states, indeed, wherever adversarial military relationships loom throughout the world.

In this sense, the question of whether arms control has outlived its usefulness is misplaced. The real question is whether arms control is doing its job effectively and can do so in future applications. The 1987 Treaty on Intermediate-range Nuclear Forces in Europe (INF) has been satisfactorily implemented with destruction of all U.S. and Soviet missiles of this type, so we seek to answer this question with regard to other European arms control agreements, starting with the Conventional Forces in Europe Treaty (CFE). It should be kept in mind that the states involved in European security issues also participate in several global arms control regimes like the Non-Proliferation Treaty, the treaties prohibiting production or use of biological and chemical weapons (the latter may enter force in 1995), and in several regimes, like the Nuclear Suppliers Group, whose aim is to restrict transfer of weapons components.

THE CFE TREATY

The Conventional Forces in Europe Treaty, signed November 19, 1990 in Paris, formally entered into effect on November 9, 1992 (by agreement, advance implementation started in July). The treaty places a top limit on the major ground and air force armaments—battle tanks, armored combat vehicles, artillery, combat aircraft, and combat helicopters—that are deployed in the CFE "area of application" from the Atlantic Ocean to the Ural Mountains by the thirty signatory states. The treaty requires the former Warsaw Pact states to reduce their combined holdings of these weapons by about 130,000 items to a "common ceiling" level equal to the combined holdings of the NATO countries after a reduction of a few thousand NATO armaments has been made.[3] Most excess weapons are to be destroyed. By agreement, naval and nuclear forces are excluded from treaty coverage. There is extensive verification. The equal levels for members of NATO taken together and for members of the former Warsaw Pact taken together are 20,000 tanks, 30,000 armored combat vehicles, 20,000 artillery pieces, 6,800 combat aircraft, and 2,000 attack helicopters. There is also a national limit on the holdings of each signatory state of these armaments. A supplementary political understanding, CFE–1A, signed in July 1992 at the Helsinki 92 Summit, requires the participating states to limit the level of full-time military personnel of their ground and air forces deployed in the CFE area of application.

The character of the CFE negotiations changed radically during their course, owing to Soviet agreement to withdraw all forces from Eastern Europe, collapse of the communist governments of Eastern Europe, German unification, formal dissolution of the Warsaw Pact, and then of the Soviet Union itself. The CFE talks took only nineteen months from beginning to conclusion. Although only two pages of formal treaty text had been approved by the end of 1989 after nine months of negotiation, a positive outcome was never in serious doubt. What was uncertain after the anti-Gorbachev coup of August 1991 and the subsequent collapse of the Soviet Union was implementation of the treaty. Persistent, skillful diplomacy by the United States and other NATO countries shepherded the Soviet successor states through tense negotiations over the allocation among them of the equipment of the Soviet armed forces and brought them to treaty ratification. However, in the turbulent circumstances of the successor states, some important questions of implementation have not been resolved.

As the CFE talks opened, the concentration of military forces in Europe was the largest in peacetime history in both size and destructive capacity—a total for both alliances of 7 million active-duty military personnel, 90,000 tanks, 125,000 armored troop carriers, 128,000 artillery pieces, 8,000 helicopters, 16,000 combat aircraft, 2,500 combatant naval vessels in the waters surrounding Europe, and about 10,000 tactical-range nuclear weapons. All this at a staggering annual cost for the NATO alliance of $300 billion a year and about $200 billion for the Warsaw Pact. Figures released by the Warsaw Pact itself in January 1989—a historic first publication of numbers on pact armed forces—pointed to a pact superiority of about 30,000 tanks, 23,000 other armored vehicles, 15,000 artillery pieces, and 1,500 launchers for surface-to-surface missiles equipped with nuclear warheads. NATO's figures using different definitions showed still higher Warsaw Pact numerical superiorities, including an advantage of about 8,000 combat aircraft.

There had long been doubts in the West as to the loyalty of the Soviet Union's Warsaw Pact allies and regarding the capacity of the Soviet Union and other Warsaw Pact governments to rapidly mobilize their forces and to move them forward for an attack. But for more than four decades, the

Warsaw Pact's numerical superiority was the basis for NATO's fears of an overwhelming pact conventional attack, especially against forces in West Germany, where NATO territory was shallowest.

Earlier efforts at negotiated reduction of the East-West military confrontation in Europe failed completely; the NATO-Warsaw Pact talks on Mutual and Balanced Force Reductions (MBFR) were closed down in February 1989 after fifteen years of negotiation without productive outcome. NATO negotiating demands in MBFR had progressively narrowed down to purely symbolic withdrawal of about 10,000 U.S. and Soviet military personnel, but the extensive verification that was still part of the deal was unattractive to the Soviet military.

By early 1986, Gorbachev and his advisers had decided the MBFR talks were too deeply mired to be pulled out, that it was necessary to add to reduction of military personnel the reduction of armaments, more easily counted and verified, and also to include in the negotiations France, Spain, and Portugal, which had not participated in MBFR. Gorbachev offered NATO a choice between expanding the MBFR talks or starting afresh. NATO chose the latter, and new negotiations began in March 1989.

The main difference between the MBFR and CFE negotiations was the political will of the Soviet leadership to get results in CFE, evidenced in Gorbachev's announcement in December 1988 of a pump-priming unilateral Soviet reduction of 500,000 soldiers plus withdrawal from Central Europe of four tank divisions. This was quickly followed by Soviet agreement in January 1989 to the "mandate" or terms of reference of the CFE talks, which established as a major goal of the talks the "elimination of disparities (i.e., superiorities) prejudicial to stability and security"; the first time ever publication by the Warsaw Pact of data on its forces (January 1989), which confirmed NATO claims of large pact superiorities; and by Foreign Minister Eduard Shevardnadze's speech at the opening session of the CFE, where he accepted the central NATO negotiating approach of reducing the major armaments of both alliances to a new equal level below that of the numerically weaker side.[4]

It is easy after the event to criticize the basic CFE concept of moving to parity at a lower level as simplistic. Clearly, equal forces do not of themselves ensure military stability or the absence of conflict. Yet at the outset of the CFE talks, NATO leaders were still reckoning with the indefinite continuation in some form of the huge East-West military confrontation that had dominated European politics for forty years. The West's military objective in the talks was to reduce the pact's large numerical superiority in armored divisions that created the possibility of a rapid blitz attack to the English Channel. The Western demand in CFE for parity reflected the basic concept of the SALT, START, and MBFR talks, to pose a serious political test of the stated willingness of Soviet leaders to place their military and political relationship with the Western countries on a wholly new footing. The parity objective was clearly understood and supported by Western public opinion. It was a blunt negotiating instrument but a durable and finally effective one.

Because of its desire to limit U.S. influence over the West's negotiating position and to avoid bolstering the international legal standing of NATO, France insisted from the outset of the CFE negotiations that they not be conducted "bloc to bloc," but rather among individual participants. In practice, however, the negotiations were conducted on an alliance-to-alliance basis until the Warsaw Pact began to crumble. At this point, some pact states, notably Hungary and Poland, urged positions helpful to the NATO stance and left the Soviet Union to negotiate on its own.

One lasting, valuable outcome of this French insistence was the treaty provision that each alliance must divide its quota of arms among its member states and notify all other signatories of these limits; Article VII establishes limits on each state's holdings of CFE equipment. These treaty obligations cannot be changed unless some other state in the same group voluntarily relinquishes part of its quota. Changes must be notified. Now that the Warsaw Pact has dissolved, these individual limits provide the enduring structure of CFE. (See Table 1.) Through allocations finally agreed on at the May 1992 meeting of the Commonwealth of Independent States in Tashkent,[5] and their subsequent ratification of the CFE Treaty, Russia and the other successor states accepted individual national limits on their holdings of treaty-limited equipment. Russia ended up with an allocation of only 6,400 tanks west of the Urals, while NATO countries are permitted 20,000 tanks, giving them a three-to-one advantage over Russian forces in the area. (But total Russian tanks, including those deployed and stored east of the Urals, are much more numerous. The International Institute for Strategic Studies estimates the total as close to 50,000.)[6]

These individual national ceilings in treaty-limited equipment, augmented by declared limits on military personnel and their ongoing verification, are the most important enduring elements of the CFE.

VERIFICATION

The verification task in CFE is immense. The treaty's area of application is 2.5 million square miles, with more than 150,000 items to be verified in thirty countries. During the CFE talks, most of the controversy over verification was inside NATO, where the United States vainly urged its allies to agree to establish controls at exit-entry points to the reduction area and at transportation choke-points. European NATO governments

TABLE 1
WEAPONS IN EUROPE AFTER IMPLEMENTATION OF THE CFE TREATY

NATO

COUNTRY	TANKS	ACVs*	ARTILLERY	AIRCRAFT	HELICOPTERS	TOTAL
Belgium	334	1,099	320	232	46	2,031
Canada	77	277	38	90	13	495
Denmark	353	316	553	106	12	1,340
France	1,306	3,820	1,292	800	352	7,570
Germany	4,166	3,446	2,705	900	306	11,523
Greece	1,735	2,534	1,878	650	18	6,815
Iceland	0	0	0	0	0	0
Italy	1,348	3,339	1,955	650	142	7,434
Luxembourg	0	0	0	0	0	0
Netherlands	743	1,080	607	230	69	2,729
Norway	170	225	527	100	0	1,022
Portugal	300	430	450	160	26	1,366
Spain	794	1,588	1,310	310	71	4,073
Turkey	2,795	3,120	3,523	750	43	10,231
United Kingdom	1,015	3,176	636	900	384	6,111
United States	4,006	5,372	2,492	784	518	13,172
Totals	19,142	29,822	18,286	6,662	2,000	75,912

TABLE 1 (CONTINUED)
WEAPONS IN EUROPE AFTER IMPLEMENTATION OF THE CFE TREATY
EASTERN EUROPE

COUNTRY	TANKS	ACVs*	ARTILLERY	AIRCRAFT	HELICOPTERS	TOTAL
Bulgaria	1,475	2,000	1,750	235	67	5,527
Czech Republic **	957	1,367	767	230	50	3,371
Slovakia	478	683	383	115	25	1,684
Hungary	835	1,700	840	180	108	3,663
Poland	1,730	2,150	1,610	460	130	6,080
Romania	1,375	2,100	1,475	430	120	5,500
Totals	6,850	10,000	6,825	1,650	500	25,825

* Armored Combat Vehicles

** Czechoslovakia divided in January 1993 into the Czech Republic and Slovakia with the Czech Republic taking two-thirds of the CFE holdings.

TABLE 1 (CONTINUED)
WEAPONS IN EUROPE AFTER IMPLEMENTATION OF THE CFE TREATY
COMMONWEALTH OF INDEPENDENT STATES***

COUNTRY	TANKS	ACVs*	ARTILLERY	AIRCRAFT	HELICOPTERS	TOTAL
Armenia	220	220	285	100	50	875
Azerbaijan	220	220	285	100	50	875
Belarus	1,800	2,600	1,615	260	80	6,355
Georgia	220	220	285	100	50	875
Kazakhstan****	0	0	0	0	0	0
Moldova	210	210	250	50	50	770
Russia	6,400	11,480	6,415	3,450	890	28,635
Ukraine	4,080	5,050	4,040	1,090	330	14,590
Totals	13,150	20,000	13,175	5,150	1,500	52,975

Source: The Arms Control Association, based on information from the ACA, IDDS, NATO, and DOD.
This Table reflects post-CFE holdings of individual signatory states, or "entitlements," as agreed by each group of states and by the CIS states among themselves.

*** Does not include 3,738 ground weapons deployed in "coastal defense" divisions and naval infantry regiments of the former Soviet Union. These weapons will be reduced according to a separate agreement to be implemented in conjunction with the CFE.

**** Kazakhstan, whose territory falls largely outside the geographical boundaries of the CFE Treaty, is not allocated any of the former Soviet Union's weapons deployed or stored west of the Ural Mountains.

considered that exit-entry and choke-point inspection would provide grounds for undesirable Soviet presence at Western ports, airports, and major rail junctions. Consequently, and perhaps unfortunately, NATO did not advance proposals on these measures.

In contrast, negotiation of the once-difficult verification subject with the Soviet Union and other Warsaw Pact states went relatively smoothly. The pact waited for NATO to make its verification proposals first and then incorporated into its own counterproposal most of the concepts and large segments of the actual wording of the NATO verification proposal. East and West agreed that verification would include noninterference with satellite imaging, repeated exchange of detailed data on the forces, and extensive on-site inspection, including a quota of challenge inspections. However, in keeping with the United States' relinquishment late in the START talks of its own concept of "anytime, anywhere" inspection, in order to protect sensitive Western installations from Soviet inspection, CFE provides for the right to refuse challenge inspection directed to sensitive objects. The theory is that a pattern of such refusals could provide warning of intent to avoid compliance nearly as well as specific evidence of noncompliance.

The main East-West controversy over verification in CFE was over how to calculate the number of inspections each country had to accept on its territory. NATO finally agreed to a Soviet proposal to compute inspections by the number of "objects of verification"—units or military organizations where treaty-limited items were held, such as ground-force brigades, air wing, or storage sites. Agreement on a key for "active" quotas—quotas for signatory countries carrying out inspections of other participating states— was made more difficult by the desire of former Warsaw Pact countries to receive part of the quotas for inspection of the Soviet Union so they could inspect their former ally.

Although NATO negotiators originally intended to include provision for aerial inspection in the CFE Treaty, this subject was dropped under pressure to ready the treaty for signature at the November 1990 Paris Summit. In any event, nearly 400 CFE inspections were carried out in the first four-month period of CFE to confirm "baseline" starting data. Only minor problems were noted.[7]

IMMEDIATE CONTROVERSY

The ink on the signature of the CFE Treaty was barely dry, however, when sharp controversy erupted over other irregularities in Soviet implementation of the treaty: The Soviets reported fewer than 900 objects of verification instead of the 1,700 they had earlier indicated. The effect was to cut in half the number of on-site inspections of the USSR under the treaty. The data provided by the Soviets at the time of treaty signature for the total numbers of their treaty limited equipment in the CFE area were about 30,000 below U.S. intelligence estimates. During the summer and early fall of 1990, the Soviets were estimated to have moved nearly 60,000 treaty-limited pieces of equipment, including enough tanks for fifty heavy armored tank divisions, beyond the Urals, out of the CFE area of application and out of treaty coverage, reducing their destruction quota by that amount. Much of this equipment was stored in the open where it would rapidly deteriorate. However, a good portion was under shelter, and more shelters were being built. The Soviets had not reported the armaments of three ground-force divisions in the CFE reduction area. They later declared these divisions to be coastal defense formations subordinated to the Soviet navy and therefore exempt from treaty coverage. This claimed exemption was a potentially serious loophole in the treaty; if left unchallenged, the Soviets or any other signatory could subordinate an unlimited number of ground-force units to the navy, removing them from treaty coverage. The Soviets had failed to report 1,700 armored combat vehicles held by the Strategic Rocket Forces and civil defense forces. As subsequent negotiation revealed, most of these actions, though not the massive eastward movement of Soviet equipment, had been undertaken by the Soviet military acting on their own.

These issues were ultimately resolved. The most serious of them, the movement of a very large number of treaty-limited armaments beyond the Urals, was declared by NATO governments to be regrettable but legal—the United States had done the same on a much smaller scale by transferring tanks and other arms to Egypt and Saudi Arabia after the Gulf War started in August 1990. (However, the United States did report in CFE data exchange the armaments of the U.S. Seventh Corps sent to the Gulf.) In June 1991, after long negotiation between the United States and the Soviet Union, the Soviets made a politically binding statement to the Joint Consultative Group, the multilateral organization established to oversee CFE implementation, committing the Soviet Union (Russia has inherited the commitment) to destroy over 14,000 pieces of treaty-limited arms beyond the Urals by 1995, not to use withdrawn equipment to create new operational units, not to keep the equipment in unit sets (like U.S. prestored equipment) where it could be issued rapidly to operational units, and to provide information on stored equipment on a continuing basis. The U.S. Senate in ratifying the treaty stated that the United States would consider failure to comply with Soviet commitments on coverage of the coastal defense units and on disposition of equipment withdrawn beyond the Urals as violations of the CFE Treaty and grounds for withdrawal from it.[8]

Western negotiators did a good job in rapidly and effectively urging Soviet successor states to sign onto the CFE Treaty after the dissolution of the Soviet Union—representatives of the successor states and Eastern Europe were in effect coopted as members of the NATO High-Level Task Force, the coordinating committee of officials that had provided policy guidance to NATO negotiators—and in informing officials of the new states, some of them completely new on the job, of their obligations of their governments under the treaty. The CFE heads of state meeting in Helsinki in July 1992 agreed to bring the treaty into effect provisionally for a 120-day period to provide extra time for ratification by Armenia and Belarus.[9] The Baltic states decided not to participate in CFE, but Russia will report and permit inspection of its treaty-limited arms still deployed in the Baltic states, and bilateral agreements have been made with the Baltic state governments to permit inspection there.

CFE–1A—LIMITS ON MILITARY PERSONNEL

The CFE–1A talks began in November 1990, a few days after signature of the main treaty. The NATO participants marked time until the implementation disputes with the Soviets were resolved. The talks then moved ahead, but had to cope with the disintegration of the Soviet Union during the second half of 1991. Despite this, negotiators reached agreement before the prescribed deadline. In July 1992, the CFE–1A agreement—not a treaty but a political agreement called "The Concluding Act of the Negotiation on Personnel Strength of Conventional Armed Forces in Europe"—was signed. In the agreement, the participating states commit themselves not to exceed after March 1996 (forty months after entry into force of the CFE Treaty) the upper limits on full-time ground and air force personnel that each participant has declared for the CFE area of application. Armenia, Azerbaijan, Georgia, and Moldova, Soviet successor states engaged in conflict with one another or internally, all failed to make official declarations of manpower limits but did so later. In addition, Iceland, which has no armed forces, reported zero, as did Kazakhstan, which has only a small sliver of its territory included in the CFE area of application.

The declared limit for Russia is 1,450,000 personnel, for Ukraine 450,000, for Germany 345,000, and for U.S. forces in the CFE area 250,000 (by 1993, the actual count of U.S. forces in Europe was down to 150,000). CFE–IA has provision for detailed exchange of data and for "evaluation" inspections rather than verification of the agreement. Evaluation includes messing and sleeping facilities for the troops. The distinction between "verification" and "evaluation," as well as the fact that CFE–1A is not a treaty, but a political agreement among participating states, arises from the view of NATO governments, especially the United States, that manpower limits are not verifiable and that commitments on them therefore should not take the form of enforceable treaty obligations. Despite this debatable distinction (German manpower limits are part of the Two-Plus-Four Treaty ratified by the U.S. Senate), the CFE–1A limits probably have considerable practical validity. (See Table 2.)

However, increases in the declared CFE–1A limits can be announced by individual signatory states. If a participant objects to a proposed increase, it can convene a conference of all participants to examine the increase in light of the explanation provided. The conference is then supposed to "seek to decide" on a future national personnel limit for the proposing country. The language here is weak. CFE–1A also requires participants that intend to call up reserve personnel numbering more than 35,000 to give advance notification of forty-two days except for "emergency situations," and to identify the units with which the called-up personnel will serve. It had been intended to include this useful "stabilizing" measure—it is really a confidence-building measure despite the pretentious vocabulary—in the CFE Treaty, but shortage of time had prevented it.

RUSSIA SEEKS CHANGES IN CFE ZONAL LIMITS

From the outset of East-West negotiations on reducing conventional forces, the NATO "flank countries"—Norway in the north and Greece and Turkey in the south—sought to protect themselves from a situation in which the Soviet Union might agree to pull back its forces on the central front only to reinforce the northern and southern border areas with the withdrawn troops. As part of the system of zonal restrictions originally designed to prevent NATO and the Warsaw Pact from concentrating forces along the border between East and West Germany, Article V of the CFE Treaty contains special flank limits covering Greece, Turkey, and Norway on the NATO side and, on the pact side, Romania, Bulgaria, and the Leningrad, Odessa, North Caucasus, and Transcaucasus military districts of the former Soviet Union. In discussions among the Soviet successor states over allocation of armaments, Russia accepted a total of 700 tanks, 1,280 artillery pieces, and 580 combat vehicles—enough equipment for two to three divisions—for both its flank areas of St. Petersburg in the north and the North Caucasus in the south.

In September 1993, after fighting had broken out in Georgia and Nagorno-Karabakh along the southern border of the North Caucasus military district, and in North Ossetia inside the district itself, Russia sent a diplomatic note to CFE signatories requesting suspension of Article V.

TABLE 2
TROOP LIMITS UNDER CFE–1A[1]

Armenia	60,000
Azerbaijan	NA
Belarus	100,000
Belgium	70,000
Bulgaria	104,000
Canada	10,660
Czech Republic	93,330
Denmark	39,000
France	325,000
Georgia	40,000
Germany	345,000
Greece	158,621
Hungary	100,000
Iceland	0
Italy	315,000
Kazakhstan	0
Luxembourg	900
Moldova	20,000
Netherlands	80,000
Norway	32,000
Poland	234,000
Portugal	75,000
Romania	230,000
Russia	1,450,000
Slovakia	46,670
Spain	300,000
Turkey	530,000
Ukraine	450,000
United Kingdom	260,000
United States	250,000

[1] The troop levels listed for Armenia and Moldova are unofficial numbers provided by the Pentagon; an official declaration has either not been made or is not accessible. There is no official nor unofficial troop level available for Azerbaijan as of mid-1994. Iceland has no armed forces. Only a small fragment of Kazakhstan territory is inside the CFE area of application, and the republic is not declaring any personnel for that area.

Russian officials argued that ongoing fighting in the south and the rise of Islamic fundamentalism threatened the security of Europe as well as Russia, and that Moscow needed a substantial increase of forces and equipment in the North Caucasus district to meet challenges in those areas. Moreover, there were unused military bases and barracks in the south that could be used to meet the acute housing shortage for forces withdrawn from Eastern Europe. Ukraine joined with Russia in asking for a suspension of Article V, declaring that the flank limits were a serious obstacle to the normal functioning of the Ukrainian armed forces; the former Odessa military district comprised 23 percent of Ukraine's territory—this includes the Crimea—but the country was permitted to station only 7 percent of its forces there.[10]

It was hard to assess objectively Russia's case for changing the treaty. On the one hand, the serious conflicts that had broken out in the Caucasus could worsen. Formally, at least, Russian troops had been "asked" to intervene in Georgia. On the other hand, it appeared that Russia might be following a deliberate policy of moving its troops back in to control the border republics; Western suspicions of Russian imperialism were strong. The United States, Turkey, and other countries declared their opposition to any change in the treaty and tried to wait out the Russians through protracted discussions in the CFE's Joint Consultative Group. In addition to concerns about Russian expansionism, they feared the breakdown of the entire shaky compromise on allocation of Soviet equipment among the successor republics. But it was unlikely Russia would abandon its insistence on adjusting the treaty limits. Some compromise would have to be found, perhaps temporary increases for peacekeeping operations.

ASSESSMENT

The CFE Treaty fully achieved NATO's objective of establishing equality between NATO and the Warsaw Pact at lower levels of armed forces. In fact, the final treaty text corresponds very closely to the NATO position paper for CFE tabled at the outset of the talks.[11] Of course, NATO's parity objective was overtaken by events—the dissolution of the Warsaw Pact, the Soviet Union's agreement by mid-1990 to withdraw the bulk of its forces from Eastern Europe, and the breakup of the Soviet Union itself. But the CFE Treaty has some solid, enduring benefits: It furnishes a literally indispensable framework for cooperation in Europe on political, economic, and security issues, and it provides useful insurance against a resurgent Russian threat, a distinct possibility as long as social and economic turmoil in Russia continues.

The Soviet Union had more than 41,000 tanks in Eastern Europe and in the USSR west of the Urals when CFE began in 1989, enough for about

125 traditional heavy armored divisions with 328 tanks each.[12] Even after the Soviet Union agreed to withdraw its troops from Eastern Europe for political reasons, in the absence of a CFE Treaty, all these withdrawn tanks and other armaments could have been deployed in western Russia and Ukraine, and Russia might well have gained control over the bulk of them even after dissolution of the USSR. Under CFE, total overall armaments of all the Soviet successor states in the CFE area will only be 30 percent of their 1989 strength. Russia, Ukraine, and Belarus combined would at most be able to equip thirty-five tank divisions of traditional size in this area (Russia alone has twenty divisions), as contrasted with nearly three times that number the USSR actually had in this territory earlier. Where the Soviet Union and its Warsaw Pact allies could muster about 8,000 combat aircraft, Russia will now have about 3,400. It is limited to 890 combat helicopters in the CFE area, as compared to NATO's 1989 estimate of 3,700 for the Warsaw Pact as a whole.

Violation of the CFE Treaty by Russia would send an unambiguous warning to the NATO states. Russia would probably need at least two years before it could build up its forces to attack proportions, which would entail moving stored equipment back across the Urals.

NATO will have to reduce almost nothing as the result of CFE. It will have to destroy about 3,000 tanks and 300 artillery pieces in addition to former East German weapons covered under the treaty whose elimination is the responsibility of the German government. But if it chooses, NATO will be allowed to add more than 1,400 armored combat vehicles and 1,300 combat aircraft, bringing its net reductions, at least on paper after "cascading" or distribution within NATO of more modern U.S. arms to NATO members like Turkey, to only 97 pieces of treaty-limited equipment—as compared with net reductions of 33,268 treaty-limited items for countries of the former Warsaw Pact.[13]

General Colin Powell, former chairman of the Joint Chiefs of Staff, estimated that, although Russia might be in a position to bring twenty to thirty additional divisions westward across the Urals for reinforcement in an offensive strike, NATO, provided it retained the ability to expand its own force levels to those of 1990 and reacted decisively to the violations (two important provisos), could defeat such an attack with conventional arms.[14] As Senator Joseph Biden pointed out during the Senate hearing for the CFE Treaty, this also meant that the United States and its NATO allies would after implementation of the treaty have valid military grounds to relinquish earlier plans for possible use of tactical nuclear weapons in the event of attack from the East.[15]

The military benefits of CFE for the NATO countries include the extensive verification provisions, which entail hundreds of on-site inspections of

Russian forces in the coming years. Monitoring the CFE Treaty will yield on a continuing basis, as former secretary of defense Dick Cheney pointed out, much greater transparency of the structure, size, and deployment of Russian and Ukrainian forces.[16] In fact, the CFE Treaty is so favorable to NATO that it was attacked as betrayal of national interests by Russian right-wingers. What these critics left out of the account is that Russia received the assurance that NATO, too, would be limited, including both U.S. and German forces. Russia and other CFE participants also benefit from the treaty requirement to notify other participants of new types and new models of armaments.

It is probable that preparations since 1986 within the Soviet leadership for sizable negotiated force reductions in CFE prepared Soviet leaders intellectually and psychologically for the even more far-reaching decisions completely to withdraw Soviet forces from Eastern Europe that followed. Moreover, the fact that German forces would be limited under CFE was a necessary precondition for reluctant Soviet agreement to German unification as well as to membership of united Germany in NATO.

CFE has provided a framework for the orderly reduction of U.S. military manpower which will save the United States at least $10–15 billion per year.[17] This estimate is highly conservative because it does not include shrinkage in the overall defense budget arising from a 75 percent cut in U.S. forces in Europe; about 50 percent of the U.S. defense budget in recent decades has been spent for the defense of Europe. In the long term, the additional warning provided by deep cuts in Russian forces and verified limits permits the further cuts in Western forces that are under way.

For East European states, CFE provides the reassurance of national force limits for countries that worry about each other, like Hungary and Romania. Article IV of the treaty prohibits the stationing of foreign forces inside the CFE area without the agreement of the host state. The participation of the NATO countries in this treaty provision, proposed by Poland, creates a valuable political guarantee of the independence of the East European states in the face of possible future pressure from Ukraine or Russia.

Without CFE limits on the conventional forces of the successor states of the Soviet Union, relationships among them would be even more strained. Limits on the size and deployment of Russian forces are very important to many neighboring republics like Ukraine and the Baltic states. As Russia's efforts to suspend Article V of the treaty show, these limits are significant. Moreover, in the absence of the CFE framework and pressures from Western CFE states, it is likely that the process of dividing up the arms of the old Soviet Union among the successor states would have taken much longer and engendered much more friction and that subsequent military relationships among the members of the Common-wealth of Independent States would have been even more suspicious and unproductive than they are. This particular assessment is supported by a report on the CFE Treaty issued by the Supreme Soviet in July 1992; it states that the treaty is "the only real instrument making it possible to pre-vent an arms race among the states of the Commonwealth."[18]

Thus, the CFE Treaty, especially through the individual national limits contained in Article VII and through the provisions for verifying these oblig-ations over the years provides predictability and assurance in military rela-tionships and an indispensable basis for cooperation among the European states, the United States, Canada, and Russia. Without the framework of CFE obligations and without NATO to back up these obligations, there would be incessant worry in all European capitals about what countries like Germany and Russia were doing in the military field, continual shifts in the composi-tion and levels of national armed forces in Europe, and ceaseless jockeying for advantage among European states, large and small. Most European gov-ernments would spend their time worrying about one another's military activities instead of thinking how they could cooperate. In this sense, CFE is necessary to the continued democratization of Russia, to the forward move-ment of the European Community, and to the operation of the CSCE.

SHORTCOMINGS

Despite these real advantages, the CFE Treaty does not go far enough. Because negotiators pegged the proposed reductions only slightly below NATO levels existing at the beginning of the talks, even the parity achieved by the talks leaves both sides with a very high level of arms. After all CFE reductions are completed in 1996, Europe would still be permitted four to five times the level of arms it had at the outset of World War II, even after Germany had rearmed and other European states increased their forces in reaction. If forces are kept at this level, it would represent an undue eco-nomic burden and security risk for CFE signatories. Of course, this will not happen. Pressed by the serious economic depression of the early 1990s, most CFE countries are reducing their forces on economic grounds. More specifically, the CFE Treaty fell considerably short of achieving the nego-tiating aim, agreed to by both sides in the mandate for the talks, of elimi-nating the capability for initiating large-scale offensive action. The high numbers of combat aircraft permitted are especially destabilizing.

The CFE Treaty does not limit Russian forces east of the Urals, where Russia has four times as many armaments as permitted it in the CFE zone in the west. NATO countries have a still greater advantage in the exemption of all U.S. territory from the treaty, and Russia has other major security concerns east of the Urals, particularly China. But the existence of numerous forces and armaments in an area abutting on the CFE area is a considerable drawback. Part of the problem arises from the fact that during the CFE talks, Western governments permitted the Soviet Union to withdraw eastward about 60,000 treaty-limited weapons, including three times as many tanks as are permitted in western Russia, saving them from destruction. This development might have been prevented by agreeing early in the talks that all arms in the CFE area at the outset of the talks would be counted for purposes of reduction and be frozen in place, with exceptions if needed. However, such a provision might also have created even more serious opposition to the treaty from the Soviet military. In any event, it was not tried.

There are no limits in the treaty on production in the CFE area of the restricted arms or on stockpiling these arms at production sites for export, although stockpiling has to be for unspecified "temporary" periods and should not deviate from "normal" pretreaty practice and excessive stockpiling could be questioned on these grounds. There is also no limit on arms stockpiled at the production site in an unfinished form that would permit rapid completion. Production of limited arms in the CFE area must be reported, but only once a year. U.S. proposals to monitor the number of completed treaty-limited arms that leave production plants were rejected by Russia and European arms-producing countries on the grounds that U.S. production would be totally excluded from monitoring.

There are no limits in CFE on potentially destabilizing modernization of treaty-limited armaments, although modifications must be notified in advance of field deployment. The treaty has no provision for reducing force projection equipment essential to forward-moving attack, including units for transport of munitions and vehicle fuel and rapid transport of tanks, mobile anti-aircraft, and prefabricated bridging. There are no limits in the treaty on the number of military units or formations, the organizations that bring together personnel and arms to create fighting forces. More specifically, there are no limits in CFE on the number of reserve units, their size, or their training, and thus no limits on force generation capability. By manning a large number of units with skeleton cadres, filling rear-echelon jobs with civilians, and training active-duty personnel as officers and noncommissioned officers as the German "Black Reichswehr" did in the 1920s and 1930s, and then mobilizing these reserves and equipping them from production stocks or equipment from outside the CFE area of application, Russia or other signatory states could expand their forces fairly rapidly. This may be a trouble area in the future.

Verification weaknesses in the CFE Treaty include the absence of checks on production, the lack of controls on entry to or exit from the CFE area—this would have been useful in order to check trans-Ural traffic— or controls at major airfields, road, and rail choke-points, and also the failure to introduce air verification measures specifically designed to monitor CFE limits. (Overflights under the Open Skies Treaty when it enters into force will be useful, but too few; they will have restrictions on loitering and circling over verification sites and will cruise at the wrong altitude for this purpose.) Further loopholes are in the suspension of force limits for seven days to provide for troops in transit, and in the provisions for the first forty-month period that allow entry of further forces into the area without numerical limit so long as they are not there when final limits are applied at the end of the period in 1996. (This provision could have been used by Russia for temporary reinforcement of the Caucasus area without a need to change the treaty as Russia sought to do.)

These problems have to be seen in perspective. They would be serious if the Soviet Union had remained intact but are considerably less so given its dissolution and the economic and internal security problems faced by Russia and other successor states. Moreover, even where no limits are specified in the CFE Treaty, large-scale changes in structure and reserve activity and production are observable and several have to be prenotified under the CSCE regime of confidence-building measures. A great deal of information on the general level and activity of armed forces will be collected by all participants in the European security system in the course of monitoring inspections and observing exercises and by people moving back and forth as long as these societies remain relatively open. For the most part, this information will be reassuring. If it is not, it will provide grounds for action.

CFE implementation faces some practical problems. Former members of the Warsaw Pact, especially Russia, obligated to destroy a huge amount of equipment in a brief forty-month period were already falling behind schedule, as Russia has also done with regard to destruction of chemical weapons. A simplified procedure for armaments destruction was adopted after Russia, Germany, and others claimed it was costing up to $15,000 to make a single tank inoperative. There have been cases of Russian monitors not showing up to carry out inspections because their system was unable to transport them. But such problems could be dealt with.

THE CSCE REGIME OF CONFIDENCE-BUILDING MEASURES AND INSTITUTIONS

Chapter 9 sketched the development of the Conference on Security and Cooperation in Europe and its new permanent institutions. In this chapter, we discuss in more detail the CSCE regime of confidence- and security-building measures (CSBMs) and the work of two institutions established to coordinate them, the Conflict Prevention Center and the Forum for Security Cooperation. Then we evaluate the capability of these measures and institutions to cope with Europe's security problems.

WHAT CONFIDENCE-BUILDING MEASURES DO

In the general sense, confidence-building measures aim to reduce mutual fear and suspicion between potential adversaries in order to reduce the risk of conflict and to promote political reconciliation. They do not of themselves affect levels or equipment of armed forces. Instead, the measures provide their participants with authorized information on the nature and activities of one another's armed forces, opportunities to discuss the implications of that information, and mutual restrictions, often called "constraints," on some portion of armed force activities. The objective is to reduce as much as possible of the secrecy with which all states shroud some aspects of their military forces, to reduce the fear of attack, and to reduce the risk of conflict caused by human error and by misinterpreting the activities of potential adversaries. The confidence generated by confidence-building measures and the authorized access to information they provide are twofold: increased trust in the intentions of the other side and—probably more important—increased confidence in one's own knowledge of the capabilities and activities of the other side.

Authorized access to information on armed forces and their activities is the core of confidence building. For thousands of years, people have believed that secrecy about their military forces was an important military asset—a belief carried to its extreme in the old Soviet Union and other totalitarian regimes. It is only in our self-analytical century that we have become aware of the many disadvantages military secrecy can also have, among them exaggerations of capabilities by others, increased impetus for arms races, heightened possibilities of errors of assessment and overreaction, and, above all, the fear and suspicion that are the seeds of hostility and war.

Confidence-building measures can be classified in five categories: information exchange, communication activities, notification of force activities, access to adversary forces for observation and verification, and constraints.[19] In actuality, four of these categories—information exchange, communication, notification, and access—involve information exchange in one form or another. CSBMs parallel and complement arms control measures aimed at reducing or limiting the level of armed forces. They broaden the range of information made available by participants in arms reduction agreements by covering the activities of armed forces as well as force levels, and they can also be used to restrict some part of those force activities.

Given the Soviet Union's great police-state success in maintaining secrecy in military affairs, from the outset one major aim of CSBMs from the Western viewpoint was to penetrate the Iron Curtain. Another was to reduce the capacity of the Soviet Union to use military maneuvers to intimidate, as it had on the Polish border in 1981, or to cover force concentration for surprise attack or invasion, as it had in Czechoslovakia in 1968.

The European CSBMs address the basic dynamic of modern land warfare: rapid, undetected massing of forces to obtain local superiority and to break through the defender's lines. If surprise can be eliminated or reduced, the defense can prepare and can concentrate its own forces against the main line of attack, the possibility of success is reduced, and attack discouraged. Information exchange and prior notification are intended to establish patterns of "normal" force activities. Departure from normal patterns serves as warning, while agreed communication channels create a possibility of discussing these deviations. Confidence-building measures deliberately avoid casting blame for political differences or past conflicts. They are neutral in nature and claim to benefit both sides equally in terms of reducing the risk of conflict. CSBMs can also be used in a postconflict situation to consolidate the peace.

THE HELSINKI BEGINNING

Civilian experts had been discussing possibilities for confidence-building measures for a long time before the CSCE came to deal with them seriously, but professional military officers generally did not like the idea. They preferred to cope with their problems through self-reliance and complete freedom of action without any agreed restrictions, through their own measures of military security on their own forces and their activities, and through covert intelligence to penetrate the adversary's secrecy. They believed they would be bound by suggested constraints while their opponents would violate them, gaining military advantage. These feelings were especially strong in the East, where Soviet military leaders considered their high level of military security compared with the lower security level of the democratic West a military advantage not to be relinquished.

These reservations account for the timid beginning of the CSCE regime of confidence-building measures in the 1975 Helsinki Accords. A lone paragraph of the accords urges participants to provide timely information on their military activities in order to reduce the risk of conflict through misunderstanding or miscalculation—a concept drawn from the conference on surprise attack of the mid-1950s. Helsinki participants were also urged in this section of the accords to notify in advance military maneuvers involving over 25,000 soldiers in the area between the Atlantic and border regions of the USSR. (Leonid Brezhnev later agreed to extension of the geographic coverage deeper in the Soviet Union to the line of the Ural Mountains and of the Ural River.) This measure, which was on a voluntary basis, was fulfilled only partially by Western countries and far less frequently by the states of the Warsaw Pact.

STOCKHOLM AND VIENNA

There matters remained for nearly a decade. The big breakthrough on confidence-building measures—renamed by NATO countries confidence- and security-building measures (the concept of "security" was added by suspicious American officials in order to emphasize that, to be accepted, measures had to increase the security of participants rather than lull them with possibly baseless confidence)—came with the emergence of Mikhail Gorbachev as Soviet leader. Gorbachev sent Soviet chief of staff Marshall Sergei Akhomeyev as his personal representative to the CSCE talks on confidence-building measures in Stockholm held between 1984 and 1986, in order to energize Warsaw Pact participants. The resulting Stockholm Document was a breakthrough, containing the first agreement for on-site inspection in the Soviet Union. The Stockholm meeting was followed by two further conferences on CSBMs whose cumulative results are set forth in the Vienna 1992 Document.

The Stockholm breakthrough did not come out of nowhere. It followed a decade of jawboning by NATO and neutral country officials with their Warsaw Pact counterparts as well as of informal East-West discussion by civilian defense and arms control experts. When Gorbachev decided to move to improve Soviet relations with the West, he and his advisers already knew what actions had to be taken on confidence building in order to make their point.[20]

CSBMs NOW IN EFFECT

The CSBMs now in effect include:

PRIOR NOTIFICATION OF CERTAIN ACTIVITIES. As set forth in Vienna 1992 Document (paragraphs 36–44), this measure provides for a forty-two-day advance notification of activities involving at least 9,000 troops or 250 battle tanks or two brigades, and amphibious or airborne activities of at least 3,000 troops. These notification thresholds have been lowered a great deal from the original Helsinki level of 25,000 personnel. A two-page list specifies items of information that are to be provided in advance.

OBSERVATION OF CERTAIN MILITARY ACTIVITIES. Observers from other CSCE member states are to be invited whenever the level of personnel or equipment involved reaches 13,000 soldiers or 300 tanks, a divisional level (Vienna 1992 Document, paragraphs 45–64). Observers are to be briefed, provided with adequate observation, transport, and communications equipment, and, if feasible, given an opportunity to view the activity from the air by helicopter or fixed-wing aircraft.

ANNUAL EXCHANGE OF MILITARY INFORMATION (Vienna 1992 Document, paragraphs 10–15.4). This exchange includes the major ground and air force armaments, military organization, and personnel levels now covered in CFE and CFE–1A. However, CSCE covers the European neutrals, which the CFE Treaty does not. On the other hand, the CSCE-prescribed exchange does not cover combat support units like combat engineers, as required in CFE. The information exchange provides each participant with a fairly comprehensive picture of the already-deployed combat potential of all other participants as well as major changes taking place.

PRIOR NOTIFICATION OF INCREASES IN PERSONNEL. The Vienna 1992 Document (paragraphs 11.3.1 and 11.3.2) requires advance notice of one year for increases of at least 1,500 personnel in active-duty units below the division level and of 2,000 personnel for reserve units, provided that the increases are to last for more than twenty-one days.

This measure moves for the first time in the CSBM regime to cover force generation and reserve mobilization. But the qualification that these increases need not be reported if they are for periods of less than twenty-one days (a requirement imposed by the Swiss, owing to the mobilization pattern of their largely reserve army) greatly weakens its effect. The related requirement in CFE–1A to notify increases of over 35,000 forty-two days in advance is not subject to this twenty-one day restriction, but the threshold for preannouncement is much higher.

PRIOR NOTIFICATION OF DEPLOYMENT OF NEW TYPES OF ARMAMENTS. Information on new types or versions of major arms is to be reported in connection with annual information on weapons deployments (Vienna 1992 Document, paragraphs 12.2 and 14–15.4). There is a parallel provision in the CFE Treaty. In a potentially important innovation, the Vienna 1992 Document (paragraphs 35–35.4) also calls on participants to arrange demonstration of new types of major weapons for military experts of other participating states prior to field deployment of these weapons.

EXCHANGE OF INFORMATION ON MILITARY BUDGETS. CSCE participants are required to exchange annually information on their military budgets for the forthcoming fiscal year (Vienna 1992 Document, paragraph 16). Other participants can submit written questions, to which participating states must make every effort "to reply promptly." As discussed below, this measure has been further developed.

INSPECTION. The Vienna 1992 Document (paragraphs 75–142) provides for up to three on-site inspections per year to cover military activities that have not been announced. In addition, the quality of annual information exchange on military forces can be "evaluated" by on-site visits. The quota of evaluation visits is also low, one per year for every sixty units in the forces of participating states. (The upper limit of fifteen per year will not provide much coverage for larger forces.) Therefore, these inspections do not provide much additional help to the more stringent regime of the CFE Treaty, though they do involve the European neutrals in the verification process.

CONSTRAINTS. The Vienna 1992 Document (paragraphs 71.1–74) expands the constraints introduced two years earlier: Military activities involving more than 40,000 personnel must be notified to other participants more than two years in advance. Participating states cannot carry out more than one such activity in a two-year period. They cannot carry out within a single year more than six activities with more than 13,000 personnel; no more than three of these may involve more than 25,000 troops. And they cannot carry out simultaneously more than three exercises exceeding 13,000 personnel. This tightened provision reduces the capability to intimidate through military maneuvers or to concentrate large numbers of forces for surprise attack under the guise of maneuvers.

UNUSUAL MILITARY ACTIVITIES. The Vienna 1990 Document contained an innovative procedure for questioning military activity by a CSCE participant that falls outside the normal pattern. Any CSCE state with concerns about "unusual and unscheduled activities of their military forces outside their peacetime location's that are militarily significant" (the language of the 1990 measure, taken over in Vienna 1992 Document, paragraphs 17–18.5) can call on the instigating state to explain the activity in writing or to send representatives to account for it before a meeting of all participating states held at the Vienna Conflict Prevention Center. This measure looked like a promising way to bring a budding Hitler to account early in his development. But as pointed out earlier, its actual use by Austria and Hungary at the outset of the war in former Yugoslavia dribbled away into nothing as the CSCE states took no follow-up action. Still, Helsinki 1992 Document usefully authorizes sending fact-finding missions to corroborate accusations of unusual military activities.

THE CONFLICT PREVENTION CENTER

The Conflict Prevention Center, already described in the chapter on CSCE, has a staff function in coordinating operation of CSBMs, including exchange of data on armed forces, and making available results of CSCE verification inspections, organizing an annual assessment of CSBMs, and operating the procedure for unusual military activities. Policy decisions in all these areas are made either by the newly established Permanent Committee or by the Forum for Security Cooperation.

THE CSCE FORUM FOR SECURITY COOPERATION

The Helsinki Summit of July 1992 finally amalgamated negotiations on force reduction and confidence-building measures into a single conference called the CSCE Forum for Security Cooperation, staffed by officials stationed in Vienna by their member governments. The two activities had been separated since the early 1970s by U.S. insistence that "hard" arms control—force reductions negotiations with the Soviet Union involving "real security" issues for NATO states—must be conducted in a tighter, more controlled alliance-to-alliance framework; "soft" arms control—confidence-building measures and the like—could be dealt with in a larger, looser forum like the CSCE. Now, full participation is extended to all members of the CSCE, including neutrals and Soviet successor states. At the same time, the forum has some operational responsibilities. It supervises and coordinates implementation of confidence-building measures, organizes discussion and clarification of the information exchanges called for in some confidence-building measures, including annual assessments of their operation, and holds seminars on military doctrine and related subjects.

Since its establishment, the forum has worked on a dozen major projects. These include standardization of obligations undertaken in the CFE and CSCE contexts into a uniform code for all CSCE member states, improving present CSBMs and creating new ones, global data exchange, nuclear and conventional nonproliferation, regional stabilization measures, and a code of military conduct. Some of these projects are described below.[21]

DEFENSE DIALOGUE. This program for transparency in defense planning, approved by the Council of Foreign Ministers in Rome in late 1993, is a highly desirable amplification of the rudimentary exchange of information on defense budgets set up by the Vienna 1992 Document framework. The concept now calls for annual advance discussion on defense planning for up to five years. Each member state would make available information describing its defense policy, strategy, allocation of financial and human resources, and major changes in planned size and structure of the forces, troop training, and major new equipment. Detailed budget figures are required, and member states will be able to raise questions about them and receive written replies. They will be permitted to conduct study visits to participating states to discuss national defense planning.

If seriously pursued, this defense dialogue could develop into one of the most important CSCE activities in the security field; though it could also become a source of friction among members. If handled well, it could provide an opportunity to explore outsiders' concerns about a nation's force posture and to influence final decisions. It could also improve parliamentary control of the armed forces by giving parliamentarians access to a broader range of information and opinion than may be available from their own authorities. It would allow for discussion of potentially destabilizing new weapons systems well before deployment. There is some overlap here with similar activities of the the North Atlantic Cooperation Council (NACC); nonetheless, it would be unfortunate if the broader CSCE measure were not fully implemented.

STABILIZING MEASURES FOR LOCALIZED CRISIS SITUATIONS. The Forum for Security Cooperation has prepared a checklist of stabilizing measures for application in regional crises—border flare-ups or small-scale wars. The CSCE Council of Foreign Ministers or Committee of Senior Officials could select appropriate measures from this catalogue tailored to a specific situation. The list could serve as a useful reference work for non-CSCE countries investigating the possibility of setting up their own confidence-building measures.

PRINCIPLES GOVERNING CONVENTIONAL ARMS TRANSFERS. In the most contentious area of its activities, the Forum for Security Cooperation worked out a set of principles governing transfer of conventional arms by CSCE states that was approved by the Council of Foreign Ministers in late 1993. CSCE membership comprises most major arms suppliers other than China and Brazil. The CSCE governments agreed at Helsinki 92 to exchange information on arms production as well as arms inventories, a step not yet covered by the UN Arms Registry project. Public opinion in favor of restrictions on arms transfers is somewhat stronger in European countries than in the United States. For example, although Great Britain is a traditional arms-exporting country, prior to the general election in April 1992, Prime Minister John Major found it expedient to be in the forefront of those advocating controls on arms transfers. The potential strength of German public opinion on the issue was demonstrated in the forced resignation in 1992 of highly respected defense minister Gerhard Stoltenberg because of lax handling by his ministry of Bundestag restrictions on arms sales to Israel and Turkey. Many smaller European countries also wish to cut back on arms transfers. Although the larger CSCE governments feel strong countervailing economic pressures to continue foreign arms sales, the activities of CSCE are more open to lobbying by public interest groups. Consequently, the CSCE may ultimately make some progress in this field.

However, progress is likely to be slow. The document of principles governing conventional arms transfers agreed to by the Council of Foreign Ministers lists conditions in recipient countries that arms-exporting countries should take into account. These conditions include the economic situation of the recipient country and whether it might use the arms to suppress human rights, to threaten the security of other states, to contravene its international commitments, or to prolong a conflict. There is provision for information exchange and discussion about national experiences, including the effectiveness of control measures. Essentially, the procedures are voluntary. Nevertheless, CSCE involvement in conventional nonproliferation has made a good start.

STANDARDIZATION OF OBLIGATIONS. The Forum for Security Cooperation is also working to "harmonize" the obligations contained in the CFE Treaty and the Vienna 1992 Document on confidence-building measures. The aim is to develop a standard set of restrictions and to apply force limits to all CSCE members that have armed forces. (Of CSCE participants, five—the Vatican, Iceland, Liechtenstein, Monaco, and San Marino—have no armed forces.)

If successful, the result of this negotiation would be to extend some limitations on military personnel and major armaments to neutral CSCE member states that are not participants in CFE. In practice, this will probably mean agreement by the neutrals not to exceed present force levels rather than a negotiated reduction.

In October 1992, NATO's harmonization proposal to the forum suggested that all CSCE participants provide information on the numbers and types of CFE-limited arms they possess, changes in organizational structures or base levels, and locations of troops and equipment. The NATO proposals also suggested that all CSCE member states make binding commitments on the level of their military manpower and major conventional arms.[22] If there is agreement, possibly at the 1994 Budapest CSCE Summit, these commitments will be regarded as politically binding rather than as treaty obligations; the neutrals seem unlikely to accept treaty commitments despite pressures from Germany and France to codify them in treaty form. An unexpected problem has developed en route to standardization of data. Switzerland, which has largely a militia army, is sensitive about divulging information on location and number of stored weapons. Sweden is in a similar situation. Some way will probably be found to exempt these countries from some of the information exchange requirements.

GLOBAL DATA EXCHANGE. The Forum for Security Cooperation is also charged with negotiating a procedure for extending information exchange on armed forces to a "global" basis, meaning that it will now cover the home territory of the United States and Canada and the whole territory of the former Soviet Union as well as Turkey. France and Great Britain also have small forces outside the CFE area that would be covered in global data exchange. The exchange will also include information on the production of military equipment. The main unresolved question has been the degree of detail that will be required of participants. When finalized, this measure could be of great value in following Russian military activities beyond the Urals, a matter of direct and continuing interest to all Western states. The exchange of information on production of arms (neither production nor current holdings are covered in the UN Arms Registry transfers that went into effect in 1993) might also supply the basis for later agreements to restrict arms transfers. Information on naval forces, long excluded from arms control in Europe, will be part of this exchange, although coverage probably will not be comprehensive. Because it moves beyond Europe to cover the territorial United States, the exchange procedure will not involve verification or force limits.

CODE OF CONDUCT. One major project of the Forum for Security Cooperation is a Code of Conduct in Matters Related to Military Security. The idea of a code of conduct on security relations originated in a German proposal designed to defuse the argument engendered by U.S. opposition to the French recommendation to convert CSCE security obligations into treaty form. Under the German proposal, major points from past CSCE agreements would be collected and arranged in a compact code of military conduct that might be useful, for example, in helping the new Soviet successor state governments understand their inherited CSCE obligations.

In accordance with this aim, many provisions of the draft code submitted by participating governments move toward establishing a body of general rules for military policy in a democratic society—a sort of smaller Copenhagen Document covering civil-military relations in a democratic society. This involves issues like parliamentary control over armed forces, restrictions on the use of armed forces in dealing with domestic unrest, and the rights of soldiers to refuse illegal orders. However, worried about their own security, Poland and the other central Eastern European states are seeking to push development of the code in the direction of a mutual defense pact for CSCE states. In this sense, other portions of the code will spell out requirements to keep armed forces to a minimum level and to base military doctrines on defensive principles. Austria, Hungary, and

Poland have also urged that the CSCE commit itself to enforce the code on refractory members governments, but this seems an unlikely development at present.

ASSESSMENT

Anyone who examines the CSCE confidence-building measures and the Forum for Security Cooperation projects described here cannot help being impressed by the persistence, ingenuity, and corporate creativity that have been displayed by officials of the participating governments in formulating them. The results give the lie to the view that government service suppresses imagination and ingenuity.

Confidence-building measures now cover most potentially threatening aspects of member-state armed forces. They have gained in sophistication as well as scope. Agreed measures now envisage comprehensive exchange of information on armed forces, prenotification of most ground-force activities, constraints on frequency of larger field activities; and in-depth examination of the military posture of participating states. Without losing its value for reducing the possibility of conflict in Europe, the CSBM regime has also made a successful transition from measures based on an adversarial relationship to those of communication, cooperation, and dialogue among senior military officers and defense officials, with emphasis on influencing positively the military evolution of Russia and other Soviet successor states.

The CSCE confidence-building regime also has some fairly obvious loopholes. Despite continual efforts of the Soviet Union, later of Russia, and of the neutral states, there is still no coverage of naval forces. The United States has been adamant in opposition, although most other CSCE states appear ready for at least a modest beginning. Elimination of super-power military competition worldwide and the Bush-Gorbachev agreement to withdraw nuclear weapons from surface ships eliminates most pressures for negotiated reduction of naval forces. But it does not obviate the need for confidence-building measures covering them.

The existing CSBM regime does not provide adequate coverage of air force activity either; there is merely a provision for notification when 200 or more aircraft sorties, including helicopters, are involved as part of ground-force activities. There is no CSBM specifically addressing air force activity. Part of the problem, of course, is the great mobility and range of aircraft. Part of it is the resistance of NATO governments to putting restraints on air forces. But aircraft remain the essential weapon for surprise attack and aggression. It should be possible, given the wide availability of ground and airborne radar, to devise some measure calling for prenotification and limitation of the number of sorties in air exercises. The North Atlantic Cooperation Council (NACC), the umbrella organization for consultation between members of NATO and of the former Warsaw Pact, continues to consider cooperation measures in East-West air control in Europe to reduce the possibility of misuse of civilian air control to cover an air attack.

The CSBM measures for prenotification of ground-force activities remain vitiated by continuing exemption of all alert and readiness exercises from prenotification (and also from observation during their first seventy-two hours). This dangerous loophole should be closed. Now that the East-West confrontation has largely dissipated, the need for this exemption, which apparently permits any number of exercises without prenotification or numerical restriction, no longer exists, and the opening should be closed off or at least restricted.[23] The CSBMs directed at controlling force generation and mobilization remain in rudimentary form.

Finally, the CSCE confidence-building regime does not escape the generic weakness of most confidence-building measures. All of these measures are peacetime measures whose greatest value is conflict prevention. Their value dissipates once conflict starts. Thus, the CSBM regime does not appear to have any value in moderating violence inside member states like that in Croatia and Bosnia and in several Soviet successor states. However, CSBMs do have a role in conflict resolution and peace building that has not yet been fully explored.

THE OPEN SKIES REGIME

The Open Skies Treaty, signed in Helsinki on March 24, 1992, has the twin objectives of encouraging reciprocal openness by participating states and enhancing confidence through enabling aerial observation of military activities and installations on their territories. It is supposed to complement satellite imaging and information exchange provided for in arms control agreements.[24]

An Open Skies proposal was advanced by President Dwight Eisenhower at the July 1955 summit with the Soviet Union as a test of the stated Soviet readiness to improve relations with the Western countries. It was turned down by the Soviet delegation, although Nikita Khrushchev, not yet in full control, was later reported as wanting to accept it. It was again advanced by President George Bush in May 1989 in the effort to provide some counterpart to balance the flood of openness proposals by President Mikhail Gorbachev and was rapidly accepted in principle by Soviet leaders.[25]

The Open Skies Treaty provides for an annual quota of overflights by unarmed aircraft equipped with four specified types of sensors over any place in the territory of the participating states, with the only limitation being conditions of aerial safety valid for all air traffic. The original signatories of the treaty are the participants in the CFE negotiations: the sixteen members of NATO, the five East European states, and Belarus, Russia, Georgia, and Ukraine. Although the CFE Treaty covers only the Atlantic-to-Urals area, the Open Skies Treaty covers all of the territory of the Russian Federation and the home territories of the United States and Canada. Participants can carry out the same number of observation flights they are obligated to receive, ranging from forty-two a year for the geographically largest and most militarily developed participants, the Russian Federation and the United States, down to two per year for the smallest, Portugal. (Benelux has a group quota of six flights.)[26]

The permitted sensors are optical panoramic and framing cameras; video cameras with real-time display; infrared line scanning devices, which can be used in the dark for registering heat sources; and sideways-looking synthetic aperture radar, which can detect vehicle movement through clouds. The permitted characteristics of these sensors are further specified in the treaty. The treaty is to enter into effect when twenty of the twenty-five signatories have ratified it, perhaps in 1995 or 1996. The treaty text (Article XVII) urges the Soviet successor states that had not done so—Armenia, Azerbaijan, Kazakhstan, Kyrgyzstan, Moldova, Tajikistan, Turkmenistan, and Uzbekistan—to sign and ratify. Some demonstration overflights have already been carried out. Following a six-month period after entry into force of the treaty, any other CSCE state may adhere to it. Later, any state anywhere in the world may apply for adherence. Even before the Open Skies Treaty was signed, Hungary and Romania concluded a bilateral agreement based on it (signed May 1991) providing for four overflights each per year; some have already taken place.[27]

ISSUES IN THE NEGOTIATIONS

The Open Skies negotiations did not receive a great deal of attention from political leaders in East or West. Absence of political interest gave intelligence and counterintelligence considerations higher salience. One great difficulty of Western negotiators was in explaining what Open Skies was for, because it was not tied to any particular arms control agreement as verification, nor did it serve any specific conflict prevention purpose. The result is a fairly modest agreement that preserves the principle of go-anywhere observer flights at the cost of restrictions on permitted sensors.[28]

The Open Skies Treaty makes a political point—by joining it, signatories demonstrate that they are open to inspection and do not pose a threat to others. It continues the process of broadening confidence-building measures on information, of legitimizing exchange of information collection on an ever wider scale, and of cutting back the areas of secrecy on armed forces. The treaty complements satellite imaging and provides the possibility of more intensive additional coverage of targets of particular interest. At a later stage, if more sensors are allowed, the treaty could help to detect chemical or nuclear weapons production, including venting of weapons tests and byproducts of tritium production. The use of aircraft can bring wider accessibility to information to smaller countries, and often more rapid processing of information, than U.S. analysis of satellite imaging, which is subject to many conflicting priorities. Wider access to information that smaller countries themselves have participated in acquiring and that they may trust more than satellite imagery provided by outside powers could make it easier to undertake common action in reaction to some disquieting overflight finding.

One benefit of the Open Skies regime is that it is being instituted before a conflict takes place. The fact that the modalities of observation have been carefully worked out in the treaty makes it easier for other countries to join the treaty regime or to use it as a model for establishing one of their own, as in the case of aerial observation between Hungary and Romania.

Open Skies procedures and experience could assist CSCE confidence-building measures like that on unusual military activities. Requiring the "offending" state to accept an aerial observation flight could be useful. In the future, Open Skies could be helpful in peacekeeping, including observing outbreaks of domestic violence within national borders, as well as in other CSCE fact-finding and postconflict peace-building activities. Aerial observation can greatly help facilitate open multilateral discussion on a suspicious activity or installation in the context of CSCE measures for prenotification of deployment of new model weapons or changes in force structure.

The Open Skies Treaty's many restrictions make it a useful beginning rather than a full-fledged instrument of aerial observation. The limits on the type and quality of sensors, as well as the prohibition against loitering and circling and against collection of intelligence by electronic means, severely reduce the potential value of Open Skies flights for verification purposes, specifically for CFE verification, where it would be valuable to be able to circle an inspection site before and during an inspection to help ensure that armaments or personnel were not being moved out of the site into hiding places on its periphery. The restrictions on sensor performance also mean that flights cannot be at U–2 altitudes, which yield very wide coverage with a single trip. At the other end of the spectrum, exclusion of helicopters as observation platforms is also a serious loss. The long lead time of seventy-two hours for prenotification gives time to conceal activities or forces. Furthermore, no data may be transmitted from observation aircraft while in flight.

IMPROVING THE CFE AND CSBM REGIMES

Can the level of armed forces in Europe be reduced by further nego-tiations to add to stability in Europe and strengthen security coopera-tion?[29] The task is very difficult. In the Europe of the mid-1990s, caught in the grip of deep economic recession which is pushing defense budgets down, confronted with the vista of increasing peacekeeping tasks in for-mer Yugoslavia and elsewhere, and infused with worry over the future of Russia, few governments are devoting much thought to further arms reduc-tion. But in calmer times—and also in worse ones—interest in negotiated force reductions will probably revive, so it is worthwhile to reflect on the subject now.

There are many practical difficulties for further negotiated force reductions in Europe. With the dissolution of the Warsaw Pact and of the Soviet Union itself, negotiating for lower equal levels between the two alliances is no longer feasible. CSCE leaders agreed at Helsinki 92 to include all CSCE members in arms control negotiations. A worthy goal, but inclusion of those neutral states with armed forces adds to the difficulty of finding a workable basis to negotiate force reductions. No reduction for-mula to fit all of the CSCE participants that have armed forces can readily be developed—the discrepancy in size and situation between tiny Malta and huge Russia is too great. Germany and the Scandinavian states want the process of negotiated reductions to continue, but the motivation of most other NATO members is low. France, Britain, Italy, and the United States have in mind out-of-area challenges and peacekeeping require-ments. They accept with reluctance that economic considerations may force further reductions, but even so, they prefer to let this process take place spontaneously and to leave determination of future force levels in the hands of national governments.

Theoretically, NATO could also use the CFE formula to seek equal-ity at lower levels with Russia as a whole, which exceeds NATO in Europe in conventional forces. But Russia too is not enthusiastic about further negotiated reductions. It is caught in a confusing, complicated process of reducing its own conventional armed forces in response to harsh eco-nomic pressures, while requirements for use of these forces appear to increase. Russia may well be reluctant to move to overall equality with NATO not only because of concerns about future relations with Ukraine and other ex-Soviet republics, but concerns also about countries on its own southern flank—Iran, India, China, Japan—not to mention the United States on a worldwide basis.

Nonetheless, given long-range worries about the Russian military role in Europe, some possibilities may be worth exploring. Two of these are equal percentage reductions and cuts based on "force density," which seek to relate the total size of forces to the size of territory defended. It may be better to try out these possibilities now with Russia while relations are relatively good than to wait and try them in an atmosphere that may have deteriorated seriously.

The equal-percentage approach takes as its starting point the assumption that it will be possible in the project of the CSCE Forum for Cooperative Security to standardize arms control obligations and make them applicable to all CSCE states; in other words, to obtain the agreement of neutral CSCE states not covered by force limits of the CFE Treaty to accept limitations on their holdings of the same arms limited by CFE and on the total level of their active-duty ground and air force military personnel. However, it should also be possible to do better than this. If the European neutrals accept mandatory limits on their forces and, as a result, all CSCE members become subject to obligatory limitations on the same force components, this could provide the basis for equal-percentage reduction of manpower and heavy conventional arms by all CSCE states.

To take account of the wide difference of size among the forces of CSCE participant states, the countries could be divided into three categories. Using criteria that are illustrative and open to further refinement, Category 1 would consist of states with over 2,000 tanks and/or 600 combat aircraft; Category 2 of states with 1,000–2,000 tanks and/or 200 combat aircraft; and Category 3 of the remaining states. Using this scale, Category 1 would include France, Germany, Greece, Italy, Russia, Turkey, Ukraine, Great Britain, and the United States (the Yugoslav states are omitted); Category 2 would include Belarus, Belgium, Bulgaria, the Czech Republic, the Netherlands, Poland, Romania, and Spain; Category 3, the remaining states.

The first group might commit itself to reduce 5 percent a year of its heavy arms as defined in CFE over a ten-year period; the second group could reduce 3 percent yearly during a ten-year period; the smallest states would reduce 1 percent per year for ten years. Levels of active-duty ground- and air-force manpower should be included in percentage reductions along with CFE-designated armaments. Naval personnel should be included in negotiated reductions whether or not a scheme for negotiated reduction of naval vessels is agreed. As a result, the disproportion in the military power of the larger countries would be considerably diminished, as would the overall level of heavy conventional arms in Europe.

Another candidate for equal-percentage reduction is the equipment essential for force projection and deep penetration into enemy territory: units for trucking ammunition and vehicle fuel, tank transporters, prefabricated bridging, field hospitals, mobile anti-aircraft, and armored communication and command vehicles. Increasingly severe cuts in this type of equipment would tilt the balance in favor of nonthreatening static defenses. Like mobile high-firepower weapons, combat aircraft, and tanks, the equipment described here is essential for the offensive, but there are many less mobile and short-range substitutes for it in defense. One objection to this approach comes from those who would maintain capability for out-of-area intervention or peace enforcement. However, reductions of this type of equipment would not be total and could allow for pooling of remaining resources for multilateral operations.

Another variation on the percentage reduction approach would require that a specified proportion of active-duty heavily armed ground-force units—armored brigades and mechanized infantry brigades—be converted to reserve status over a fixed period of time. At the end of the process, for example, only one battalion per regiment or brigade would be on active duty. The reserve components could in turn be limited as to percentage of active-duty manpower and frequency and nature of training, and it would require a considerable time before the entire force could be made combat ready.[30] A version of this approach is being carried out in Germany, which plans that only seven brigades of a total of twenty-eight will be operational at all times.

It might also be worthwhile to examine the possibility of applying the percentage approach to reducing the total number of ground- and air-force units, both active-duty or reserve, held by CSCE participants. During the CFE talks, reduction of force structure (that is, of units and formations) was fiercely resisted by professional officers in all CSCE states. But if enduring reduction of military capability is the aim, then reductions in force structure are essential. Significantly, when the Western allies wanted to limit the size of the new postwar German armed forces, they imposed unit limits; the Brussels Treaty put a top limit of twelve divisions on German ground forces. Building a new combat unit from the ground up takes a long time. Consequently, eliminating units from the force structure and placing a no-increase ceiling on remaining units is a long-enduring form of force reduction. Conversely, allowing countries to retain unlimited force structure even if it is manned only at a low level means that they retain the capacity for rapid force expansion. It should be kept in mind that the objective of most arms control measures and constraints is to gain time for defensive actions against potential aggressors, ranging from the few hours gained by requiring an attacker to cross a weapons-free zone, to the eighteen months or more gained by making him build an armored brigade from the ground up or to restart a plant for production of treaty-limited armaments.

A different reduction method, proposed by Soviet and German proponents of nonoffensive defense[31] and then developed further by U.S.

researchers, would establish a ratio of forces to an area to be defended. One approach would allocate one brigade and one squadron of combat aircraft per 100 kilometers of border to be defended in a central zone and one brigade per 300 kilometers of border in Russia east of the Urals.[32]

This approach has the advantage of reducing and limiting the total number of units as well as major armaments. It would require Russia to make very large cuts, but they would be equal in percentage terms to cuts taken by several other participants. This particular proposal makes no specific allowance for stationing U.S. forces in Europe; presumably, these would be allocated a portion of the forces permitted to NATO countries. However, applying this method would also result in cuts in NATO so severe that defense against a resurgent Russia would be difficult unless the scheme were applied to the whole of Russia. This in turn raises questions of inclusion of the home territory of the United States. The approach could in theory be applied to the United States, but both the United States and Russia might insist on special allowances with regard to other large countries like China and India. Despite these difficulties, this approach merits further study.

IMPROVED VERIFICATION AND OBSERVATION

There is room for improvement in CSCE verification. There ought to be a dedicated CSCE aerial verification program to monitor force limits and evaluate data exchange. This regime should enable monitor aircraft to take position over a ground site scheduled to be inspected and over the surrounding area before, during, and after the ground inspection, preventing unobserved movement of arms and personnel out of the site into surrounding areas before an inspection takes place.

At the same time, verification should be standardized and made cheaper, with more sharing of results. The CSCE Conflict Prevention Center should be expanded to provide analysis of monitoring and verification results from member states that desire it. CSCE member states should earmark and place at the disposal of the CSCE, through the Conflict Prevention Center, pilots, observer crews, and aircraft to help with fact finding and with operation of procedures on unusual military activities. The WEU will eventually have satellite capability. In the meanwhile, the United States and Russia should provide more satellite imagery to the Conflict Prevention Center for common CSCE use. The United States, other NATO countries, and Russia should detail air and satellite photo interpretation personnel to the center. Shared information will facilitate common decisions.

SOME NEW CONFIDENCE-BUILDING MEASURES

Europe has been and remains a laboratory for the entire world in confidence-building measures, including constraints on force activities and transparency measures allowing authorized access to military information and activities. But some omissions in the existing CSBM regime should be made good, and several additional measures should be considered.

Actions to redress shortcomings in the present regime should include eliminating the exception for alerts, which remains a disquieting loophole permitting sudden force concentrations and exercises designed to intimidate.[33] If countries like Switzerland and Sweden, historically very heavily dependent on mobilization of reserves, do not wish to cooperate, a high ceiling of size for notification could be used that would omit most Swiss and Swedish exercises, or "regional" measures could be constructed that cover other CSCE states. The possibilities for advance notification of a pending alert to other CSCE states, but not to the troops participating in the alerts themselves, should be investigated. The annual number, duration, and location of these exercises should be limited by agreement. At the least, alert exercises should be opened to observers from the outset, instead of only after seventy-two hours.[34] Use of helicopters and fixed-wing aircraft to observe exercises, now optional for host countries, should be made obligatory.[35]

Among the options for new constraints, one would be to confine all or a large portion of the equipment critical to cross-border attack, like bridging, armored command vans, and mobile anti-aircraft, to monitored storage from which removal would have to be pre-announced.[36] Troops could exercise with simulations or substitutes. If negotiated reduction of armaments of this kind is not feasible, this constraint would be a useful partial measure. Equipment like this could be kept in cheap monitored storage, for example, by using small teams of enlisted personnel in a jeep for perimeter patrol, or fiber-optic perimeter cable with warning devices checked by periodic helicopter visits. CFE participants did not have time to work out details of such storage, but it should be analyzed further. Use of low-cost monitored storage could also provide a longer period of time for destruction of treaty-limited arms and reduce its excessive cost.

A second constraint would confine larger exercises to designated areas by pre-agreement rather than waiting for possible problems in these areas to develop.[37] Exercises could be excluded from specified border areas. Several proposals have been advanced to demilitarize or thin out deployments in border areas. Such measures can serve to delay attack by a limited although valuable amount of time. Their real value in political crisis situations is to limit contact between opposing military forces that could lead to conflict. In selected cases, the ban could extend to deployment of paramilitary forces. In extreme cases, zones of this kind can be used to deploy outside monitors or buffering peacekeeping forces. Some zones of this kind have already been instituted in Europe on a bilateral basis. In December 1991, Turkey and Bulgaria concluded an agreement to constrain military activities in border areas. In 1989, Hungary proposed creation of border zones to Italy, the former Yugoslavia, and Austria, from which mobile offensive units would be excluded. However, no action was taken. In mid-1991, Greece proposed to establish similar zones on its borders with Bulgaria and Turkey.[38]

A further group of possible constraints would reduce the readiness level of reserve forces and thus stretch out the time needed to prepare for aggressive attack. Such measures might also affect preparation for defense, although a higher degree of training is needed more for long-range forces like mobile armored units than for localized defenses.

CSCE and CFE provide for prenotification of some types of reserve activities.The Vienna 1992 Document (Measure VII 71.1) limits exercises larger than 40,000 personnel, whether of active-duty forces or reserves, to one in every two-year period. But, aside from the absence of restrictions in CFE or in the CSBM regime on the number of reserve units, there are also no restrictions on the levels of active-duty personnel that reserve units may have (otherwise they can become reserve units in name only), on the amount of equipment they may have, or on the nature of their training. To deal with this issue, a new constraint could provide that the proportion of active-duty personnel serving in a given reserve unit would be held to 10 percent or lower of the authorized combat strength of the unit. (The Vienna 1992 Document defines a "nonactive" or reserve unit as those manned with from 0 to 15 percent of their authorized combat strength.) This means that, unless they have given advance notice of call-up of reserve personnel, CSCE reserve units should when inspected not have more than 10 percent of their wartime personnel strength on hand. It could also be required that equipment of reserve units be held in separate monitored storage.

A good case can be made for requiring prenotification of independent air exercises over a certain size and for the presence of observers at command centers for directing these exercises. Negotiations are under way in Europe for coordinated control of military and civil air flights. This control system, together with AWACS-type aircraft and ground radar sites, could be used to monitor air exercises.

There are no valid grounds to continue to exclude coverage of naval exercises from confidence-building measures. Those exercises involving a specified number of vessels should be prenotified and opened to observation from command ships or centers and by air. Data exchange should cover naval vessels, including those in eastern Russia and in waters around the United States and Canada.

UN Secretary General Boutros Boutros-Ghali has pointed out that confidence-building measures can have an important role in postconflict peace building, together with procedures like constraints on force levels and deployments and information exchange. In fact, the intellectual genesis of confidence building is to take traditional armistice terms and to apply them before conflict rather than after it. More analysis is needed to identify confidence-building measures especially valuable for postconflict situations.[39]

New Regional Centers

Despite its considerable ingenuity in devising new institutions and measures, CSCE has not acted to exploit the decision in Helsinki 92 to carry out arms control on a regional basis. There is evident need for the regional approach in the security relationship between Russia and Ukraine. CSCE states should think of a new type of regional operation, which combines thus far separate CSCE activities of mediation, conflict resolution, confidence-building measures, and negotiated force reductions and applies them to a specific area, perhaps in a resident center in Kiev. Similar regional centers are needed in Bosnia and Croatia.

A Defensive Code for Europe

We have reviewed the work of the CSCE Forum for Security Cooperation on a code of conduct governing mutual relations of member states in the field of security. In addition to the content already described, such a code should provide agreed criteria by which the armed forces of member states could be structured.

The beginning of this chapter described some of the problems that have arisen from following the traditional axiom "If you wish peace, then prepare for war": One of the most telling criticisms of the Warsaw Pact force posture during the cold war was that the pact had equipped itself not only to defend its home territory but, following the cardinal principle laid down by Carl von Clausewitz, also to move rapidly to seek decisive victory over NATO armed forces on NATO's own territory. Post–cold war evidence confirmed that this was the approved strategy of the Soviet Union and the reason for forward deployment of so many Soviet tank divisions in East Germany and Czechoslovakia. This strategy, although understandable in light of the destruction of the Russian homeland in German attacks in two world wars, led to very heavy arming by the pact, to a continuing NATO competitive response, and to steady increase in the size and dangers of the East-West military confrontation. The existence of armed forces on both sides equipped for deep penetration attack on adversary territory created the risk of preemptive action in a crisis situation and intensified political hostility.

In place of this unstable posture, European advocates of nonoffensive defense have urged enlightened self-restraint in formulating defense aims. Under their approach, defense objectives would be limited to defense of the home territory. The objective of seeking to annihilate adversary forces on their own territory would be deliberately relinquished, together with forces sized, equipped, and organized for this purpose.

As the numerically weaker of the two alliances and as a coalition of democratic states devoted to self-defense, NATO for years had as its objective in the event of conflict the restoration of the status quo ante before the attack, rather than defeat of the adversary on its home territory. NATO's new strategic concept issued in November 1991 retains this idea, stating, "The forces of the allies must therefore be able to defend alliance frontiers, to stop an aggressor's advance as far forward as possible, to maintain or restore the territorial integrity of allied nations, and to terminate war rapidly by making an aggressor reconsider his decision, cease his attack, and withdraw."[40]

These ideas could be fitted into a CSCE code of conduct. In addition to other principles already described, the code could commit CSCE participants:

1. Not to make first use of military force, that is, to use military force only in response to attack, except in a multilateral peacemaking context. This concept, axiomatic for a defensive posture, was suggested by General Klaus Naumann, inspector general (chief of staff) of the German armed forces.[41]

2. Not to make first use of nuclear weapons. This is an old idea whose time has come. As pointed out in our chapter on NATO, NATO governments still resist a no-first-use commitment on the grounds that uncertainty on the part of an aggressor as to when NATO might use nuclear weapons is a valuable deterrent to attack. That argument had some validity. But now that the Soviet Union and its conventional superiority have faded away, NATO forces could deal by conventional means with a conventional attack by a resurgent Russia. The urgent objective now is to inhibit use of nuclear weapons by the Soviet successor states against European targets. A mutual no-first-use pledge could

provide a useful even though not insurmountable obstacle to such use. A worldwide no-first-use commitment could be undertaken by the United States, Russia, France, Great Britain, and China in connection with an advance decision by the UN Security Council to take joint action against governments or groups initiating or threatening the use of nuclear weapons.

3. Participants would pledge not to use their forces outside national borders except for collective defense and multilateral peacekeeping or peacemaking.

4. The objectives of defense would be restricted to the defense of national territory, including restoration of territorial integrity after attack. Deep cross-border attack would be renounced.

As this survey has shown, great ingenuity has been applied to limiting and controlling the armed forces of the European states. The resulting agreed measures contribute an indispensable infrastructure of knowledge and confidence about military relationships essential to all forms of political and economic cooperation in Europe. That is the great and continuing achievement of these agreements. They may also yet prove useful in heading off future interstate conflicts. But they have not prevented the eruption of organized armed violence in the Yugoslav states or in the states around Russia, nor have they as yet made a decisive contribution to resolving those internal conflicts. We turn in the final section of the book to some ideas that may have value for this purpose.

PART IV

EVALUATION

13

EUROPEAN SECURITY INSTITUTIONS
OF THE TWENTY–FIRST CENTURY

The main institutions of European security—NATO, the Western
European Union (WEU), and the Conference on Security and
Cooperation in Europe (CSCE)—all have their own strengths and weaknesses. The WEU does not include the United States or Russia in its membership and has no prospect of doing so. In its present form, NATO does
not include the European neutrals, the Eastern European states, or Russia
and other Soviet successor states. CSCE has all of these as participants, but
is weak and based on the voluntary cooperation of a large and disparate
membership.

To obtain more perspective on the strengths and weaknesses of these
organizations, let's look at their capacity to cope with the security tasks
confronting them now and possibly in future: If the task is ensuring against
a resurgent Russia, then NATO is the logical organization at this time;
however, perhaps in the long term, WEU could do this job. If the task is
integrating Russia into a Western security structure, WEU is not a candidate.
For this, a transformed NATO might provide a framework through the
North Atlantic Cooperation Council (NACC) or, in the very long run, possibly a retooled CSCE with armed forces of its own. If the task is coping with
renewed instability in the Persian Gulf, NATO could meet the requirements now, as could an ad hoc coalition of the United States and European
states; eventually, WEU might take on this task, although it probably would
still need help from the United States, at least for intelligence and logistics.

Staving off nuclear dangers in Russia and other successor states calls for the United States operating in NATO with its allies. To deal with present or future ethnic wars in Europe, including conflicts in the Soviet successor states, we need either NATO, NACC, a more developed WEU, or a much strengthened CSCE. In theory, NATO could do most of these jobs but for that, the Clinton administration would have to be willing to undertake much greater responsibility for European developments and France and other European countries would have to give up their long dream of a European Union that was self-sustaining in defense. Neither condition is likely to be met. As things stood in the mid-1990s, none of the existing organizations could perform all these functions and none could do so effectively without further large-scale transformation.

A MIXED RECORD OF PERFORMANCE

In parallel decisions in mid-1992 to take on responsibility for peace-keeping, NATO, WEU, and CSCE sought to organize themselves to cope with the most pressing security problem of post-cold war Europe—continuing ethnic violence in the Balkans and in the Soviet successor states. The decision was right, but implementation was defective.

Led by the United States with its steadfast refusal to commit its own ground forces, British, Italian, and other European governments also repeatedly rejected commitment of ground-force contingents large enough to head off or damp down the fighting in Croatia and Bosnia. All of the institutions concerned with European security—the CSCE, the EC, NATO, and WEU, and the UN too—suffered in reputation and prestige as the result of their inability to stop the fighting in Yugoslavia. When President François Mitterrand made a solo dash to Dubrovnik in June 1992, he said his dramatic trip was necessary because the EC's repute was being destroyed by its ineffectiveness in the former Yugoslavia. In the French referendum of September 1992 on the EC Treaty, opposition leaders often cited the weak performance of the EC in Yugoslavia as grounds for opposing the Maastricht Treaty, and this conclusion was reflected in public opinion polls. NATO, the CSCE, and the UN suffered equally, especially in European opinion.

Discussion of improvements in European security institutions, of "security architecture for Europe," is in one sense academic and diverts attention from the real problem: The failure of European security institutions to cope with their present challenges cannot be ascribed either to the intrinsic difficulty of the problem, considerable as that difficulty is, or to the lack of machinery or resources. As fighting erupted in the Yugoslav Federation, the NATO countries together accounted for two-thirds of the world's gross national product. They had been spending close to $500 billion a year on their armed forces, which, counting those of the United States, numbered close to 4 million at the beginning of 1992. They had overwhelming force at their disposal. In Bosnia, they were opposed only by remnants of the Yugoslav armed forces and by armed local bands of small size. The CSCE sent useful civilian observer missions to sensitive minority areas of Serbia, helped to enforce economic sanctions against Serbia, and sent repeated observer-mediation missions to Moldova, Georgia, and Nagorno-Karabakh. But in these festering trouble spots, nothing more came of the decisions of all three organizations to go in for peacekeeping. The problem in all these cases was not lack of machinery or resources, but of political will to use them.

A possible worst-case outcome of the developments we have been reviewing so far is that NATO, WEU, and the CSCE continue to fail to get a grip on post-cold war ethnic conflict in Europe. These conflicts continue and spread, some of them developing into limited interstate wars. Russia and the successor states drift toward autocratic rule with aggressive tendencies. The bulk of U.S. forces leaves Europe under conditions of friction with European NATO governments. The existing multilateral institutions for European security are further discredited in public opinion. NATO exists, but as an empty shell. Europeans continue to talk about building up WEU, but do nothing serious. CSCE becomes a discussion club for the disillusioned and pessimistic.

Under conditions like these, almost inevitably, if unobtrusively and by slow degrees, European governments would become less engaged in multilateral security organizations and, step by step, would move toward greater reliance on their own resources and their own armed forces. In a word much used in Europe, defense would become "renationalized." Multilateral security ties would slowly loosen or atrophy and the individual states of Europe find it increasingly difficult to work together. Organizations for multilateral security, including the European Union itself, would seize up internally, unable to reach decisions. The integrating bonds of half a century would slowly unravel. It would be a more dangerous security environment.

It would be a long time before such a situation was reached—but it is possible to envisage it as a worst case. The bonds of cooperation among the European and North American states are too strong to permit it easily. Moreover, NATO moved during late 1993 and 1994 to closer engagement in the former Yugoslavia, and it further developed its outreach program to the East, although not without controversy. The CSCE performed inventively in mediation and conflict avoidance in the Yugoslav states and the Soviet successor states; perhaps it would be able to do still more to control the aims and tactics of Russian intervention in neighboring republics. The WEU performed valuable functions in the Yugoslav states and extended its own capabilities. The Western countries may finally be able to help in bringing the major fighting in Bosnia to an end and provide help, including NATO peacekeeping forces, for the long, bitter period of knitting together the fragments. Success, even partial success, may restore the prestige of European security institutions and encourage member governments to continue supporting them.

It is already evident, even though the long-term future is less certain, that the European security system and its component institutions will in fact survive their first hard test in the former Yugoslavia and the Soviet successor states. But what effects will the testing experience have on these institutions, and how they might be developed to perform more effectively in future? Will the outcome, instead of gradually weakening the institutions of European security, be the emergence of a zone of order and prosperity in western Europe and of a zone of continuing disorder and deprivation in the eastern part of Europe? In other words, will Europe be redivided?

Western European Union

Some experts believe that the Western European Union would not have reemerged in the early 1990s from its reserve status into its new status as the defense arm of a future European Union if the United States had acted earlier in a more enlightened way to "Europeanize" NATO, deliberately cutting back on U.S. dominance, transferring NATO command to European countries, starting with France—in effect making a transformed NATO and not WEU the defense organization of the European Union. Yet the top U.S. military and political leadership was not psychologically able to make this jump, and there were some reasons for this inability. The U.S. leadership had talked itself into the not entirely baseless conviction that Europe could not handle the leadership role, the change to a European orientation would have had to have been made while the dangers of the cold war still appeared acute, and there was also considerable risk that the American public and Congress would in response have slackened in their support for NATO.

Some observers believe the WEU problem could have been solved in another way—if the United States itself had become a member of an expanded European Community in a modern version of Atlantic federalism. Then NATO would have been the joint defensive force of a larger transatlantic community. But among other factors, this outcome underrates the strength of national feeling in the United States and the American sense of a worldwide role reaching far beyond Europe, and it also underrates the strength of "Euronationalism" among the European political elite.

These developments did not take place. Instead, the WEU moved steadily ahead in the 1990s until it achieved assured institutional status as the designated defense organization of the European Union, although by no means military capability comparable to that of NATO. How can we assess the possibilities of WEU for the future? Will the competition between NATO and WEU go on indefinitely if at a less abrasive level, or will the two institutions ultimately develop genuine complementarity? In the abstract, all the participants, the United States and the European states, want complementarity. In their hearts, U.S. officials probably prefer continuing, unquestioned predominance of NATO. But most European governments genuinely want both an augmented defense identity for the European Union and strong transatlantic ties. Will WEU continue to grow by accretion? Will it serve as the means by which the European Union ultimately becomes self-sustaining in defense, able to meet all major challenges: a resurgent Russia, a new crisis in the Persian Gulf, and fielding of sizable peace-enforcement forces under multilateral auspices in Europe or outside it?

Some observers believe that this will not happen, that the WEU will remain a shell without much real content for a long time to come. They cite the assessment of U.K. prime minister John Major and others that that the two Maastricht Treaties were the high-water mark of a now-receding movement for European integration, and that the European Union Treaty's aim of a unified defense policy was premature and ill prepared. In this view, European integration will for a long time to come be limited to economics, without serious movement into institutionalized integration of foreign policy and defense. Even in the field of economics, according to these analysts, the project of economic and monetary union set forth in the Maastricht Treaties will not be reached on schedule and possibly not at all.[1] Observers who take this view believe that worries over Russia, concerns over possible alienation of the United States, decreasing European defense budgets, the inertia of staying with NATO's proven record and superior capabilities, and decision-making difficulties arising from absorbing new members into the EC will all inhibit development of WEU.

The other view, which is at least as plausible as the first—in fact, more plausible—is that European integration will continue to make headway in the foreign policy and defense areas as well as in economics—although now far more slowly—and that the WEU will move forward with the European Union in an incremental process of expanding capability.

In the past, progress of the European Community has been very uneven, with new projects blocked for months and years by opposition of some member states, followed by far-reaching breakthroughs. Examples of these breakthrough moves are the 1957 agreement to establish the European Economic Community after the terrible defeat of the proposal for a European Defense Community, the 1965 decision to consolidate the three existing communities, the 1973 decision finally to admit the United Kingdom, and the decision in 1986 to move toward a genuine common market without national veto through the Single European Act. Political elites in the core European countries—France, Germany, Italy, and Benelux—continue strongly integrationist, as are the institutional elites of business and banking, which have enormous stakes in the success of the European Union. Though the general public may be less sanguine, influential opinion still matters greatly on issues of European integration.

On balance, therefore, it seems probable that some movement toward further European integration will continue. As in the past, the integration process will move more slowly and irregularly than the hopes and plans of its activists and more rapidly than the doubts of its skeptics. The blows of 1992–93 to the European integration process left the United Kingdom and some other states unwilling and unable to make a commitment to economic and monetary union. At the same time, the core EC countries—France, Germany, Italy, and Benelux—are unlikely to relinquish this goal. The prospect is for a two-speed Europe, whether informally or explicitly.

The European Union is likely to continue not only to deepen, if solely in a core group, but also to broaden. As a result, WEU is likely to have fourteen full members by 1995–96 following entry of Norway, Finland, Sweden, and Austria into the European Union, although public opinion in Norway or Sweden might turn down membership in the European Union in referendums. However, if Finland, Sweden, Austria, and possibly Norway enter the EU in the second half of the 1990s and become members of WEU, it is unlikely under present circumstances that the same states will also become full members of NATO.

If they are able to maintain democratic polities in the face of economic pressures and move further toward functioning free-market economies, the Czech Republic, Hungary, and Poland might join the EU within a decade. If this happens, they too will join WEU as full members, although the United States might question full WEU membership for these states on the grounds that their membership would mean an indirect extension of NATO defense guarantees. The Baltic states are also likely to follow in European Union and WEU membership. By the end of the century, the European Union and the WEU will both in some form be the direct neighbor of Belarus, Ukraine, and Russia.

Although not wholly excluded in the very long run, it is unlikely that the Soviet successor states will become members of the European Union in the foreseeable future or that they will develop close association with the WEU. Most EC leaders are convinced that the Soviet successor states are too turbulent, with too uncertain a political and economic future, to qualify for European Union membership and that Russia and Ukraine are too large to absorb in the EU even if they could someday meet its conditions of functioning free-market and democratic institutions.

The European Union will feel some obligation ultimately to include the shattered republics of Yugoslavia, and also Romania, Bulgaria, and Albania as member states if they too can some day meet these qualifying standards. But to accept these countries as full members, the EU would probably also have to accept Turkey, whose uncertain status in human rights, social policy, and capacity to withstand the influence of Islamic fundamentalism has kept it outside the gates of the EU despite a long-standing application for membership. The resultant difficulty of making a package deal covering all the Mediterranean and Balkan states may well keep the entire area (plus Cyprus, divided between Greek and Turkish inhabitants) out of the EU for a long time to come.

Nonetheless, by the year 2010, European Union membership could be well over twenty (the twelve EU members as of 1993, plus Austria, Finland, Norway, Sweden, the three Baltic States, Poland, the Czech Republic, and Hungary, and possibly Switzerland and the Slovak Republic). It is probable that by that time, the project for political union will have regained momentum. Even if this is not the case, all the new EC members will probably also be full or associate members of the WEU, making its membership more numerous than NATO's current sixteen members. Thus enlarged, WEU might gain considerably in potential military capability. In recent years, François Mitterrand has several times suggested that France and Britain should ultimately place their nuclear weapons at the disposal of the European Union. It will be a long time before this actually occurs; in the mid-1990s, France and Great Britain were moving very slowly toward somewhat greater bilateral coordination of their nuclear forces, but Great Britain had also withdrawn from the early stages of a joint program to produce a new nuclear-tipped air-to-surface missile. But at some point in the future, in some form of decision-sharing, the EU is likely to become a world nuclear power with a link to the WEU.

No one can tell how far the WEU will actually develop. But it appears to have become a permanent feature of the European security system. The sensible course for the United States now is to accept facts and to give WEU ongoing help in its further development and to further defuse the WEU-NATO competition by seeking a political understanding with France about the future of both organizations. Unless this is done, both will remain to some extent hobbled by mutual animosity.

Fortunately, it appears that the government of Prime Minister Edouard Balladur and the Clinton administration have moved far toward such an understanding. By the end of 1993, France had accepted NATO's Partnership for Peace program aimed primarily at meeting Eastern European security concerns, and it was taking the lead in urging a larger role for NATO air forces in peacekeeping in Bosnia. In a decision announced in early 1994, France said it would send its defense minister and chief of staff to those NATO meetings that discussed the possible use of French forces, for example, in the Yugoslav states or Eastern Europe or in operations involving the WEU. For its part, at the January 1994 NATO Summit, the Clinton administration took three important steps toward the French position: It endorsed the concept of a separate European defense identity; it agreed that NATO could place its logistics and infrastructure at the disposal of WEU for WEU operations; and it agreed on the establishment of flexible operational structures in which France could cooperate without rejoining the NATO integrated command it had left in 1966.

The declaration of the NATO heads of state and government issued at the end of the Brussels meeting endorses the European Security Identity—the common foreign and defense policy called for in the Maastricht Treaty—which "might in time lead to a common defense," and also the Western European Union. It states that NATO's organization and resources will be adjusted to facilitate development of the WEU as the defense component of the European Union. It forecasts that NATO and WEU might hold joint council meetings of both organizations to address future contingencies. In future, NATO will be prepared to make collective NATO assets available, following consultation in the NATO Council, for WEU military operations undertaken in pursuit of the European Union's common foreign and security policy. Finally, the Declaration endorses the establishment of a staff for Combined Joint Task Forces. These task forces could coordinate contingency operations, like peacekeeping, of ad hoc coalitions, including non-NATO states.[2]

U.S. motivation for these actions was not only to assure a more cooperative relationship with France. Clearly, these moves were intended to devolve part of U.S. defense responsibilities and to make it possible for Europe to take on more of its own. This summit, prepared by high level Franco-American consultations over the previous year, was far removed from the caustic Bush-Mitterrand exchange about the European defense identity at the 1991 Rome NATO Summit.

Following the 1994 NATO Summit, U.K. defense minister Malcolm Rifkind took the initiative to invite the French and German defense ministers for a discussion of cooperation of the three countries in WEU. Coming from the European country that had most consistently resisted French efforts to build up the WEU on the grounds that such efforts could weaken NATO, this U.K. initiative, together with the U.S. endorsement of

WEU at the summit, was significant evidence that the Western European Union was now an accepted part of the European defense scene.

Of course, as pointed out after the 1994 NATO Summit by Alain Lamassoure, France's minister for European affairs, the European Union still lacked a developed apparatus to prepare and execute joint policy like political-military action in Bosnia. There are fragments of an apparatus in the Council of Ministers secretariat and in the policy unit that has been established in the European Commission by political affairs commissioner Hans van den Broek, but the commission has no policy planning staff or think tank. Still more serious, many of WEU's potential future activities could be severely circumscribed by the unresolved German dispute about deployment of German forces outside German borders. Moreover, as the French defense minister pointed out with Gaullist consistency, as far as France was concerned, WEU use of NATO's logistic and intelligence capabilities would only be an interim measure until Europe developed its own capabilities; in the medium and long term, NATO would have outlived its usefulness. Despite these continuing problems, there has been real progress toward developing a productive relationship between WEU and NATO.[3]

In 1990, Secretary of State James Baker proposed a U.S.-EC treaty of cooperation that would also cover security issues. This idea encountered resistance from some EC members and it was not carried out. Foreign Minister Hans Dietrich Genscher proposed a similar agreement before his resignation in 1992. In a similar vein, WEU secretary general Willem van Eekelen has argued for a "Transatlantic Bargain," possibly in treaty form, where NATO would be given priority to act first in cases requiring military intervention if the United States were prepared to participate in the intervention with its own ground forces. If not, then WEU might undertake the mission, but with U.S. logistics and intelligence support. More generally, the United States might commit itself on a long-term basis to a minimum military presence in Europe that would include reinforcement capability, the nuclear function, long-range airlift command control and intelligence.[4]

Given the understandings reached at the 1994 NATO Summit, developments appeared to be moving in this direction. Thanks to the United States's preoccupation with domestic reform, the associated emphasis on burden-sharing with allies in defense issues, and its rejection of committing ground forces in Croatia and Bosnia, the United States had accepted the decision of the European Union countries that the Union will have its own military organization. At the same time, inveterate NATO-baiter France has admitted that, at this point, WEU is far from having the capability to organize and direct the actions of a Western air fleet over Bosnia and that NATO should do the job. Things were looking up in this area.

NATO's FUTURE

That the prestige and future prospects of NATO were severely damaged by NATO's failure to take more far-reaching and effective action to stop the fighting in Croatia and Bosnia is widely accepted. This conclusion led several critics to argue that only a last-ditch intervention in Bosnia could save NATO. For example, Paul Warnke, former director of the U.S. Arms Control and Disarmament Agency, argued that a strong NATO response to the Bosnian crisis would justify NATO's post-cold war existence, but that lacking such a response, NATO "will lump along, but will no longer be taken seriously as the leading instrument of international or even European security." Senate minority leader Robert Dole asserted that the weak NATO response in Bosnia thus far "conveys the impression that the NATO alliance may have outlived its usefulness." He too urged large-scale intervention. Manfred Wörner, secretary general of NATO, said continued inaction in Bosnia would harm the alliance. "If the international community does not effectively handle this conflict, it will damage all international organizations including my own." "Exit NATO, the Western Alliance is dead," wrote James Chace, an astute American commentator. "Bosnia was the death rattle of a cold war relic."[5] In Congress, skeptics as to NATO's usefulness supported an amendment to the 1994 defense authorization bill that would require the European allies to pay all the costs of maintaining U.S. forces in Europe. The bill's sponsor, Representative Barney Frank, said "Bosnia has shown there is no real role for U.S. troops in Europe."

These comments were justified at the time; relative U.S. and NATO inaction in the Yugoslav civil wars from their outset in mid-1991 up to the end of 1993 incurred much discredit for both. Yet NATO's role in the February 1994 ultimatum to the Bosnian Serbs to draw back their artillery from Sarajevo and NATO action at the end of that month in shooting down four Serb aircraft bombing a Muslim target somewhat redeemed its reputation. If some measure of peace comes to Bosnia and NATO has an important role in the peacemaking process, its earlier inaction may to an extent be forgotten or forgiven.

Some political leaders and experts urged that NATO should act to rescue its future through expanding its membership to include Eastern Europe, and, in some versions, to Russia and Ukraine. Attending his last meeting of the NATO defense ministers as secretary of defense, Richard Cheney warned his colleagues in December 1992 that "an organization which does not address these concerns" about security in Eastern Europe "is not going to survive long term."[6] In an eloquent speech before the Overseas Writers Club, Senator Richard Lugar, who had earlier argued for more vigorous intervention in Bosnia, called for a new transatlantic strategic bargain that would extend "collective defense and security arrangements to the areas in the east and south of Europe where the seeds of future conflict are . . . NATO will either develop the structure and strategy to go 'out of area,' or it will go out of business."[7] Stephen Rosenfeld, editorial writer of the *Washington Post*, urged: "The West should see to it that NATO stops dithering and reinvents itself promptly as the Atlantic club of democratic nations. Military NATO will stew for years over what sort of threats to prepare for. Political NATO should offer membership to the countries, reformed or new, that earn it. Poland would be first."[8]

Although eastward extension would at the outset be a political and organizational action, not a military one, these critics grasped the essential point: NATO's role of protecting Europe against a resurgent Russia was necessary defense insurance for the West. However, this role, essential as it was, was far smaller than NATO's cold war mission had been. Standing alone, it did not represent a sufficient claim on tight national budgets and political support to keep NATO alive and healthy. Some new function and activity was needed for that purpose. In theory, NATO itself had already supplied the answer in the form of the North Atlantic Cooperation Council (NACC) that it established in late 1991 as an outreach organization to Eastern Europe. Yet NATO had not acted to exploit and develop NACC. Pursuing the old feud, France had blocked many of its activities. Apparently, something new was needed.

The view that both security needs and NATO's own future made extension of NATO membership to the east desirable had been widespread in the State and Defense departments since the collapse of the Soviet system. "We would like to see integration from Vancouver to Vladivostok and the forces of those countries as a united commonwealth of nations," Deputy Secretary of State Lawrence Eagleburger told the NATO Eurogroup in May 1991. This view was reinforced by ever more frequent calls for NATO membership from the Eastern European states. In 1992–93, faced by a shaky situation in Ukraine, political instability in Moscow as Yeltsin faced a nationalistic parliament, evidence of increasing Russian military intervention in surrounding republics, and increased nervousness from their Polish, Czech, and Hungarian neighbors, senior German officials, including Minister of Defense Volker Ruehe, began to urge specific action to extend NATO membership to the east, beginning with these three countries. In a speech to the North Atlantic Assembly in May 1993, Ruehe said that there were no reasons of principle precluding extending NATO membership to Eastern Europe; in the next period the membership structure of NATO would be as decisive as its political strategy for its long-term future.[9] For Germany, extension of NATO to Poland, the Czech Republic, and Hungary on the east and southeast would bolster political stability in those countries and bolster German security. The benefits here were clear. But how would the Russians react to NATO extension eastward?

Three Rand Corporation analysts (Ronald Asmus, Richard Kugler, and Stephen Larrabee), among the most articulate promoters of extending NATO membership to the East, argued that NATO should open the prospect of ultimate full membership to Eastern European states. The process of achieving membership should be stage by stage and conditional on fulfilling a series of requirements specified in advance. Candidate members should first become "associate members" of NATO, which would enable them to participate in consultations under Article 4 of the North Atlantic Treaty.[10] Article 4 provided the basis for NATO's 1992 decision to place its forces at the disposal of the CSCE and UN for peacekeeping purposes, and it would provide the basis for out-of-area military intervention by NATO or a coalition of NATO members outside the territory of NATO members.

The Rand analysts suggested that the criteria for NATO membership for new states include conditions similar to those formulated by the EC Council for EC membership for the Eastern European states: "Commitment to democratic rule; renunciation of all territorial claims; respect for the rights of minorities; and willingness to participate in the full range of future NATO activities from peacekeeping to collective defense."[11] If these conditions were ultimately satisfactorily met by the new associate members, they would become full members of the alliance, with the benefits of the pledge of collective security in Article 5 of the North Atlantic Treaty. It was argued that the step-by-step procedure toward the desired goal would hearten the Eastern European states from the outset and would enable NATO members to satisfy themselves that these states were acting responsibly before finally committing to the defense of the new member states.

In the summer of 1993, in response to the surge of interest in Washington and Eastern European capitals in expanding NATO, senior officials of the State Department diplomatically indicated that they were open-minded and studying the possibility of enlargement with several specific questions in mind: Would the present allies be willing to commit their troops to the defense of Eastern Europe? Would the Eastern European countries make a real contribution to the common defense? Would NATO work as effectively if enlarged? What would be the effect of including or excluding Russia and Ukraine from membership?[12] Most proposals of membership expansion envisaged the exclusion or nonmembership of Russia.

Public and intragovernmental discussion of NATO expansion in the United States and in Western and Eastern Europe intensified still further in fall 1993. A NATO Summit was in the offing, the first for new U.S.

president Bill Clinton and the membership issue was on the agenda. In Russia, Yeltsin had closed down the parliament and had used force to empty the parliament building. The Polish, Czech, and Hungarian governments lobbied energetically for membership. Then in December, only a month before the Brussels Summit, came another event to fuel the drive for membership—the impressive election showing of the Russian hardliners with Vladimir Zhirinovsky at their head. The resulting last-minute push for expanding NATO membership almost carried the day.

Although President Boris Yeltsin gave the idea of extending NATO membership to Poland, the Czech Republic, and Hungary, lukewarm endorsement in visits to Prague and Warsaw in August 1993, Russian statements of opposition to extension of NATO membership to the three Eastern European states increased in frequency and vehemence as the supporters of expansion made their case. Proponents of limited expansion like German defense minister Ruehe claimed that they could deal with adverse Russian reactions, but they were short on specifics as to how to do so. Exclusion of Russia from a NATO that had expanded to include its most important former Warsaw Pact allies would surely activate Russian paranoia, strengthen criticism of Yeltsin's foreign policy among Russian nationalists and make it harder to integrate Russia into the European security system.

By fall 1993, increasing political controversy over the project to expand NATO membership to a select group of Eastern European states had brought NATO's two main functions—providing insurance against a resurgent Russia and helping the new Russia move toward democracy through military cooperation and integration—into conflict with one another. The conflict was unnecessary because membership expansion to the three Eastern European states would in reality serve neither of these main functions. It would alienate Russia and make it more dangerous to the West and more resistant to cooperation in the military field. The underlying difficulty was that extending membership to Eastern Europe now might definitively foreclose the possibility of democratic development in Russia at a later point.

Fortunately, wiser heads prevailed. Instead of offering associate membership in NATO to a select few, the leaders at the NATO Summit invited all Eastern states without distinction to join the new Partnership for Peace. The summit declaration on the Partnership for Peace opens with the statement "We expect and would welcome NATO expansion that would reach to democratic states to our East, as part of our evolutionary process, taking into account political and security developments in the whole of Europe." The declaration invites all countries of Eastern Europe and the Soviet successor states to sign individual contracts ("framework documents") with NATO. In doing so, the signing states commit themselves to transparency in the national defense and budgeting processes, ensuring democratic control of armed forces, and developing with NATO joint planning, training, and exercises to strengthen their ability to participate in peacekeeping operations. In return, NATO will assist with multinational training. Furthermore, NATO commits itself in the contract "to consult with any active participant in the Partnership if that partner perceives a direct threat to its territorial integrity, political independence or security." NATO committed itself to carry out joint peacekeeping exercises, to invite partnership participants to send liaison officers to NATO headquarters, and to establish a planning staff located at the top NATO military command at Mons, Belgium, "the Partnership Coordination Cell." (The peculiar nomenclature emerges from the desire not to give the partnership planning staff greater status "than the WEU planning cell.")[13] By the spring of 1994, nearly all European countries including the neutrals had either joined the Partnership for Peace or had indicated they would join. In May, Russia said it would join. There were only two holdouts—neutral Austria, and Tajikistan, which had declined on grounds of cost.

The original scheme for "associate membership" for Poland, the Czech Republic, and Hungary was not well thought out. It is doubtful that real security advantages would have come to these Eastern European countries through associate member status. Only full NATO membership would guarantee the territory of the new members. And full NATO membership would require amendment of the North Atlantic Treaty by member-state legislatures. These legislatures were very unlikely to act to guarantee the security of even friendly nations like Poland and Hungary because of contested borders and substantial friction-producing minorities in neighboring countries.

On the other hand, the losses from extending associate membership to the three Eastern European states would have been substantial. President Boris Yeltsin had written to Western governments and spoken before the NATO Council to warn that bringing central Europe into NATO while leaving Russia out would be divisive and would undermine hopes for increasing cooperation with the Russian military. The divisiveness Yeltsin warned against would apply not only to Russia but to Ukraine, the Baltic states, and other states of Eastern Europe. The NATO states could not effectively pursue a long-term policy of seeking to integrate these countries into a functioning European security structure while at the same time seeking to impose on them a three-class system—full NATO members, associate members, and nonmembers. However, debate on the issue had one benefit: both Russia and the Eastern European states could understand from it that, if Russia clearly goes downhill to nationalist authoritarianism, decisively dispelling the hopes of democratic development that motivated the West's restraint, NATO governments would rapidly extend effective security coverage to Eastern Europe.

Meanwhile, it is not clear whether the Partnership for Peace, a somewhat watered-down, more universal version of the proposal for associate membership, will really add to European security or whether time will prove it merely an effort on the part of the Clinton administration to create the impression of achievement at the NATO Summit. In practical terms, the Partnership for Peace is a system of bilateral relationships between NATO and individual Eastern governments that will be managed by the Partnership Coordination Cell at Mons. The cell will promote programs of democratic control over armed forces, including discussion of defense budgets, that duplicate work now being done by the CSCE and the North Atlantic Cooperation Council. But the cell will also discuss structure, organization, and equipment of Eastern forces. To the extent that individual governments cooperate in the latter project, it will become easier for NATO to cooperate with NATO forces in joint peacekeeping missions, perhaps coordinated by one of the planned NATO Combined Joint Task Forces. In time, if the Partnership for Peace program is seriously pursued, some Eastern forces would become compatible with NATO forces in organization, equipment, and doctrine.

Evidently, the Partnership for Peace program could be helpful for the event of definitive turn of Russia to an aggressive policy. In such circumstances, existence of the partnership should make it easier for the NATO countries to extend additional guarantees and to cooperate with the forces of partnership countries in practical defense. But can NATO make good on its pledge of full membership if Russia remains relatively cooperative and, after four to five years of fulfilling NATO suggestions, the more assiduous and worried Eastern countries ask NATO to fulfill its pledge? In this situation, Russia is likely to maintain its opposition to NATO membership and to be listened to by the U.S. and other Western governments.

A second problem of the Partnership for Peace program is its overlap with the functions of the North Atlantic Cooperation Council and its unclear relationship with that organization, founded in 1991 to promote cooperation on security issues between NATO members and the Eastern states. If it had not been for the desire of the Clinton administration to make a mark of its own at the 1994 NATO Summit with the Partnership for Peace, the more logical course would have been to combine a declaration of NATO's willingness to contemplate expanded membership in future with actions aimed at building up the North Atlantic Cooperation Council. Now both the Cooperation Council and the Partnership for Peace will send representatives and share common facilities at NATO's political headquarters in Brussels, but only partnership signatories will have access to the more military

Partnership Coordination Cell and detail staff officers to it. In the last year the Cooperation Council, although understaffed and underbudgeted, has done some good practical coordination of peacekeeping preparations. If the partnership is to be mainly bilateral, the Cooperation Council could give the partnership a multilateral dimension. But for operational purposes, so could a combined joint task force.

Because of its comprehensive membership, the NACC is highly suited to the goal of extending the web of Western European security and stability eastward. It already provides an opening for emergency consultation with the North Atlantic Council, supposedly the main benefit for new members of the project for associate membership as well as of the Partnership for Peace. The detailed program for cooperation in peacekeeping, including joint maneuvers, staff exercises, and logistical planning agreed at the NACC meetings in June and December 1993 should not be lost. The NACC, operating under the aegis of the UN or the CSCE, could also provide some noncombatant help in some of the many ethnic conflicts, like Nagorno-Karabakh, which are undermining the possibility of democratic development in the former Soviet Union. NATO will also have to solve the problem of whether non-NATO countries, especially Russia, will accept for their units command by a NATO combined joint task force over the postconflict peacekeeping forces which someday will be needed in the former Yugoslavia and elsewhere in Europe.

Promoting the North Atlantic Cooperation Council, which has the potential ultimately to become a pan-European security organization integrating all the states of Europe, or some better thought through amalgam of the Cooperation Council and the Partnership for Peace, could convert the Partnership for Peace from a slogan to a meaningful contribution to European security. Despite this confusion over roles, after the Brussels Summit, it was at least assured that NATO's program of military cooperation with the Eastern states would receive better attention and funding.

CSCE's FUTURE

The logical destiny for the CSCE is to become a real regional United Nations. In theory, the CSCE already covers all the same areas of activity as the UN. It is more advanced than the UN in some respects, including human and minority rights, conciliation, and mediation. But it has a long way to go before it achieves the authority within Europe that the UN enjoys. The big issue facing the CSCE now is whether to move from its present status as an organization based on a network of intergovernmental political understandings to a treaty-based institution of collective security with some supranational characteristics, as urged by France and Russia.

Of the many proposals to this effect, one of the best is the proposal developed by the Hamburg Institute for Peace Research and Security Policy for a "European Security Community," or ESC.[14] An especially worthwhile feature of the Hamburg Institute proposal is its carefully worked out separation of powers, designed to prevent dominance by any of the ESC institutions while preserving the organization's ability to decide and to act in nearly all circumstances. The principal body of the ESC, the Security Council, is the assembly of all member states. It votes on major issues like sanctions or possible military intervention by simple majority to assure that it can decide. The ESC's twenty-member Standing Commission includes members of the UN Security Council—the United States, France, Great Britain, and Russia (and Germany, if the latter gets a Security Council seat)—as permanent members without a veto, with other members rotating. The Standing Commission is subordinate to the all-member Security Council. The task of the commission is to formulate in specific terms how decisions of principle by the Security Council to impose sanctions or to intervene militarily should be carried out. But its decisions can be over-turned by a two-thirds vote of the all-member Security Council. The pow-erful secretary general would have the authority to deploy preventive peacekeeping forces immediately—a highly desirable feature—but only the Security Council can commit these forces to combat. It can also reverse decisions of the secretary general by qualified majority. Objections that the non-European members of CSCE, the United States and Canada, would have against joining a European organization with such powers are resolved by giving these countries a special status exempt from some requirements.

The ESC plan also has many useful, innovative individual compo-nents, among them the use of radio and satellite television to inform the population in a conflict area of developments in the conflict and in the outside world; the broad peacekeeping training foreseen for ESC person-nel including public order, maintaining essential services, refugee care, medical services, and food distribution; and also the novel idea that the ESC should have the capacity to incur debts on international financial markets in the name of member states that are delinquent in their pay-ments to the organization or failing to live up to other commitments—in short, a system of hefty fines.

There are many obstacles to the development of the CSCE into a treaty-based organization with supranational powers as proposed by the Hamburg Institute. One of the most serious is similar to that encountered by the project to extend NATO membership to Eastern Europe: All mem-bers of the European Security Community would have to guarantee the present borders and territorial integrity of member states and agree to move with joint military forces against those who seek to change these borders forcibly, many already heavily contested.

But the CSCE does not have to adopt the treaty obligations proposed by the Hamburg Institute in order to make progress toward a point where it can become a regional UN. For this, the immediate need is improvement of CSCE's capacity to reach rapid, effective decisions on particularly difficult questions. The CSCE foreign ministers already have the authority to adopt the organizational components of the ESC plan described here—Security Council assembly, Standing Commission, and enhanced authority for the secretary general. They should give serious study to the possibility.

CONCLUSIONS

In this chapter, we have been searching to define a more productive relationship among NATO, WEU, and CSCE that will permit them to contribute more effectively to a solution of current European security problems. Desirable as it would be to have a single, cohesive, well-organized European regional peacekeeping organization that functioned effectively, this is unlikely to happen anytime soon.

Of the various concepts that have been advanced, the most practical synthesis would call for improvement of CSCE decisionmaking; for building up the North Atlantic Cooperation Council and the Partnership for Peace, expanded to include interested neutrals, to carry out peacekeeping operations under the auspices of the CSCE; and for promoting the long-term development of the WEU. In the very long term, if democracy in Russia one day succeeds in establishing firm roots, NATO, having also fulfilled its new post-cold war functions, could transfer its infrastructure and other assets to WEU as the main military defender of the European Union states. At the same time, the North Atlantic Cooperation Council or a new NATO enlarged to include Russia as a member could be melded with CSCE as its pan-European security arm. For the long interim until something like this could materialize, NATO itself would continue its separate role as overall guarantor against major war in Europe, while the WEU and the North Atlantic Cooperation Council and Partnership for Peace were being expanded and improved.

In addition to the main condition of achieving enduring democracy in Russia, two basic conditions remain to be fulfilled if this long-term possibility is ever to materialize: First, there must be an even deeper understanding with France over the WEU-NATO relationship that gives full weight to the progress of integration of the European Union on the one hand and to the development potential of the North Atlantic Cooperation Council on the other.

Second, and more important, governments and publics must acknowledge that changes of machinery are not a substitute for more effective efforts to cope with the conflicts that are now going on in Europe and those that threaten to erupt soon. It is legitimate and necessary to learn from past difficulties and to try to prevent their return through proposing new structures and measures. But what is the real use unless the existing resources of European security institutions are actively used, including, where necessary, in peacemaking enforcement operations to contain conflicts now taking place?

A policy that in reality consists of permitting existing conflicts to burn themselves out while establishing still more elaborate mechanisms to cope with the next outbreak of organized violence is both cruel and illusory. Cruel because it awakens hopes that will not be fulfilled; unless the hurdle of committing adequate forces to peacemaking can be surmounted, the cycle of violence will recur. Illusory, because as the killing goes on and the towns and villages continue to burn, public and legislative support for the security institutions of Europe will also be consumed in the flames.

14

MOVING TOWARD A LESS VIOLENT WORLD—TEST CASE, EUROPE

This book is a report card on the most ambitious attempt yet launched to prevent and control war and armed conflict, an attempt whose success or failure can have decisive effects on the peace and security of our planet. The authentic heroes of the book—however appealing or unappealing in other contexts—are Mikhail Gorbachev, Eduard Shevardnadze, Boris Yeltsin, Ronald Reagan, George Shultz, Margaret Thatcher, George Bush, James Baker, Helmut Kohl, Hans Dietrich Genscher, and François Mitterrand. Assisted by skilled and creative subordinates, their achievement was to effect political change of epochal dimensions almost entirely free of violence and bloodshed. It is unparalleled in human experience that change of this significance—eclipse of the cold war nuclear confrontation, elimination of Stalinist rule in the USSR, withdrawal of Soviet forces from Eastern Europe, and German unification—should take place without armed conflict.

This achievement made possible the sudden emergence of a functioning if rudimentary global security system based on the United Nations, bolstered by regional security organizations. It can also inspire the nations and peoples of the world to renew efforts to move toward the old dream of a world without war.

In the past, most people thought of war between nations and armed violence inside nations as a natural disaster, like earthquakes, floods, or forest fires—a disaster with which people would seek to cope after it happened.

But our century, largely because it has been the bloodiest in recorded history, has broken with the tradition of accepting war as an incurable affliction of humanity. Drawing on the lessons of history, military experience, and social psychology, a broad range of measures has been developed to prevent conflict, to contain conflict if it occurs, and to end it. The spectrum includes conflict prevention, mediation, conflict resolution and peacekeeping, confidence-building and transparency measures, restrictions on deployment and activities of armed forces, negotiated force reductions and limitations, and control over weapons production and proliferation. Even applying these measures more widely and systematically than heretofore, it will probably not be possible to end all armed conflict. But it has become more feasible to think about preventing specific conflicts and about bringing them to a more rapid end if they do occur and in this way gradually to lower the level of violence throughout the world. Moving toward this goal is an enormously hopeful yet practical activity for governments and peoples everywhere.

At the same time, it is obvious from the many actual and potential wars described in this book that the complex of European regional security institutions that emerged so rapidly from the cold war is already on trial. This system will either continue growing in capacity or it will wither into formalism and ultimately be replaced by a system that neorealist political scientists believe reflects the natural state of international relations—a system based on the competitive interaction of individual states trying to maximize their security through expanding their own military capabilities, perhaps including nuclear capabilities, moving in and out of alliances and coalitions in a ceaseless search for balance and stability—behavior that, historically, has prevented some wars but caused many others.[1]

The jury that is monitoring this test and that will reach the verdict on the future of the multilateral security approach is composed of the governments and publics of the world's industrialized states, large and small, including nonnuclear Sweden, Belgium, Italy, and Germany, as well as several states outside Europe—Japan, Taiwan, and South Korea. The countries in this group are the world's main consumers of "security services." In the past, many of them depended on protection given by the United States, but they now increasingly rely on a broader multilateral system. These countries have strong military potential, including the capacity to produce nuclear weapons far more rapidly and effectively than the Irans or Iraqs of this world.[2] At present, they prefer on the ground of rational considerations of better results and less cost to entrust their security to multilateral systems of cooperative security.

These industrialized states keep the international system going. Over the next decades, the European states in this group will make up their minds about the performance of the multilateral European security system and its capacity to meet their main security interests. Their two chief requirements are effective control over nuclear weapons in all their aspects and a reasonably safe international environment, providing increasingly effective assurances against loss of life and destruction of economic resources through conflict, especially in their own region.

Europe is the test case for the workability of the new global system as well as the chief laboratory for trying out institutions and measures of multilateral security. On the one hand, Europe has the worst security problems of any of the world's regions. The problems of control over nuclear weapons and proliferation, although worldwide, are at their most acute in the former Soviet Union. The outcome there, even more than in Iraq or North Korea, will be decisive in determining whether nuclear weapons will continue to shrink in number and significance or once again become the dominant feature of global politics as they were during the cold war, but this time spreading into many hands. Europe, still drenched with the blood of two world wars, is also the scene of some of the world's worst outbreaks of ethnic violence.

On the other hand, Europe also has the world's most developed array of institutions and measures to cope with armed conflict and war. NATO, with its overwhelmingly strong armed forces, has reorganized itself for crisis management and peacekeeping. Creatively, NATO officials have established the North Atlantic Cooperation Council and the Partnership for Peace to form active links with the countries of Eastern Europe and the former Soviet Union. The Conference on Security and Cooperation in Europe, which takes in nearly all the European states plus the United States and Canada, has created a broad array of institutions and procedures, many of them highly innovative, for conciliation, mediation, conflict prevention, and protecting the rights of national minorities. A revitalized Western European Union, designated by the European Union as its defense arm, also has some experience in peacekeeping, with the potential for further development. The European Union itself, despite disagreements over the degree of future integration, is still expanding its membership and has taken on additional responsibilities for European security. It has played an active role in mediating and monitoring in the former Yugoslav republics. The United Nations too is deeply involved in the Yugoslav states and, increasingly, in conflicts in the former Soviet Union.

European security is a test for global security because the governments supporting this impressive institutional lineup, including those of the United States, the European Union, and Russia as well, together control the world's greatest military and economic resources. If these governments and the multilateral security institutions that the governments have tried so hard to improve cannot cope effectively with Europe's security problems, then what can make such a security system work, in Europe or worldwide?

Sadly, the heroes that brought about the cold war builddown, as well as their successors, are also responsible for the failure of the new European multilateral security system to cope more effectively with the problems that have emerged as the cold war confrontation splintered into scores of explosive fragments. Human lives were saved in the relatively bloodless process of dismantling the Soviet imperium, but were sacrificed by the thousands in ethnic violence in the former Yugoslavia and the Soviet successor states. An eruption of nationalistic animosity between Russia and Ukraine put at stake the entire regime of nuclear arms control. Ethnic tensions surrounding Albanian residents of Serbia and Macedonia could trigger interstate war.

THE NUCLEAR ELEMENT

Even after the end of the cold war, nuclear weapons remain the chief danger to both the United States and the European states, either through direct attack by a known or secret nuclear weapon state, or through collapse of the nonproliferation regime and deterioration of the international environment to one composed of a score of nuclear weapons states competing against one another to maximize their own security.

These dangers do not have the immediacy of the nuclear Armageddon that could have erupted within minutes during the cold war. Nonetheless, they are serious. The United States and the European states could suffer immense devastation from direct attack from a nuclear weapons state like Russia or China or from concealed weapons brought into their major cities.

The combination of ethnic conflict and political instability with large nuclear arsenals has resulted in Europe's most serious security problem. Russia and three other Soviet successor states with nuclear weapons are moved by strong currents of nationalism; their economies are tottering. Each has a government on which unreformed communists and right-wing nationalist groups already have considerable influence. The only major argument about Russia's instability is whether it will last ten, twenty, or thirty years; more possibly, the latter.

In its first years, the Clinton administration did a good, although incomplete, job in nuclear arms control. As described in Chapter 4, the administration actively pursued proliferation dangers in Ukraine as well as in North Korea, and pressed for early implementation of the START treaties. It has also urged negotiation on a comprehensive ban on testing of nuclear warheads, and proposed an international agreement on ending production of fissile material for weapons. It energetically promoted the indefinite extension of the Non-Proliferation Treaty.

If all these projects can be successfully carried out, there would be a more effective nonproliferation regime, development of new nuclear weapons would be made more difficult, and operational deployment of strategic-range nuclear weapons by the United States and Russia would be cut back to levels that existed when the Non-Proliferation Treaty entered into force in the early 1970s. A treaty ending production of fissile material for weapons could bring an upper limit on the maximum size of the arsenals of the nuclear weapons states, both declared and undeclared.

These achievements would be very important. The big loophole in U.S. policy, however, is that the administration has not yet put forward a long-term program of nuclear arms control that would comprehensively address the dangers of the Russian nuclear arsenal and result in its irreversible reduction. The large holdings of the nuclear weapons states, especially Russia, and the United States as well, create two main problems. One is their significance for the future success of the nonproliferation regime: Without a sense that the world supply of nuclear weapons is steadily contracting and that the possibility of actual use of nuclear weapons is steadily lessening, it will not be possible over time to enlist the voluntary cooperation of scores of nonnuclear states necessary for effective operation of the nonproliferation regime.

The second, more immediate problem is the serious dangers that arise from the incomplete nature of the current U.S.-Russian nuclear arms control regime and, to a lesser extent, from the failure so far to involve China—and Britain and France as well—in negotiated reductions of their nuclear arsenals. These shortcomings have to be remedied or the nuclear dangers from Russia will continue to threaten Western security, and the opportunity brought by the end of the cold war for radical departure from nuclear confrontation may be lost. Time is not on the side of the Western states in this matter: Russia is moving to the right politically and its willingness to agree on far-reaching steps on nuclear weapons may already have decreased in the upsurge of national feeling reflected in the December 1993 election results.

What is needed is to articulate a Western nuclear arms control program that can cope better with current dangers and, by defining a long-term goal, can also infuse nuclear arms control and nonproliferation activities with purpose and direction during the coming decade or more. The first, most urgent step toward this goal is to begin now with reciprocal monitoring and irreversible builddown of Russian and U.S. arsenals, using measures and techniques that can later be applied to all nuclear weapons states.[3]

DANGERS FROM EXISTING ARSENALS

The Clinton administration has continued the Bush program of buying up to 500 tons of highly enriched uranium from Russian nuclear weapons to be converted into fuel for nuclear reactors through diluting it with natural uranium. This is a valuable program for bringing about enduring reduction of the Russian arsenal. However, statements by Russia's minister of atomic energy Viktor Mikhailov indicate that both Russian stocks of highly enriched uranium for weapons and Russian weapons totals are considerably larger than originally estimated in the West. Moreover, the buyout program will take up to twenty years to complete.[4]

The United States and Russia are also engaged in dismantling warheads of tactical-range delivery systems withdrawn from operational deployment by informal agreement between the Bush and Gorbachev governments. But there is no formal agreement on this subject between the two governments, as yet no verification or monitoring of the dismantling process or of resulting stocks of fissile material. The United States has funded the design of a new long-term storage facility in Russia for nuclear weapons and fissile material, one aspect of which is increased transparency on what is being stored. But after construction starts on this facility, it too may take a decade to complete.

In an important innovative proposal raised by President Bill Clinton in his speech at the UN in September 1993, the administration has said it would as a unilateral gesture place weapons-grade fissile material excess to its military needs under international supervision.[5] A month before President Clinton presented his proposal, the Russian delegate at the Geneva-based conference on disarmament made a similar suggestion. The size of the stock of fissile material to be retained by the United States as a strategic reserve was not decided at the time of the proposal, but it is sure to be sizable. The administration intends this program of handing over plutonium and highly enriched uranium to internationally supervised storage as a demonstration project to encourage similar action by other nuclear powers on a voluntary basis. At the January 1994 Moscow Summit, President Yeltsin indicated willingness to consider parallel action but did not then undertake a specific commitment. He did agree to establishment of a United States-Russian working group to examine the possibility. However, even if Russia does decide to hand over a portion of its fissile material to international supervision, this will not of itself give insight into what Russia is retaining or any control over it.

All of this activity is valuable. However, it circles around the periphery of the main problem, what to do now about Russia's huge stockpile of already-fabricated weapons and already-produced fissile material, more than 30,000 warheads, 1,000 tons of highly enriched uranium, and 100 tons of weapons-grade plutonium.[6]

The main effect of the U.S.-Russian START nuclear arms control agreements is to withdraw a large portion of U.S. and Russian strategic nuclear forces from operational field deployment to stored, reserve status. These agreements merit every support because they greatly decrease the short-term risk of nuclear war. But, with the exception of the twenty-year project to purchase enriched uranium from Russia, the reductions foreseen in the START Treaties are not permanent or irreversible. There is no agreed limit on the number of existing weapons in storage or the amount of weapons-grade fissile material that the two countries may retain in their stockpiles, nor is there any exchange of data on or verification of these stockpiles, as there is under the START Treaties for warheads and delivery systems still deployed in the field. In March 1994, Secretary of Energy Hazel O'Leary concluded a tentative understanding with Minister Mikhailov to exchange observers to look at warhead dismantling in the two countries on a trial basis.[7] This was a breakthrough in principle, but it was not clear whether the observers would in time become part of a wider systematic approach to the problem or this development would remain symbolic. If the proposed multilateral agreement to end production of fissile material for weapons is achieved and goes into effect in several years, it will cap the growth capability of nuclear arsenals, but it will not apply to present holdings either.

Some missile launchers—submarines equipped to fire ballistic missiles and silos for withdrawn missiles—will be destroyed under START I. The United States has already destroyed many silos; Russia even more. However, there is also no Russian-American agreement, aside from the important provision in START II requiring destruction of the Russian SS–18 heavy-load missiles, to destroy the actual intercontinental-range missiles withdrawn from operational deployment under reduction agreements or to restrict their production. Like warheads withdrawn from the field under reduction agreements, these missiles can be stored for later deployment. START I contains a verified upper limit on the number of mobile missiles that can be stored by Russia, but it is a generous one. Ukraine and Kazakhstan have insisted that missiles deployed on their territories be destroyed rather than returned to Russia for possible future use, but aside from the SS–18s, there is no commitment by Russia to destroy the strategic-range missiles deployed on its own territory.

The December 1993 Russian elections moved the country to the right and brought into sight the possible emergence of authoritarian government in Russia, whether by parliamentary means or by coup. Such a government could at some point use its reserves of warheads, missiles, and fissile material to organize rapid, large-scale expansion of Russian nuclear forces, reinstituting the nuclear competition that was the most frightening aspect of the cold war. Moreover, although a decisive move to the right could come suddenly at any time, it will be many years before it can become clear that functioning democratic institutions have really taken root in Russia and have a real chance of surviving. This means that, unless there is decisive bad news sooner, the unstable political conditions of Russia and Ukraine will probably last for decades.

Problems of instability in Russia are intensified by rising rates of crime and official corruption, including in the armed forces, as well as the depressing economic conditions that affect rations and pay of the forces and account for very low morale. In 1992, some 40,000 charges of corruption were brought against members of the Russian armed forces. In the same year, the Russian defense ministry reported 4,000 cases of theft of conventional weapons from military depots and nearly 6,500 cases in 1993.[8] Continuing ethnic clashes in Russia and the neighboring republics add to the problem: In 1990, extremists tried to take over a storage site with tactical nuclear weapons near the capital of Azerbaijan.

In these conditions, the risk of forcible seizure of nuclear warheads or weapons-grade fissile materials by extremists and of theft or illegal sale of weapons or fissile material will remain unacceptably high, as will the possibility of leakage of nuclear knowledge or components through ineffective export controls or hiring Russian weapons experts. North Korea has already sought to do in the field of missile construction. In presenting the National Academy of Sciences report on plutonium disposal in January 1994, Professor Wolfgang Panofsky said members of his panel were of the unanimous view that in present conditions the Russian nuclear stockpile constitutes a clear and present danger to U.S. security.[9] Russian officials insist that strict control has been maintained over warheads and that they have been able to frustrate some attempts to steal fissile material in order to sell it. But Washington has no direct knowledge of the situation. There is no monitoring, no data exchange, and no verification arrangements.

Panofsky's remarks about the dangers of the Russian stockpile for the United States are even more applicable to Europe. Short of outright attack with nuclear weapons, most of the dangers of the Russian arsenal—theft, illegal sale, forcible seizure by extremist groups, accidental discharge, or even use in local conflict, say, between Russia and Ukraine—pose a greater risk to Europe than to the United States. Unless action is taken to deal with it, Western countries are going to be faced by a dangerous situation as concerns nuclear weapons in Russia for decades to come, a period in which continuing Western worry over this topic is likely to be repeatedly punctuated by dramatic, worrisome incidents. This situation is dangerous in its own right, potentially highly so. Beyond that, it will almost certainty sap and undermine Western willingness to continue the economic help and political support essential for long-term development of democracy in Russia, thus helping to perpetuate the underlying dangers. The logical solution to this problem is to get as many of these weapons and as much fissile material as possible out of Russia, or at least out of exclusive Russian control, at the necessary cost of reciprocal actions by the United States. This is precisely what future Western nuclear arms control policy should seek to do.

In sum, there is far more danger both to the United States and to the European states from already existing Russian nuclear weapons and fissile materials than there is from the possibility of their future covert development by Third World countries. North Korea, bad as it is, may have two or three warheads; Russia has at least 30,000. Further START-type reductions that withdraw weapons from field deployment with the option of storing them indefinitely are not an adequate answer to these problems of stocks of tens of thousands of nuclear warheads, hundreds of tons of highly enriched uranium, and tons of plutonium in Russia and at least six other countries.

Relevant to this issue, of course, is the future nuclear strategy of the United States and of Great Britain and France. What purposes will nuclear weapons serve in future? The study of long-term nuclear weapons policy for the United States begun in the fall of 1993 by former secretary of defense Les Aspin could be a useful contribution to answering this question, although first indications were that it might be a fairly orthodox endorsement of a classic deterrence posture. Perhaps it can be agreed that the main justification for nuclear weapons now is to discourage war of any kind between the nuclear weapons states and to deter use of nuclear weapons by declared or clandestine nuclear weapons states through the capacity to retaliate. If so, these reasons indicate that nuclear weapons will be with us for a long time to come.

As long as the threat is one from rational governments concerned over the welfare of their populations, this deterrence approach may hold. However, if the fear is that unstable governments headed by political extremists or extremist groups outside government may gain control of nuclear weapons, then the traditional deterrence approach becomes less convincing, and measures directed at better control over the weapons themselves become even more important. The alternative is to deploy a larger U.S. nuclear force indefinitely to cope with contingencies arising in other nuclear weapons states, especially Russia and China. But this alternative is more dangerous, less effective, and, in the long run, more costly in economic and political terms than reducing the arsenals of all the nuclear weapons states and tightening the nonproliferation regime.

A potential answer to these problems is an approach with three stages: a stage making the START reductions irreversible, a post-START arms control program, and a third stage that we can call the "final stage of nuclear arms control." All three stages would share three common features missing from the current administration program. First, they would provide for bilateral or multilateral monitoring of storage of warheads and fissile material. Second, instead of simply storing warheads reduced by agreement or fissile material from these weapons in the hands of the owner government, they would provide for dismantling all reduced warheads and transferring their fissile material to bilaterally or multilaterally monitored storage. Finally, they would provide for destruction of most reduced missiles and drastic restrictions on their future production.

MAKING START IRREVERSIBLE

The necessary steps in this first stage are:

1.   To establish a reciprocal U.S.-Russian system of monitoring stocks of warheads and fissile materials produced for weapons in both countries through a portal-perimeter system similar to that still used in the treaty on intermediate-range nuclear missiles and applied to existing storage sites. The bilateral monitoring system would be superimposed on existing custody arrangements. Russian and U.S. personnel would continue guarding their own weapon storage facilities. The system would be designed solely to assure that warheads and fissile material are not withdrawn from storage without authorization previously agreed by the two governments. Access to details of weapons design would not be necessary.

The presence of monitors would help to inhibit the main dangers: forcible seizure, theft, illegal sale, or use of stored fissile materials to make more weapons. Monitors can be overpowered but not without giving warning. The director of the Pantex plant in Amarillo, Texas, the United States' only weapons assembly plant, has publicly stated that Russian monitoring of his plant is feasible without access to design information.[10] The priority recommendation of the National Academy panel on disposal of fissile material is to set up a reciprocal U.S.-Russian regime for stockpile monitoring.

The administration has been considering transparency measures to be applied at some future point to storage sites in Russia and the United States and some degree of monitoring in a weapons plant in each country. Why not go the whole way and monitor all warhead and fissile material storage in both countries, meeting the risks in Russia now, while they are at their peak, and possibly in Ukraine as well? These measures would also provide useful precedents and experience for subsequent monitoring of storage of warheads and fissile material in other nuclear weapons countries.

2. Comprehensive data exchange between the United States and Russia on holdings of warheads (deployed and stored) and of fissile material for weapons. The Biden Condition (named after its sponsor, Senator Joseph Biden, and agreed to by the U.S. Senate in ratifying START I for application to START II and subsequent agreements) requires reciprocal inspections, data exchanges, and other cooperative measures to monitor the number of nuclear stockpile weapons on the territory of both countries and the location and inventory of facilities for producing or processing fissile materials. There have been repeated proposals over the years for data exchange, warhead tagging, and so on, so far to no effect.

3. Agreement between the United States and Russia to dismantle all strategic warheads withdrawn from operational deployment under the START Treaties and subsequent agreements, as well as tactical warheads withdrawn unilaterally, not to reuse their fissile material for weapons, and to transfer this material to storage monitored bilaterally or by the International Atomic Energy Agency (IAEA), or preferably, by a combination of bilateral and IAEA monitoring, using both sensors and continuous on-site personnel. The purpose of transferring the fissile material from reduced warheads to monitored custody is to confirm that the owner country is definitively renouncing the right to use this material for weapons. The owner country would maintain the right to withdraw the highly enriched uranium in order to downgrade it for use in its own power reactors or to sell it. In theory, the same arrangement could be applied to plutonium. But it would be far preferable to make permanent the transfer of weapons-grade plutonium to monitored storage. Storage of plutonium would be monitored until long-term methods of disposing of this uniquely dangerous material were agreed. To make the transfer measure effective, both countries would formally agree not to produce further fissile material for weapons. (Neither is doing so now except for Russia's production of plutonium in

three reactors also used for city heating, which would be safe-guarded.) This bilateral pledge would boost prospects for a multilateral ban on production of fissile material for weapons, which would later replace the bilateral commitment.

Verification of this scheme as it applies to dismantling strategic warheads need not be complicated: The number of deployed weapons prior to reductions has been computed for START. It should be possible to agree on the amount of fissile material contained in each type of warhead to calculate the total amount to be turned over to monitored storage. Whether it would be feasible to move the stored fissile material, especially the plutonium, out of the territory of the owner country to some internationally controlled storage site, is a separate question for later study. This move would be desirable.

For the United States, a pledge to reduce strategic weapons would probably require expansion of dismantling facilities or the use of extra teams to permit use of existing facilities for longer hours. At current work rates, the United States' sole facility is fully occupied with dismantling warheads from tactical-range delivery systems. Russia is believed to have additional facilities that could be used for dismantling. Expanded dismantling would provide more work for jobless Russian weapons experts.

4. At the same time, the two governments should agree to destroy all missiles withdrawn from field deployment to comply with reduction agreements and to end production of these missiles. In both cases, an exception would be made for a limited agreed number for space launch purposes. All actual space launches would be inspected prior to launch. Missile testing would end. Successful fulfillment of the requirement in the INF Treaty calling for destruction of all U.S. and Russian missiles of this class has brought valuable experience for verifying such an agreement. A Russian-U.S. missile reduction agreement could serve as the basis for a worldwide treaty to ban production or deployment of missiles with ranges over one hundred kilometers except for carefully verified space launch purposes. It would at the least give added authority and effectiveness to multilateral efforts to restrict sale of missile components.

5. In this next stage of U.S.-Russian nuclear arms control, the two governments could also move toward what one expert calls "zero alert," a situation where still-deployed warheads are

dismounted from missiles as well as aircraft and separately stored and missile launching submarines are delayed by agreed measures in preparations to fire their missiles. If a comprehensive system of U.S.-Russian nuclear monitoring has already been agreed, separate storage of warheads under zero alert could also be bilaterally monitored.[11]

The U.S. and Russian governments have both adopted the vocabulary of irreversible reductions. At the January 1994 Moscow Summit, the administration proposed and Russia agreed to establish a working group "to consider steps to ensure the transparency and irreversibility" of nuclear reductions. The first task of the working group was to review the administration proposal to place a portion of weapons-grade fissile material of the United States—and Russia if it agrees—under international monitoring. This proposal is a potential first step in the direction of warhead dismantling and builddown of stocks of fissile material, but it will be voluntary and it will rest on unilateral decisions by Russia and the United States on how much of its fissile material stocks each wants to transfer to international monitoring. Instead, this process should be made obligatory, perhaps by administrative agreement between the two governments, while the Russian government is still in a position to do so. Halfway measures, such as further negotiated warhead reductions of the START type, will not suffice. An unstable Russia with a thousand still-deployed strategic warheads and thousands more in reserve would still be lethally dangerous.

It will not be easy to gain agreement to this concept of irreversible builddown of nuclear arsenals. Atomic Energy Minister Mikhailov wants to use weapons-grade plutonium from nuclear weapons to fuel Russian energy reactors. Moreover, both U.S. and Russian military leaders would strongly prefer to stockpile warheads and fissile material against future contingencies than to give them up for good. They want to do the same thing with strategic-range missiles. But that approach would perpetuate the dangers of the Russian arsenal.

An alternate approach has been informally suggested by some representatives at the Geneva-based UN Conference on Disarmament. They have in mind a treaty that would follow conclusion of an accord ending production of fissile material for weapons or complement it. The new treaty would obligate its signatories to turn over to international custody a portion of their overall holdings of weapons-grade fissile material, whether in deployed weapons, stockpiled warheads, or unweaponized fissile material, that is excess to a negotiated level. The level would be periodically lowered over a period of years until stockpiles were very low or perhaps fully depleted. The obligation to transfer a portion of present stocks could also be applied at some point to stocks of weapons-usable plutonium for power reactors or highly enriched uranium from research or naval reactors. This idea deserves consideration for later use. However, rather than undertaking a cumbersome and time-consuming project to draft and negotiate a new international treaty at this point, it seems simpler and more practical to begin with bilateral Russian-American agreement to transfer to monitored storage the fissile material from dismantled weapons and then to extend this practice to other nuclear weapons states. In the case of Russia and the United States, already-fabricated weapons constitute more than half of estimated stocks of highly enriched uranium and weapons-grade plutonium. Stocks of stored fissile material not yet fabricated into weapons could be dealt with at a later, more transparent stage.

FIVE-POWER DISARMAMENT

If agreement has been reached on this bilateral U.S.-Russian program, the next logical stage of nuclear arms control should combine deep negotiated cuts in the arsenals of all five declared nuclear weapons states with moves to make these reductions irreversible. Russia has already pointed out that negotiated nuclear reductions beyond the START levels would have to include Great Britain, France, and China.

This stage is based on the assumption, despite present uncertainties, that Ukraine's and North Korea's problems will be resolved, START II is ratified and both START Treaties are on their way to implementation, a comprehensive test-ban treaty has been concluded, together with a treaty ending production of fissile material for weapons covering the five nuclear powers and also the three undeclared nuclear weapons states—Israel, India, and Pakistan—and that agreement has been achieved on extending the Non-Proliferation Treaty either indefinitely or for a considerable period.

This sequence of actions may not come off. In particular, ratification of START II by the new Russian Duma is open to many doubts. At best, the ratification process will be difficult and it may require renegotiation of some aspects of the treaty, especially those which eliminate the Russian SS–18 heavy missiles while permitting a large preponderance of submarine-launched missiles for the United States. If the Duma fails to ratify START II, the two governments might be willing to act to carry out many of its provisions by executive agreement, but it is likely that pressures from the Duma and also the U.S. Senate would place limits on such actions. In such a situation, a bilateral U.S.-Russian agreement to monitor stocks of warheads and fissile material would be all the more needed. If renegotiation is required, the two governments should move directly to a still more advanced reduction agreement that prescribes even more drastic reductions than START II's 3,000-warhead level, cutting more deeply into U.S. submarine-based missiles and that has the features of irreversibility described here. In the circumstances, such a new agreement might be more acceptable to the Duma than START II.

If START II or a replacement is ratified, the post-START stage of nuclear arms control should consist first of agreement by the United States and Russia to continue with negotiated irreversible reduction of their own arsenals, followed by action to draw Great Britain, France, and China into the reduction process. As suggested by several leading experts, the United States and Russia could first reduce to 1,000 warheads.[12] Then they would join the other three countries in a series of further reduction steps. In addition to agreement on step-by-step reduction of arsenals to low levels, the other three countries would also agree to conditions similar to those of the U.S.-Russian disarmament program. In this stage, stockpiles of plutonium for civilian reactors could also be transferred to monitored custody so that those countries that operate plutonium reactors for power would not have weapons-usable stocks of fissile material at their disposal; the material could still be withdrawn on a supervised basis when needed for energy production.

A final stage of nuclear arms control short of a possible later decision to eliminate the weapons entirely could be subsequently achieved through an agreement among the five nuclear powers to reduce their total arsenals to no more than 200 warheads each, to separate these warheads from their delivery systems, and to place both the warheads and the delivery systems under multilateral control on the territory of the owner states. The level of 200 warheads is selected for reasons of negotiability as slightly lower than the British nuclear arsenal and considerably lower than the French or Chinese levels, thus requiring some reduction by all. All declared nuclear powers would commit themselves to dismantle the warheads reduced to reach the 200-warhead level and to place all weapons-grade fissile material from them as well as their remaining stocks of fissile material for weapons under international monitoring as reductions are carried out.

Publicly defining this final stage of nuclear arms control will create understanding and support for the many necessary intervening steps. Once nuclear weapons are actually neutralized as suggested here, they will cease to be a major factor in international security or international politics. Neutralizing the weapons will create conditions in which still further improvements in the nonproliferation regime can be pursued, the ultimate future of nuclear weapons can be dispassionately discussed, and in which, most importantly, the lengthy task of building an international security system of greater effectiveness can be more seriously addressed.

Our pursuit of ways to reduce the dangers to the West of nuclear weapons in Russia has brought us to the path of a comprehensive nuclear arms reduction scheme. But this broad approach, which enlists all five nuclear weapons states in drastic, irreversible builddown of nuclear weapon capability, neutralizing the small remaining arsenals by placing their warheads under international monitoring, is probably the only way to gain a secure grip on Russian dangers.

How feasible is this scheme? If the five nuclear powers were asked to sign on to it today, all would very likely refuse outright. However, bilateral monitoring of the Russian and U.S. nuclear stockpiles is not a futuristic idea, but a present necessity in the interest of the security of Europe and the United States. Russian-U.S. agreement to dismantle warheads reduced under the START treaties and to give up their right to reuse the fissile material would be a very big step. Yet both countries are dismantling tactical nuclear weapons withdrawn from operational deployment. Russia has agreed to dismantle the warheads brought from Ukraine, Belarus, and Kazakhstan and to transfer a large amount of highly enriched uranium from dismantled weapons to the United States. The United States and also Russia have agreed in principle to transfer some weapons-grade fissile material to international custody. Both governments are at least using the vocabulary of making reductions irreversible. The prospects are good for ultimate agreement on a multilateral treaty to cut off production of fissile material. Russia itself has in the past proposed both mutual monitoring of warhead stocks and mutual dismantling of reduced weapons. In February 1992 at the Geneva Conference on Disarmament, foreign minister Andrei Kozyrev proposed U.S.-Russian exchange of data and monitoring of stocks of warheads and fissile material. Prior to the conclusion in 1987 of the INF Treaty, Mikhail Gorbachev proposed destruction of the warheads of reduced missiles. Although the United States did not take up these suggestions when they were made, it should do so now.

YUGOSLAV ERRORS

The new and strengthened institutions of the European security system foundered seriously in the former Yugoslavia. The countries of the NATO alliance and of the former Warsaw Pact, pledged to cooperative peacekeeping in the CSCE and the NACC, with combined military forces of well over 5 million men, were unable to put a stop to fighting involving no more than 1 or 2 percent of that number at any given time. NATO, the CSCE, the European Community, the Western European Union, and the United Nations itself all failed in this mission.

Despite what NATO and the UN may still be able to do in peacekeeping in Bosnia, some enduring damage has been done to the confidence of governments and public opinion in these institutions. This is especially true for millions in Eastern Europe and in the former Soviet Union and around the world whose hopes that the European security institutions and the UN would be able to keep the post-cold war peace have been sorely disappointed. In a speech to the General Assembly of the Council of Europe in October 1992, Czech president Vaclav Havel said the conflict in the former Yugoslav republics had been the first great test for Europe in the post-cold war era. Europe's response, he said, was a failure on the same scale as its historic failures to cope with Nazism and Soviet tyranny.[13]

What went wrong with Western policy in the former Yugoslavia? Are there lessons to be learned for the future? Future analysts will develop their own lists of errors, but some can be identified now.

As regards the Western political approach to the dissolution of Yugoslavia, the Western countries were not ready with a negotiating framework of their own when the talks among the Yugoslav republics began to founder in the spring of 1991. The republics should have been kept in continuous negotiating session, as Peter Carrington, Cyrus Vance, David Owen, and Thorvald Stoltenberg all tried to do later. At the beginning, Yugoslav republic leaders were more impressionable than they became later and such a Western effort could have been effective. Western recognition of Slovene and Croat sovereignty under German pressure at the beginning of 1992 was a mistake because it triggered serious fighting in Croatia by Serbs against Croats. Even more damaging, with the experience of Croatia behind them, was the failure of the Western countries to persevere with the EC negotiations on the status of Bosnia before they recognized it as an independent state or at the very least to insist that, before Western recognition, a political understanding of some kind be reached among the Serb, Croat, and Muslim inhabitants of Bosnia. Given the probability that further ethnic conflicts will erupt in Europe, the continuing absence of agreement among Western countries on procedures for dealing with minorities seeking autonomy remains a dangerous gap in Western policy.

As regards peacemaking in the Yugoslav states, there is wide agreement that the Western powers missed an opportunity for effective military intervention at the outset of fighting in Slovenia and in Croatia when intervention could have prevented the outbreak of fighting or stifled it in its early stages. Perhaps the worst of these errors was the failure of the Western states, with the experience of bloody fighting in Croatia before their eyes, to fail to agree on the preventive deployment of a NATO or UN peacekeeping force in Bosnia before they recognized it as an independent state. In each of these cases, emphasis should have been on early action to prevent conflict from taking place or to extinguish it rapidly if it did break out, with minimum casualties to any of the forces involved, including the peacemakers.

There is plenty of hindsight corroboration that errors of this kind were made. Secretary of State Warren Christopher said in February 1993 that the West had missed repeated opportunities to engage in early effective ways that might have prevented the conflict in former Yugoslavia from deepening. The two senior officials of the Bush administration most responsible for policy in this area agreed after leaving office that early peacekeeping intervention could have been effective. In January 1993, General Brent Scowcroft, national security adviser to President Bush, told editors of the *Washington Post* that if a military force had been put in along the Croatian-Serbian border at the very beginning, it might have stopped the fighting before it got going. Former secretary of state Lawrence Eagleburger told a *Post* reporter in February that early coordinated multilateral action might have headed off the conflict. As reported in Chapter 6, NATO commander general John Galvin had the same view.[14]

Among other lessons of the former Yugoslavia are that effective early intervention designed to head off or contain organized violence must include a substantial ground-force component. The job cannot be done without it. Peripheral measures—sanctions, banning of air flights, and naval blockades, even air attacks—cannot stop killing on the ground. In the former Yugoslavia, the Western countries drew the wrong lessons from history to justify their reluctance to make a serious ground-force contribution. Neither the experience of the United States in Vietnam nor the German experience in the Balkans in World War II was applicable, militarily or politically, to the situation in this area in the 1990s. In Bosnia, UN forces were not trying to achieve foreign domination over the entire life of a country, but pursuing the far more modest goal of bringing about a durable cease-fire to save lives and improve prospects for negotiating a settlement. In Bosnia, there were no major outside powers, as there were in Vietnam and also in World War II Yugoslavia, to help indigenous forces against UN or NATO peacekeepers. To the contrary, Serbia and Montenegro were surrounded by an increasingly effective blockade. NATO forces had complete sea and air superiority, to a far larger extent than in Vietnam or World War II Yugoslavia. Despite these decisive differences, both Germany and the United States remained captives of their own past histories because their governments insisted, in order to excuse their own inaction, that there was a close comparison between past situations and that in the Yugoslav states.

THE LEADERSHIP PROBLEM

Because of the Bush administration's deliberate restraint as regards participation in the Yugoslav crisis, there was a leadership vacuum in the Western coalition. Multilateral coalitions need leadership and that leadership must fully participate in all activities of the coalition.

It was practical domestic politics that a U.S. administration entering a presidential election campaign should seek to pass off responsibility for Yugoslavia to the European Community. But it was not practical foreign policy. Earlier we have described how the main leadership function in the European Community, now the European Union, has been exercised by France and Germany in cooperation. Together, these two governments have the weight to push through difficult decisions. However, this team could not function on Yugoslavia. It was clear to all from the outset of difficulties there that, on the issue of deploying military forces beyond national borders, German decisionmaking was paralyzed by the difficult effort to come to terms with the German historical past. Franco-German cooperation could not work here. American complaints that the Yugoslav case demonstrated inherent weakness in European leadership capabilities are not justified. The fact is that the Western alliance could probably have come to effective decisions on Yugoslavia if either of its major members, the United States or Germany, had been willing to participate fully in agreed actions there. But in this case, both held back from participation, as to a lesser extent did Great Britain. France, which came closest to the right policy on intervention, was too weak to sway the alliance on its own.

Subsequently, the Clinton administration sporadically tried to exercise leadership on Yugoslavia. But here, it often led from behind, refusing to commit even a limited ground-force contingent for delivery of humanitarian supplies. Effective leadership requires willingness to make equal sacrifice with other coalition partners and to make a military contribution at least the equal of theirs.

The efforts of the EU, the United States, and Russia to propose potential solutions in the Yugoslav states were poorly coordinated and entailed an element of competition. The United States did not conceal its distaste for the solutions suggested by the EU-UN team of Owen and Stoltenberg and pushed their approach aside for a new concept of a Bosnian-Croat deal after the NATO air threat in early 1994 had secured the withdrawal of heavy Serb arms from Sarajevo. The bickering between the United States and other NATO countries and Russia in connection with these events and with NATO's decision two months later to apply the same approach to the siege of Goradze was vociferous and damaging. Only after these developments did the United States, the UN, the EU, and Russia move toward the coordinated, cooperative approach they should have had two years earlier.

Despite the undeniably positive motives of the Western countries, the net effect of their sometimes clashing policies was to prolong the fighting in the former Yugoslavia: The allies refused to intervene decisively to stop the fighting. Several of them, including the United States, encouraged the Bosnian government to continue its resistance to the system of ethnic cantons proposed by the EC before Bosnian independence, which is largely what the Bosnian government was negotiating on more than two years later. U.S. actions also encouraged the Bosnian Muslims to believe they would ultimately receive military assistance from the United States and increased their resistance to negotiated settlement. Western deliveries of food inevitably also sustained the troops of each ethnic faction; sometimes, in order to get food to hungry civilians, the UN itself was forced to distribute rations directly to the combatants.

Western governments, this time with the United States in the van, partially redeemed themselves at the end of 1993 and in early 1994 with a greater display of military determination and negotiating creativity. Yet their earlier mishandling of the Yugoslav problem had already had important negative consequences. The governments lost an important opportunity to consolidate and strengthen the rudimentary post-cold war security system through effective action in the former Yugoslavia. Given the smooth and nearly bloodless end of communist domination in the Soviet Union and Eastern Europe, the evident willingness of all states of Europe to cooperate in maintaining peace, the continuing military strength of the United States and of NATO, the impressive success of the Western coalition in the Gulf War, and an encouraging unity of purpose in the UN Security Council, European and world opinion was justified in expecting to see effective Western and East-West cooperation to stifle the fighting in the former Yugoslavia and to move on to meeting other peacekeeping challenges in Europe. Instead, ineffective Western actions dealt a serious blow to the prestige, authority, and effectiveness of these institutions and left the way open for continuation of ethnic violence in the Yugoslav states, elsewhere in Eastern Europe and in Russia and the neighboring republics. Disappointment over failure of the Western governments to make good on these widespread expectations was part of the pain of the former Yugoslavia.

IS PEACEKEEPING A NATIONAL SECURITY INTEREST?

Nonetheless, Western governments were caught in a painful squeeze in Croatia and Bosnia. On the one hand, the wide disparity between their superior military capabilities and their declared principles of peace and world order and the daily televised evidence of continued wholesale killing made the governments appear incompetent. The other jaw of the vise was the evident unpopularity Western governments would incur with their own voters if they committed their citizen-soldiers to televised combat and possible casualties in a situation that the governments themselves asserted had no connection to national security interests. To cope with these pressures, governments took refuge in peripheral military activities in the Yugoslav states.

Despite these very understandable inhibitions against committing armed forces to combat situations, the effectiveness of a multilateral peacemaking system ultimately depends on the willingness of its member states to use military force, risking the lives of their own soldiers, to prevent or contain organized violence. If its participating governments do not have this determination, the new European security system may go the way of the League of Nations, which collapsed when its member states could not summon the resolve to act together against the initial aggressive actions of Mussolini and Hitler. After that failure, most league members did not openly reject multilateral security or withdraw from the organization; they continued to the end with pro forma adherence to its institutions. But their commitment to multilateral security slackened, and important decisions on security issues were guided by the silent conclusion that the only sure defense was individual national action or, at best, joining opposing military alliances.

In the Yugoslav case, what was missing was neither soldiers nor institutions for multilateral decisionmaking. What was missing was the conviction on the part of Western governments that the damage to their national interests from continued fighting was sufficiently great to overcome inhibitions against sending their troops into potential combat situations. By insisting, wrongly, that stopping the fighting in the former Yugoslavia was not a national security interest, Western governments sharply circumscribed their own capacity to commit their forces for multilateral peacemaking operations there.

Subjecting citizen-soldiers to injury and death through deliberate governmental decisions to use military force is a very serious responsibility of the state, probably its most serious one. Such responsibility must be exercised with the greatest restraint. In democracies, the problem is still greater. Democratic governments are accountable to legislatures, the media, and public opinion for their decisions on this subject. The cold war confrontation, which threatened the existence of Western countries, provided a convincing rationale for these decisions. After the cold war ended, this problem became far more difficult for Western governments. Today, they are faced by commendable resistance of their publics to use of military force, intensified in the case of the United States by the conviction that earlier administrations tragically erred in making this decision with regard to Vietnam. When this normal public resistance is amplified by televised coverage of combat, government decisions to commit armed forces must have a very clear justification.

The idea of "national security interest" is the concept that governments have traditionally used to justify committing their military forces to potential combat situations other than straightforward defense of the national territory. Historically, definitions of the national security interests of individual states have shifted, reflecting changing consensus among political elites in their perceptions of the circumstances of the time. In democracies, of course, the public has to share these perceptions to a significant degree; democratic governments are continually engaged with their publics in a dialogue over defining national security interests. The concept of national security interest is linked in turn with the concept of "political will," a concept that has become familiar in discussion of the reluctance of Western governments to use their immense military superiority to end the fighting in the former Yugoslavia. Political will—the determination to act even when action may be attended by serious costs—flows from the conviction of governments that certain issues do affect their national security interests.

Thus, beyond errors of policy with regard to the Yugoslav states themselves, political leaders in both the United States and Europe failed in their function of defining the issues at stake for their publics. Leaders did not make clear that this crisis was not only a humanitarian crisis of lost lives and suffering, but that their own security environment and interests were directly affected. National security interests were and are affected not only from the viewpoint of possible consequences in the spread of war to other countries in the Balkan region and in encouragement of other ethnic aggressors, but from the equally important viewpoint of damage to the credibility and effectiveness of the institutions and organizations that will be called on to guard those security interests in the future. These institutions must sometimes take setbacks. But they cannot often accept defeat and failure, because in that event, who will trust them with their security?

By the time of the crisis over Goradze in the spring of 1994, the conclusion that the credibility and standing of the UN, NATO, and other European institutions had suffered serious damage in Bosnia was publicly admitted even by Western governments. In justifying his request to NATO for further air strikes after the Bosnian Serbs, ignoring two limited strikes, continued the siege of Goradze, President Clinton said the request was necessary to maintain "NATO as a credible force for peace in the post-cold war era."[15] But the damage to the prestige of NATO and the UN from their ineffectiveness in Bosnia—and as regards the UN, in Somalia, Haiti, and Rwanda—did not stop with these institutions. It unavoidably extended to their principal backers—the Clinton administration, the EU governments, even the Yeltsin government, which admitted it had been gulled by the Bosnian Serbs. In fact, the damage extended beyond the prestige of serving governments to strike at the credibility of the countries themselves. When doubts over the decisiveness and competence of governments reach a certain intensity, they damage the roots of national power—in this case, the authority, capability, and power of the United States, the United Kingdom, France, and Germany as nation states. Without a reputation for competence in foreign and military policy, the United States, for example, would lose much of its capacity to influence others and to deter negative developments without actual use of force. Once the European security institutions and the UN become deeply involved in a problem—and in Yugoslavia, a European CSCE state bordered by two members of NATO and the EU, deep involvement was inevitable—the international standing of the main member states also becomes directly engaged. Governments cannot withdraw from this co-responsibility without damage to their credibility, as was shown in the case of U.S. withdrawal from Somalia and the turnabout of the U.S. navy ship carrying a peacekeeping contingent to Haiti. Clearly, the maintenance of credibility and authority of this kind is a primary national security interest for each state.

But, instead of defining the effectiveness of peacekeeping institutions in Bosnia and elsewhere as an issue involving national security interests, President Clinton and his senior officials claimed the opposite. In October 1993, mistaken tactics in Somalia brought the defeat of an elite U.S. army unit, the death of eighteen U.S. soldiers, and the collapse of efforts to disarm the warlords in the Somali capital of Mogadishu. The Clinton administration, at its outset a strong proponent of multilateral peacekeeping, took cover from a firestorm of congressional and public criticism behind a barricade of stringent conditions about future U.S. participation in peacekeeping. This rout sent a dismaying message about the future of peacemaking around the world. It caused UN secretary-general Boutros Boutros-Ghali to comment, "Politically and economically, the international community is now in retreat."[16]

In an important speech at Johns Hopkins University in fall 1993, National Security Adviser Anthony Lake defined U.S. national interests under the Clinton administration to include enlarging the area of democracy and free-market economies, defending U.S. allies, and coping with autocratic states seeking weapons of mass destruction. This definition was reasonable as far as it went, but Lake explicitly left peacekeeping outside this new definition of U.S. national interests. He made quite clear that for this reason, U.S. participation in peacekeeping would be optional. The United States would participate in some peacekeeping operations and refuse to participate in others, "Ultimately, on these and other humanitarian needs, we will have to pick and choose." In his September 1993 speech at the UN, President Clinton warned the UN against taking on too many peacekeeping assignments. "The United Nations must know when to say no."[17]

The Clinton administration had in this way placed peacekeeping outside the sphere of national interests and had made U.S. participation optional. Once this was done, in order to avoid the appearance of an open-ended commitment to humanitarian peacekeeping, it was also necessary to make clear that future U.S. participation in peacekeeping would be subject to stringent conditions and requirements. Among these requirements are an identifiable threat to peace, clear objectives, an identifiable end of involvement, calculable costs, participation of other countries, willingness of combatants to agree to a cease-fire, U.S. command in missions involving combat, and advance agreement of Congress.[18] At U.S. initiative, most of these demanding requirements were endorsed in a September 1994 statement by the five permanent members of the UN Security Council.

Individually, these requirements are reasonable. They would also be reasonable qualifications of a previously announced vision of a long-term approach for reducing the frequency of conflict in the world. However, when applied together in the absence of some positive general vision of peacekeeping aims, the requirements become forbiddingly negative. For example, they would preclude U.S. participation in rapid preventive deployment of peacekeeping forces designed to head off conflict or to contain it right at its outset—activities where preconditions like those about calculable costs and an identifiable end of involvement cannot be met because the situation at the outset of conflict is nearly always incalculable. Taken together, the requirements promise that future U.S. participation in general peacekeeping will be rare.

The notion that peacekeeping is optional, "humanitarian," and outside the realm of national interests appears to be based on several unstated premises: One is that armed conflict in and between human societies is in fact endemic, and that its outbreak is uncontrollable and haphazard, a kind of natural disaster. We have argued here that this is not the case. It is not at all probable that all armed conflict will ever be eliminated. But early preventive action—identification of incipient conflict situations, negotiation, mediation, preventive deployment as with the U.S. and Scandinavian units in Macedonia, even military intervention to require a cease-fire in place at the outset of conflict—can prevent or contain specific conflicts and thus lower the overall level of organized violence in the world.

A second silent premise of the present U.S. position on peacekeeping is that, because the risk of global war has dissipated along with the cold war and all wars have consequently become regional wars—a correct assumption—countries located outside the regions of conflict are immune to the consequences of regional wars—an incorrect one. Along these lines, in a provocative, often exasperating book, Max Singer and

Aaron Wildavsky argue that the rich industrialized countries of the world are free of the threat of war among themselves and can continue to live in peace and plenty while the remainder of the world suffer in "zones of turmoil." The authors believe these zones may straighten themselves out on their own after a century or two of conflict through the operations of the free-market economy, although the industrialized countries may from time to time decide on an optional basis to participate in peacekeeping operations in them.[19]

But, even leaving aside the real risk of some nuclear complication with Russia or China, there are serious faults in this reasoning. Because a distant regional conflict may be a matter of indifference to U.S. or European public or political opinion, this does not mean either that such a conflict does not affect the national interests of countries in the affected region or that countries in the "zones of peace" are completely insulated from negative developments in the "zones of turmoil." To the contrary, most Western governments correctly attach highest priority among their national security interests to effective nuclear nonproliferation, regarding proliferation as a direct threat to national security. But unless security requirements are satisfied in regions that may be distant from the industrialized countries, the ultimate result may be fairly widespread proliferation and the development of a direct threat to Western states, for example, from the Mideast or North Africa.

Given the experience in the Yugoslav states, Western governments should undertake at least three actions: They should seek to blunt the potential clash between their own domestic public opinion and the requirements of peacekeeping by making arrangements that will make it easier to send preventive peacekeeping forces in the early stages of possible conflict when they can be most effective. They should seek to defuse future ethnic conflicts by establishing institutions and procedures to facilitate nonviolent achievement by qualified minorities of regional autonomy within national borders. And they should deliberately launch a fundamental debate with their own publics about the nature and prospects of an effective international peacekeeping system and its relevance to national security interests.

A Readiness Force

We have described the problems caused by reluctance of the Western governments to approve preventive intervention in situations where a conflict appears ready to erupt in order to block the conflict and to restore conditions for mediation and negotiated settlement. A partial solution—and only a partial one—is to create conditions that insulate the decision to commit rapid intervention forces from domestic political reactions to the extent possible. What is needed for rapid response is not only units composed solely of volunteer personnel, but also advance approval by national legislatures of states of the use of such troops for authorized peacemaking purposes. States contributing manpower to a rapid reaction force would in effect transfer their right to control use of these particular troops to one of the multilateral security organizations. Under present conditions, it takes from three to six months after agreement has been reached to carry out a peacekeeping operation to gather together the forces and financial support for it. By that time, conflict has often broken out or intensified to such an extent that it would take major force to deal with it.

The simplest and most direct solution of this problem is for the permanent members of the UN Security Council (whose number should be expanded by the addition of Brazil, Egypt, Germany, Japan, India, and Nigeria) to move toward fulfilling their obligations under Articles 43 and 45 of the UN Charter on earmarking ground and air forces for peacekeeping. Each permanent member should designate one readiness brigade of ground forces and appropriate air combat and air transport units, specially trained for peacekeeping missions and available on immediate call. These units would be composed only of volunteers. Their expenses would be paid by their own countries until committed to a peacekeeping operation. These forces should be directed by an improved UN command structure now under discussion by a number of member governments. In Europe, the Allied Command Europe mobile brigade and its air unit should be so designated. A second ground brigade with its air contingent should be formed by the North Atlantic Cooperation Council, drawing on battalion-sized units from Western and Eastern Europe and the Soviet successor states, to serve on peacekeeping missions at the request of the UN Security Council or the CSCE.

It is desirable for reasons of equal risk-sharing and an adequate role in deciding on their possible use that the United States contribute one of these brigades directly. Congress in legislating this U.S. contribution should explicitly preapprove use of these troops for peacemaking operations following a decision by the UN Security Council, the CSCE Council of Ministers, or the NATO Council. Other national legislatures need to take parallel action for their contributions. There should be general public understanding that these troops will be used for rapid intervention if the necessity presents itself. In cases that appear to call for early preventive intervention, the U.S. government and other contributing governments could then vote in the UN, CSCE, or NATO councils with greater focus on the merits of the case itself, less influenced by domestic political considerations than is now the case. This exemption from immediate legislative oversight would of course affect only the brigades proposed for the readiness force and the air force units assigned to them and would not apply to other force contributions for peacemaking operations.

Financing of peacekeeping brigades should not be dependent on ad hoc assessments on member states as at present. Instead, operations carried out by these brigades should be financed by the proceeds of a tax on international travel collected by member governments and turned over to the UN. There should also be a possibility of direct financial contribution to the brigades by individuals throughout the world. National tax legislation and UN accounting procedures should be changed to permit tax deductible contributions to the readiness brigades or to individual peacemaking operations. Provisions like this might not bring in much income, but people in the United States and throughout the world should be in a position to vote their support for their UN force with their own money.

The United States and some other Western governments do not support the idea of a UN rapid response force because designating even a few brigades might add to the supranational character of the UN; it would be a beginning that might be built on further. This "disadvantage" actually seems a strong advantage of the scheme. These governments also oppose the scheme because they believe the existence of these forces might add to pressures for UN intervention in undesirable situations; in other words, that it could diminish their influence in reaching a UN, NATO, or CSCE decision on peacekeeping. But preventive deployment requires rapid early decisions.

Next, we turn to some possible measures for defusing ethnic frictions before they become conflicts.

HEADING OFF ETHNIC CONFLICT

With the end of cold war totalitarian repression, the longing of many peoples in Europe to live in a country of their own burst out of suspended animation into potentially destructive vitality. This longing takes two main forms: One is the desire of ethnic minorities within the borders of a single state to have their own homeland. The second is the desire of ethnic groups separated by national borders to unite in one homeland. Yugoslavia was so complicated because it combined both forms. This book has described over twenty potential cases of these two types in Eastern Europe, and there are more than that number in the Soviet successor states. Both the European and global security systems lack procedures for coping with the desires of those ethnic minorities that insist on autonomy, national independence, or unification and for heading off the armed violence that is so often a product of these desires.

It is worth calling to mind that Yugoslavia under Marshal Tito had a relatively enlightened if despotic system for protecting the rights of minorities and for giving them a role in national decisions. After Tito died, it did not work. Even before the Serbs dismantled it, other groups lost confidence in it. However, if there had at the time been a recognized international authority in Europe to appeal to and a recognized procedure to go through to achieve regional autonomy within national borders, violence in the former Yugoslavia might have been averted. Certainly such an authority and such procedures could be useful in averting violence in numerous other ethnic quarrels that could erupt in Europe.[20] In his speech at the June 1993 Athens meeting of the North Atlantic Cooperation Council, Russian foreign minister Andrei Kozyrev said it was necessary for countries concerned with security in Europe to step up their opposition to aggressive nationalism through prevention of domestic conflicts and defense of the universal rights of the individual and of ethnic and other minorities.[21] Kozyrev was right. It is time for the countries concerned with European security to do even more: to face the sovereignty issue head on and formally to agree that ethnic conflict within state borders is a deadly enemy of economic and political development and a potential threat to international security and that it must therefore be addressed by specific preventative measures.

The CSCE has already done work in this field that puts it ahead of all multilateral institutions. Logically, it ought to be the vehicle for further development. A special CSCE Commission for Minorities should be set up with three tasks: ensuring the full application of existing CSCE agreements on minority rights, providing a framework for formal hearings of minority claims of mistreatment, and developing for approval by the CSCE Council of Foreign Ministers and later application by the commission itself a more extensive Code of Minority Rights, to include procedures for achieving regional autonomy within national boundaries by nonviolent means.

The commission would be composed of qualified senior personalities from six to eight CSCE member states and would be headed by the CSCE high commissioner for minorities (the first commissioner, former Netherlands foreign minister Max van der Stoel, was appointed in 1993). It would assist the commissioner in overseeing the implementation in member states of the broad range of principles for minority protection contained in the CSCE Copenhagen Document. The Copenhagen principles include the right to preserve and develop ethnic, cultural, linguistic, and religious identity and to protect it against involuntary assimilation. They also cover the right to use the minority language in official transactions; the right to found educational, cultural, and religious organizations, both on a voluntary basis and through public support "in accordance with the national legal system"; the right of individuals to develop contacts inside and outside their borders with members of their own ethnic group; and the right to distribute and have access to information in their own language.

However, these activities may not violate the territorial integrity of their state.[22] All CSCE member states are committed to maintain the provisions of this document.

The commission would also hear complaints of individuals or minority representatives over alleged violations of these principles and summon member governments to account for questionable practices. To deal with the small number of hard cases in which there has been a long, documented struggle for autonomy or independence, the commission should formulate for ministerial approval an extension of the Copenhagen principles in the form of a CSCE Code of Minority Rights. The principal content of this code would be a prescribed set of steps through which those minorities that insist on a greater degree of autonomy, that deliberately seek outside assistance, and that pledge themselves to nonviolent means, would have to go in order to qualify for outside support from the CSCE states. The code procedure would culminate in regional autonomy within national borders, plus some form of power sharing at the center, in those cases where the minority, supervised by the CSCE commission, has been able to complete all prescribed steps without initiating organized violence. The absence of violence is a categorical requirement in this scheme, whose objective is to reduce the incidence of conflict in Europe.

The required procedure could include such steps as (1) a proven record of earlier good-faith efforts to achieve greater autonomy and self-governance; (2) two or more referendums five years apart demonstrating desire for changed status and greater autonomy by a qualified majority (75 percent) of adults in the ethnic group concerned and a majority of at least 60 percent of the entire adult population of the region in question; (3) an explicit, detailed code of protection for other minorities living inside the region; (4) responsible negotiation with national authorities giving clear evidence of willingness on the part of the petitioning minority to pay a fair share of the economic costs of autonomy, including the costs of possible voluntary resettlement of populations; (5) agreed measures of power-sharing at the center of government, including such possibilities as participation in national parliaments through proportional representation, assured representation in coalition governments and executive departments of government, and some form of federalism or, in extreme cases, confederation.[23]

The CSCE Commission for Minorities would apply this code in qualifying cases and also follow through on its implementation. There is a precedent for activity of international organizations in formulating and monitoring agreements for the protection of minorities. It is the minority protection treaties developed by the League of Nations with Poland, Yugoslavia, Czechoslovakia, Romania, and Greece. Any member could draw the attention of the league to alleged violations or pass on the dispute to the international tribunal.[24]

On the basis of the Code of Minority Rights, the CSCE commission would seek to limit pressure tactics or violence against a minority by its national government through formal or informal commission complaints to the host government, fact-finding investigations, and other CSCE human rights procedures described earlier. It should have the authority to summon the offending government for confidential or public hearings. On occasion, the tribunal might also hear government complaints about use of violence by minorities on their territories and call leaders of minority groups to account.

In time, if this approach were successful, CSCE states could go even further. They could define steps and actions through which a government could be declared by the CSCE Council of Ministers to have undermined the legitimacy of its sovereignty over a given area or territory, such as repeated violations of individual human rights, failure to provide protection to minorities (or entire populations), lack of effective control, repressive actions, and failure to respond to efforts to open discussion or negotiation on any of these topics. The CSCE could agree that, in such cases, it would warn the offending state and seek to negotiate with it on improving the situation. In an extreme case it might apply economic sanctions. Theoretically, it would be possible to go still further and to agree among CSCE members that the CSCE might temporarily assume administrative powers over a minority area, but only in those cases where the government of the state concerned was willing to agree to this action.

Actions of this kind, with considerable intrusiveness of outside organizations, would stress the concept of sovereignty even further than it has been weakened in recent years. However, UN actions in the Yugoslav states, on behalf of the Kurds of northern Iraq, and in Somalia have established that external intervention is accepted by world governments when internal developments create a potential threat to international security, when there is systematic violation of human rights, and for humanitarian reasons, when a government fails in its obligation to provide for basic wants of its population or there is no effective government.

The possible CSCE actions to defuse potential ethnic conflict described here go far, but they remain voluntary except for the possibility of economic sanctions. Some have suggested that the CSCE should seek treaty status to use force against errant members; variants of this idea were discussed in the last chapter. But such a stage is far beyond the level of consensus that today pertains among CSCE member states. Nor is it suggested here that a CSCE Code of Minority Rights should attempt to establish procedures to cover secession and establishment of new, independent states. The answer to ethnic conflict is not fragmentation of existing states or establishing more ministates. The international community should not be called on to support groups with a population of the size of a medium-sized city, like the Abkhazians or Ossetians of Georgia, in their efforts to achieve independence by force of arms.

It is evident that a number of CSCE member states with actual or potential minority problems like Russia, France, Great Britain, and even the United States with its growing Hispanic population in the Southwest, would have strong reservations about even the more limited suggestions here for achieving regional autonomy. But organized ways of defusing ethnic tensions in Europe before these tensions reach the stage of organized violence are urgently needed. If necessary, these procedures could be restricted at the outset to those CSCE member states willing to apply them voluntarily, as was done on the CSCE project for an arbitration tribunal. If CSCE governments cannot agree because of the political sensitivity of this subject that their officials should carry out serious study of the concept of an autonomy code for minorities, they should at least commission one or more nongovernmental organizations linked to the CSCE to do so, or one of these organizations should volunteer to undertake the task.

However, there is no time in some of Europe's most urgent problem areas to take the leisurely road to eventual consensus among CSCE countries on a procedure for defusing ethnic violence. Three of the shakiest and potentially most explosive ethnic-nationalistic problems in Europe are in Ukraine and in two areas of former Yugoslavia with large Albanian populations, Kosovo, and Macedonia. Civil war in East Ukraine and the Crimea followed by large-scale Russian military intervention would deliver a very serious blow to long-term prospects of democracy in Russia and to Western willingness to help Russia in the difficult effort to achieve democracy. Conflict between Albanians and Macedonians or Albanians and Serbs could bring widespread interstate war with Serbia, Albania, Bulgaria, Greece, and Turkey as possible participants.

There is a need for extraordinary Western measures to head off these developments. These are areas where some form of regional autonomy with outside guarantees of impartial application needs to be negotiated rapidly, as Russia and the Western powers have been seeking to do in Bosnia and in the Krajina area of Croatia. The dangers in Ukraine are sufficiently acute to justify some sort of buy-back provision like incorporation in Russia of Eastern Ukraine and the Crimea in return for a very large Russian payment in long-term energy resources—natural gas, oil, and uranium for reactors—or at the least a special status that would permit Russian residents of these areas to move freely in and out of Russia and to do business with Russia without impediment.

Second, a new CSCE institution, a CSCE Regional Conflict Prevention Center, should be established in Ukraine and also in Macedonia and Kosovo with participation of senior officials and militia advisers from the host state, all neighboring states and from larger CSCE member states from outside the region like the United States, France, and Germany—and Russia in the case of Macedonia and Kosovo. (As a neighboring state, Russia would be an essential member of the center in Ukraine.) These centers would apply the whole spectrum of CSCE's potential measures. They could use the conflict prevention and mediation measures that CSCE has developed for its resident missions and they could apply in a regional conflict prevention context a set of the military confidence-building measures CSCE has already developed for regional crises. They could provide assurance of impartial administration of whatever understandings have been reached on regional autonomy, or the code of regional autonomy described above if something like it is approved at a later time. Together with the EU, these CSCE centers could coordinate and promote economic aid to their host countries.

Eduard Shevardnadze's plea for a UN presence in Georgia rather than a CSCE presence may well reflect his view that at this point the UN is a more capable institution than the CSCE for peacemaking and for placing some limits on the activities of the Russian military in Georgia. If this view is widespread, then perhaps instead of a CSCE regional conflict prevention center, a similar United Nations center should be established with participation of senior officials from the host country and neighboring countries. Which organization is chosen is not the issue, although in time CSCE must develop further as a regional organization of the UN. These centers, backstopped by the CSCE's Permanent Group in Vienna, would provide a coordination point for bilateral efforts of the United States and the EU countries to cope with those crisis areas. However, as the early stages of the Yugoslav states' conflict already demonstrated, the requirements of conflict prevention exceed the capacity of bilateral relationships, important as these can be, and call for a multilateral approach, applied in these urgent cases through an authoritative presence on the scene.

SUMMING UP

A series of seismic historical shifts—dissolution of the Soviet Union, shrinkage of Moscow's military potential, and replacement of a Marxist-Leninist regime by prodemocratic governments in Russia and most other successor states—have reduced the danger of major war in Europe to a distant prospect. At the same time, the two main challenges to European security are the continuation of large nuclear arsenals in the hands of

Russia and three other unstable republics and the eruption of ethnic-nationalist conflicts in Eastern Europe and also around the borders of Russia (which have sometimes resulted at least in part from Russian actions). Either issue or a combination of them could result in interstate conflicts, which in turn could trigger major war.

However, the problems of European security described here, forbidding as many are, represent a far smaller threat to the security of Europe and the United States than the risk of global nuclear war that was at the core of the cold war confrontation. In addition, leaving aside the outcome of Russia's hesitant progress toward democracy, all the security problems discussed in this book are soluble or at least can be coped with.

The issue of controlling nuclear weapons in Russia is still far from resolved. There have been some important successes and some important failures. But possible long-term solutions of the kind described here are in sight. The European security institutions also have had a mixed record in preventing or containing the outbreak of large-scale armed violence in the region. On one hand, these organizations have prevented fighting in Croatia and Bosnia from spreading to highly inflammable neighboring areas—a very important achievement. Under the impact of the fighting, they have made many organizational innovations, potentially valuable for the future, including operational coordination between the UN and NATO. They have played a generally helpful role in providing a negotiation framework for the combatant groups, a useful if limited military role in what could be the wind-down phase of the Bosnian conflict, and they could play an indispensable role as peacekeepers once a settlement was reached there.

But this record is also besmirched by the deaths of up to 200,000 people in the Yugoslav states and of tens of thousands of deaths in the states neighboring Russia. True, tens of thousands of people have also died in recent conflicts outside Europe—for example, in Liberia, Angola, the Sudan, Rwanda, Burundi, and Sri Lanka—but these areas do not have the benefit of a NATO, a European Union, or a CSCE. When the UN and other international security organizations have operated at all in these areas, they have had fewer pretensions about their capability and, consequently, less respect and authority to lose if they did not fulfill their commitments.

One conclusion to be drawn, especially from the Yugoslav experience, is that Western governments should learn to view their national security interests in two complementary dimensions. The first dimension is the traditional one of defense of the home territory against direct threats to it, even distant ones. The second dimension is one of concern for the cohesion and effectiveness of the European (and international) security system as such, for the wider environment of national security.

The European security system can in time meet the hopes and expectations of its supporters only by establishing a record of effectively heading off or containing conflict—here, "conflict" means both interstate war and armed violence inside state borders. A European or an international security system that is limited to sending peacekeepers to guard the ruins of burned-out conflict cannot elicit the confidence and ongoing support of participating governments or their publics. Unless governments can break through their inhibition against involvement in peacekeeping and peace enforcement in cases where defense of home territory is not involved but where there is a possibility of casualties to their peacekeeping forces, the European security system will remain useful machinery for managing armed violence at its margins but not a cooperative system to which states will entrust more and more responsibility. In its place, member states will have to continue to rely mainly on their own armed forces for defense. The same conclusions apply to the global security system in the United Nations.

The point is a central one and bears repetition: If multilateral security organizations cannot cross the barrier to greater effectiveness and dependability in preventing organized violence and instead remain caught in the old pattern of reacting only after conflict erupts, then they can never gain the full trust and support of peoples and governments, support that would give these organizations the strength and authority needed to grow still further in the same capabilities. Instead, people and governments everywhere will remain trapped in the vicious cycle of treating organized violence as a natural phenomenon of the human condition and reacting to it only after it occurs.

On the other hand, where there is a two-dimensional definition of national interest, the prestige and effectiveness of multilateral security organizations will be considered an integral part of the state of national defenses. And wherever there is a real threat either to traditional national security or to the effectiveness of the multilateral security system, governments would consider intervention. To regard the effectiveness of regional or global security systems as a national security interest is not sentimentality but hard-headed calculation. In today's world, there is a direct connection between the effectiveness and credibility of these organizations and that of the principal countries supporting them. Where the organizations suffer loss in authority and influence, the governments do also. In the long run, the level of this authority and credibility makes a decisive difference in the nature of the international environment in which all countries must live.

Among the practical consequences of this approach for both the United States and the European countries are that peacekeeping should be viewed as an integral part of national defense planning and that national contributions to financing peacekeeping should become a normal part of national defense budgets. No one is suggesting that the United States and its major allies should themselves intervene in every armed squabble. What is needed instead is a long-term objective, widely understood by the public, of gradually lowering the incidence of conflict in the world through step-by-step improvement in the capabilities of a worldwide network of regional security organizations headed by the United Nations.

These regional organizations—the CSCE in Europe, backed by NATO and the European Union, the Organization of American States, the Organization of African Unity, the Association of South East Asian Nations, and possibly two additional organizations for South Asia and for the North Pacific, as often proposed by Australia, Canada, and the United States, should be strengthened or established. Each should have peacekeeping capability of its own, to include developed mediation capability and a small early intervention force with its own source of financing through an international tax. The United States and the European states should adopt a policy of systematically building up the peacemaking capability of these regional organizations. As the regional organizations gain peacekeeping competence, the need for intervention by the UN itself or the larger powers will decrease, and along with it, ultimately the national defense budgets of the major member states. Clearly, this is an enterprise that will take many years to carry out, but it is one that, properly articulated, could command great public support in all Western countries and throughout the world as a practical way to reduce the frequency of conflict.

Europe is a test case for international security in two senses: On the one hand, success of the European security system will create a powerful new international force with the European Union at its core supporting the progress of democracy and free-market economies in Eastern Europe and in Russia and the other former Soviet states, even if that progress is slow and uneven. This development could also provide impetus for a quantum jump in the effectiveness of the global system of multilateral security institutions to a higher plateau of conflict prevention and containment.

On the other hand, the failure of the European system of multilateral security institutions would probably mean the failure of the UN-linked system of multilateral security as well, both by force of example and because the main actors are the same in both cases. In both cases, "failure" would not mean instant collapse but slow desiccation. If the industrialized states conclude that the multilateral approach has failed to serve their main interests—control over nuclear weapons and limiting the amount of violence in the world, especially in their own regions—they will increasingly strike out on their own, confirming the forecasts of the neorealists. The process would probably not be dramatic at the outset, but at the end of that road, there may be up to a score of nuclear-armed countries engaged in an unending and ever-shifting search for a dependable balance of power. This would be a more dangerous, nuclearized multipolar world system rather than one based on increasing resort to multinational cooperative security: a world in which the possibility of lethal conflict is endemic. The stakes in the European test case are indeed high.

NOTES

CHAPTER 1

1. Mikhail Gorbachev, *Perestroika,* 1st ed. (London: William Collins, 1987).

2. Moshe Lewin, *The Gorbachev Phenomenon,* exp. ed. (Berkeley: University of California Press, 1991).

3. In this book, I do not intend to document each statement of fact or opinion with already published material, but to do so selectively. For this chapter, the most valuable background sources are the excellent series of reports on Gorbachev's perestroika prepared by the Congressional Research Service, including F. Mike Miles, "Soviet Restructuring Under Gorbachev: A Chronology, January 1985–June 1987"; Charlotte Kea, "Glasnost and Perestroika Under Gorbachev, a Chronology, July 1987–December 1988"; Theodore S. Dagne and Steven J. Woehrel, "Soviet Glasnost and Perestroyka, a Chronology, January–October 1989"; Theodore S. Dagne, "Soviet Glasnost and Perestroyka, a Chronology, November 1989–February 1990"; Francis T. Miko, "Gorbachev Reform Program After the 1988 Party Conference," February 28, 1989; Steven J. Woehrel, "Soviet Union: An Assessment of Recent Republic and Local Elections," July 20, 1990; Jim Nichol, "The 28th Soviet Communist Party Congress: Outcomes and Implications," August 2, 1990; Stuart D. Goldman, "The New Soviet Legislature," September 20, 1990; Vita Bite, "The Baltic Republics' Push for Independence," updated January 30, 1991; Joseph G. Whelan, "Gorbachev's World View on the Eve of the Washington II Summit, May 1990," May 20, 1991; Stuart D. Goldman,"Soviet Perestroyka: Political and Economic Change Under Gorbachev," updated February 5, 1991, "The Soviet Union in Crisis," updated May 22, 1991, on the Soviet economy; John P. Hardt, "Soviet Transition to a Market Economy," updated December 13, 1990; International Monetary Fund, "The Economy of the USSR," December 1990; Central Intelligence Agency and Defense Intelligence Agency, "Beyond Perestroyka: The Soviet Economy in Crisis," May 14, 1991; and Deutsche Bank, "The Soviet Union at the Crossroads: Facts and Figures on the Soviet Republics," October 1, 1990. A very useful check is provided by the annual chronologies of events in the Soviet Union and Eastern Europe published by *Foreign Affairs,* New York.

4. Martin Malia, "The Yeltsin Revolution," *New Republic,* February 10, 1992.

5. These ideas are summarized in chapters 3–7 of *Perestroika* and in Gorbachev's impressive speech of December 8, 1988, to the UN General Assembly, published in Foreign Broadcast Information Service, SOV–88–236, December 8, 1988.

6. FBIS, SOV–91–164, August 23, 1991.

7. Minsk FBIS, SOV–91–237, December 10, 1991; Alma-Ata, FBIS, SOV–91–246, December 23, 1991.

8. *Washington Post,* December 26, 1991.

9. Robert Cullen, Twilight of Empire (New York: Atlantic Monthly Press, 1991), p. 75.

10. Corelli Barnett, *The Collapse of British Power* (Atlantic Highlands, N.J.: Humanities Press International, 1986), originally published in 1972.

Chapter 2

1. *Perestroika,* updated ed. (London: William Collins, 1988), p. 165.

2. Mark Frankland, *The Patriots' Revolution* (London: Sinclair Stevenson, 1990), p. 223.

3. Karl Kaiser, *Deutschlands Vereinigung* (Bergisch-Gladbach: Bastei Lubbe, 1991), p. 35.

4. *Pravda,* July 11, 1990.

5. For background, see my articles "Federal Germany After the Euromissiles," *Bulletin of the Atomic Scientists,* December 1983; "How to Lose Germany," *Foreign Policy,* Summer 1984; "Directions in Inner-German Relations," *Orbis,* Fall 1985; "Will the Two Germanies Solve the Problem of European Security?" *SAIS Review,* Summer–Fall 1988.

6. Among the sources for this section of the book are Kaiser, *Deutschlands Vereinigung;* Hans Adomeit, "Gorbachev and German Unification," *Problems of Communism,* July–August 1990; Elizabeth Pond, "A Wall Destroyed," *International Security,* Fall 1990; Stephen Szabo, *The Diplomacy of German Unification* (New York: St. Martin's Press, 1992); Ronald D. Asmus, *German Unification and Its Ramifications,* Report, no. R–4021–A (Santa Monica, CA: Rand Corporation, 1991); the chapter on the German unity in my book *Watershed in Europe* (Lexington, MA: Lexington Books, 1987). (I also have drawn on several of my own articles on Germany, including four sources previously cited—under the "German Unification" section of this chapter: "Federal Germany after the Euromissiles," *Bulletin of the Atomic Scientists,* December 1983; "How to Lose Germany," *Foreign Policy,* Summer 1984; "Directions in Inner-German Relations," *Orbis,* Fall 1985; and "Will the Two Germanies Solve the Problem of European Security," *SAIS Review,* Summer–Fall 1988.) Also useful are Wilhelm Bruns, "Die Ausseren Aspekte der Deutschen Einigung," *Forschungsinstitut,* Friedrich-Ebert-Stiftung, September 1990. Bruns, my late friend, was an eminent analyst of the

German unity issue. Gerard Holden, "The End of an Alliance," Peace Research Institute, Frankfurt, December 1990. A valuable aid to chronology is the weekly *Deutschland Nachrichten* and its English-language companion, *This Week in Germany*, published by the German Information Center, New York, as well as the annual *Foreign Affairs* chronologies.

7. Jonathan Dean, "Reviving 4-Power Rights in Germany," *Washington Post,* January 17, 1990.

8. Adomeit, "Gorbachev and German Unification," p. 15.

9. Details of the Stavropol meeting are in FBIS, SOV–90–139, July 19, 1990.

10. The text of the treaty is in *Arms Control Today,* October 1990.

CHAPTER 3

1. S. Frederick Starr, *Prospects for Stable Democracy in Russia* (Columbus: The Mershon Center, Ohio State University, July 1992).

2. See, for example, Steven Erlanger, "Russian Premier's Star is Rising Fast," *New York Times*, January 26, 1994.

3. Michael Dobbs, "Study Predicts Social Strife as Russia Ends Price Control," *Washington Post*, January 1, 1992.

4. Robert Gates, statement before the House Armed Services Committee Defense Policy Panel, December 10, 1991.

5. "Never Say Die," *Economist*, March 27, 1993; John Lloyd, "Pressing Ahead on the Long Road of Reform," *Financial Times*, May 27, 1993; Andrew Gowers, "A Relentless Slide in Oil Production," *Financial Times*, May 27, 1993.

6. John Lloyd, "Fuse Burns Low on Unemployment Time-Bomb," *Financial Times*, October 7, 1993; "Reforming Russia's Economy," *Economist*, December 11, 1993; Fred Hiatt, "Yeltsin Promises to Hold Course Despite Election," *Washington Post*, December 23, 1993; Jeffrey Sachs and Charles Wyplosz, "How the West Should Help Russian Reform," *Financial Times*, January 11, 1994; Leyla Boulton and John Lloyd, "Chernomyrdin Promises Caution in Progress Toward Economic Reform," *Financial Times*, January 12, 1994; Jurels Martin and John Lloyd, "Yeltsin May Step Up Reforms," *Financial Times*, January 14, 1994; R. W. Apple, "Clinton, in Russia, Is Firm in Support of Yeltsin's Aims," *New York Times*, January 14, 1994; "Russia in Need,"*Economist*, January 15, 1994.

7. "A Battle, Not the War," *Economist*, May 1, 1993.

8. Anders Aslund, "Go Faster on Russian Reform," *New York Times*, December 7, 1992; Jeffrey Sachs and David Lipton, "Russia on the Brink," *Financial Times*, October 16, 1992; John Parker, "Russia—the Sixth Wave," *Economist*, December 5, 1992.

9. Quote cited in John Lloyd, "Barely Afloat on a Cruel Sea," *Financial Times*, March 3, 1993.

10. Margaret Shapiro, "Price of Russian Freedom Includes a Surge in Crime," *Washington Post*, February 27, 1992; Associated Press, "Russian Crime Rise Laid to Economic Ills," *Washington Post*, July 29, 1992; Leyla Boulton, "Moscow Forced to Fight Mafia," *Financial Times*, December 30, 1992.

11. Edward Balls, "Economic Transformation Is Under Way," *Financial Times*, May 27, 1993; Leyla Boulton, "Deficit Reined Back in Revised Russian Budget," *Financial Times*, July 1, 1993; "Russia on the Line," *Economist*, July 3, 1993; Celestine Bohlen, "Russian Economy Bears Good News," *New York Times*, July 4, 1993; Stanley Fischer and Jeffrey Sachs, "Remove Roadblock to Russian Reforms," *Financial Times*, July 6, 1993; Chrystia Freeland and Edward Balls, "Climate of Reform Brings the Rouble Back from the Dead," *Financial Times*, July 23, 1993.

12. Times Mirror Center for the People and the Press, "The Russians Rethink Democracy," January 27, 1993.

13. Steven Erlanger, "What Russia Wants: Less Pain, a Strong Hand," *New York Times*, April 18, 1993.

14. John Parker, "Russian Reform," *Economist*, December 5, 1992.

15. John Parker, "Russia—the Sixth Wave," *Economist*, December 5, 1992.

16. Peter Reddaway, "Russia on the Brink," *New York Review*, January 28, 1993, and "Russia in Turmoil," *Economist*, March 27, 1993.

17. Report of Russian Procurator-General Valentin Stepkanov, cited by Reddaway, "Russia on the Brink."

18. John Lloyd and Leyla Boulton, "Gaidar Returns to Cabinet in Boost for Reform," *Financial Times*, September 17, 1993; the text of Yeltsin's speech dissolving the parliament is published in the *New York Times*, September 22, 1993; "All or Nothing," *Economist*, September 25, 1993; "Russia Turns Its Back on Parliament," *Economist*, September 25, 1993; Fred Hiatt and Margaret Shapiro, "Yeltsin Defies Legal Trap Set by His Opponents," *Washington Post*, September 26, 1993; Fred Hiatt and Margaret Shapiro, "Troops Move in to Put Down Uprising," *Washington Post*, October 4, 1993; Serge Schmemann, "Yeltsin Calls Army to Moscow," *New York Times*, October 4, 1993, "Army Ousts Yeltsin Foes from Parliament," *New York Times*, October 5, 1993; Margaret Shapiro, "Army Shellfire Crushes Moscow Revolt," *Washington Post*, October 5, 1993; "The Battle for Russia," *Economist*, October 9, 1993; Serge Schmemann, "Tarnished Knight on a Darker Stage, *New York Times*, October 10, 1993.

19. John Lloyd and Dmitri Volkov, "Yeltsin Seeks Unfettered Powers for Presidency," *Financial Times*, October 29, 1993; John Lloyd, "A Constitution for Yeltsin's Time," *Financial Times*, November 11, 1993; Margaret Shapiro, "Russians Approve New Constitution," *Washington Post*, December 13, 1993; John Lloyd, "Voters Hand Great Powers to President," *Financial Times*, December 13, 1993; "Framework or Frameup?" *Economist*, December 18, 1993. The text of the constitution has been translated by FBIS. John Lloyd, "Moscow Devolves Power to Tatarstan Republic," *Financial Times*, February 17, 1994.

20. The results were as follows:

PROREFORM PARTIES

Russia's Choice	76 seats
Pres	30 seats
Yabloko	28 seats
Liberal Democratic Union	26 seats

160 seats

CENTRISTS

New Regional Block	65 seats
Democratic Party of Russia	15 seats

80 seats

ANTIREFORM

Liberal Democratic Party	64 seats
Agrarian	55 seats
Communist Party	45 seats
Women of Russia	24 seats

188 seats

INDEPENDENTS	21 seats
VACANT	1 seat
TOTAL	*450 seats*

John Lloyd, "Voters Fed Bolshevik Slogan of Bread and Peace," *Financial Times*, November 26, 1993; Lee Hockstader, "Yeltsin Threatens to Yank Television Time from Opponents," *Washington Post*, November 27, 1993; Fred Hiatt, "Russians Choose a Direction," *Washington Post*, December 12, 1993; Celestine Bohlen, "Nationalists Move Far Out in Front in Russian Voting," *New York Times*, December 14, 1993; Lee Hockstader, "Zhirinovsky Vows to Seek Yeltsin's Job," *Washington Post*, December 15, 1993; Above figures are from "The Final Tally," *Economist*, January 8, 1994, as modified in "Diversity in the Duma," *Economist*, April 30, 1992.

21. John Lloyd, "Political Uncertainty Leaves the Public Without a Prop," *Financial Times*, January 20, 1994; Fred Hiatt, "Yeltsin Names Cabinet Short on

Reformers," *Washington Post*, January 21, 1994; Lee Hochstader, "Russian Foreign Policy Reaffirmed," *Washington Post*, January 22, 1994; "What Is About to Be Lost," *Economist*, January 22, 1994; Steven Erlanger, "Russian Premier's Star Is Rising Fast," *New York Times*, January 26, 1994; "The Road to Ruin," *Economist*, January 29, 1994; Thomas Friedman, "US Asks Allies to Help Speed IMF Aid to Russia," *New York Times*, February 1, 1994, "IMF Head Defends Russia Loan Policy Against Criticism," *New York Times*, February 2, 1994.

22. Jim Hoagland, "The Empire Strides Back," *Washington Post*, June 2, 1992.

23. Foreign Broadcast Information Service, SOV–93–087, May 7, 1993.

24. John Lloyd, "Russian Defense Ministry Turns on Kozyrev," *Financial Times*, July 9, 1992.

25. A full summary of the Russian armed forces doctrine is in FBIS, SOV–93–2225, November 19, 1993.

26. David White, "Assault Tactics Puzzle Experts," *Financial Times*, October 5, 1993; Serge Schmemann, "Russia Drops Pledge of No First Use," *New York Times*, November 4, 1993; Fred Hiatt, "Russia Shifts Doctrine on Military Use," *Washington Post*, November 4, 1993; for text of the Basic Provisions of the Military Doctrine of the Russian Federation see FBIS, SOV–93–222–S, November 19, 1993; Serge Schmemann, "Russia's Military, a Shriveled and Volatile Legacy," *New York Times*, November 28, 1993; Associated Press, "Yeltsin Said to Scale Back Plans to Slash Army's Size," December 30, 1993.

27. John Lloyd, "Russia's Love Affair with West Ends in Disappointment," *Financial Times*, February 25, 1993; Andrew Gowers, "Russia Attacks UN Vote on Serbia," *Financial Times*, April 21, 1993; Michael Littlejohns, "Russia Uses Veto on Cyprus Force," *Financial Times*, May 13, 1993; Andrew Lawler and Daniel Sneider, "US, Russia Quarrel Over Missile Exports," *Defense News*, June 21, 1993; Michael Gordon, "US Warns Russia on Missile-Fuel Sales," *New York Times*, June 23, 1993; Michael Dobbs, "Russian Premier Delays US Visit," *Washington Post*, June 25, 1993; Daniel Williams, "Russia Wary of Following US Lead on Policies," *Washington Post*, July 2, 1993.

28. Fred Hiatt, "Ex-Soviet States End Joint Forces," *Washington Post*, June 16, 1993.

29. Schmemann, "Russia's Military."

30. Adi Ignatius, "Russia Now Fields a Potemkin Military," *Wall Street Journal*, July 2, 1993; Elaine Sciolino, "Moscow Won't Send More Troops to Balkans," *New York Times*, June 12, 1993.

31. Steven Erlanger, "Russia's Workers Pay Price as Military Industries Fade," *New York Times*, December 13, 1993.

32. Thomas Lippman, "Ex-Soviet Arms Exports Plunge," *Washington Post*, June 13, 1993.

33. George Lardner, Jr., "Republics' Procurement of Arms Said to Plunge," *Washington Post*, January 23, 1992.

CHAPTER 4

1. The figures are: Estonia, 0.5 million; Latvia, 1 million; Lithuania, 0.3 million; Belarus, 1.3 million; Ukraine, 11.4 million; Moldova, 0.6 million; Georgia, 0.3 million; Armenia, 0.7 million; Azerbaijan, about 0.4 million; Kazakhstan, over 6 million; Turkmenistan, 0.4 million; Uzbekistan, 1.6 million; Tajikistan, 0.4 million; and Kirghistan, 0.8 million. These figures are rough ones, reflecting considerable migration of ethnic Russians from the outlying republics into Russia, which is continuing. Deutsche Bank, "The Soviet Union at the Crossroads," 1991; "Russians Abroad: Pawns or Knights," *Economist*, July 10, 1993.

2. Based in part on International Institute for Strategic Studies, *Military Balance*, 1993–94; Steven Erlanger, "Troops in Ex-Soviet Lands: Occupiers or Needed Allies," *New York Times*, November 30, 1993.

3. FBIS, SOV–93–222–S, November 19, 1993.

4. "Azerbaijan Chief Offers to Resign," *New York Times*, June 8, 1993; Serge Schmemann, "War and Politics Clog Azerbaijan's Road to Riches," *New York Times*, July 9, 1993; James Rupert, "Civil Wars in Ex-Soviet Republics Draw Russia into Troubled Morass," *Washington Post*, July 15, 1993; "Azerbaijan Claims Armenians Seized a Key Town," *New York Times*, September 5, 1993; "Alarm in Kaukassus," *Frankfurter Allgemeine Zeitung*, September 8, 1993; John Lloyd, "Azeris May Join CIS and Improve Chances of Peace," *Financial Times*, September 7, 1993, "Azeris Offer Peace Talks," *Financial Times*, September 8, 1993; "Refugees on Move in Azerbaijan War," *New York Times*, September 16, 1993; "Kozyrev Warns Armenia Over Aid," *Financial Times*, November 23, 1993; "The Bear Pauses," *Economist*, December 11, 1993.

5. David White, "The Empire Splits Up," *Financial Times*, December 22, 1992; John Lloyd, "Georgia Peace Negotiations Break Down," *Financial Times*, July 13, 1993; David Kakabadse, "Im Transkaukasus Kreuzen sich viele Interessen," *Frankfurter Allgemeine Zeitung*, September 8, 1993; Celestine Bohlen, "Moscow Sidesteps a Role in Georgia," *New York Times*, September 24, 1993; Thomas Goltz, "Besieged Georgia City Reinforced but the Intense Fighting Continues," *New York Times*, September 27, 1993; Serge Schmemann, "In Crushing Blow to Georgia, City Falls to Secessionists," *New York Times*, September 28, 1993; Celestine Bohlen, "Shevardnadze's Fight With Rebels Links His Fate to Georgia's Future," *New York Times*, October 3, 1993; Serge Schmemann, "Around Russia's Rim, a Fear of Events at the Center," *New York Times*, October 3, 1993; "Georgien will der GUS Beitreten," *Frankfurter Allgemeine Zeitung*, October 9–10, 1993; Thomas Goltz, "Fears Raised for Refugees in Caucasus," *New York Times*, October 10, 1993; John Lloyd and Steve LeVine, "Hungry Russia Watches Georgia Carve Itself Up," *Financial Times*, October 20, 1993; "Georgia Troops Move Into Rebel Stronghold," *New York Times*, October 25, 1993; Raymond Bonner, "Shevardnadze Enters Stronghold Recaptured from Foes in Georgia," *New York Times*, November 8, 1993, "Georgian Talks of New War With Separatists," *New York Times*, November 19, 1993;

Frances Williams, "UN Talks on Abkhazia," *Financial Times*, December 1, 1993; Raymond Bonner, "Pact with Russia Bedevils Georgian," *New York Times*, December 9, 1993; Frances Williams, "Abkhazia Talks Make Progress," *Financial Times*, January 13, 1994; "Georgia and Abkhazia Sign Pact," *Financial Times*, January 14, 1994.

6. Chrystia Freeland, "Russia Hints at Attacks Across Afghan Border," *Financial Times*, July 21, 1993; Raymond Bonner, "Asian Republic Still Caught in Web of Communism," *New York Times*, October 13, 1993, "Why All Eyes are on a Place Called Tajikistan," *New York Times*, November 7, 1993, "Tajik Civil War Fades, but the Brutality Goes On," *New York Times*, November 26, 1993; "Tajikistan: Lost Freedom," *Economist*, December 4, 1993.

7. John Lloyd, "Moscow Back Pedals in Row Over Baltic Troops," *Financial Times*, January 20, 1994.

8. Leslie Gelb, "Yeltsin as Monroe," *New York Times*, March 7, 1993.

9. "European Leaders Voice Concerns Over Possible Russian Expansionism," special to the *Washington Post*, February 6, 1994.

10. "Remaking the Soviet Union," *Economist*, July 13, 1991.

11. Mark Smith, *The Soviet Fault Line: Ethnic Insecurity and Territorial Dispute in the Former USSR* (London: Royal United Services Institute for Defense Studies, 1991); Stephen Van Evera, "Managing the Eastern Crisis: Preventing War in the Former Soviet Union," *Security Studies,* Spring 1992.

12. "Warnings from Massandra," *Economist*, September 11, 1993; "Russian Warns of Nuclear Risk in Ukraine," *Washington Post*, November 6, 1993; "Russia Warns Ukraine on Decay of Warheads," *New York Times*, November 6, 1993; Steven Erlanger, "Ukraine's Hedging on A-Arms Angers Russia," *New York Times*, November 22, 1993; John Lloyd, "Kiev Faces Sanctions in Nuclear Row," *Financial Times*, November 24, 1993; "Ukraine: Bomb Huggers," *Economist*, November 27, 1993; "Ukraine Nuclear Arms Deactivated," *Financial Times*, December 2, 1993; Leyla Boulton, "Yeltsin Attacks 'Evil' of Ukraine's Nuclear Delays," *Financial Times*, December 16, 1993; Jill Barshay, "Ukraine Nears Nuclear Deal," *Financial Times*, December 20, 1993; Michael R. Gordon, "Kiev Acts Quickly on Pledge to Remove Warheads," *New York Times*, December 21, 1993; Jill Barshay and George Graham, "Kiev Confident of Deal on N-Arms," *Financial Times*, December 22, 1993; Ann Devroy, "Pact Reached to Dismantle Ukraine's Nuclear Force," *Washington Post*, January 1, 1994; R. Jeffrey Smith, "U.S., Ukraine, Russia Near Deal on Arms," *Washington Post*, January 9, 1994; Jurek Martin and John Lloyd, "Ukraine to Give Up N-Weapons," *Financial Times*, January 11, 1994; R. W. Apple, Jr., "Ukraine Gives in on Surrendering Its Nuclear Arms," *New York Times*, January 11, 1994; Jane Perlez, "Ukraine Hesitates on Nuclear Deal," *New York Times*, January 12, 1994; John Lloyd, "Ukraine Offers Debt Swap in N-Deal," *Financial Times*, January 13, 1994; Ann Devroy and Margaret Shapiro, "Clinton Pledges U.S. Support for Russia's Revival," *Washington Post*, January 15, 1994.

13. Daniel Williams, "Japan Hedges on Nuclear Arms Treaty," *Washington Post*, July 9, 1993.

14. Cited by Sir Solly Zuckerman, "A Nuclear Weapon-Free World—Feasible? Desirable?" *New York Review of Books,* June 24, 1993.

15. William J. Broad, "Russia Has Far More A-Fuel Than US Thinks, Study Finds," *New York Times,* September 11, 1992.

16. Richard Cheney, speech to the American Political Science Association, August 29, 1992.

17. Robert Daniels, review of *Comrades* by Brian Moynahan, *New York Times Book Review,* May 3, 1992.

18. John Lloyd, "Pressing Ahead on the Land Road of Reform," *Financial Times,* May 27, 1993.

19. See *Economist Book of Vital World Statistics* (New York: Times Books-Random House, 1990), p. 31. Spain was calculated to be at about 50 percent on the UN index of purchasing power parity, with the United States at 100 percent.

20. David Roche (Morgan Stanley International), in "Russia Looks at the World," *Economist,* July 4, 1992; Jacek Rostowski, "Why the West Must Plug Russia's Gap," *Financial Times,* January 20, 1994.

21. William J. Perry, Senate Confirmation Hearing, Answers to Advance Questions. Text in *Inside the Pentagon,* February 3, 1994.

22. FBIS, SOV–92–241, December 15, 1992.

23. Text in the *Washington Post,* February 22, 1990; statement of William Perry before the Senate Armed Services Committee, February 2, 1994.

CHAPTER 5

1. To claim greater affinity with Western Europe and greater distance from Russia, Poland, the Czech Republic, Slovakia, and Hungary like to call themselves East Central Europe or even Central Europe. In this terminology, Romania, Bulgaria, Albania, and the Yugoslav states are the Balkans. But Ukraine, as well as Romania and Bulgaria, like to call themselves part of Eastern Europe. This survey uses the term *Eastern Europe* to refer to all the countries between Germany and the former Soviet Union.

2. Cited by Brooke Unger, "Poland," *Economist,* April 16, 1994.

3. Stephen Engeberg, "East Bloc Treading Water in a Sinkhole of Lethargy," *New York Times,* April 8, 1992; Abraham Brumberg, "Mitteleuropa Blues," *New York Times Book Review,* June 14, 1992.

4. Mary Battiata, "Polish Police Files Provoke Political Mud Slinging," *Washington Post,* July 9, 1992; "Eastern Europe's Past: The Complexities of Justice," *Economist,* March 21, 1992.

5. Frances Williams, "A New Economic Order Eludes Eastern Europe," *Financial Times,* April 6, 1992; John Parker, "Eastern Europe," *Economist,* March 13, 1993.

6. See inter alia Deutsche Bank, "Privatization in Eastern Europe: A Status Report," 1991; "Business in Eastern Europe," *Economist,* September 21, 1991;

William Ryrie, "Free-Market Preaching in a World with No Marketplace," *Washington Post,* July 28, 1991.

7. "Europe: Crossing the East-West Chasm," *Economist,* May 16, 1992.

8. "East European Economies," *Economist,* December 19, 1992; Anders Aslund, "The Triumph of Capitalism," FBIS, WEV–93–016, January 27, 1993; Parker, "Eastern Europe," p. 160; Anthony Robinson and Christopher Bobinski, "Poland Poised to Be a Post-Communist Success Story," *Financial Times,* February 24, 1993; Konstanty Gebert, "'Shock' Crock: Plan's Overrated Reforms," *Washington Post,* May 2, 1993.

9. Richard Stevenson, "East Europe Says Barriers to Trade Hurt Its Economies," *New York Times,* January 25, 1993; "Poor Relations," *Economist,* May 1, 1993; European Council Copenhagen Communique, text extracts, *Financial Times,* June 23, 1993; Alan Riding, "European Community Sets Terms for 6 Former Soviet Allies to Join," *New York Times,* June 23, 1993.

10. Gillian Tett, "Poor Prospects Seen for Incomes in Eastern Europe," *Financial Times,* September 22, 1993.

11. Frances Williams, "Modest Recovery in Eastern Europe Foreseen," *Financial Times,* April 18, 1994.

12. As quoted in Bruno Schoch, "To Strasbourg or to Sarajevo," Peace Research Institute, Frankfurt, Report no. 28, September 1992, a thoughtful and valuable discussion of the overall problem.

13. Parker, "Eastern Europe," p. 18, has a useful chart of minorities. See also "That Other Europe," *Economist,* December 25, 1993.

14. F. Stephen Larrabee, "Long Memories and Short Fuses," *International Security,* vol. 15, no. 3 (Winter 1990–91); Daniel N. Nelson, "Europe's Unstable East," *Foreign Policy,* Spring 1991; Hugh Miall, *New Conflicts in Europe* (Oxford: Oxford Research Group, Current Decisions Report no. 10, July 1992).

15. Schoch, "To Strasbourg or to Sarajevo," p. 167.

16. Pal Dunay, "Das Alte Ungarn im Neuen Europa," Peace Research Institute, Frankfurt, Report no. 2, 1993; Judith Ingram, "Boys Impatient for Greater Hungary to Take Wing," *New York Times,* January 15, 1993; Stephen Engelberg and Judith Ingram, "New Hungary Adds Its Voice to the Ethnic Tumult," *New York Times,* January 25, 1993; Hansjakob Stehle, "Heiliger Schachsinn," *Die Zeit,* January 29, 1993.

17. Schoch, "To Strasbourg or to Sarajevo," p. 167.

18. Ibid.

19. "Gag Rule in Romania," *New York Times,* March 9, 1993.

20. David Ottoway, "Romania Seeks to Ease Ethnic Tensions," *Washington Post,* April 3, 1993; David Binder, "Romanians and Hungarians Building a Bit of Trust," *New York Times,* July 20, 1993.

21. "Romania's Iliescu Holds Talks with NATO's Woesner," ROMPres, Bucharest, cited in FBIS, SEU–93–032 February 19, 1993.

22. "Out of Frying Pan, into Fire," *Economist,* April 2, 1994; "Albania; Just for Show," *Economist,* April 9, 1994.

23. Kerin Hope, "Albania Rattles a Diplomatic Sabre at Greece," *Financial Times,* April 15, 1994.

24. Henry Konnir, "Life Remains Grim for the Albanians," *New York Times,* June 20, 1993.
25. Text is in FBIS, WEU–91–056, March 22, 1991.
26. Quoted in *Economist,* June 29, 1991, pp. 16–17.

CHAPTER 6

1. For background on the Yugoslav crisis, see James Gow, "Deconstructing Yugoslavia," *Survival,* vol. 33, no. 4 (July–August 1991); Jonathan Dean, "Coping with Europe's Security Problems: The First Tests," in Eric H. Arnett, ed., *New Perspectives for a Changing World Order* (Washington, DC: American Association for the Advancement of Science, 1991); Peter Billing, Der Bürgerkrieg in Jugoslawien, Hessische Stiftung-Friedens-und Konfliktforschung Report no. 1, 1992; James B. Steinberg, *The Role of European Institutions in Security after the Cold War: Some Lessons from Yugoslavia,* Report no. CAN–3445–FF (Rand Corporation, Santa Monica, CA, 1992); John Newhouse, "Dodging the Problem," *New Yorker,* August 24, 1992; John Zametica, *The Yugoslav Conflict,* Adelphi Paper 270 (London: International Institute of Strategic Studies, 1992); John Newhouse, "No Exit, No Entrance," *New Yorker,* June 28, 1993.
2. Barry Posen, "The Security Dilemma and Ethnic Conflict," *Survival,* vol. 35, no. 1 (Spring 1993), citing Ivo Banac, "Political Change and National Diversity," *Daedalus,* vol. 119, no. 1 (Winter 1990).
3. Ibid.
4. David Binder, "Yugoslavia Seen Breaking Up Soon," *New York Times,* November 28, 1990.
5. In an Aspen Institute conference in Berlin in March 1991, I advocated preparing a NATO force for intervention if Slovenia and Croatia seceded. Within several Western governments, officials were suggesting the same thing.
6. Cited in Anthony Lewis, "What Might Have Been," *New York Times,* January 10, 1994.
7. U.S. Commission on Security and Cooperation in Europe, "The Referendum on Independence in Bosnia-Herzegovina," March 12, 1992.
8. Chuck Sudetic, "Yugoslav Groups Reach Accord," *New York Times,* March 19, 1992. The text of the draft agreement is in FBIS, EEU–92–054, March 19, 1992.
9. John F. Burns, "Bosnia 1992," *New York Times,* December 31, 1992; Elaine Sciolino, "U.S. Fears a Sharp Rise in Balkan Refugee Flow," *New York Times,* July 13, 1993.
10. Blaine Harden, "UN Pleads for Help for Bosnian Refugees," *Washington Post,* July 23, 1992.
11. Anthony Lewis, "The End of Pretending," *New York Times,* February 7, 1994.

12. Details are in UN Security Council document S 25050 of January 6, 1993, the Report of the Secretary General on the Activities of the International Conference on the former Yugoslavia.

13. Secretary of State Warren Christopher, opening statement at press conference of February 10, 1993, text in *Dispatch* 4, no. 7, March 1993, Department of State.

14. Paul Lewis, "Bosnian Muslims Join Croats in Accepting Peace Plan," *New York Times,* March 26, 1993.

15. Peter Maass, "Bosnian Serbs Bar UN Peace Plan," *Washington Post,* April 3, 1993.

16. Paul Lewis, "Balkan Negotiator, in Shift, Backs Plan Dividing Bosnia," *New York Times,* June 18, 1993; David B. Ottaway, "Mediator Backs Partition for Bosnia," *Washington Post,* June 18, 1993.

17. Paul Lewis, "Two Leaders Propose Dividing Bosnia into Three Areas," *New York Times,* June 17, 1993; Paul Lewis, "Serb-Croat Plan to Split Up Bosnia Worries Mediators," *New York Times,* June 24, 1993; David Ottaway, "Bosnian Partition Plan Echoes Earlier Proposal," *Washington Post,* July 27, 1993.

18. "Bosnia: They Call It Peace," *Economist,* August 28, 1993; John F. Burns, "Bosnia Legislators Reject Peace Plan in a Lopsided Vote," *New York Times,* September 30, 1993; Eugene Robinson, "EC Negotiator Says U.S. 'Killed' Plan for Bosnia," *Washington Post,* November 27, 1993; William Drozdiak, "EC Pressing Bosnia Plan—Again," *Washington Post,* November 29, 1993; David Ottaway, "Serb-Muslim Deadlock Stalls Bosnia Talks," *Washington Post,* January 19, 1994; Laura Silber, "Bosnia Partition Talks Collapse," *Financial Times,* January 20, 1994; John Kifner, "Foe's Troops Pouring In, Bosnia Says," *New York Times,* January 31, 1994; Laura Silber, "Zagreb Denies Troops in Bosnia," *Financial Times,* January 31, 1994; John Kifner, "Bosnian Serbs Order General Mobilization for 'Conclusion of War'" *New York Times,* February 1, 1994; "Bosnia: Lift the Embargo Now," editorial, *New York Times,* February 6, 1994; Richard Burt and Richard Perle, "The Next Act in Bosnia," *New York Times* op-ed, February 11, 1994.

19. Craig Whitney, "NATO Air Strikes in Bosnia: A Catch-22," *New York Times,* July 17, 1993; William Drozdiak and Daniel Williams, "NATO Warms to East, Splits on Bosnia Action," *Washington Post,* January 11, 1994; "The Cost of Weakness," *Economist,* January 29, 1994; Craig Whitney, "Putting Force Behind Talk," *New York Times,* February 11, 1994.

20. Alex Morrison, executive director of the Canadian Institute of Strategic Studies, cited in Anne Swardson, "Canada, with Troops in Bosnia, Stands Firm against Airstrikes," *Washington Post,* January 14, 1994.

21. David Ottaway and Julia Preston, "UN Rejects Airstrikes in Bosnia; Talks Break Up," *Washington Post,* January 20, 1994; Thomas Lippman, "NATO Allies Losing Resolve for Airstrikes," *Washington Post,* January 23, 1994; Elaine Sciolino, "U.S. Rejects Plea to Act in Bosnia," *New York Times,* January 25, 1994; "The Bosnia Stall," *Economist,* February 5, 1994; Julia Preston, "Boutros-Ghali Backs Airstrikes in Bosnia," *Washington Post,* January 29, 1994; John Goshko, "U.S. Endorses NATO Role in UN Plan for Bosnia," *Washington Post,* February 1, 1994;

David Ottaway, "NATO Gives Serbs Airstrike Deadline," *Washington Post,* February 10, 1994; Elaine Sciolino with Douglas Jehl, "As U.S. Sought a Bosnia Policy, the French Offered a Good Idea," *New York Times,* February 14, 1994; NATO Press Communique M–NAC–1(93) 38, Final Communique, Ministerial Meeting of North Atlantic Council, June 10, 1993; NATO Press Communique M–1(94) 3, Declaration of the Heads of State and Government, January 11, 1994; John Pomfret, "UN, NATO, in Dispute over Bosnia," *Washington Post,* February 14, 1994, "UN, U.S. Differ on Ultimatum," *Washington Post,* February 15, 1994; Steven Erlanger, "Yeltsin Adamant on Role in Bosnia," *New York Times,* February 16, 1994; Daniel Williams, "Maneuvering over Bosnia Puts U.S.-Russian Harmony at Risk," *Washington Post,* February 20, 1994.

22. John Pomfret, "Croatia, Serbs Sign Cease-Fire," *Washington Post,* March 30, 1994.

23. Daniel Williams and Thomas Lippman, "Muslims and Croats Link Territories," *Washington Post,* March 2, 1994.

CHAPTER 7

1. *Economist Book of Vital World Statistics* (New York: Random House, 1990), pp. 31, 33.

2. "So Much Power, So Little Purpose," *Economist,* July 3, 1993.

3. Marc Fisher, "Germany Groans under Huge Cost of Unification," *Washington Post,* July 2, 1991; *Economist,* January 18, 1992; Roger Cohen, "The Growing Weight of German Reunification," *New York Times,* March 8, 1993.

4. "The Bank They Love to Hate," *Economist,* January 18, 1992.

5. *Focus: Germany,* no. 77, April 2, 1992; Unification Issues, Economic Forecasts for 1992, December 1991, Deutsche Bank; Norbert Walter, "The Wages of German Success," *New York Times,* May 22, 1992.

6. "Germany Recounts the Cost," *Economist,* June 29, 1991; "Kohl's Debterdämmerung?" *Economist,* April 4, 1992; Richard E. Smith, "German Sea Change as the Bills Come In," *International Herald Tribune,* October 21, 1991; Cohen, "The Growing Weight of German Unification," p. 225.

7. *Economist,* March 23, 1991; Marc Fisher, "Economy Migrates in Germany," *Washington Post,* February 27, 1992.

8. Robert J. Samuelson, "Europe's Boom Has Come and Gone," *Washington Post,* February 12, 1992; Christoph Bertram, "Go Easy on Worried Germany," *New York Times,* May 12, 1992.

9. Craig Whitney, "Germans Feel Pain of Unity," *New York Times,* February 19, 1993; Ariane Genillard, "West German GDP Could Fall by 1.5%," *Financial Times,* April 15, 1993.

10. John M. Berry, "Europe's Plan for Monetary Union at Risk," *Washington Post,* July 31, 1993.

11. Ferdinand Protzman, "Germany Moves to Make First Cut in Social Programs," *New York Times*, August 12, 1993.

12. Quentin Peel, "Forced to Find Common Ground," *Financial Times*, December 8, 1992; Christopher Parkes, "'Crash Landing' Predicted for W. German Economy," *Financial Times*, March 1, 1993; Quentin Peel, "Bonn Acts to Curb Deficit With $12 Billion Spending Cut," *Financial Times*, July 14, 1993; "The Stiff Man of Europe Loosens Up," *Economist*, July 17, 1993.

13. Marc Fisher, "On German Birthday Easterners Await Happy Returns," *Washington Post*, September 29, 1991; "The Weight on Kohl's Mind," *Economist*, April 6, 1992; Stephen Kinzer, "As Euphoria of Unity Fades, Eastern Germans Feel Scorned and Excluded," *New York Times*, April 18, 1992.

14. Cited in Kinzer, "As Euphoria of Unity Fades."

15. "Deutschland 2000," *Sueddeutsche Zeitung*, January 1, 1991.

16. Cited in Ronald Asmus, *Germany in Transition*, Report no. D–7767 (Santa Monica, CA: Rand Corporation, 1992).

17. Marc Fisher, "On Trial for Death at the Berlin Wall," *Washington Post*, September 10, 1991, "East German Guards Convicted," *Washington Post*, January 21, 1992.

18. Rick Atkinson, "Three Ex-Eastern Officials Sentenced," *Washington Post*, September 17, 1993.

19. "Parteien einigen sich auf Regeln zum Umgang mit STASI-Akten," *Frankfurter Allgemeine Zeitung*, April 26, 1991; Peter Jochen Winters, "In den Akten und in den Koepfen" *Frankfurter Allgemeine Zeitung*, May 21, 1991; Ferdinand Protzman, "Ex-East German Chief Quits Politics," *New York Times*, September 7, 1991; Stephen Kinzer, "German MP's Face Background Checks," *International Herald Tribune*, October 19, 1991; Marc Fisher, "Bonn Closing Books, Opening Controversy," *Washington Post*, November 13, 1991; "Bad Spirits," *Economist*, December 21, 1991; Marc Fisher, "East Germans Face Pain of Redefining Pasts," *Washington Post*, January 19, 1992; "Not All He Seemed," *Economist*, January 25, 1992; John Tagliabue, "Eastern Germany Is Investigated," *New York Times*, February 5, 1992; Stephen Kinzer, "Germans Anguish over Police Files," *New York Times*, February 20, 1992.

20. German Information Center, *This Week in Germany*, March 29, 1992; Judy Dempsey, "Cracks behind the Unity," *Financial Times*, November 16, 1992.

21. "Zachert, Nicht Nur Randgruppen," *Frankfurter Allgemeine Zeitung*, June 16, 1993; "German Democracy on Guard," Konrad Adenauer Stiftung, Washington, DC, January 1993; German Information Center, New York, "Focus on Right-Wing Radicalism in Germany," February 1993, *This Week in Germany*, June 18, 1993.

22. Craig Whitney, "Disabled Germans Fear They'll Be the Next Target," *New York Times*, January 19, 1993; Marc Fisher, "Turks' Deaths Dash Optimism in Germany," *Washington Post*, May 31, 1993.

23. Stephen Kinzer, "Bonn Parliament Votes Sharp Curb on Asylum Seekers," *New York Times*, May 27, 1993.

24. Stephen Kinzer, "Germany Closing Migrants' Hostels," *New York Times*, September 8, 1993.

25. Jane Perlez, "Prague Fears Being Migrant Trail's Last Stop," June 30, 1993.

26. Quentin Peel, "Kohl Moves to Review German Citizenship Laws," *Financial Times*, June 17, 1993; Stephen Kinzer, "Kohl Plans to Ease the Path for New Citizens," *New York Times*, June 17, 1993.

27. Marc Fisher, "2,000 Neo-Nazis March in Dresden," *Washington Post*, June 16, 1991, "Anti-Immigrant Violence Grows in Germany," *Washington Post*, September 30, 1991; Stephen Kinzer, "Anti-Foreign Passions Boil in Northern Germany," *International Herald Tribune*, October 9, 1991; Marc Fisher, "Germans' Kristallnacht Observance Ends in Clash of Leftists, Neo-Nazis," *Washington Post*, November 10, 1991; Frederick Kempe, "Germans Try to Stem Right-Wing Attacks on Foreigners," *Wall Street Journal*, December 4, 1991; German Information Center, "Reform of Asylum Law," *This Week in Germany*, January 10, 1992; Associated Press, "German Social Democrats Signal Openness to Limits on Refugees," *New York Times*, March 13, 1992; German Information Center, "State Elections: CDU Loses in the South, SPD in the North, Far Right Gains in Both," *This Week in Germany*, April 10, 1992; "Bleibt es beim Rechtsruch?," *Der Spiegel*, no. 18, April 1992.

28. "Zachert, Nicht Nur Randgruppen," *Frankfurter Allgemeine Zeitung*, June 16, 1993.

29. Wolfgang Roth, "Anonyme Beiträge für Extremisten," *Sueddeutsche Zeitung*, October 9, 1993.

30. John Pomfret, "Europe's Rio Grande Floods with Refugees," *Washington Post*, July 11, 1993.

31. "Berufsverbot für Republikaner der Falscherweg," *Sueddeutsche Zeitung*, December 2, 1993.

32. David Marsh, "Regretful Note over Unity's Path," *Financial Times*, September 9, 1993.

33. "On Second Thoughts," *Economist*, March 14, 1992.

34. "CSCU Erteilt 'Europa-Euphorie' Eine Absage," *Sueddeutsche Zeitung*, October 9, 1993; Quentin Peel, "Bavaria's PM Exposes Split on European Union," *Financial Times*, November 3, 1993; Rick Atkinson, "Germans Debating European Union Again," *Washington Post*, November 12, 1993.

35. Claus Gennrich, "Hoffnung auf eine Versoehnung Mit Polen," *Frankfurter Allgemeine Zeitung*, May 2, 1991; Marc Fisher, "German and Poland Sign Border Treaty," *Washington Post*, June 18, 1991; Claus Gennrich, "Deutschland und Polen besiegeln die Neugestaltung der Beziehungen," *Frankfurter Allgemeine Zeitung*, October 18, 1991.

36. Christopher Parkes, "Germany Plans Sharp Cuts in Spending on Military," *Financial Times*, January 13, 1992; Quentin Peel, "Bundeswehr Set for Radical Cutback," *Financial Times*, February 20, 1992; Foreign Broadcast Information Service WEU–92–034, February 20, 1992.

37. German Information Center, *The Week in Germany*, February 12, 1993; *Atlantic News*, February 10, 1993; *Atlantic News*, February 12, 1993.

38. Robert Gerald Livingston, "Good Morning, Germany," *Der Spiegel*, January 20, 1992.

39. John J. Mearsheimer, "Back to the Future," *International Security* 15, no. 1, (Summer 1990).

CHAPTER 8

1. Eugene Robinson, "Worldwide Migration Nears Crisis," *Washington Post*, July 7, 1993.

2. Edward Mortimer, "Convenient Cracks in the Wall," *Financial Times*, April 15, 1993; Henry Kamm, "In Europe's Upheaval Doors Close to Foreigners," *New York Times*, February 10, 1993.

3. Alan Riding, "Tougher Rules on French Citizenship Approved," *International Herald Tribune*, May 14, 1993; "France, Zero Option," *Economist*, June 12, 1993; Roger Cohen, "French Immigration Curbs Provoke Cabinet Rift," *New York Times*, June 23, 1993; William Drozdiak, "Rolling Up a Worn-Out Welcome Mat," *Washington Post*, July 13, 1993.

4. David Buchan, "EC Urged to Offer Free Trade to Maghreb Countries," *Financial Times*, April 3, 1992.

5. Michel Debré, "The Threat Is from the South," *Le Quotidien de Paris*, June 26, 1990, cited in Foreign Broadcast Information Service, WEU–90–150, August 3, 1990; Edward Mortimer, "Is This Our Frontier?" *Financial Times*, April 3, 1992; Judith Miller, "The Islamic Wave," *New York Times Magazine*, May 31, 1992.

6. The literature on Islamic fundamentalism is very large and rapidly growing. Among useful sources are John Esposito, *The Islamic Threat* (New York: Oxford University Press, 1992); Mark Juergensmeyer, *The New Cold War?* (Berkeley: University of California Press, 1992); Ghassan Salame, "Islam and the West," *Foreign Policy*, Spring 1993; the three volumes of the Fundamentalism Project of the American Academy of Arts and Sciences, described in the *Fundamentalist Project Newsletter*, Spring 1993; George Perkovich, "Insecurity and Islam," *Tikkun*, May–June 1993; Judith Miller, "The Challenge of Radical Islam," *Foreign Affairs*, Spring 1993; Charles Butterworth and I. William Zartman, eds., *Political Islam*, annals of the American Academy of Political and Social Science, November 1992.

7. William Drozdiak, "Turmoil in Algeria Alarming Europeans," *Washington Post*, December 17, 1993; "Algeria, No Place to Be a Foreigner," *Economist*, December 18, 1993.

8. Jonathan Randall, "Tunisia Appears to Have Defused Its Militant Fundamentalist Surge," *Washington Post*, June 6, 1991; "Soviet Central Asia, the Next Islamic Revolution," *Economist*, September 21, 1991; William Drozdiak, "Iran and Turkey Vie for Political, Economic Influence in Soviet Muslim States," *Washington Post*, November 24, 1991; Martha Brill Alcott, "Central Asia or Bust," *New York Times*, December 30, 1991; "Algeria Votes for Islam," *Economist*, January 4, 1992; M. J. Akbar, "At the Center of the World," *New York Times*, January 10, 1992; Jonathan Randall, "Algeria's President Quits, Imperiling Power Shift to Moslems," *Washington Post*, January 12, 1992; "Algeria, the Soldiers Cut In," *Economist*, January 18, 1992; Amos Perlmutter, "Wishful Thinking about Islamic Fundamentalism," *Washington Post*, January 19, 1992; "Sudan, Islam's Star," *Economist*, February 1, 1992; Jennifer Parmelee, "Sudan Denies Khartoum-Tehran Axis to Promote Islamic Regimes in Africa," *Washington Post*, March 12, 1992; "Islam Resumes Its March," *Economist*, April 4, 1992; Steve Call, "Afghan Crisis Turns Inward," *Washington Post*, April 19, 1992.

9. Roberto Aliboni, "European Security across the Mediterranean," Institute for Security Studies, WEU, Chaillot Paper, no. 2, March 1991.

10. Count de Marenches and David A. Andelman, *The Fourth World War* (New York: Morrow, 1992).

11. "Algeria and the Bomb," *Economist*, January 11, 1992; Jack Anderson and Michael Binstein, "An Iranian Bomb," *Washington Post*, January 12, 1992; R. Jeffrey Smith, "Gates Warns of Iranian Arms Drive," *Washington Post*, March 28, 1992.

12. Graham Fuller, "Islamic Fundamentalism: No Long-Term Threat," *Washington Post*, January 13, 1992, *Islamic Fundamentalism in the Northern Tier Countries*, Report R–3966–USDP (Santa Monica, CA: Rand Corporation, 1991); "Algeria Retreats," *Economist*, January 18, 1992; David Ignatius, "Islam in the West's Sights: The Wrong Crusade?" *Washington Post*, March 8, 1992; "Living with Islam," *Economist*, April 4, 1992.

13. Pervez Hoodbhoy, "The 'Islamic' Bomb," *Bulletin of the Atomic Scientists*, June 1993.

14. David Buchan, "EC Urged to Offer Free Trade to Maghreb Countries," *Financial Times*, April 30, 1992; Aliboni, "European Security across the Mediterranean."

CHAPTER 9

1. Helsinki Document 1992, para. 22.

2. A note on sources for this chapter. The main sources for the analysis of CSCE are the "Documents," the summaries of conclusions reached after each major CSCE session. Cumulatively, the Documents are the rules that CSCE member states have agreed should guide their actions. I have been following CSCE closely since its outset, and much of the material in this chapter is from my notes of many conversations with diplomats and officials dealing with CSCE. Of other published sources, John J. Maresca's book, *To Helsinki* (Durham, NC: Duke University Press, 1985), is invaluable for the early period. Much useful information is contained in *Focus on Vienna*, periodic reports issued by the Austrian Committee for European Security and Cooperation (Lederergasse 23/3/27 A 1094, Vienna); *CSCE Events since 1972*, pamphlet issued in 1992 by the Finnish National Committee for European Security (Ruoholahdenkatu 14, 00180 Helsinki), which contains a valuable chronology of CSCE developments; in the five *CSCE Helsinki 92* bulletins issued by the NCES; and in the many publications by the Commission on Security and Cooperation in Europe of Washington, DC, especially *An Overview of the CSCE Process, Recent Meetings, and Institutional Development*, February 1992, and *From Vienna to Helsinki: Reports on the Inter-Sessional Meetings of the CSCE Process*, April 1992. Documents of the CSCE can be obtained from the United States commission. For current structure and future of the CSCE, a helpful source is Norbert Ropers and Peter Schlotter, *The CSCE*, Study no. 14, Foundation for Development and Peace, Bonn, 1993.

3. Albania, Armenia, Austria, Azerbaijan, Belarus, Belgium, Bosnia and Herzegovina, Bulgaria, Canada, Croatia, Cyprus, Czech Republic, Denmark, Estonia, Finland, France, Georgia, Germany, Greece, Holy See, Hungary, Iceland, Ireland, Italy, Kazakhstan, Kyrgyzstan, Latvia, Liechtenstein, Lithuania, Luxembourg, Malta, Moldova, Monaco, Netherlands, Norway, Poland, Portugal, Romania, Russia, San Marino, Slovakia, Slovenia, Spain, Sweden, Switzerland, Tajikistan, Turkey, Turkmenistan, Ukraine, United Kingdom, United States, Uzbekistan (Yugoslavia suspended).

4. The figure is from *CSCE Events since 1972*, p. 25.

5. Egon Bahr, "Sicherheit durch Annährung," *Die Zeit,* July 6, 1990.

6. Harald Müller, "A United Nations of Europe and North America," *Arms Control Today,* January–February 1991.

7. Richard H. Ullman, *Securing Europe* (Princeton, NJ: Princeton University Press, 1991).

8. Charles A. and Clifford A. Kupchan, "Concerts, Collective Security and the Future of Europe," *International Security,* Summer 1991.

9. David Ottaway, "Summit Tries to Protect Minorities," *Washington Post,* October 10, 1993; Edward Mortimer, "Europe to Speed Setting of Rights," *Financial Times,* October 11, 1993.

10. Mortimer, "Europe to Speed Setting Rights."

11. Text obtained from Ambassador Kampelman, at the office of Fried, Frank, Harris, Shriver & Jacobson, 1001 Pennsylvania Avenue NW, Washington, DC, 20004.

12. CSCE Summary of Conclusions of the Stockholm Council Meeting, December 15, 1992; *Focus on Vienna,* no. 29, April 1993, Austrian Committee for European Security and Cooperation; Ropers and Schlotter,

13. Helsinki Document 1992, Section III, paras. 22, 23, 30.

14. Helsinki Document 1992, Section III, paras. 36, 37, 52, 53.

15. James Rupert, "Diplomats on Lonely Mission to End Tensions in Yugoslav Regions," *Washington Post,* June 9, 1993.

16. Assembly of Western European Union, *United Nations Operations,* Document 1366, May 19, 1993.

17. *CSCE 94,* Bulletin of the Finnish National Committee for European Security, STETE (Ruoholahdenkatu 14, 00180 Helsinki).

18. Theresa Hitchens, "CSCE Tries to Preserve Shaky Azerbaijan Peace," *Defense News,* June 21, 1993.

19. CSCE, *Decisions by the Rome Council Meeting,* December 1, 1993; Anthony Robinson, "CSCE Defers Peace Mandate," *Financial Times,* December 2, 1993; December 2, 1993; "Keine Einigung Uber Russlands Einsaetze," *Sueddeutsche Zeitung*; Foreign Minister Andrei Kozyrev, "Russia Is Bearing the Burden of Actual Peacemaking in Conflicts on the Perimeter of Its Borders Virtually Alone, and No One Will Do This for Her," Foreign Broadcast Information Service, SOV–93–183, September 23, 1993.

20. "Plan for European Security Conference Soon," *Financial Times,* November 18, 1993.

CHAPTER 10

1. In this chapter, I am not going to discuss NATO's structure at any length, but will provide a brief oversight here as background. NATO's sixteen member governments (Belgium, Canada, Denmark, France, Germany, Greece, Iceland, Italy, Luxembourg, Netherlands, Norway, Portugal, Spain, Turkey, United Kingdom, and the United States) are represented at NATO headquarters in a suburb of Brussels by diplomatic and military personnel organized into a series of committees or working groups. The North Atlantic Council is the principal authority of the alliance. Its members consist of the ambassadorial permanent representatives of the member states, acting under direction of their home governments, and chaired by NATO secretary general Manfred Wörner of Germany. The permanent representatives of the North Atlantic Council meet at least weekly. The council meets each six months at the level of foreign ministers, and from time to time at the level of heads of member governments ("Summits"). The council coordinates member-state positions on new issues and on NATO's ongoing activities. Under it come the Defense Planning Committee (DPC) and the Nuclear Planning Group, composed of the defense ministers of member states except for France. France withdrew from the DPC and from NATO's integrated staff in 1966. NATO has about forty major standing-committees and perhaps two hundred subordinate ones, including some, like the Central European Pipeline System, which are full-time implementing organizations. The most senior of these committees, the Military Committee, consists of the chiefs of staff of participating countries (usually represented by permanent military representatives of general officer rank from all member countries—except Iceland, which has no armed forces, and France). Under the general supervision of the Defense Planning Committee, the Military Committee provides guidance on military questions both to the NATO Council and to NATO military commands. The Military Committee is assisted by the International Military Staff (about 150 officers, 100 civilian employees). NATO now has two main military commands: (1) Supreme Headquarters Allied Powers Europe (SHAPE), headed by a U.S. General, who in wartime commands all ground, air, and naval forces assigned to NATO, and in peacetime organizes, trains, and prepares contingency plans for possible use of the forces; this command now has three major ground and air force subordinate commands; (2) the Allied Command Atlantic (Norfolk, Virginia), with six subordinate commands headed by an American admiral, has responsibility for guarding the Atlantic sea lanes. With the exception of air defense and multinational rapid-reaction forces, the NATO military command has no forces permanently under its command in peacetime. Forces assigned to NATO remain under national command until their governments turn them over to NATO. Details on NATO organization can be found in the annual handbook *The North Atlantic Treat Organization of Facts and Figures,* published by the NATO Information Service.

2. NATO Press Communique S–1(91) 85, November 7, 1991.

3. Ibid., para 21.

4. "NATO Plans Greece's Return to Revamped Southern Flank," *Defense News,* July 12, 1993.

5. Department of Defense, hearings on CFE Treaty, S. HRG. 102–288, March 1991, p. 225; Address of Assistant Secretary of State Stephen Oxman before the Atlantic Council, Washington, DC, August 12, 1993.

6. Theresa Hitchens, "NATO to Devise New Force Requirements," *Defense News,* July 5, 1993.

7. Secretary of Defense Les Aspin, statement before the House Armed Services Committee, March 30, 1993.

8. NATO Press Communique S–1(90) 36, July 6, 1990.

9. NATO Press Communique M–1(91) 42, June 6, 1991, para 3.

10. Text of Lawrence Eagleburger speech made available by the U.S. Department of State.

11. "Rome Declaration on Peace and Cooperation," NATO Press Communique S–1(91) 86, para 11.

12. Alan Cowell, "Bush Challenges Partners in NATO over Role of US," *New York Times,* November 8, 1991. See also Frederick Kempe, "NATO Leaders Prepare to Expand Ties to Ex-Warsaw Pact Countries," *Wall Street Journal,* November 4, 1991; and Alan Riding, "NATO Chiefs Seek to Define Its Role," *New York Times,* November 7, 1991.

13. NATO Press Communique M–NACC–1(91) 111, December 20, 1991.

14. Barbara Crossette, "NATO Eyes Military Role to Halt Azerbaijan Feud," *New York Times,* March 11, 1992.

15. William Drozdiak, "NATO States, Ex-East Bloc Meet for Talks," *Washington Post,* March 11, 1992.

16. Eagleburger, loc. cit.

17. Stanley R. Sloan, "The NATO Strategy Review," *Congressional Research Report* 91–379 RCO, April 30, 1991.

18. Agence France Presse, cited in Foreign Broadcast Information Service, WEU–93–106, June 4, 1993.

19. NATO Press Communique M–NACC–1(93) 40, June 11, 1993, and M–NACC–2(93) 73, December 3, 1993.

20. Rome Communique, see note 11 above (paras. 55 and 57).

Chapter 11

1. Assembly of Western European Union, "Western European Union Information Report," February 1993.

2. Willem F. van Eekelen, *Future European Defence Co-Operation—the Role of WEU,* European Strategy Group Occasional Paper, London, September 1989; Ian Gamble, "Prospects for West European Security Cooperation," Adelphi Paper, no. 244, International Institute for Strategic Studies, London, Autumn 1989.

3. Gamble, "Prospects for West European Security Cooperation," p. 30.

4. Emilio Colombo, "European Security at a Time of Radical Change," *NATO Review,* June 1992.

5. Catherine Guicherd, "A European Defense Identity: Challenge and Opportunity for NATO," Congressional Research Service, Report 91–478RCO, June 12, 1991.

6. Text is in Foreign Broadcast Information Service, WEU–90–238, December 11, 1990.

7. Text of the letter is in FBIS, WEU–91–202, October 18, 1992, and in *Bulletin of the Federal German Government,* S117/S 929, October 18, 1992.

8. Text of the Treaty on European Union, issued in the United States by UNIPUB, Lanham, MD, p. 126.

9. Para. 1 of the Declaration; the text of the Declaration is in pages 240–46 of the Political Union Treaty.

10. Author's own notes of discussion with a senior WEU official, April 1992.

11. NATO Press Communique (93)41, June 8, 1993.

12. Willem F. van Eekelen, "Security in a Changing World," paper distributed in a session of the Academy for Security and Cooperation in Europe, Washington, DC, April 24, 1992.

13. Willem F. van Eekelen, "Transatlantic Relations in a New Context," talk for the Bergeporfer Gesprachskreis, Ditchley Park, U.K., May 22, 1993.

14. Text of the Petersburg Declaration is printed in the "Information Letter of the Assembly of Western European Union," no. 12, July 1992.

15. Daniel Franklin, "The European Community," *Economist,* July 3, 1993.

16. Ian Davidson, "An American Row in Paris," *Financial Times,* July 6, 1992.

17. Ian Gamble, "European Security Integration in the 1990s," Chaillot Paper no. 3, Institute for Security Studies, WEU, November 1991, pp. 8–15.

18. Guicherd, "A European Defense Identity," p. 62.

19. Nicole Gnesotto, "European Defense: Why Not the Twelve?" Chaillot Paper no. 1, Institute for Security Studies, WEU, March 1991.

20. Ian Davidson, "An American Row in Paris,"*Financial Times,* July 6, 1992, and "Platform for Historic Ambitions," *Financial Times,* June 22, 1992.

21. Gamble, "Prospects for West European Security Cooperation," p. 41.

22. "Say Yes. Yes to What? Stop Arguing," *Economist,* August 8, 1992.

23. Guicherd, loc. cit., pp. 57–61.

24. Marc Fisher, "Germans Caught in US-French Rift," *Washington Post,* June 27, 1992.

CHAPTER 12

1. See, for example, Victor Hansen, *The Western Way of War: Infantry Battle in Classical Greece* (New York: Oxford University Press, 1989).

2. All these activities have the same stated objective, to prevent, limit, or end armed conflict. Consequently, they should be viewed as belonging to the same category. Ivo Daalder has a useful definition of arms control as occupying a middle position on a spectrum of possible political relations among states, where war is

at one end of the spectrum and peace at the other. In both extreme conditions, arms control is valueless, but in intermediate positions, arms control has value in preventing movement toward war or help in transforming political relations in the direction of multilateral security cooperation. Ivo Daalder, "The Future of Arms Control," *Survival,* vol. 34, no. 1 (Spring 1992).

3. Following the dissolution of the Soviet Union, the Russian Federation and seven other successor states became CFE signatories. Treaty participants are Armenia, Azerbaijan, Belarus, Belgium, Bulgaria, Canada, Czechoslovakia, Denmark, France, Georgia, Germany, Greece, Hungary, Iceland (no military forces), Luxembourg, Moldova, Netherlands, Norway, Poland, Portugal, Romania, Russia, Spain, Turkey, Ukraine, United Kingdom, and United States; Jonathan Dean and Randall Forsberg, "CFE and Beyond," *International Security,* Summer 1992, p. 87.

4. For details on the early phases of CFE, see my book, *Meeting Gorbachev's Challenge* (New York: St. Martin's Press, 1989). The published sources for the CFE talks are good. Very useful are the *Vienna Fax* series of bulletins issued by the Institute for Defense and Disarmament Studies, Cambridge, MA; the coverage provided in the *Arms Control Reporter* published by the same institute; *Focus on Vienna* bulletin series issued by the Austrian Committee for European Security and Cooperation (Lederergasse 23/3/27 A 1094, Vienna); the *BASIC Reports on European Arms Control,* published by the British American Security Information Council (Suite 302, 1601 Connecticut Avenue, Washington, DC 20009, and 8 John Adam Street, London, WC2N 6 EZ), and periodic bulletins published by the Arms Control Association (Suite 250, 11 Dupont Circle NW, Washington, DC 20036–1207). In addition, Pal Dunay, a highly knowledgeable arms control expert and periodic member of the Hungarian CFE delegation, has published a report: *The CFE Treaty: History, Achievements, and Shortcomings,* Peace Research Institute, Frankfurt, Report no. 24, October 1991. For official accounts by U.S. government officials, the series of reports by the Foreign Relations Committee are the standard authority for U.S. aspects of the treaty; Treaty Doc. 012–8, 102nd U.S. Congress, Senate contains the text of the treaty with administration comment on each article. S.HRG. 102–288 contains the record of Senate hearings on the treaty. Senate Exec. Rept. 102–22 contains the report on the treaty of the Senate Foreign Relations Committee to the full Senate, with its evaluation and recommendations.

5. *Arms Control Reporter,* 1992, p. 407.B.473.

6. *The Military Balance 1992–1993,* International Institute for Strategic Studies, London, Autumn 1992, p. 97.

7. *Arms Control Reporter,* February 1993, p. 407.B.483; *Arms Control Reporter,* November 1992, p. 407.B.478.

8. Report of the Senate Foreign Relations Committee on the CFE Treaty, Senate Exec. Rept. 102–22, November 19, 1991, pp. 63–69, 80–81.

9. *Arms Control Reporter,* 1992, p. 407.B.476–77.

10. The text of the Russian note is in the *Arms Control Reporter,* November 1993, p. 407.D.85–86. Zonal limits are described in pp. 407.B.492–93 of the same issue.

11. Text of that paper is in Dean, *Meeting Gorbachev's Challenge*, p. 385.

12. Senate Exec. Rep. 102–22, p. 66.

13. Randall Forsberg and Steve Lilly-Weber of the Institute for Defense and Disarmament Studies. See Dean and Forsberg, "CFE and Beyond," Table 1.

14. Senate Hearing 102–288, pp. 88–89.

15. Ibid. p. 93.

16. Ibid. p. 82.

17. Senate Exec. Rep. 102–22, pp. 39–40.

18. *Arms Control Reporter*, November 1992, p. 407.B.477.

19. *General and Complete Disarmament: Defensive Security Concepts and Policies*, UN General Assembly, Department A/47/394, September 22, 1992, para. 172.

20. Text of the Stockholm Document and an evaluation of its content can be found in Dean, *Meeting Gorbachev's Challenge* (chapt. 6). Texts of further CSCE decisions on CSBMs are found in the Vienna Document 1990; the Paris Charter 1990; Vienna Document 1992, which contains a description of currently valid CSBMs incorporating the content of the Stockholm and Vienna 1990 measures; and in the Helsinki Document 1992.

21. Many of the details on the work of the Forum are drawn from *Focus on Vienna*, Austrian Committee for European Security and Cooperation, no. 29, April 1993, and no. 30, August 1993; see note 2, chapt. 7. See also John Borawski and Bruce George, "The CSCE Forum for Security Cooperation," *Arms Control Today*, October 1993.

22. *Arms Control Reporter*, November 1992, p. 402.B.311.

23. See the suggestions in Dean, *Meeting Gorbachev's Challenge*, p. 117.

24. This description of the treaty objective is drawn from the position paper adopted by the NATO Council in December 1989 prior to the opening of the Open Skies negotiations in February 1990. The text is in *Arms Control Reporter*, 1990, pp. 409.D.1–409.D.4.

25. *Arms Control Reporter*, 1990, p. 409.B.1; Jonathan B. Tucker, "Open Skies: Back to the Future," *Arms Control Today* 20, no. 8 (October 1990).

26. Annex A, Section I of Open Skies Treaty text.

27. *Arms Control Reporter*, 1991, p. 409.B.25.

28. A good review of the issues early in the talks is contained in Lewis Dunn and Brett Henry, "Open Skies and CFE Aerial Inspection," Science Applications International Corporation, McLean, VA, August 30, 1990.

29. Further discussion of issues raised in this section can be found in Ashton B. Carter, William J. Perry, and John D. Steinbruner, *A New Concept of Cooperative Security*, Brookings Occasional Papers (Washington, DC: Brookings Institution, 1992); Ivo Daalder, "The Role of Arms Control in the New Europe," in *Arms Control* vol. 12, no. 1 (May 1991); Daalder, "The Future of Arms Control"; Lynn E. Davis, "The Future of Conventional Forces and Arms Control in Europe," in Harold Brown, ed., *Changing Roles and Shifting Burdens in the Atlantic Alliance* (Washington, DC: Johns Hopkins Foreign Policy Institute, 1991); Thomas Hirschfeld, "Helsinki II," *The Future of Arms Control in Europe*, Report no. R–4174–FF/RC (Santa Monica, CA: Rand Corporation, 1992); Paul B. Stares and

John D. Steinbruner, "Cooperative Security in the New Europe," in Paul B. Stares, ed., *The New Germany and the New Europe* (Washington, DC: Brookings Institution, 1992); Jenonne Walker, "New Thinking about Conventional Arms Control," *Survival*, January–February 1991; as well as in Dean and Forsberg, "CFE and Beyond"; Jonathan Dean and Stanley R. Resor, "The CFE Negotiations," in Kurt Gottfried and Paul Bracken, eds., *Reforging European Security* (Boulder, CO: Westview Press, 1990); Jonathan Dean, "Building a Post-Cold War European Security System," *Arms Control Today*, June 1990; and Jonathan Dean, "The CFE Negotiations, Present and Future," *Survival*, July–August 1990.

30. Hirschfeld, "Helsinki II," p. 48.

31. Prominent among them are Alexei Arbatov and Albrecht von Müller.

32. Stares and Steinbruner, "Cooperative Security in the New Europe."

33. The exception is set forth in Measure IV, 39 of the Vienna Document 1992.

34. Dean, *Meeting Gorbachev's Challenge*, pp. 118–19; Hirschfeld, "Helsinki II," p. 36.

35. Vienna Document 1992, measure 61.4.

36. Davis, "The Future of Conventional Forces and Arms Control in Europe."

37. Daalder, "The Future of Arms Control."

38. UN General Assembly Report, A/47/394, para. 205.

39. Boutros Boutros-Ghali, "Post-Conflict Peace Building," in *An Agenda for Peace* (New York: United Nations, 1992); Fred Tanner, "Postwar Arms Control," *Journal of Peace Research* 30, no. 1 (1993).

40. NATO Press Communique S–1(91)85, November 7, 1991.

41. The original source is General Klaus Naumann, "Doctrines and Force Structures," in Ian Culbertson and Peter Volten, eds., *The Guns Fall Silent* (New York: Institute for East-West Security Studies, 1990), cited by Davis in "The Future of Conventional Forces and Arms Control in Europe."

CHAPTER 13

1. David Marsh, "EC Banks Skeptical on Single Currency," *Financial Times*, November 4, 1993.

2. Text of the "Declaration of the Heads of State and Government Participating in the Meeting of the North Atlantic Council Held at NATO Headquarters, Brussels, on 10–11 January, 1994," NATO Press Communique M–1(94)3, January 11, 1994.

3. Erika Platt, "France Cultivates Closer Ties to NATO but for Own Reasons," *Defense News*, September 8, 1993; David Buchan, "Paris to Strengthen Its Role within NATO," *Financial Times*, January 6, 1994; Steven Greenhouse, "NATO Clears Plan for Task Forces," *New York Times*, January 6, 1994; "Declaration of

the Heads of State and Government," NATO Press Communique M–1 (94)3, January 11, 1994; William Drozdiak, "Summit Shows U.S. Easing Grip on NATO," *Washington Post,* January 12, 1994; Lionel Barber, "Concern at Weak EU Foreign Policy," *Financial Times,* January 18, 1994; David Buchan, "France Goes on the Defensive Offensive," *Financial Times,* January 24, 1994; David White, "UK Seeks Role in European Defence Plans," *Financial Times,* January 25, 1994.

4. Willem F. van Eekelen, "Security in a Changing World" (see chap. 11, note 12).

5. *Washington Post,* May 23, 1993; Bob Dole, "Bosnia: It's Not Too Late," *Washington Post,* August 1, 1993; Theresa Hitchens, "Bosnia's Fallout Threatens NATO," *Defense News,* May 31, 1993; James Chace, "Exit, NATO," *New York Times,* June 14, 1993.

6. Richard Cheney, cited by David White, "The Empire Splits Up," *Financial Times,* December 22, 1993.

7. Washington, DC, June 24, 1993.

8. *Washington Post,* November 13, 1992.

9. "Ruehe Offen Für Neue NATO-Mitglieder," *Frankfurter Allgemeine Zeitung,* May 22, 1993.

10. Article 4 of NATO Treaty reads, "The Parties will consult together whenever, in the opinion of any of them, the territorial integrity, political independence or security of any of the Parties is threatened."

11. Ronald Asmus, Richard Kugler, and Stephen Larrabee, "Building a New NATO," *Foreign Affairs,* September–October 1993; Zalmay M. Khalilzad, "Extending the Western Alliance to East Central Europe," Issue Paper (Santa Monica, CA: Rand Corporation, May 1993).

12. Address by Assistant Secretary Stephen Oxman before the Atlantic Council, Washington, DC, August 12, 1993.

13. NATO Press Communique M–1 (94)2, January 10, 1994.

14. Institut für Friedensforschung und Sicherheitspolitik, *Vom Recht Des Starkeren zur Starke Des Rechts,* Hamburg, April 1993, issued in English as *From the Law of the Strongest to the Strength of the Law.*

Chapter 14

1. See Kenneth N. Waltz, *Theory of International Politics* (New York: McGraw-Hill, 1979); John Mearsheimer, "Back to the Future," *International Security,* Summer 1990.

2. The relative rapidity of nuclear weapons development by this group of states is evaluated in a report by the U.S. Energy Research and Development Agency, cited by Joseph A. Yager, "Prospects for Nuclear Weapons Proliferation in a Changing Europe," Center for National Security Negotiations, vol. 4, no. 1, Science Applications International Corporation (SAIC), McLean, VA.

3. A more detailed description of the proposals for U.S.–Russian and five power nuclear disarmament discussed in this chapter can be found in Jonathan Dean, "The Final Stage of Nuclear Arms Control," *Washington Quarterly,* vol. 17, no. 4 (Autumn 1994).

4. William J. Broad, "Russian Says Soviet Atom Arsenal Was Larger Than West Estimated," *New York Times,* September 26, 1993.

5. President Clinton, address to the UN General Assembly, September 27, 1993.

6.

CURRENT NUCLEAR WEAPONS STOCKPILES
(estimated as of December 1993)

	WARHEADS	ACTIVE	WARHEADS IN THE INACTIVE RESERVE	RETIRED WARHEADS	INACTIVE AND RETIRED WARHEADS
United States		10,500	400	5,850*	
Russia		15,000			17,000†
United Kingdom	200				
France	525				
China	435				

*(peaked at 32,500 warheads in 1967)
†peaked at 45,000 warheads in 1986

Source: "Nuclear Notebook," *Bulletin of the Atomic Scientists,* December 1993.

HEU, Pu STOCKPILES
(estimates as of 1990)
NUCLEAR WEAPONS STATES

United States: 550 tonnes HEU in total stockpile, 285 tonnes of which are in weapons; 89 tonnes of weapons-grade Pu (from 1993 DoE data); 127.3 tonnes of PU in spent fuel. (Figures here are in metric tonnes of 1,000 kilograms each, slightly larger than U.S. tons.)

Russia: 720 tonnes of HEU in total stockpile, 480 tonnes in actual weapons (assuming 32,000 warheads, 15 kg per weapon); 125 tonnes of weapons-grade Pu, 70.7 tonnes of Pu in spent fuel

United Kingdom: 10 tonnes of HEU in total stockpile, 3.0–4.5 tonnes in actual weapons (assuming 200–300 weapons, 15 kg per weapon); 11 tonnes of weapons-grade Pu, 26.1 tonnes of Pu in spent fuel

France: 15 tonnes of HEU in total stockpile, 7.5–9.0 tonnes in actual weapons (assuming 500–600 nuclear weapons, 15 kg per weapon); 6.0 tonnes of weapons-grade Pu, 67.2 tonnes of Pu in spent fuel

China: 15 tonnes of HEU in total stockpiles, 6.0 tonnes in actual weapons (assuming 300 weapons, 20 kg per warhead); 2.5+/-1.5 tonnes of weapons-grade Pu

Israel: 330 kg of weapons-grade Pu

India: 290 kg of weapons-grade Pu

Pakistan: 130–220 kg of HEU

Note: There is little evidence that Israel and India have developed adequate facilities to produce HEU for use in nuclear weapons. Pakistan does not yet appear to have developed a capacity to produce separated plutonium in quantities necessary for a plutonium-based nuclear weapons program.

Source: Except as noted, figures are from David Albright, Frans Berkhout, and William Walker, *World Inventory of Plutonium and Highly Enriched Uranium 1992*, Stockholm International Peace Research Institute (New York: Oxford University Press, 1993).

7. Thomas Lippman, "Accord Set on Nuclear Inspections," *Washington Post*, March 16, 1994, "Russia Set to Close Three Reactors," *Washington Post*, March 17, 1994.

8. "The High Price of Freeing Markets," *Economist*, February 19, 1994.

9. National Academy of Sciences, *Management and Disposition of Excess Weapons Plutonium* (Washington, DC: National Academy Press, 1994), pp. 27–28.

10. R. Jeffrey Smith, "Reporters Granted First Look at Texas Nuclear Weapons Facility," *Washington Post*, January 14, 1993.

11. Paper by Bruce G. Blair, "Global Zero Alert for Nuclear Forces," Brookings Institution, revised March 15, 1994.

12. Andrew J. Goodpaster, "Further Reins on Nuclear Arms," Atlantic Council, Washington, DC, August 1993.

13. Cited by Raymond Calamoro, "Balkan Crisis Comes between Friends," *Financial Times*, November 26, 1993.

14. *Washington Post*, January 19, 1993; Don Oberdorfer, "A Bloody Failure in the Balkans," *Washington Post*, February 8, 1993.

15. Reuters text of President Clinton's news conference, April 20, 1994, *New York Times*, April 21, 1994.

16. Cited in Daniel Williams and Ann Devroy, "U.S. Limits Peace-Keeping Role," *Washington Post*, November 25, 1993.

17. President Clinton, address to the UN General Assembly, September 27, 1993; Secretary of State Warren Christopher, statement before the Senate Foreign Relations Committee, November 4, 1993; Secretary of Defense Les Aspin, remarks before the National Academy of Sciences, December 7, 1993; Anthony Lake, assistant to the president on national security affairs, address at Johns Hopkins University, School of Advanced International Studies, Washington, DC, September

21, 1993; U.S. ambassador to the UN Madeleine K. Albright, remarks to the National War College, Washington, DC, September 23, 1993.

18. U.S. ambassador to the United Nations, Madeleine K. Albright, statement before the Senate Foreign Relations Committee, October 20, 1993.

19. Max Singer and Aaron Wildavsky, *The Real World Order: Zones of Peace, Zones of Turmoil* (Chatham, NJ: Chatham House Publishers, 1993).

20. A valuable treatment of this subject is in Norbert Ropers and Peter Schlotter, *The CSCE*, Study no. 14, Foundation Development and Peace, Bonn, 1993.

21. Federal Broadcast Information Service, SOV–93–112, June 14, 1993.

22. Document of the Copenhagen Meeting of the Conference on the Human Dimension of the CSCE, June 29, 1990, para. 30–40.

23. See *Survival*, vol. 35, no. 1 (Spring 1993), especially David Welsh, "Domestic Politics and Ethnic Conflict," and John Chipman, "Managing the Politics of Parochialism"; Kamal Shehadi, "Ethnic Self-Determination and the Break Up of States," Adelphi Paper no. 283, International Institute of Strategic Studies, December 1983. All three are excellent.

24. Norbert Ropers and Peter Schlotter, op. cit., p. 28.

INDEX

ABOUT THE AUTHOR

Jonathan Dean, a former U.S. Foreign Service officer, is now the adviser for international security issues at the Union of Concerned Scientists, one of the largest public interest groups of natural and social scientists. Ambassador Dean's foreign service assignments included helping to establish new German armed forces after World War II; negotiating with the Soviet Union to assure access to Berlin; negotiating with the Warsaw Pact countries on reduction of conventional and nuclear forces in Europe; and working with UN peacekeepers in the field and in the U.S. Department of State. This is his third book on European security issues.